T0325034

Supply Chain Management:
Issues in the New Era of Collaboration and Competition

William Y. C. Wang, University of South Australia, Australia

Michael S. H. Heng, Universitas 21 Global, Singapore

Patrick Y. K. Chau, The University of Hong Kong, Hong Kong

IDEA GROUP PUBLISHING

Hershey • London • Melbourne • Singapore

Acquisitions Editor:	Michelle Potter
Development Editor:	Kristin Roth
Senior Managing Editor:	Amanda Appicello
Managing Editor:	Jennifer Neidig
Copy Editor:	Jane Conley
Typesetter:	Jessie Weik
Cover Design:	Jane Conley
Printed at:	Integrated Book Technology

Published in the United States of America by
     Idea Group Publishing (an imprint of Idea Group Inc.)
     701 E. Chocolate Avenue
     Hershey PA 17033
     Tel: 717-533-8845
     Fax: 717-533-8661
     E-mail: cust@idea-group.com
     Web site: http://www.idea-group.com

and in the United Kingdom by
     Idea Group Publishing (an imprint of Idea Group Inc.)
     3 Henrietta Street
     Covent Garden
     London WC2E 8LU
     Tel: 44 20 7240 0856
     Fax: 44 20 7379 0609
     Web site: http://www.eurospanonline.com

Library of Congress Cataloging-in-Publication Data

Supply chain management : issues in the new era of collaboration and competition / William Y.C. Wang, Michael S.H. Heng, and Patrick Y.K. Chau, editors.
    p. cm.
  Summary: "In the current business landscape, many business firms compete in one project and cooperate in another related project, and they do so at the same time. Even more interesting is that certain members of these firms are involved in both projects. This book examines this new business landscape"--Provided by publisher.
    ISBN 1-59904-231-2 -- ISBN 1-59904-232-0 (softcover) -- ISBN 1-59904-233-9 (ebook)
  1. Business logistics. I. Wang, William Y. C., 1974- II. Heng, Michael S. H., 1948- III. Chau, Patrick Y. K.
  HD38.5 .S89607
  658.5--dc22
                    2006010099

British Cataloguing in Publication Data
A Cataloguing in Publication record for this book is available from the British Library.

All work contributed to this book is new, previously-unpublished material. The views expressed in this book are those of the authors, but not necessarily of the publisher.

Supply Chain Management:
Issues in the New Era of Collaboration and Competition

Table of Contents

Preface vi

Section I:
The Impacts and Challenges of Supply Chain Management

Chapter I. Implementing Supply Chain Management in the New Era:
A Replenishment Framework for the Supply Chain Operations
Reference Model 1
William Y. C. Wang, University of South Australia, Australia
Michael S. H. Heng, Universitas 21 Global, Singapore
Patrick Y. K. Chau, The University of Hong Kong, Hong Kong

Chapter II. An Investigation into the Barriers to Introducing Virtual
Enterprise Networks 23
Angela Lin, University of Sheffield, UK
David Patterson, Business Link South Yorkshire, UK

Chapter III. Information Flows in a New Zealand Sheep Meat Supply
Chain 45
Andreas Schroeder, Victoria University of Wellington,
  New Zealand
Beverley G. Hope, Victoria University of Wellington,
  New Zealand

Chapter IV. Virtual Integration: Antecedents and Role in Governing Supply Chain Integration 63

    Jeffrey C. F. Tai, National Central University, Taiwan
    Eric T. G. Wang, National Central University, Taiwan
    Kai Wang, Ming Chuan University, Taiwan

Section II:
The Participants' Roles in Supply Chain Management

Chapter V. Trust and Transparency in Supply Netchains: A Contradiction? 105

    Gert Jan Hofstede, Wageningen University, The Netherlands

Chapter VI. Integration of Global Supply Chain Management with Small and Medium Suppliers 127

    Asghar Sabbaghi, Indiana University South Bend, USA
    Ganesh Vaidyanathan, Indiana University South Bend, USA

Chapter VII. Strategic Alliances of Information Technology Among Supply Chain Channel Members 165

    H. Y. Sonya Hsu, Southern Illinois University, USA
    Stephen C. Shih, Southern Illinois University, USA

Section III:
Implementation of Channel Integration

Chapter VIII. A Process Model of Inter-Organisational SCM Initiatives Adoption 191

    Yu Ni Ham, University of Melbourne, Australia
    Robert B. Johnston, University of Melbourne, Australia

Chapter IX. Factors Affecting Inter-Organisational Information Management Systems in Australian Food Processor Chains 226

    Christine Storer, Curtin University of Technology, Australia

Chapter X. The Application of Soft Systems Methodology to Supply Chain Management 254

    Ross Smith, Deakin University, Australia
    David Mackay, Deakin University, Australia
    Graeme Altmann, Deakin University, Australia
    Lucas Merlo, Deakin University, Australia

Chapter XI. Integrated E-Enterprise Supply Chain Security Design and Implementation 286

Stephen C. Shih, Southern Illinois University, USA
Michael Camarata, University of Akron, USA
H. Joseph Wen, Southeast Missouri State University, USA

Section IV:
Performance Control and Risk Issues

Chapter XII. Monitoring Supply Chain Flows through Improved Performance Measurement of Extended Processes 313

Marco Busi, SINTEF Industrial Management, Norwegian
    University of Science and Technology, Norway and
    University of Strathclyde, UK

Chapter XIII. Supply Chain Risk Management: A Game Theoretic Analysis 355

Thorsten Blecker, Hamburg University of Technology, Germany
Wolfgang Kersten, Hamburg University of Technology, Germany
Hagen Späth, Hamburg University of Technology, Germany
Birgit Koeppen, Hamburg University of Technology, Germany

Chapter XIV. Smart Integrated eOperations for High-Risk and Technologically Complex Assets: Operational Networks and Collaborative Partnerships in the Digital Environment 387

Jayantha P. Liyanage, University of Stavanger, Norway
Mike Herbert, ConocoPhillips, Norway
Jan Harestad, OilCamp AS, Norway

About the Authors 415

Index 425

Preface

Viewed from the perspective of history, supply chain has been around for a long time. Even in prehistoric times, logistics was pressed into service in the conduct of war. Many accounts of electronic commerce have tried to locate the roots of commerce by discussing the famous Silk Route. Supply chain began to acquire immense significance in world history with the advent of capitalism and colonialism. The idea of international division of labour was systematically applied to obtain raw materials from the colonies to feed the factories of the colonial masters, and to export manufactured goods to the colonies. Such a canned version of history of supply chain management (SCM) serves as a gentle introduction to illustrate the economic, political, societal and global significance of SCM. Of course, the details of such impacts would not be the same today with Internet-based SCM. But we believe that modern day SCM continues to influence the economic and political landscape while it is shaped by the wide array of forces known collectively as globalization. It is beyond the scope of this short preface to do full justice to such big issue. Indeed, it will require many volumes to provide the stage for the complexity and fascinating nature of the topic to be revealed in its full glory.

What we set out to do here is much more modest. We want to contribute to this interesting global phenomenon by collecting together in one volume well-researched works that illuminate SCM issues in the e-business environment in varying degrees of brightness and from various angles. This task is not easy, for our call-for-paper has to complete with a host of high quality journals and conferences. In order to select a meaningful theme, we begin by asking ourselves what may be conceived as pretty distinctive in current SCM as opposed to what was in good currency some years ago. Three observations come to mind. First, it has often been noted that the e-business environment has brought about a new kind of competition. Instead of the traditional mode of firms competing against firms, we have now supply chains competing against supply chains. This has brought about a very complex and intriguing relationship between the core firm of a supply chain and other members. Second, for those of us schooled in the competitive model of Michael Porter, we cannot help but notice that in an SCM environment, Porter's competition represents only one side of the proverbial coin. In fact, the current business landscape has many stories of business firms competing in one project and cooperating in another related project, and they do so at the same time. Even more interesting is that certain members of these firms are involved in both projects. The point suggested here is that Porter is not so much wrong as incomplete. Third, the nature of competence has changed. Traditionally, competence of a firm refers to its ability to produce quality goods at low costs. What is in good currency today refers to a firm's ability to identify the right suppliers to execute a given activity in the value chain, to organize such activities, and to manage its relationship with these suppliers. It is with this new business landscape in background that we frame the title of this book as *Supply Chain Management: Issues in the New Era of Collaboration and Competition*.

The layout of this book is based on the four major aspects in SCM: impacts and challenges, the role of the SCM participants, the implementation of channel integration, and performance control and risks.

Section I: The Impacts and Challenges of Supply Chain Management

Chapter I reviews the literature of SCM from several angles that can be the basis of a proposed framework for the SCM knowledge within academic and managerial contexts. By introducing the supply chain operations reference (SCOR) model, which was developed by the Supply Chain Council and is recognised as a diagnostic tool for SCM worldwide, the chapter identifies the limitations of contemporary SCM design and implementation. This chapter surveys the literature of performance control and risk issues in SCM and SCOR model and discusses the proposed framework for the future research. This chapter implies the needs of further investigation of the above areas, which explains the layout of this book.

Chapter II is a preliminary investigation into the development barriers of a virtual enterprise network in the Creative Digital Industries sector in South Yorkshire, United Kingdom. The authors contend that the key factors in delivering an integrated virtual value chain are trust and the control of risk by taking the concept of virtual organization as its theoretical basis. They have provided the evidence of the connection between trust and the control in the context. On the one hand, the three dimensions—competence, integrity, and benevolence of trust—were used by the small and medium enterprises (SMEs) in this study as the criteria for choosing their business partners. On the other hand, risks such as poaching, stealing, transaction-specific, information asymmetries, and loss of resource control were confirmed by these SMEs as the main concerns that led to their resistance to participation in a virtual value chain. They suggest that managers should pay attention to trust building and the control of risks at all stages while developing and participating in a virtual value chain based on the research result.

Chapter III focuses on downstream information flows by interviewing six major stakeholders in the meat supply chain of New Zealand to determine their information needs and the information they provide to their downstream partners. It is one of the few supply chain studies in the agricultural industry, which is quite different from the service industry and manufacturing industry. Drawing attention to the impact of livestock diseases, it details the various information flows and information media used, identifies redundancies and deficiencies, and makes recommendations for improvements.

Chapter IV provides a framework to identify the issues related to how virtual integration along the supply chain can affect the channel coordination. It surveys the related supply chain integration literature, theoretical foundation, and research frameworks and then develops the research hypotheses and a structural model. The model is tested with adequate research method and measurement, followed by statistical data analysis in order to show the interrelationships between influential factors. This study suggests that information and communications technology (ICT)-enabled collaboration can be regarded as alternative governance mechanism, that is, virtual integration. With ICT-enabled collaborative operation, execution, and process planning and control, virtual integration supports both value creation and transaction cost reduction. Therefore, virtual integration is a particularly effective and useful governance mechanism for integrating supply chain under the condition of significant asset specificity.

Section II: The Participants' Roles in Supply Chain Management

Chapter V analyzes the effects of increased transparency in supply chain and business network. The chapter differentiates three levels of transparency: history transparency, operations transparency, and strategy transparency. Using an example in the Dutch egg sector, the chapter shows how the role of the individual company changes in a supply chain and discusses the implications. Though technology push makes transparency feasible and economically attractive, social-psychological barriers exist. A brief review of cases from several continents shows that these barriers vary across cultures, depending on prevailing attitudes towards relationships and authority. Transparency may run counter to tradition, to trust and to entrepreneurial freedom in the supply chain, but it also offers opportunities for creating supply chains that are profitable for all participants. To grasp these requires vision on the part of those involved.

Chapter VI develops an integrated framework for global SCM as viewed from the strategic aspects of small and medium-sized enterprise (SME) suppliers. Primary consideration is given to characteristics of the integrated supply chain and the necessity for adaptation in managing the supply chain in order to attain competitive advantage. A review of the current literature and an analysis of the supply chain in changing global markets emphasize the relative importance of strategically managing the supply chain process given the limited resources of the SMEs. Managing the supply chain through the development of market-specific strategies allows an SME to be proactive as opposed to reactive in its strategic planning, which can greatly benefit customer satisfaction levels and thus enhance the performance of the firm.

Chapter VII explores novel ways of improving flexibility, responsiveness, and competitiveness via strategic IT alliances among channel members in a supply chain network. To gain competitiveness, firms have to constantly update their operational strategies and IT through collaborative efforts of a "network" of supply chain members rather than through the efforts of an individual firm. The foci of the chapter are: (1) an overview of SCM issues and problems, (2) supply chain coordination and integration, (3) the latest IT applications for improved supply chain performance and coordination, and (4) strategic IT alliances.

Section III: Implementation of Channel Integration

While the benefits of adopting inter-organisational supply chain management (IOSCM) have been widely reported within industry, its adoption has been slow and below industry expectations. There is lack of theory within the literature to explain this problem in IOSCM initiatives adoption. Employing an inductive case-study approach to theory building, **Chapter VIII** develops a process model that captures the complexity of intra-industry interactions in the course of adoption and argues for a normative path to achieve the increasing levels of integration envisioned in IOSCM. The model proposes three sets of requirements that have to be met to achieve a certain level of integration: supply chain integration, inter-organisational structures, and relationship intimacy. However, to achieve the higher levels of integration, it is necessary to have mastered the lower levels of integration demanded by earlier initiatives. This path dependence constitutes a major barrier to adoption of more advanced IOSCM initiatives.

Good communication systems between organisations increase customer satisfaction and relationship behaviour in SCM. However, not much is known about the details of how information is used to manage relationships and coordinate customers and suppliers. In earlier stages of the research, a dynamic model of inter-organisational information management systems (IOIMS) and relationships was developed. An evaluation of this model was based on a survey of Australian food processors and a case study. **Chapter IX** also reports an evaluation of a revised version of this model. A strategic oriented IOIMS was positively associated with IOIMS satisfaction, which was in turn positively associated with perceived current outcomes (satisfaction with performance, perceived responsiveness, and strength of relationship trust). However, (attitudinal) commitment to developing long-term customer/supplier relationships was not significantly associated with the IOIMS, IOIMS satisfaction, or current outcomes. Results were moderated by the nature of the business environment—power/dependency, experience, and market uncertainty.

Chapter X reflects upon techniques that might facilitate improved strategic decision making in an SCM environment. In particular, it presents the integration of a selection of techniques adapted from the soft systems methodology (SSM). The results indicate that SSM techniques can complement existing SCM decision-making tools. In particular, this chapter outlines a framework for integrating some SSM techniques with approaches based upon the supply-chain operations reference model.

To gain competitive advantages, e-enterprises need to integrate the entire lines of business operations and critical business data with external supply chain participants over the Web. However, this introduces significant security risks to the organizations' critical assets and infrastructures. **Chapter XI** reports a case study of e-service security design and implementation at a leading U.S. company. It reviews security concerns and challenges in front-end e-business and back-end supply chain operations. This is followed by an analysis of the company's e-service and its security problems. The case then presents an integrated e-enterprise security methodology to guide the company toward meeting its security needs. The results provide IT security professionals with practical steps and sustainable solutions for tackling the unique security challenges arising in an open, unbounded e-enterprise supply chain environment.

Section IV: Performance Control and Risk Issues

Increasing strategic importance of logistics related processes demands higher integration of performance management and SCM. **Chapter XII** goes beyond existing work and develops an understanding of the issue of performance management from an SCM perspective. The aim is to understand how today's manufacturing systems and processes could be measured and managed in the context of the extended business—back through the supplier chain and forward into the distribution and customer chain. The chapter's major outcomes are a clearer understanding of the concept of SCM through performance, and a process for designing a supply chain performance measurement system.

Chapter XII introduces a game-theoretic approach to supply chain risk management. The study described focuses on the risk of a single supply chain member defecting from common supply chain agreements, thereby jeopardizing the overall supply chain performance. It introduces a manual supply chain game, by which dynamic supply chain mechanisms can be simulated and further analyzed using a game theoretic model. The model helps to identify externalities that negatively impact supply chain efficiency. Incentives are necessary to overcome these externalities in order to align supply chain objectives. The game theoretic model, in connection with the supply chain game, provides an informative basis for the future development of incentives by which supply chains can be aligned in order to reduce supply chain risks.

The oil and gas production in Norway is a challenging area for applying SCM to solve complex problems. Since 2003, oil and gas (O&G) production business on the Norwegian Continental Shelf entered a new development path, which is described in **Chapter XIV**. Smart integrated IT-based operation is seen as the way forward. It is intended to re-engineer the industry structure within the next few years with new policies and practices establishing operational networks and collaborative partnerships between O&G producers, and the service-support-supply market through active integration for effective and efficient management of offshore production assets. Adaptation of this approach is largely stimulated by rapid development in application technology, large-scale information and communication platforms, and the foreseen substantial commercial benefits of well-integrated collaborative industry infrastructure. This is a novel macro-scale program and the Norwegian O&G industry has already launched major initiatives in this regard to realize its fully functional status by the year 2010. The sophisticated information and communication platform and onshore support centres represent major Norwegian initiatives in this digital era.

Acknowledgments

Here we would like to express our deep gratitude to all the contributors. All submissions have gone through the normal process of double-blind review and the efforts of our reviewers deserve our many thanks. We must also thank the editorial team of Idea Group Inc.—Dr. Mehdi Khosrow-Pour and his colleagues, Ms. Jan Travers and Ms. Kristin Roth—who have worked closely with us in this project.

To what extent have we succeeded in achieving our modest goal? You as reader of this book are the best judge, and we certainly welcome your critique and comments, which we would seriously study as useful input for our future work.

Section I:

The Impacts and Challenges of Supply Chain Management

Chapter I

Implementing Supply Chain Management in the New Era:
A Replenishment Framework for the Supply Chain Operations Reference Model

William Y. C. Wang, University of South Australia, Australia

Michael S. H. Heng, Universitas 21 Global, Singapore

Patrick Y. K. Chau, The University of Hong Kong, Hong Kong

Abstract

Combining with the collaborations between business customers and suppliers, traditional purchasing and logistics functions have evolved into a broader concept of materials and distribution management, namely, supply chain management (SCM) (Tan, 2001). This chapter reviews the literature of SCM from several paths that can be the basis of a proposed framework for SCM within academic and managerial contexts. In addition, it includes the approaches of supply chain operations reference (SCOR) model, which was developed by the Supply Chain Council and is recognised as a diagnostic tool for SCM worldwide. This chapter also summarises the literature of performance control and risk issues in SCM and the SCOR Model and discusses a proposed framework for the future research.

Introduction

A supply chain is established when there is an integration of operations across its constituent entities, namely, the suppliers, partners, and business customers (Narasimhan & Mahapatra, 2004). It is an observation that individual firms compete as integral parts of supply chains in the global markets. Moreover, the evolution of information technology (IT) has particularly generated growing attention on searching for ways to improve product quality, customer services, and operation efficiency and remaining competitive by supply chain collaboration. As noted by Strader, Lin, and Shaw (1999), ". . .there has been a general movement towards organizing as partnerships between more specialised firms or business units as IT enables the costs of coordination decrease" (p. 361), implying the impact of IT and potential advances of supply chain management (SCM). A number of researchers and practitioners have, therefore, devoted their efforts to various approaches to manage the constituents and activities of a supply chain since the early 1980s. Yet conceptually, the management of supply chains has not been well organised or understood. Academia has continuously highlighted the necessity for clear definitional constructs and frameworks on SCM (Croom, Romano, & Giannakis, 2000; New & Mitropoulos, 1995; Saunders, 1997).

However, SCM research, which draws on industrial economics, information systems, marketing, financing, logistics and interorganisational behaviour, has a fragmented nature and lacks a universal model. Hence, what we set out to construct in this chapter are the general theoretical and managerial domains of SCM, thereby, attempting to contribute to the development of such discipline. The literature is surveyed to identify the cognitive components of the current subject, as it is a key question for any applied social research that concerns the strategic approach taken to its mapping (Tranfield & Starkey, 1998).

Theoretical models are needed in order to inform the understanding of the supply chain phenomena. An illustration of industrial dynamics in Forrester's (1958) model in fact instantiates the possibility of such applications that aid the comprehension of material flows along the supply chain. Further, it has remarkably laid the foundation for subsequent advancement of supply chain analyses and understandings (e.g., Min & Zhou, 2002; New & Payne, 1995; Sterman, 1989; Towill, Naim, & Wilker, 1992). SCM is not only concerned with the extraction of raw materials to their end of useful life, it also focuses on how firms utilise their suppliers' processes, technology, and capability to enhance sustainable competitive advantage (Farley, 1997). When all organisational entities along the supply chain act coherently, operation effectiveness is achieved throughout the systems of suppliers. Cooper, Ellram, Gardner, and Hawk (1997) advocate such a concept, and further indicate that much of SCM literature is predicated on the adoption and extension of extant theoretical concepts.

Our chapter is not so much a critical review of the literature as a taxonomy with which to map the subsequent research. In this context, it is our intention to try to provide a framework for conducting a project of supply chain management.

This chapter is organised into five sections corresponding to the initial idea of the book layout. In the first section, the supply chain operations reference (SCOR) model is introduced (SCC, 2001), underlying the common aspects and approaches, as it has gradually become a widely accepted standard of supply chain management in industry from its initial launch in 1996. One of the goals in this chapter is to identify the limitations of the SCOR Model and, therefore, to suggest a framework and supply chain implementation. Aligning with the SCOR model, we map the possible research areas by proposing a framework as a domain of research in supply chain design and for the managerial concerns in a project of supply chain management. The next section considers the bodies of literature associated with the stakeholder theory and network theory in organisational studies, which are applied to the interorganizational context (e.g., Premukumar, 2000; Rogers, 2004; Windsor, 1998). Then, we focus on the how to bridge the gaps towards the integration of the supply chain. We further explain the elements for facilitating transformation of the supply chain associated with business processes, organisation structure, and performance control in the following section. The chapter concludes with a summary with some conclusions that can be drawn from the content in terms of moving towards a coherent approach to supply chain management.

Finding the Supply Chain Challenges with the SCOR Model

There is a profusion of literature related to the landscape of supply chain management. Various aspects can be found as the constituents of this subject, which leads to a confusion of meaning (New & Payne, 1995), thus causing difficulty in laying out the scope and content of supply chain design. The term *supply chain management* has not only been associated with logistics activities in the literature but also with the planning and control of materials and information flows of an enterprise, both internally and externally. Additionally, strategic issues, resources, interorganizational relationships, and even governmental intervention have been addressed in extant studies (e.g., Thorelli, 1986; Wang & Heng, 2004), and others discuss the effects of network externality (e.g., Gulati, 1999). These research domains are indeed relevant to the understanding of supply chain context; however, in this chapter, we consider the direct challenges that an enterprise may encounter in order to implement supply chain management. Therefore, the issues in the subsequent discussion follow the logical sequences of SCOR that have been widely adopted by industries such as AT&T, Boeing, and ACER for supply chain diagnosis and design.

The Supply Chain Operations Reference Model

Developed in 1996, SCOR is a standard model of supply chain processes and is used similarly to International Organization for Standardization (ISO) documents for intra-enterprise processes. The SCOR model also builds on the concepts of business process reengineering (BPR), performance measurement, and logistics management by integrating these techniques into a configurable, cross-functional framework. It is a model that links business processes, performance indicators (metrics), and suggested actions (best practice and the features). It was developed to be configurable and aggregates a series of hierarchical process components that can be used as a common language for enterprises to describe the supply chains and communicate with each other (Huang, Scheoran, & Keskar, 2005; SCC, 2001).

The SCOR model follows a set of "top-down" procedures, commencing from the corporate-level strategy that the procedures can help to identify thousands of business activities inside an organisation and spanning across the boundaries of the supply chain entities. The document of the SCOR model includes the following elements as a communicative platform among enterprise owners, project leaders, and corporate consultants of the supply chain planning activities:

- Standard descriptions of each business process along the supply chain that are categorised as "Plan," "Source," "Make," and "Delivery." There are also other two categories defining the product return as "Return"[1] and the supportive activities as "Enabler."
- Key performance indicators (KPI) are defined and classified by the attributes accompanying with each of the business processes; for example,

"Total Source Cycle Time to Completion" is a KPI in the attribute of "Supply Chain Responsiveness" of Source activities.

- Best practices are brought up in the SCOR model as recommendations if the diagnosis of certain processes by KPI shows the necessity for improvement.

- Identification of the associative software functionalities that can enable the best practices for business processes reengineering.

This SCOR model consists of four levels as the analytical stages leading to the implementation of an effective SCM strategy. The five distinct business processes, Plan, Source, Make, Deliver, and Return, are within the Level 1 stage and should be further decomposed into processes categories pending on the activities involved. Hence, Level 2 defines the core process categories that can be found in an actual and idealised supply chain around an enterprise. For example, the "source" category includes "source stocked products," "source made-to-order (MTO) products," and "source engineered-to-order (ETO) products" (Table 1). These different types of channel activities derive from the three major customer demands. Making stocked products corresponds to the situation of unknown demand quantities and expects easily procurement of the raw materials, while making MTO and ETO products requires the accuracy of demand forecasting and transparent market estimation.

Because of the customer-oriented nature, the delivery processes actually affects the associated Make and Source activities, and hence the SCOR model spans at least the interactions of information and material flows from the understanding of aggregate demand to the fulfillment of each order. To portrait the business

Table 1. Supply chain activities based on SCOR level 1 & 2 (Adapted from SCC, 2001)

Plan		Source		Make		Deliver	
P1	Plan Supply Chain	S1	Source Stocked Product	M1	Make-to-Stock	D1	Deliver Stocked Product
P2	Plan Source	S2	Source MTO Product	M2	Make-to-Order	D2	Deliver MTO Product
P3	Plan Make						
P4	Plan Deliver	S3	Source ETO Product	M3	Engineering-to-Order	D3	Deliver ETO Product
Source Return				**Deliver Return**			
SR1	SR2	SR3		DR1	DR2		DR3
R1: Return Defective Product			R2: Return MRO Product			R3: Return Excess Product	

processes by recording down the Level 1 and Level 2 activities of current supply chain is also called "As-Is" stage, which requires the project team to canvas the business environment of an enterprise that should normally include two ties from the core firm (the centre of a supply chain, definition can be seen in Banerji & Sambharya, 1998, and Wang & Heng, 2002), that is, "the customer's customer" and the "supplier's supplier."

To begin with, it suggests an analysis to prepare the Level 1 document as to geographical context so as to reveal the transportation costs and trading relationships between the legal entities. Then, the diagram at Level 2 can be developed to describe the information flows of forecasts/orders and the material flow with the types of goods produced and delivered by connecting the business processes involved. Software has recently been developed to computerise the SCOR elements in enacting the interrelations of the processes, for example, ScorWizard, IBS Business Intelligence (BI), and i2 Enterprise Resource Planning (ERP) solutions. These are relatively helpful in simulating different scenarios based on the business strategies.

The SCOR model at Level 1 and Level 2 reveals the supply chain in a simplified way, thus enhancing its overall flexibility (Huang et al., 2005). Level 3 represents the decomposition of Level 2 processes in an interrelated way. For instance, there are four Level 3 components decomposed from P1 (Plan Supply Chain), as shown in Figure 1:

- P1.1 – identify, prioritize, and aggregate production requirements
- P1.2 – identify, assess, and aggregate supply chain resources
- P1.3 – balance supply chain resources with supply chain requirements
- P1.4 – establish and communicate supply chain plans

To accomplish the Level 3 activities, the "To-Be" (future) processes model is developed to support strategic objectives that should work within the new supply chain configuration at Level 2. At this level, all SCOR processes are interconnectively designed and running as an operation cycle of planning, execution, and enabling by certain frequency. The supply chain components at Level 4 are acting as the work statement that is expected to be set up by the project team without standardised documents. Eventually, the completed four levels become the guidelines for implementing supply chain management.

The SCOR model has become a topical issue, attracting not only the interest of enterprises themselves, but of industrial associations and government. Contrary to the industrial emphasis, there is a scarcity of academic literature regarding the application, adoption, benefits, and limitations of SCOR model, except for very

Figure 1. The "top-down" approach in implementing the SCOR model (Adapted from SCC, 2001)

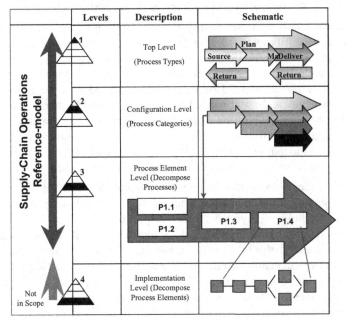

Notes: *P1.1—Identify, prioritize, and aggregate supply-chain requirements; P1.2—Identify, assess, and aggregate supply-chain requirements; P1.3—Balance production resources with supply-chain requirements; P1.4—Establish and communicate supply-chain plans*

few reports such as Huang et al. (2005) and Wang, Ho, and Chau (2005). The aspects of the framework that are of interests for further study in the literature are discussed in the subsequent sections.

The Participants' Role in Supply Chain Management

When configuring a supply chain, it is necessary to identify who the stakeholders within the channel context are. However, an inclusion of all potential partners might complicate the analysis of the complete supply chain, since it may explode the number of partners added from one tier to another (Cooper et al., 1997; Min & Zhou, 2002). The key is to target the supply chain entities that are critical to the value-added processes and are manageable by the core firm, that is, the centre of a supply chain targeted and is influential and powerful to its affiliate firms (Banerji & Sambharya, 1998; Wang & Heng, 2002).

As noted by Lambert, Cooper, and Pagh (1998), marketing research has contributed to identifying the members in a supply chain context, describing the needs for channel coordination, and drawing a marketing network. There are also studies with similar aspects from the area of strategic alliances and business network (e.g., Liu & Brookfield 2000) that are concerned about the germination of channel structure and participants. Lambert et al. (1998) further claim that the extant literature has not built on early contributions to put an emphasis on the complete supply chain from suppliers, manufacturers, distributors, and product brand owners. Indeed, one of the major weaknesses of SCM literature is the assumption that everyone knows the participants within the scope of SCM.

In a complete supply chain, there are primary stakeholders of SCM who actually perform operational and managerial activities in the channel processes and secondary stakeholders playing the roles of supporting entities such as the banks and freighters (Lambert et al., 1998). Although such classification may not be clear in all cases, it helps to identify the key customers who trigger the supply chain flows from demands and the major suppliers for value-added activities. From this starting point, the current SCOR model that only spans two tiers of the core firm becomes insufficient for analytical purpose, since the channel structure is quite often not a linear type and the supporting participants are not included in the analysing scope of the SCOR model.

Understanding the structural dimension of supply chains is a prerequisite for analysing and configuring the process links among channel members (Min & Zhou, 2002). The supply chain is derived from the interrelationships of its stakeholders that actually cause a multidimensional structure. Lambert et al.'s (1998) supply chain network indicates that there are two structural dimensions: horizontal and vertical, as shown in Figure 2. The horizontal structure represents the numbers of tiers along the analytical scope of a supply chain, and the vertical structure represents the number of partners within each tier.

Based on such aspect, a change of channel partners will alter the dimension of the supply chain. For example, the horizontal spectrum may become narrower when some entities merge with others. Outsourcing decisions may further change the scope and structure of supply network. In fact, some outsourcing firms can form various network formations other than the tier structure, such as rings, stars, or fans (Liu & Brookfield, 2000; Wang & Heng, 2002). The shifting of the supply chain scope (or, in some literature, the boundaries of the business network), which is normally caused by the strategic moves toward channel partners, eventually affects existing design and current managerial performance of SCM. A recent example is the case of the ACER Group which is associated with the shifting of channel structure that is reported by Wang and Ho (2005).

Figure 2. Supply chain network structure

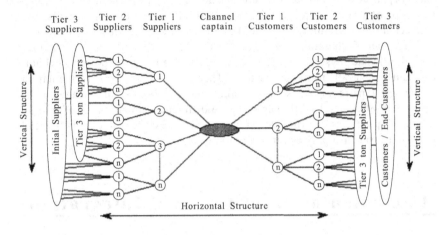

Despite a delicate design and implementation of global SCM and ERP systems, the ACER Group has suffered from a low retention rate of IT professionals of ERP systems and a lack of patterns for business processes reallocation in new manufacturing bases. These challenges are actually due to insufficient ante-consideration of potential business reallocation. When a sudden rundown occurred at several subordinates with reduced production volume in The Philippines and operation scale in Canada, it was somehow too late to adjust the plans of SCM. Therefore, it is necessary to identify the proper scope for a SCM project with the entities involved and then determine which aspects (e.g., geographical ranges and time period) of the supply chain network should be configured (Min & Zhou, 2002). Comparing the SCOR model, there are at least three limitations that can be found; they are:

- SCOR can only present business flow in between legal or geographical entities, not any matrix organisational structure or the concept of "virtual enterprise".

- SCOR is limited to the presentation of one single supply chain, while most enterprises may be associated with multiple channels of markets and products.

- The activities of collaborative design and customer relationships management are not defined in SCOR.

In brief, modeling a supply chain requires the analysis of relationships among channel participants and the structures formed. Thus, a clear picture for defining the scope of a SCM project can be presented. Moreover, these processes may connect multitiered supply chains as the core firm is actively involved in tier one and a number of other links beyond it. The direct involvement of a core firm may not only allocate physical resources but also interorganizational powers, technology, and knowhow to its trading partners. There is also indirect involvement from non-integral parts of the supply chain structure, but it can influence the operations of channel participants. Those different characteristics of trading relationships affect the firms' decisions regarding resource allocation that lead to the concerns in supply chain configuration.

Implementation of Channel Integration

The Transformation toward the "To-Be" Stage

Subsequent to the right analysis and design of supply chain management, this section discusses issues in the implementation of SCM. Using the terminology of the SCOR model, it is the "To-Be" stage. Figure 3 shows the most common goals and components of the transformation that involves human factors, business processes, and the technology, so as to build up a unified order desk, purchasing channels, delivery tracking, and so on, for the support of supply chain decision. Although the SCOR model is a widely adopted industrial standard—and possibly the only one—it has not successfully addressed a transforming framework from the stages of "As-Is" to "To-Be" for SCM projects. In particular, it merely handles the components of business processes and technology without tackling any social factors or human issues.

The previous section has portrayed the "top-down" approaches by utilising SCOR model as a standard. That approach requires the team of a SCM project to lay out existing business processes and use the suggested SCOR metrics to diagnose current problems for the implementation of ideal SCM. At least the Level 1 and Level 2 business processes should be confirmed so that hundreds of metrics can be then applied to measure the current operation excellence along the specific supply chain, such as "day of inventory" (Level 2) in the category of cash-to-cash cycle time (Level 1) and "supplier on time and in full delivery" (Level 2) in the category of delivery performance (Level 1). The step of measuring KPI of the supply chain activities belongs to the second stage of SCOR, namely "gap analysis," which underpins the design of "To-Be" processes. In other words, the differences between current status and ideal

Figure 3. The components of implementing SCM projects from As-Is to To-Be

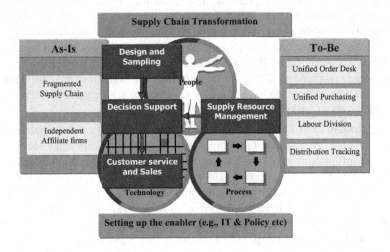

performance are actually the opportunities for improvement based on the expectation of target firms and on the comparison with competitors.

Nevertheless, such a way of bridging the gap between "As-Is" and "To-Be" might not be applicable to many circumstances. There are at least two reasons, as discussed below. First, the KPI analysis, which depends on recording operation outcomes, is actually a measuring tool from a basis of productivity, efficiency, and profitability. There is a myth that the figures of operation excellence and actual responsibility can and should be combined in an ideal business situation. However, it is clear that they are at least partially contradictory.

First, on the one hand, the business units within a supply chain must try to achieve operation excellence for survival, and each of the enterprises has the pressure and duty to earn a higher return on its shareholders' equity than occurred before the SCM project. The KPI figures that are made create trust on the part of investors and are usually reflected in short-term operation efficiency, making it easier to project to an image of corporate success. These indicators are not only a sort of management result, but also a source of enterprise competitive health and wealth at a supply chain context.

On the other hand, supply chain participants are networks of parties that work together by trading relationships toward both a shared goal and individual interests without being merely economic machines. Although an SCM initiator (mostly the core firms) represents a major role of the value of channel participants, it does not necessarily have enough power to force its partners to follow the integration contents. Likewise, it is also important for trust to develop between the SCM initiator and its external partners and other interest groups. Such trust can only be built up from ensuring that the perceived value of all entities and stakeholders along the supply chain are taken into account. However, it may be difficult to have a unique standard of KPI measurement across the boundaries of enterprises.

Second, the KPI of SCOR is not always available in the SCM initiator, particular when it involves the sharing of interorganizational information. It may be caused by lack of information readiness in other trading partners (Iacovou, Benbasat, & Dexter, 1995; Lee, Clark, & Tam, 1999; Wang et al., 2005). For instance, the calculation for the indicator of "Complete Manufacture to Order Ready for Shipment Time" might need the information of several tiers of suppliers and collaborative manufacturers, since there are usually several working segments before the delivery of final products. As such, the SCM initiator must gather operation information from various suppliers in time for a precise estimation of this KPI. Unfortunately, in the brick-and-mortar world, it is not easy to ensure equal systems readiness between an SCM initiator and its trading partners, albeit even the headquarter may find it difficult to obtain confidential information from its subordinators because their interests are potentially contradictory.

Last but not the least, KPI analysis has a limitation in corresponding to the strategic choices. For example, a SCM initiator may consider "Perfect Order Fulfil Rate" to be the most important target in the very beginning, when the distributors have equal or much more power than it does. This occurs in the supply chain of the Taiwanese IT industry (e.g., Wistron, Accton, and Asus); many of them initiate their projects of global logistics management with the major players such as Dell and IBM. They have to give in to the benefits of reducing inventory level for channel competency. Only when they ensure the higher bargain power with their customers would they adjust the ratio of some KPI evaluations along the supply chain.

Major Approaches of the Transformation

In a matrix of two-dimensional content analysis, Croom et al. (2000) highlight four major categories of supply chain elements for trading exchanges by summarising the extant literature. These categories are assets, information, knowledge, and relationships. In Croom et al.'s (2000) framework, SCM elements are further divided into three levels of dyadic, chain, and network forms. These elements are much richer than those defined in the SCOR model, which are very limited in the categories of assets and information and still less than the two-dimensional framework just mentioned. For example, SCOR does not include the analysis of total cost ownership (asset), business network redesign (information), human resource planning (knowledge), or trust/power/ commitment (relationship). However, there is, in particular, a scarcity of research on knowledge elements for SCM that lead to their unclear and inconsistent presence in the literature. The few examples are the subjects of knowledge with time-based capabilities in production activities (Handfield & Nichols, 1999) and configure-to-order for customised sales (Ton & Liao, 2002). The last category of Croom et al.'s (2000) framework is associated with "soft" elements, since relationship is a social tie existing among the supply chain entities. Although there have not been any widely accepted methods in industry (nor in SCOR) for managing the supply chain relationships, some scholars have considered it to be the most important figure in SCM. For example, Handfield and Nichols (1999) indicate that the efforts of other elements for implementing SCM in managing the flows of information and materials are likely to be unsuccessful if there is not a solid foundation of effective relationships in the channel context.

In order to mark up the insufficiency of the SCOR model and to map the Croom et al.'s (2000) elements, we propose a method in bridging current gaps for the SCM transformation processes. As shown in Figure 4, there are four major approaches, namely, KPI analysis, problem/opportunities analysis, expectation/ constraints, and the experts' opinions, which can be amended to the SCOR model as explained next.

Figure 4. Bridging the gap of the supply chain transformation

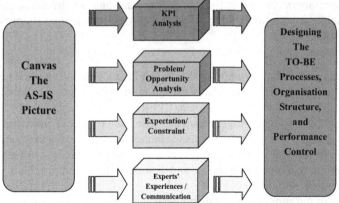

- **KPI analysis:** This approach follows the typical "top-down" SCOR analytical processes and is relevant when most operation figures are recorded and updated regularly. Since it requires information across the boundaries of firms, the SCM adopters may often encounter difficulties by merely using such an approach. It is even true in the situation in which most channel participants are subordinates or in joint ventures of a particular adopter because of unequal readiness of IT infrastructure or conflictions of management interests.

- **Problem/opportunity analysis:** When identifying the processes "gaps" by KPI information becomes less achievable, it is possible to find out the existing problems and difficulties by interviewing the employees from both upstream and downstream of the supply chain. Contrary to the KPI analysis that starts by enacting the supply chain strategy and comparing existing performance and the targets, problem/opportunity analysis is rather a "bottom-up" approach. It is suggested that the SCM project participants record various feedback and then map them into the different levels of SCOR processes. For instance, the KPI of "day sales receivable outstanding" in the Delivery element of SCOR Level 2 is related to the processes performance of the sales department. The same goal of identifying the SCM gaps can thus be achieved by directly finding problem/opportunity through individual interviewing and observation.

- **Expectation/constraint:** One of the successful key factors in implementing an SCM project is the participants' attitude with commitment to collaborative improvements. It will affect the information gathering for KPI and problem analyses and the subsequent actions for supply chain modification that is sometimes accompanied by the adjustment of existing benefits among channel members. For example, the delivery routes, supply chain policies of pricing and return of goods, and requirements of forecasting between buyers-suppliers may be altered after the SCM implementation. It is, therefore, necessary to find out the expectations/constraints of channel participants so as to avoid the potential conflictions among supply chain entities.

Another example is that examining the demand management processes of the SCM initiator might lead to a tentative solution of implementing collaborative planning, forecasting and replenishment (CPFR) systems as suggested by SCOR model. However, doing so might require the adoption of new IT infrastructures and cause changes to the existing demand management processes in some of the suppliers. It is inevitable that compromises will have to be made in order for the transformation to happen in upstream and downstream of a supply chain. There are a few points should be considered when identifying the expectations and constraints of the supply chain stakeholders:

- Enterprise as a participant in a business ecosystem and supply network
- Cluster of firms that gradually evolves as a group—the coevolution effects
- Gradual development of shared vision—centred around a product or product group
- Further, the role of clusters in competitiveness

The experts' experiences/communication: The last approach for the supply chain transformation is to adopt an expert opinion from a third party. A SCM project covers the areas of channel collaboration in material management, production planning, sales/distribution, quality control, assets management, and cost controlling, and requires the knowledge of a business processes enabler, such as the adoption of information systems. Acquiring expert opinions is vital to the successfulness of any SCM project, not only because of the need for the above expertise, but also in the pre-selection adoption methods, business processes design, training, and customised IT systems. That means, most likely, that firms have to get the help of consulting companies to enact the proper adoption methods and learn from others' successful experiences. Nevertheless, the SCM project owners have to interact with outside consultants who are not always familiar with the "know-how" of a particular industrial context.

Quanta Computer Inc., one of the major players in the IT industry of global market, has a sales volume of USD 10 billion in 2004. Its implementation of SCM has become a legendary story in the Taiwanese IT industry, as Quanta Computer Inc. accomplished the supply chain processes redesign with its trading partners and established its ERP systems (a modified version of SAP) in only half a year. It is a monumental SCM implementation project, not only because of such a short period of time, but also because of the success of building up the global supply network to dramatically achieve the target of cost cutting through low-level inventories. An interesting thing was, although the consultants for the SCM project of Quanta Computer Inc. had a strong background in SAP systems, only the project manager was initially conversant with the production line of IT products. Communication and exchange of ideas thus played a significant role before the commencement of SCM adoption. In addition, Quanta Computer Inc. and its trading partners have cooperated with consultants from various global regions throughout the adoption period.

In short, the transformation of existing supply chain processes and structure relies on identifying the gaps and opportunities for improvement. Both "top-down" and "bottom-up" approaches are keys to the success of supply chain configuration now and in the future. Moreover, it is necessary to discreetly survey the stakeholders' expectations from the standpoint of various supply chain entities in order to ensure substantial benefits and learn from the anatomy of successful/failed cases via the experiences of the experts from the third party.

Combining the Performance Control into SCOR Analysis

The important leverage gained from the supply chain integration is the mitigation of risk by certain control (Min & Zhou, 2002). It is generally believed that the implementation of an SCM project consumes considerable resources of human labour, materials, and time. It will definitely have an impact on the enterprise and its trading partners. Therefore, a part of reasonable performance control is to ensure that the supply chain operates right on track.

For such consideration, there are hundreds of KPI (metrics) mapping the levels of business processes defined in the SCOR model. Whether the KPI information of the supply chain entities is available for calculation or not, it is possible to find out the existing problems and difficulties of supply chain configuration, as suggested in previous section. The recorded "As-Is" process, as illustrated in Figure 5, can be labelled in the format of normal flowchart.

Then, each of the codified processes should be analysed by a set of SIPOC diagrams (Pyzdek, 2003), which were originally used as quality control tools and can detail the information deliver (supplier), data sent (input), data generated (output), and information receiver (customer) for the purpose of systems development. This instrument allows us to see the opportunities for improving

Figure 5. Example of current processses coding in the flowchart

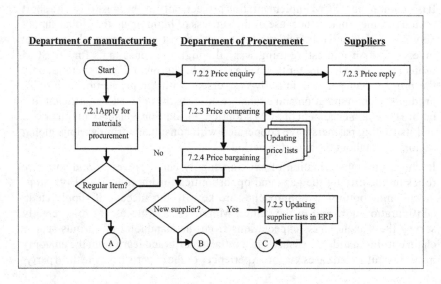

current communication interfaces among departments and trading partners. The previously identified "gaps" should be then codified, grouped, and prioritised, since some of them may cause similar problems, affect related business processes and supply chain entities, or be overcome by integrated solutions. The grouped and prioritised "gaps" thus become the basis for creating "To-Be" scenarios that are associated with the adjustment of corporate policies, organisation structures, business flows, and information systems.

As previously discussed, most of the KPI items are naturally related to existing business processes because of their formulas for calculation. For instance, the KPI "day sales receivable outstanding" in the D element of SCOR Level 2 is related to the processes performance of sales department. As most of the SCOR metrics are related to the business processes of a single organisation, we recommend an extended table to map the cross-functional channel activities for performance monitoring encompassing the supply chain entities within the scope of an SCM project.

Formulated in another way, the business processes can be divided into two types—the planing and coordinating activities owned by the supply chain group and the operational activities of individual firms. Staff in the department of procurement in one firm might often play the role of directly and indirectly taking care of the purchasing decisions of other collaborative participants in the supply

Table 2. The control panel of planning and decision-making activities

Collaborative activities			Individual Supply Chain Entities				
Business Processes	SCOR Code	'To-Be' SCOR KPI	Core firm (SCM initiator)	Distributor	Supplier 1	Supplier 2	Current Business Processes Code
Supply Chain Planing	P1	Provided by SCOR documents (should be further selected	V				Recorded in 'As-Is' analysis and should be
Plan Sourcing	P2	based on the top managers'	V	V			mapped into the planning
Plan Making	P3	opinion).	V		V	V	processes.
Plan Delivering	P4		V	V			

Notes: The level 3 SCOR code and the related departments of each supply chain entities should be shown on a real control panel. They are omitted in this table because of consideration of simplicity.

chain structure. The supply chain coordinating team may also negotiate with the customers' team to manage the suppliers' inventory level (Lambert & Pohlen, 2001). Ideally, it means that they should be evaluated both by the KPI of their original firms and the KPI of the suppliers and customers, based on certain percentages in order to monitor the two types of business processes. A control panel is thus generated in Table 2 for designing the KPI measurement and monitoring the supply chain performance.

Table 2 is an example of the control panel for planning and decision-making activities that maps the existing processes and "To-Be" processes in a project with four companies. It entails the information of how to control the supply chain functions across the boundaries of firms based on the selected KPI that are predefined by the SCOR standard. More importantly, this table contains the implications that the "gaps" between the current and future infrastructures of information exchange might be overcome by combining the current business processes codes that are embedded with SIPOC analyses and the responsible supply chain entities. One of the benefits is, for example, this joint process-metrics analysis of customer, supplier, and distributor will capture how the repositioning of inventory control improves total supply chain performance, whereas the information of inventory turns does not reflect any of the trade-offs that occurred in the channel links (Lambert & Pohlen, 2001). Consequently, it amends the insufficiency of using current SCOR metrics in the dyad and network supply chain structure.

Conclusion

We have stated in the foregoing sections that SCM plays a role in influencing the economic behaviour by the way business processes are managed. This, in itself, is certainly a very significant point, as it influences the costs of inventory holding, goods delivery, and manufacturing processes. In particular, it affects performance in customer fulfillment and cash-to-cash cycling, which are vital to enterprise survival (Garrison & Noreen, 2003). Achieving effectiveness of SCM does not only rely on process tuning, but also just-in-time communication and decision making through the enablers as performance measurement and information systems. Despite its importance, however, there is not much literature on the implementing framework, and most of the existing reports are individual case studies (Croom et al., 2000).

The SCOR model has been the most widely adopted standard and may be the only one for the analysis of SCM implementation. It has been modified several times since its first announcement by the Supply Chain Council in 1996. There

Figure 5. The sequence of SCM implementation

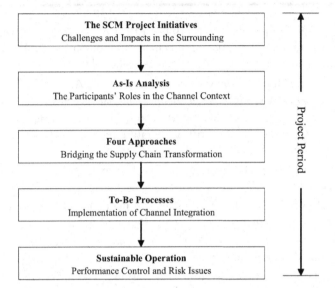

is yet another point deserving the attention of academia and practitioners, namely, it is not a complete framework for implementation of an SCM project, but merely a referential tool for assigning business processes and associated factors of performance measures. It may actually be dysfunctional without considering the stakeholders' value/expectation and embedding the mutually owned processes into performance measurement. Therefore, we have amended its weakness by discussing the supply chain configuration and transformation and the implementation procedures.

Future research is required to test the proposed framework in actual business settings, including different industries and regions. Other barriers and limitations to SCM implementation and how they shall be overcome need to be further identified. These may consist of the demand up-size and down-size from order changes, for example, emergent orders or order cancelling, and the calculation of KPI for nonfinancial figures from the operation activities. To the extent that similar difficulties and solutions are identified in various supply chain context, it is possible that a refined framework can be developed for practitioners. Finally, progress should be tracked over time to prove the long-term benefits derived from implementing SCM based on such a framework.

References

Banerji, K. ,& Sambharya, R. B. (1998). Effect of network organization on alliance formation: A study of the Japanese automobile ancillary industry. *Journal of International Management, 4*(1), 41-57.

Cooper, M. C., Ellram, L. M., Gardner, J. T., & Hank, A. M. (1997). Meshing multiple alliances. *Journal of Business Logistics, 18*(1), 67-89.

Croom, S., Romano, P., & Giannakis, M. (2000). Supply chain management: An analytical framework for critical literature review. *European Journal of Purchasing & Supply Management, 6*, 67-83.

Farley, G. A. (1997). Discovering supply chain management: A roundtable discussion. *APICS – the Performance Advantage, 7*(1), 38-39.

Forrester, J. W. (1958). Industrial dynamics: A major breakthrough for decision makers. *Harvard Business Review, 36*(4), 37-66.

Garrison, R. H., & Noreen, E. W. (2003). *Managerial accounting* (10th ed.). Boston: McGraw-Hill Irwin.

Gulati, R. (1999). Network location and learning: The influence of network resources and firm capacities on alliance formation. *Strategic Management Journal, 20*(5), 397-402.

Handfield, R.B., & Nichols, E.L. (1999). *Introduction to supply chain management*. Upper Saddle River, NJ: Prentice-Hall International Editions.

Huang, S. H., Sheoran, S. K., & Keskar, H. (2005). Computer-assisted supply chain configuration based on supply chain operations reference (SCOR) model. *Computers & Industrial Engineering, 48*, 377-394.

Iacovou, C. L., Benbasat, I., & Dexter, A. S. (1995). Electronic data interchange and small organizations: Adoption and impact of technology. *MIS Quarterly, 19*(4), 465-85.

Lambert, D. M., Cooper, M. C., & Pagh, J. D. (1998). Supply chain management: Implementation issues and research opportunities. *International Journal of Logistics Management, 9*(2), 1-19.

Lambert, D. M. & Pohlen, T. L. (2001). Supply chain metrics. *International Journal of Logistics Management, 12*(1), 1-19.

Lee, H. G.., Clark, T., & Tam, K. Y. (1999). Research report: Can EDI benefit adopters? *Information System Research, 10*(2), 186-195.

Liu, R. J., & Brookfield J. (2000). Stars, rings and tiers: Organisational networks and their dynamics in Taiwan's machine tool industry. *Long Range Planning, 33*, 322-348.

Min, H., & Zhou, G. (2002). Supply chain modeling: Past, present, and future. *Computer and Industrial Engineering, 43,* 231-249.

Narasimhan, R., & Mahapatra, S. (2004). Decision models in global supply chain management. *Industrial Marketing Management, 33,* 21-27.

New, S., & Mitropoulos, I. (1995). Strategic networks: Morphology, epistemology, and praxis. *International Journal of Operations and Production Management, 16*(4), 19-34.

New, S. J., & Payne, P. (1995). Research frameworks in logistics: Three models, seven diners and a survey. *International Journal of Physical Distribution and Logistics Management, 25*(10), 60-77.

Premukumar, G. P. (2000). Interorganization systems and supply chain management: An information processing perspective. *Information Systems Management, 17*(3), 56-69.

Pyzdek, T. (2003). *The six sigma handbook, revised and expanded: The complete guide for greenbelts, blackbelts, and managers at all levels* (2nd ed.). New York: McGraw-Hill.

Rogers, S. (2004). Supply management: 6 elements of superior design. *Supply Chain Management Review, 8*(3), 48-54.

Saunders, M. J. (1997). *Strategic purchasing and supply chain management.* London: Pitman.

SCC. (2001). *Supply chain operations reference model: Overview of SCOR Version 6.2.* Pittsburgh, PA: Supply-Chain Council, Inc.

Sterman, J. D. (1989). Modeling managerial behavior: Misperceptions of feedback in a dynamic decision making experiment. *Management Science, 35*(3), 321-329.

Strader, T. J., Lin, F. R., & Shaw, M. (1999). Business-to-business electronic commerce and convergent assembly supply chain management. *Journal of Information Technology, 14,* 361-373.

Tan, K. C. (2001). A framework of supply chain management literature. *European Journal of Purchasing & Supply Management, 7,* 39-48.

Thorelli, H. B. (1986). Networks: Between markets and hierarchies. *Strategic Management Journal, 17,* 37-51.

Ton, L. L., & Liao, M. H. (2002). Optimized simulation of SCM: Cases on NB and PCB industries. In *Proceedings of the PCB Conferences on Production and Management.* (In Chinese)

Towill, D. R., Naim, M. M., & Wikner, J. (1992). Industrial dynamics simulation models in the design of supply chains. *International Journal of Physical Distribution and Logistics Management, 22*(5), 3-13.

Tranfield, D. & Starkey, K. (1998). The nature, social organization and promotion of management research: Towards policy. *British Journal of Management*, *9*, 341-353.

Wang, W. Y. C., & Heng, M. S. H. (2002). Boundaries of business network in supply chain: Overcoming SMEs barriers in implementing business-to-business integration. In *Proceedings of the 4th International Conference on Electronic Commerce*, Hong Kong.

Wang, W. Y. C., & Heng, M. S. H. (2004). Bridging B2B e-commerce gaps for Taiwanese SMEs: Issues of government support and policies. In B. J. Corbitt & N. Al-Qirim (Eds.), *E-business, e-government & small to medium-sized enterprises: Opportunities and challenges* (pp. 244-268). Hershey, PA: Idea Group Publishing.

Wang, W. Y. C., & Ho, Michael, S. C. (2005). Information systems dispatching in the global environment: ACER, a case of horizontal integration. *Journal of Cases on Information Technology, 8*(2), 45-61.

Wang, W. Y. C., Ho, M. S. C., & Chau, P.Y. K. (2005). A process-oriented methodology for the supply chain analysis of implementing global logistics information systems. In *Proceedings of the 2nd International conference on Innovations in Information Technology*, Dubai, UAE.

Windsor, D. (1998). *The definition of stakeholder status*. Presented at the International Association for Business and Society (IABS) Annual Conference, Kona-Kailua, HI.

Endnote

[1] Addition to the processes introduced in this chapter, the Supply Chain Council has recently announced DCOR and CCOR models to define the design and customer service activities to amend SCOR model. Some professionals have considered them to be part of the enablers of existing SCOR processors.

Chapter II

An Investigation into the Barriers to Introducing Virtual Enterprise Networks

Angela Lin, University of Sheffield, UK

David Patterson, Business Link South Yorkshire, UK

Abstract

This chapter reports on a preliminary investigation into the barriers related to the development of a virtual enterprise network in the creative digital industries sector in South Yorkshire, United Kingdom. Based on the concept of a virtual organization, it is argued that the key factors in delivering an integrated virtual value chain are trust and the control of risk. The connection between trust and the control of risk is demonstrated. Trust can be examined along three dimensions: competence, integrity, and benevolence. These dimensions of trust were used by the small and medium-sized enterprises (SMEs) in this study as the criteria for choosing business partners. Risks such as poaching, stealing, transaction-specific, information asymmetries, and loss of resource control were confirmed by the SMEs as the main sources of their resistance to participation in a virtual value chain. It is proposed that managers should pay attention to trust building and the control of risks at all stages of the development of a virtual value chain in order to drive collaboration forward

Introduction

Business Link South Yorkshire (BLSY) is a UK Government-funded organization dedicated to the support of small and medium-sized enterprises (SMEs) in South Yorkshire. The South Yorkshire region is currently undergoing a significant economic reconstruction after the decline of the traditional coal and steel industries during the 1980s. Prior to the 1980s, the coal and steel industries were the main employers in the region, and they were typically nationalized and large in size. This distinctive historical background is reflected not only in the fewer number of SMEs in South Yorkshire than in the rest of the Yorkshire and Humberside economic region but also in its significantly lower gross domestic product (GDP) than the rest of the UK. Hence, South Yorkshire's economic redevelopment and reconstruction concentrates on fostering enterprise among SMEs.

Within the scope of this regional redevelopment project, supply chain development was identified as a key to improving the competitive profiles of SMEs in South Yorkshire. BLSY was aware of the concept of the Virtual Enterprise Network (VEN), developed by the regional development agency, Yorkshire Forward. The aim of the VEN is to introduce new levels of collaboration among businesses beyond the traditional "back-to-back" supply chain contracting process and to encourage SMEs to join a VEN to tender for a large project and deliver it jointly.

This chapter presents a preliminary study to identify the challenges of implementing the concept of the virtual value chain in the creative and digital industry in South Yorkshire and to draw some lessons for further development of virtual supply chain management.

The organization of the chapter is as follows. The next section outlines the theoretical assumptions of the concept of the VEN and introduces the components of the model of the VEN developed by Yorkshire Forward. Then, the research design of this work is described, followed by the data analysis. The discussion section synthesizes and presents the findings. A concluding section outlines the implications of the research for future research and practices.

Background

This section presents the framework of VEN developed by Yorkshire Forward that is used by Business Link South Yorkshire to promote collaborative supply chain management among local SMEs. The section briefly reviews the concept of the virtual organization upon which the VEN framework was built, and this is followed by the introduction of the VEN framework.

Virtual Organization

The concept of a virtual organization emerged in the early 1990s to reflect the needs for a new form of organization that is speedy, flexible, fluid, and able to foster information and communication technologies (ICT) in order to face the challenges imposed by an ever-faster changing business environment (e.g., greater competition and globalization, Itrona, 2001a). Despite the fact that the concept of a virtual organization is much talked about both in academe and in commerce, there is still no cohesive vision of what a virtual organization should consist. The lack of a standard definition of the concept of a virtual organization is perhaps due to the fact that there are different ways of interpreting the term "virtual."

Views of "virtuality" can be categorized into those that emphasize the management changes supported by technology and those that emphasize technologies. The former regards virtuality as the management or organizational capacity that coordinates different groups of people or organizations to work together towards a common goal in an ad hoc manner. Information and communications technology advances this idea by providing tools and platforms to make coordination easier. From the technological driven point of view of the virtual organization, virtuality is about collaborating in distributed locations through computer-mediated virtual platforms; that is, virtuality refers to the virtual reality in the computing sense (Hughes, O'Brien, Randall, Rouncefield, & Tolmie, 1998).

From the organizational perspective (Venkatraman & Henderson, 1994, as quoted in Sieber, 2001), virtuality is:

[...] the ability of the organization to consistently obtain and coordinate critical competencies through its design of value-adding business processes and governance mechanisms involving external and internal constituency to deliver differential, superior value in the marketplace. (p. 251)

The description of the virtual organization given by Hughes et al. (1998) offers a comprehensive definition that gives equal consideration to both the organizational and technological issues embedded in the concept.

These "virtual" organizational arrangements consist of networks of workers and organizational units, linked by information and communication technologies, which will flexibly coordinate their activities and combine their skills and resources in order to achieve common goals but without very much by way of traditional hierarchical modes of central direction or supervision. Such arrangements will form and reform as problems arise, so providing a flexibility of response to changing circumstances and organizational needs.

The challenges of establishing the virtual organization include control and supervision of work, awareness and coordination of the efforts, and trust and collaboration. These challenges are magnified when one is building a virtual organization at the industrial level. This is because this type of virtual organization may not have a definite and well-defined organizational boundary and companies within it are loosely coupled. Often, the companies involved may see that the "organization" is "out there" instead of feeling that they are part of the organization (Pollock & Cornford, 2004); that is, companies may see the organization as "them" and never "us," and, as a result, the organization remains "virtual" (Pollock & Cornford, 2004).

A virtual organization raises concerns about how the work and the quality of the work produced by the companies involved can be controlled and supervised. It also raises the issue of what mechanisms would need to be in place to raise the members' awareness of which work tasks are ready and made available to others, and to coordinate the efforts of different members in order to ensure that separate activities and tasks come to have coherence (Hughes et al., 1998). In order to work together, companies are required to share information and to an extent make their internal processes transparent to other members (Hart & Saunders, 1997). This inevitably raises the question of corporate privacy and business confidentiality.

Barriers to Virtual Organizations

It is noted that there are a number of barriers to forming virtual organizations and to making virtual organizations work effectively. The two significant barriers—trust and risk—will be outlined in this section.

Trust

A virtual organization such as a virtual supply chain transcends conventional organizational boundaries to bind participants together on a temporary basis. A virtual organization encompasses various business interests and operations, organizational cultures and contexts, and business and social networks. Hence, by default, a virtual organization embraces uncertainties and risks caused by the conflicting interests that exist among its participants. "Trust is the foundation upon which commerce is built, and in the virtual world it may be the fuel for the

Table 1. Summary of trust dimensions

Trust dimension	Description
Competence	A company has the ability to deliver its promises to clients.
Integrity	A company acts in a consistent, reliable, and honest manner when delivering on its commitments.
Benevolence	A company has its 'heart' in right place and puts its clients' interests ahead of its own.

locomotion" (Tang et al., 2003, p. 342). Trust can be defined as "the willingness of a party to be vulnerable to the actions of another party based on the expectation that the other will perform a particular action to the trust or, irrespective of ability, to monitor or control that other party" (Mayer, Davis, & Schoorman, 1995).

Generally speaking, trust can be examined in three dimensions: (1) competence, (2) integrity, and (3) benevolence (Chen & Dhillon, 2003, Gefen & Silver, 1999, Hart & Saunders, 1997) (Table 1). Through its continual development, a trustful relationship changes over time from initiating, developing, building, and maintaining, to declining. Conditions that influence the development of such relationships include individuals' propensity for risk, the cost of failure, and past experience (Chen & Dhillon, 2003; Introna, 2001b).

If, as described, "trust is a social capital that may need a significant reciprocal social investment from the partners" (Introna, 2001b, p. 270), a virtual organization that emphasizes speedy, flexible, and temporary is obviously against this principle. A virtual organization requires cooperation and coordination between different parties. Trust acts as a foundation for such cooperation and coordination. Trust is also an indicator that can be used to assess and predict the future behavior of other parties in order to reduce the uncertainties and risks inherent in the business relationship. As suggested, trust can act to reduce ambiguities and uncertainties in business relationships so that cooperation and coordination can take place.

Trust is not always developed from scratch (McKnight, Cummings, & Chervany, 1998). It is suggested that trustworthiness, which is a belief that comes before trust, will determine how willing participants are to commit to developing a relationship. Trustworthiness is formed on the basis of the participants' initial encounters with each other, institutional expectations of how each other should and will behave, and preexisting dispositions. It is then argued that initial trustworthiness has a direct, positive relationship with early trust building (Jarvenpaa, Shaw, & Staples, 2004).

Risk

As outlined in the above discussion, risks are embedded in any interorganizational relationships. Two types of risks associated with the virtual organization are covered here: (1) risks in pooled information resources, and (2) risks in value/supply-chain (Kumar & Dissel, 1996, p. 291) (Table 2). The risks associated with pooled information resources include poaching and stealing. Poaching occurs when commonly held resources are diverted by participants for their own private use and private gain. Stealing occurs when participants are able to access information about business partners' customers and to deliberately entice customers away from those partners.

The risks associated with value/supply chain can be examined from a transaction perspective based on transaction cost theory. Transaction costs can be defined as "the costs of managing the interaction while keeping the opportunistic

Table 2. Summary of risks

Risks	Definition
Risks in pooled information resources	**Poaching:** commonly held resources are diverted by participants for their own private use and private gain. **Stealing:** previously private information is accessed by others for private gain.
Risks in value/supply-chain	**Transaction specific:** investment is specific to the project and cannot be reused in other projects. **Information asymmetry:** performance is difficult to monitor thereby encouraging opportunism among participants. **Loss of resource control:** resource control is lost when resources are passed onto a next party.

behavior under control so that ongoing cooperation between the units can be sustained" (Kumar & Dissel, 1996). Transaction risk refers to the risks associated with exposure to being exploited in the relationship (Kumar & Dissel, 1996). Three kinds of transaction risk are identified: transaction specific, information asymmetric, and loss of resource control (Clemons & Row, 1992). Transaction-specific risk occurs when the investments (e.g., capital) in the project cannot be used elsewhere; that is, where the investments are not reusable, portable, or compatible. Information-asymmetric risk refers to the risk caused by the fact that performance by the participants is difficult to monitor, thereby increasing performance shirking by opportunists at the expense of others. Loss of resource control occurs when resources are transferred between different parties as part of the relationship. There are two types of resources subject to loss of control; one is the physical resources that one party relies on others to supply in order to accomplish the work, and the other is the intellectual property, such as knowhow and information, which is unique to the party.

Risks are inevitable in the virtual organizations. This is because the ties between the participants are not always close and the chance of opportunism taking place is greater. Thus, the importance of trust building becomes significant when risks are perceived by the participants of the virtual organization.

Virtual Enterprise Network by the Business Link South Yorkshire

Building upon the concept of the virtual organization, a framework for a VEN is a conceptual model that outlines the strategies that government agencies and SMEs can take to create virtual organizations among themselves to work towards a common goal. There are two main parts to the VEN framework. One focuses on the development to form the basis of the virtual organization, and the other focuses on the levels of virtual supply chain development. The underlying assumption of the VEN model is that the assembling of a virtual enterprise will achieve resource efficiency, market efficiency, and process efficiency. These efficiency objectives can be achieved through mechanisms that develop relationships between companies. These mechanisms include: networking, special interest groups, one-to-one trading, recommending suppliers, nominating suppliers, and partnering.

* **Networking:** This is perhaps the first step towards virtuality as it aims to bring businesses into contact with other businesses in the same sector. It is believed that the knowledge of and relationships with other businesses through networking will be the foundation of a VEN.

- **Special interest groups (SIGs):** It is to believe that special interest groups will emerge from the initial networking. The SIGs have typically become "industry-led" with companies taking the initiative in developing the group. These groups have typically focused on common technical issues faced by businesses.

- **One-to-one trading:** This is often the desired outcome of the networking and special interest groups. It is also a critical step to establishing a long-term relationship.

- **Recommending suppliers:** This reflects whether a company prepares to recommend other business(es) to its business associates to form a larger network.

- **Nominating suppliers:** This reflects the willingness of a company to nominate other supplier(s) to complete the job.

- **Partnering:** This is a network of strategic alliances. Partners in a virtual enterprise network are mutually dependent and rely on each other to achieve specific goal (e.g., a specific project).

It is worth noting that relationship development does not always reflect the duration of the time businesses have known each other. In practice, it depends on the business opportunity that is available as that may speed up the development, for example, going from the stage of the networking directly to the stage of the partnering.

The second part of the framework focuses on evaluating and measuring the type of supply chain developed among businesses. There are four types of supply chain recognized by the framework. These types can be categorized according to the sophistication of the supply chain involved:

- **Historical relationship-driven:** The supply chain is formed on the basis of businesses relationships with each other in the past.

- **Price-driven:** The supply chain is formed on the basis of a quote-driven relationship(s), principally focused on a reduction in price against given specifications.

- **Best value-driven:** The supply chain is formed on the basis of a relationship that seeks to deliver additional benefits over and above those of price, including metrics-based measurement of different suppliers' performance.

- **(Advanced) Supply Chain Management:** The supply chain is formed on the basis of the application of innovative techniques, such as just-in-time (JIT), collaborative planning, forecasting and replenishment (CPFR), or the concept of an extended enterprise. This type of supply chain is formed in order to deliver significant reductions in transaction costs, to improve information exchange, and to reduce inventory levels.

BLSY is currently focusing its attention on the first part of framework, helping to establish a range of face-to-face forums in order to create opportunities for businesses to meet and form relationships. BLSY hopes that it is through such relationship development opportunities that collaboration between businesses will eventually take place.

Research Design

The overall aim of this study was to understand the mechanisms that SMEs in the creative and digital industries use to develop their business networks and, from there on, an integrated supply chain.

This research employed the case study approach to address challenges of implementing the concept of the virtual enterprise network (VEN) in the creative and digital industries sector within the South Yorkshire region. The creative and digital industries sector was chosen for the study for two main reasons. First, the sector is one of the business clusters that is thought to be a key to the regional regeneration in South Yorkshire, and while the business community has seen a wide range of networks and support organizations emerge within the sector in recent years, anecdotal evidence suggests that the sector remains fragmented in its supply chain development. Second, companies in the creative and digital sector appear to be more interested in and willing to consider using a VEN compared to those in more traditional sectors such as the advanced metals and materials industry.

The data was collected through multiple sources of information. Background knowledge of VEN was formed through participation in presentations and meetings where the framework was developed by Yorkshire Forward. The semi-structured interviews with some stakeholders, including a Business Link South Yorkshire advisor and some local SMEs in the creative and digital sector, were the main source of data. Interviews were designed to collect data on issues such as how SMEs associate with other comparable businesses, how they go about developing relationships with other businesses, what the issues are around rivalry and collaboration with other businesses, and how SMEs in the sector go about developing their supply chains. The questions were also asked with an attempt to identify SMEs' attitudes towards joining a VEN. A range of people

Table 3. Summary of the interviews

Interviewees	Company	The nature of the business
Barker	Ascension Design	Web developer offers leading edge bespoke Web design and e-commerce solutions.
Walker	Metatek	Technology consultancy business. Also acts as Technology director for a new business being launched.
Vernon	Epitomy	Software development business provides Internet based parts catalogues and supply chain management solutions principally to the automotive industry.
McEwen	ACS (UK) Ltd	Hardware and software reseller and ICT support business operating across the North of England
Gilbert	Business Link	Adviser

in the creative and digital sector were contacted for interviews. Due to the accessibility (i.e., the willingness and availability) of these individuals, a total number of five interviews were carried out. Table 3 outlines the background of the interviewees.

This is an exploratory case study; therefore, it adopted a categorical aggregation data analysis approach (Stake, 1995) with which "the researcher seeks a collection of instances from the data, hoping that issue-relevant meanings will emerge" (Creswell, 1998, p. 154). As this study is interested in the challenges of implementing VENs among the regional SMEs, the data analysis focused on stakeholders' attitudes towards and views of the VEN and the challenges that the stakeholders expected to face when implementing the VEN framework.

Data Analysis

The analysis is organized under the two headings: (1) networks and (2) barriers to VENs. Networks were identified by the SMEs as the major source of business collaboration. Currently, SMEs rely on extension of the existing social networks to form business partnerships. This, however, limits the scope of the network; hence, the concept of building business networks through VENs was appealing to some. The barriers identified by the SMEs to building a VEN or participating in one were mainly associated with issues such as trust, risks, and ownership of resources. The SMEs argued that until these issues can be solved there is always going to be hesitation in taking a part in a VEN.

Networks

As with other business sectors, both formal and informal networks were valued highly by SMEs in the digital and creative industries. SME representatives interviewed believed that having a good position in the right networks gave them good access to resources and business opportunities. Three different types of networks were identified as being used by SMEs to gain access to business opportunities: social networks, business networks, and established public networks.

Social networks were said to be critical to all the SMEs in the study. These networks provided SMEs with the initial contacts that enabled them to meet potential clients and raise people's awareness of their existence. The networks were regarded as critical assets in the early stage of the establishment of the businesses.

Initially I set up business as a sole trader, a friend of mine who had been an IT contractor for years, took me under his wing as a mentor sort of thing. Recently it has just been people who I am happy to come across. Very recently, I began to get in touch with the South Yorkshire Digital Network and talked to people there about what we do and then we sort of agreed to keep in touch with each other. Basically, it is through people I formed friendship with. (Interview with Barker at Ascension Design)

In order to maintain the networks and to establish reputation within the networks, the SMEs then concentrated on making sure that the quality of their delivery meets or even goes beyond their clients' expectations.

If you have done a good job with one or two or three it is very nice because you build the reputation. Even if you miss the boat on one, people realised that you aren't not doing your jobs or not good at getting the funding. It is just really the case of that you cannot win them all. That is nice you establish yourself within a network as someone who can deliver and knows their business within that particular area. The network is extremely important to me. (Interview with Walke at Metatek)

However, the SMEs realised that simply relying on existing social as well as business networks may not enable them to grow at the rate that they expected, and, as such, they were willing and prepared to move away from an informal to a more formal business setting. In addition, through cross networks networking, businesses were able to crosscheck companies that had already been known to them and to learn about other unfamiliar companies. Actively participating in the networking forums and special interest groups initiated and organised by BLSY is the evidence on one hand. On the other hand, the SMEs were keen on talking to advisers in the BLSY or other similar organizations to seek for potential opportunities.

It has been interesting to hear what people say about, obviously people talking to people about what people do. [...] I want to make sure that businesses that I work with are certain body as well. The network is good because you can actually get an idea about what people are like, it is quite useful to listen to what people say and get a feel for that. (Interview with Barker at Ascension Design)

Club UK Online (A BLSY managed project) is very useful; we collaborate on projects where ACS cannot quite deliver everything, only perhaps 60%, so we have to collaborate people in the network. (Interview with McEwen at ACS [UK] Ltd)

Although the SMEs appreciated the size of each network they were counting on the depth of each business relationship. That is, instead of developing close relationships with other similar businesses horizontally, the SMEs in the study preferred to develop close relationships vertically with their clients. As explained, having good relationships with clients could often lead to other long-term contracts and opportunities to be recommended to other companies by the current clients. For example, the interviewee from Ascension Design said:

[...] because the relationship that we have there [the name of the company] we know unless that we really have to mess up the relationship before they could somewhere else. So again, that is the way we work with people, and the organizations are pretty confident with our work. (Interview with Barker at Ascension Design)

Barriers to VEN

The SMEs relied on networking as a tool to establish contacts, and most of them admitted that they would not commit themselves to a VEN unless they knew what the commitments and benefits were in advance. The main concerns that seem to influence the SMEs' decision about joining a VEN and collaborating with companies who are unknown to them to bid on large projects include: trust, intellectual property right, and risks.

Trust

The aim of the VEN framework is to encourage companies that have specific knowledge and capacity to work collectively to bid on and deliver large projects that they would be unable to do on their own. It was, however, pointed out during the interviews that a VEN would only work if there were trust relationships among the companies working together and between companies and the organization that manages the VEN. "Trust—that is everything" (Interview with Walke at Metatek).

It is noted that "trust" is a mechanism that helps people associate with each other and build relationship within the networks. Indeed, the SMEs would only be willing to trade and collaborate with others if a trust relationship exists.

If people get a sniff you are not in there for them, I think you are fighting a loosing battle. That is not to say you are in it for the good of your health, they understand you are in there to run your own business but they want to know that you also have their concerns at the forefront. (Interview with Walke at Metatek)

Very few people would buy from completely unknown companies particularly buying the service which has high people content. You will not do so without some form of familiarity i.e. from the buying process itself or through the network. (Interview with Vernon at Epitomy Solutions)

Trust also serves as a mechanism that enables the SMEs to share information and encourages them to be creative. The SMEs expressed that they would be happy to share information and collaborate with people or companies that they know but would be cautious about what to share when they work with strangers. "It would be inhibited especially if they are responsible for their own actions and information could be held against them" (Interview with Vernon at Epitomy Solutions). This is believed to discourage people from being creative.

If someone tells you something or you see something is done you cannot just unlearn. Although they may not steal your ideas with intention but once they see something is done in the new way you cannot ask them to unlearn about it. Besides, being a part of the VEN they can access to resources (e.g., in-depth knowledge). [...] Often the clients would come with the requirements and we would say no you don't want to do that. We would suggest other ways and that is the part of services that we offer. I think that if there is issue about intellectual property right I think that more people might just give what the clients are asking for. (Interview with Baker at Ascension Design)

The data suggested that trust is particularly important in the creative and digital sector because the product contents are people-intensive, and people working together on the same project need to be at the same level (e.g., with regard to technical know how) in order to ensure quality.

A large project or large client usually demands high level of commitment and high quality. [...] Every partner should be at the same level. (Interview with Barker at Ascension Design)

Within the framework model, information is expected to flow freely within the supply chain and the SMEs are encouraged to recommend and/or nominate suppliers to their clients when they cannot deliver the project alone. However, the interviewees did not seem to be warm to this idea. They explained that recommendation or nomination involves risks of losing business to rival companies and of damaging their own reputation.

I would not introduce anyone into the network if I thought they will take businesses away. That is why I really need to know people and trust them before I work with them. That is important. If I thought that that is likely to happen I probably wouldn't work with them. (Interview with Barker at Ascension Design)

We generally would not recommend anybody who hasn't done some work for us. We are quite funny about that. It does take a lot for us to recommend someone else, because again we have recommended and it hasn't gone well, so it's once bitten, twice shy. (Interview with McEwen at ACS [UK] Ltd.)

Intellectual Property Rights

Unlike the traditional manufacturing sector, one of the main concerns that the SMEs in the creative and digital sector have is intellectual property rights (IPR). This is perceived by the interviewees in this study as the second obvious barrier to joining the VEN. The IPR issue within the context of VEN is who owns the IPR to the final deliverable, which is the product of a joint effort under the umbrella of the VEN? The direct impact of this concern will be reflected in the amount of effort that participating companies put into the project and in the willingness to be creative and share information with others. Traditionally, protecting IPR is difficult for most SMEs because they do not have resources (e.g., legal expertise and finances) to do so. Hence, IPR is said to concern the SMEs more than it does larger sized companies. In this sense, until it is demonstrated that there is a strategy of managing potential conflicts caused by IPR issue among companies within a VEN, it would be difficult to convince the SMEs to join a VEN.

Risks

The concerns discussed above have their roots in the SMEs' perceptions of uncertainty and risks that they associate with joining a VEN. The SMEs suggested that they can only be convinced to participate in a VEN if good project and risk management is in place. An individual SME's efforts to build trust relationships with its clients and collaborators in the same supply chain are specifically intended to minimise the risks of financial loss, zero return on its commitment to the project, and bad reputation. Similarly, the concern about IPR is associated with the concern about risk of losing overall control of the product development. Nevertheless, if the organization that manages the VEN will take care of coordination issue, the interviewees expressed that they would not be so concerned about who their collaborators are.

The VEN framework is intended to encourage companies within a VEN to compete and bid to contribute to a specific part of a large project. The issue that the interviewees were concerned about was who will be in charge of quality inspection along the supply chain? In the immediate term, poor project delivery would cost the SMEs because they may need to commit resources to redo the project. In the long term, poor delivery would damage the companies' reputations.

We are very attached to the clients so for that reason if it is grounded working for VEN I would be less bothered with the people who I am working with because in the of the day it was VEN's responsibility if things go wrong. If that is the case I would be less bothered because I would expect that the people who are in charge of the VEN would handle the client relation and they would be the people who are bothered about who work together. I would say that it is not my role to do that. From that point I would be very happy to work with other people. (Interview with Barker at Ascension Design)

Other issues identified by the interviewees were the boundary definition and project audit. Boundary definition refers to defined responsibilities of each working party in a VEN.

From that point I would be very happy to work with other people. Obviously, my concern in that would be perhaps having just very clear boundary about who does what and how that is done because inevitably you will have a large involvement on that and obviously the work that we do/ handle would depend on what other people would do... .(Interview with Barker at Ascension Design)

The question is who controls the project; who controls the discussions with the client; who schedules the work; who you are collaborating with; and what sort of knowledge base they have. When things start to get messy who is going to pick up the pieces? (Interview with McEwen at ACS [UK] Ltd.)

Once the responsibility of each working party is defined, the next key issue is project audit, which addresses to need to audit and control the work at each stage of the value chain. ACS (UK) Ltd. has been participating and collaborating with companies within Club UK Online to deliver projects and argued that the framework of VEN could work if the project audit of a VEN is in place.

Club UK Online has very really good audit in place which ensures that businesses deliver what they say the will deliver. [...] we get the peace of mind, as been through same process as we have. [...] If you haven't got control of everything, there is always a likelihood (no matter what it says on paper) that something somewhere will go wrong, its just a question of how bad it will go wrong. (Interview with McEwen at ACS [UK] Ltd.)

Interestingly, it was suggested by the interviewee at Epitomy Solutions that the project control in itself presents a potential risk. It was explained that any potential structures imposed by the VEN organizer could create interorganizational conflicts, especially when the members of the VEN have to compete to bid for work. This, as described, may create a hostile environment that is contradictory to the idea of virtual enterprise network.

Networks perform best when willing members collaborate independently without being imposed and I don't think, speaking from my past experience, it does not necessarily be a recipe of success because it could lead to interorganizational conflicts. [...] the members of the bidding party should be allowed to coalesce naturally not having it as an imposed procedure. Therefore, I would thought that in the name of the virtual enterprise network is to create non-hostile environment in which that the enterprises would coalesce to be in the position to bid a larger orders and not to have them to compete individually for that. (Interview with Vernon at Epitomy Solution)

Discussion

This study has identified that networks, trust, perceived risks, and intellectual property rights are the key factors that influence SMEs' decisions about joining a virtual enterprise network in the creative and digital industries sector. These issues, except for intellectual property rights, have been identified as obstacles to the implementation of a virtual organization elsewhere in the literature (Chesbrough & Teece, 1996, Marshall, Burn, Wild, & Mckay, 1999). On the surface, SMEs in the study rely on networking to gain access to resources and to be "competitive." On closer scrutiny, however, it is apparent that SMEs use networking as a means to building a trusting relationship; that is, networking is only a means used to achieve an end, that of trust building. This supports the argument that trustworthiness is crucial in terms of initiating a trustful relationship. Indeed, the VEN framework takes this into account and encourages collaboration to be developed from special interest group meetings.

Trust and risk are inseparable. From the data analysis, it is apparent that collaboration will only take place if trust exists in the relationship and if the risks will be effectively managed. The incentive for SMEs to participate in a virtual enterprise network is not, as assumed by BLSY, being able to obtain a bigger contract—although the idea is attractive. Rather, it is the assurance that SMEs are able to form a mutual, trusting, and long-term business partnership with others. This is because SMEs traditionally rely on the face-to-face networks to pursue business opportunities.

Participation in a virtual value chain requires SMEs to coordinate and trust each other's output and share information with each other to an extent in order to deliver a common product. Although the interviewees in the study did not use the term "trust" explicitly, they emphasized the importance of "knowing who they are working with." "Knowing who they are working with" means knowing partners' competence, integrity, and benevolence in advance. These were three important criteria for choosing business partners. SMEs, for example, would like to know if the partners perform at the same level (e.g., have good knowledge) as they do. As pointed out by the SMEs, the interdependence between business partners in terms of inputs and outputs makes it difficult to identify an individual partner's responsibilities and efforts. Thus, entering into a "wrong" network may expose them to the risks of damaging their own reputation, which is particularly important for small to medium-sized businesses. This explains why the SMEs in the study were more willing to form a VEN with businesses with which they already had dealings and why they were less willing to participate in a VEN where the participants were unknown to them.

It was noticed that the major resistance to the virtual value chain is caused by uncertainty and control of the risks that are perceived to be involved. It was also noticed that trust relates to how risks are perceived by participants. In general, the data suggests that the more developed the trustful relationship is among partners, the less likely participating in a virtual value chain is perceived to be risky, and vice versa. The risks that the SMEs were concerned about include poaching, stealing, information asymmetries, and loss of resource control. For example, intellectual property is regarded as the most important asset in the creative and digital industries sector; hence, it is not surprising that the SMEs feared that entering a virtual enterprise network may expose them to risk. This is the main reason for the SMEs not wanting to collaborate with strangers as they worry that unfamiliar business partners may exploit collaboration for private gain (e.g., poaching or stealing resources).

Risks may be magnified when collaborators are mainly SMEs and none of them is the leader of a supply chain. Traditionally, SMEs have limited resources compared with larger sized enterprises; hence, in order to survive, SMEs need to ensure that their resources are allocated efficiently. Any risks that are perceived potentially endanger resource optimization and would not be welcomed by SMEs. In this sense, risk management can be used as a mechanism to compensate a lack of mutual trust in the virtual supply chain, and issues such as who will bear the cost and consequences of risks associated with interorganizational collaboration and how the risks are managed and controlled will determine the developmental dynamics of a VEN.

Future Trends

Recommendations for Practitioners

The technology that supports interorganizational coordination with an aim of achieving efficient supply chain management has been around a long time. The slow takeoff of the technology (such as EDI) among business has traditionally been blamed on the cost of the investment in the technology itself. Nevertheless, it was apparent in this study that whether or not and what technological platform will be used to coordinate the efforts among business partners are not perceived to be the keys that drives collaboration forward. What drive collaboration forward are the fundamental business issues of trust building and risk management. Thus, in order to develop effective interorganizational supply chain management, suppliers and business champions (e.g., the network leader, government agency) should consider the following strategies:

- Develop a robust and non-hostile environment where business associates are able to be familiar with and get to know each other and then gradually develop a trust relationship.

- Provide incentives to attract companies to work together towards a common goal. The incentives include terms of conditions and rewards for collaboration. It is important that the champion of the supply chain management explains how the collaboration will work and what and why specific commitment and risks will be expected. This will help participating companies reduce uncertainty and form realistic expectations for the outcome of the collaboration.

- Trust and risk are two sides of the same coin and one has impacts on the other. If, like the VEN model suggests, companies work on the project basis where trust relationship cannot be boosted and developed in a short time, risk management may have to be in place to replace trust relationship at the outset. This management mechanism can be gradually removed when companies begin to develop trust relationship.

Recommendations for Future Research

Given that supply chain management is rapidly evolving thanks to the development of information technology, further research in the areas of business relationships between organizations and the value of information sharing will be particularly useful. First, more research should focus on the business relationship development between organizations within the context of supply chain management, especially in the area of trust and power relationships, and collaboration and cooperation behaviors. Second, information is vital to coordinate business activities among partners but asking businesses to share information is always a challenging task. Hence, more studies should be carried out to examine the information requirements associated with different types of business relationships and the drivers that would encourage businesses to share information to achieve an effective supply chain.

Conclusion

The framework of VEN seems to work in the area of bringing different businesses together to explore the possibility of working together to develop new projects (e.g., product or business development). However, taking the framework a step further will require further hard work by BLSY, for example, to review its role in the virtual supply chain branded with VEN. Currently, BLSY is not considering taking on any managerial roles in any VEN project; rather, it sees itself as a broker who is bridging the different networks. However, the lessons from the interviews suggest that this approach will not be successful overall, but remains as a framework if BLSY does not have a stake in implementing VENs.

References

Chen, S., & Dhillon, G. (2003). Interpreting dimensions of consumer trust in e-commerce. *Information Technology and Management, 4*(2/3), 303-318.

Chesbrough, H. W., & Teece, D. J. (1996). When is virtual virtuous? *Harvard Business Review, 74*(1), 65-73.

Clemons, E., & Row, M. (1992). Information technology and industrial cooperation: The changing economics of coordination and ownership. *Journal of Management Information Systems, 9*(2), 9-28.

Creswell, J. W. (1998). *Qualitative inquiry and research design: Choosing among five traditions.* Thousand Oaks, CA: Sage Publications.

Gefen, D., & Silver, M. (1999, July 4-7). Lessons learned from the successful adoption of an ERP system. In *Proceedings of the 5th International Conference of the Decision Sciences Institute* (pp. 1054-1057). Athens, Greece: Decision Science Institute.

Hart, P., & Saunders, C. (1997). Power and trust: Critical factors in the adoption and use of electronic data interchange. *Organization Science*, *8*(1), 23-42.

Hughes, J., O'Brien, J., Randall, D., Rouncefield, M., & Tolmie, P. (1998), Some "real" problems of "virtual" organization. Published by the Department of Sociology, Lancaster University (UK). Retrieved March 7, 2005, from http://www.comp.lancs.ac.uk/sociology/papers/Hughes-et-al-Probhlems-of-Organization.pdf

Introna, L. (2001a). Defining the virtual organization. In S. Barnes & B. Hunt (Eds.), *E-commerce and V-business: Business models for global success* (pp. 43-52). Oxford, UK: Butterworth-Heinemann.

Introna, L. (2001b). Recognizing the limitations of virtual organizations. In S. Barnes & B. Hunt (Eds.), *E-commerce and V-business: Business models for global success* (pp. 268-277). Oxford, UK: Butterworth-Heinemann.

Jarvenpaa, S. L., Shaw, T. R., & Staples, D. S. (2004). Towards contextualized theories of trust: The role of trust in global virtual teams. *Information Systems Research*, *15*(3), 250-267.

Kumar, K., & Dissel, H. (1996). Sustainable collaboration: Managing conflict and cooperation in interorganizational systems. *MISQ, 20*(3), 279-330.

Marshall, P., Burn, J., Wild, M., & Mckay, J. (1999, June 23-25). Virtual organizations: Structure and strategic positioning. In *Proceedings of the 7th European Conference on Information Systems* (pp. 482-495). Copenhagen, Denmark: Copenhagen Business School.

Mayer, R. C., Davis, J. H., & Schoorman, F. D. (1995). An integrative model of organizational trust. *The Academy of Management Review, 20*(3), 709-734.

McKnight, D. H., Cummings, L. L., & Chervany, N. L. (1998). Initial trust formation in new organizational relationships. *The Academy of Management Review*, *23*(3), 473-490.

Pollock, N., & Cornford, J. (2004). ERP systems and the university as "unique" organization, *Information Technology and People*, *17*(1), 31-52.

Sieber, P. (2001). Virtuality in the IT industry. In S. Barnes & B. Hunt (Eds.), *E-commerce and V-business: Business models for global success* (pp. 250-267). Oxford, UK: Butterworth-Heinemann.

Stake, R. (1995). *The art of case study research.* Thousand Oaks, CA: Sage Publications.

Tang F. F, Thom, M. G., Wang, L. T., Tan, J. C., Chow, W. Y., & Tang, X. (2003). Using insurance to create trust on the Internet. *Communication of ACM, 46*(12), 344-377.

Chapter III

Information Flows in a New Zealand Sheep Meat Supply Chain

Andreas Schroeder, Victoria University of Wellington, New Zealand

Beverley G. Hope, Victoria University of Wellington, New Zealand

Abstract

Recent outbreaks of Bovine Spongiform Encephalopathy (BSE), foot-and-mouth disease, and bird flu have heightened awareness of traceability and information flows in agricultural industries. Existing supply chain research has focused on supply chains for manufactured goods, but the agricultural industry differs from manufacturing, being characterized by horizontal alliances and imprecise output predictions arising from uncontrollable factors such as weather and rates of natural increase. This chapter explores the downstream information flows in a sheep meat supply chain. It identifies stakeholders and the nature and efficiency of their information exchanges. Findings show that important information is generated in several tiers along the supply chain, but this information is not always shared and opportunities for increased supply chain competitiveness are lost. The lack of information sharing is explained by the unwillingness of partners to commit to tight contractual agreements, the lack of adequate technological infrastructure, and the absence of regulations mandating certain information flows.

Introduction

New Zealand, once known as "Britain's farm," is a world leader in production of quality beef, sheep, and dairy products. For more than a hundred years, New Zealand sheep meat has been produced for local consumption and export. Although it is less dependent on primary industries today than in the past, sheep meat is still a major export earner for New Zealand and its production and processing provides many employment opportunities.

A carefully coordinated supply chain would provide New Zealand's sheep meat industry with new capabilities and efficiencies in production and processing, as well as an increased responsiveness to consumer preferences. In addition, and more importantly, it would prepare the industry to meet increasing international requirements for traceability. A key element in agribusiness supply chain operation is the integration of information flows that not only facilitate operations but also add value to products and provide confidence to consumers. A sophisticated supply chain would lead the New Zealand's sheep meat industry into the 21st century and better prepare it for future competition in international markets.

The research reported in this chapter focuses on downstream information flows. We interviewed major stakeholders in the supply chain to determine their information needs and the information they provide to their downstream partners. In the remainder of this chapter, we report the various information flows and information media used, identify redundancies and deficiencies, and make recommendations for improvements.

Information Flows in the Supply Chain

Competitive environments create pressure on organisations to collaborate. Supply chain management governs these collaborations by integrating "key business processes from end users through to original suppliers that provide products, services, and information that add value for customers and other stakeholders" (Lambert & Cooper, 2000, p. 66). Information flows are critical to these collaborations and their improvement is a major incentive in supply chain integration (Buhr, 2000). Such flows creates closer collaboration between the supply chain members (Mariotti, 1999), have positive impacts on customer satisfaction (Singh, 1996), and can lead to the creation of new products and services, new marketing approaches, and advanced operations (Hoek, 1998).

Supply chain information flows can be upstream, from retailers toward producers, or downstream, from producers toward retailers. The upstream flow may comprise information ranging from order details to the sharing of customer requirements and strategic decisions (Sahin & Robinson, 2002). The objectives of these upstream flows include desire for cost-savings through inventory reduction, decreased order magnification, and reduced time delays in fulfillment (Lee et al., 1996, as cited in Zhao, Xie, & Zhang, 2002). Downstream flows may comprise product details, product origin and destination, shipment details, and invoicing information (Sahin & Robinson, 2002). Though most research concentrates on upstream flows, both upstream and downstream flows are crucial for supply chains (Singh, 1996)

Information technology is the backbone of a supply chain (Sanders, 2002). Sophisticated software and hardware components provide flexibility of operation to handle last-minute orders, order changes, mechanical failures, picking and packing errors, coordination failures, and data corrections (Hull, 2002). However, technology only enables information exchange; humans are the source of information and the drivers of technology. Consequently, people still play the pivotal role in supply chain environments and the relationship between buyers and suppliers remains a vital element of a successful supply chain (Kannan, 2002; Mariotti, 1999).

Supply Chain Management in the Agricultural Industry

Supply chain management first emerged in the manufacturing industry, and the processes of modern supply chain management reflect this origin. In considering supply chain management in the agricultural industry, we need to take into account differences in the business environment, product characteristics, and importance of downstream information flows.

The agribusiness environment is characterised by horizontal alliances such as cooperatives, rather than the vertical partnerships most often found in the manufacturing industry (Hobbs & Young, 2000). In addition, agricultural product sale and distribution is often carried out through intermittent auctions or less involving regulated markets. The horizontal alliances and product distribution mechanisms reduce the direct interaction between producer and buyer and inhibit development of close relationships (O'Keeffe, 1998). An additional factor inhibiting supply chain integration in the agricultural industry is the lack of information technology experience and confidence of some members (Salin, 2000). This inexperience, coupled with perceptions of high costs and risks, forms a considerable obstacle to the development of a sophisticated supply chain (Bailey, Norina, & Cassavant, 2002).

Product characteristics also provide a point of differentiation between agricultural and manufacturing industries. In manufacturing, production can be scheduled with relative precision so that output can be known in advance or adjusted to meet changing demand. By contrast, output of agricultural products cannot be precisely known in advance due to vagaries of weather, disease, and rates of natural increase. Furthermore, the time required to raise animals for consumption means it is impossible to adjust supply at short notice. Product quality is also a critical concern in agribusiness, necessitating high standards in handling, storage, and transportation (Jongen & Meulenberg, 1998). Consumers can be very sensitive to specific attributes of agricultural products and marketing needs to cater to local preferences in terms of product presentation, variety, and packaging. This is particularly important where a product is destined for international distribution (Jongen & Meulenberg, 1998). The product characteristics described create unique challenges for the coordination of an agricultural supply chain.

The agribusiness environment and product characteristics also create specific requirements for information flows. In many manufacturing supply chains, the focus is on *upstream* information flows signalling demand fluctuations. In the agricultural industry, equal or greater emphasis is placed on *downstream* information flows concerned with ensuring that hygiene, safety, and quality requirements are met. Using information systems to signal production conditions (e.g., organically fed) and product handling (e.g., halal meat preparation) facilitates the development of consumer trust by verifying that the product meets certain criteria or preferences (Dorp, 2003; Jongen & Meulenberg, 1998). Downstream information flows assist in providing traceability of product, which contributes to food safety and communicates diligent operations to the consumer (Dorp, 2003; Wilson & Clarke, 1998).

The meat industry, in particular, has employed information technology to process downstream information flows to enable traceability (Mousavi, Sarhadi, Lenk, & Fawcett, 2002). For example, the Scottish Borders Traceability and Assurance Group (TAG) initiative provides for full product traceability along the cattle beef supply chain using radio frequency identification (RFID) ear tags. The tags identify individual animals and link to records in a central database containing, among other things, date and place of birth, veterinary records, cattle movements, purchases and sales, and deaths on any farm where the beast has been held (Pettitt, 2001). Third parties, such as slaughterhouses or meat processors, may automatically read this information and update their own information databases. The RFID tag provides a system to deal with statutory record keeping, serves as a farm management system, and facilitates government control in the event of animal health emergencies such as recent BSE outbreaks.

Information technology has also been used for traceability in the Belgian poultry industry (Viaene & Verbeke, 1998). A central database registers all movements of poultry product from the reproduction facility and hatchery to the slaughterhouse. Using this database, the veterinary authority can investigate the source and spread of any disease outbreaks. In contrast to the Scottish Borders TAG initiative where individual tagging is used, the Belgian poultry initiative identifies on a flock basis because there are too many birds to trace individually. With the exception of a few elite products, traceability in the Belgian poultry industry is lost at the slaughterhouse (Fallon, 2001).

In summary, the unique business environment, product characteristics, and need for traceability distinguish agricultural products and supply chains from the manufacturing products and supply chains. The agricultural industry has a need for downstream information flows, which creates a challenge for supply chain management.

Agricultural Supply Chains in New Zealand

New Zealand's geography, climate, and long history in agricultural exporting have made it one of the world's most efficient producers of quality agricultural products (Ministry of Agriculture and Forestry, 2002). It achieves this efficiency without employing formal supply chain management principles to the extent seen in some other Organisation for Economic Co-operation and Development (OECD) countries (Basnet, Corner, Wisner, & Tan, 2003). The relative lack of supply chain management in New Zealand's industry in general may be attributed to its small and thinly spread population, its lack of any supply chain-intensive manufacturing industry to provide an example, and the "relative lack of leverage of New Zealand firms to bring about change" (Basnet et al., 2003, p. 63). Yet meat industry products, including sheep meat, contribute strongly to the New Zealand economy by being the second largest export income earner (Statistics New Zealand, 2000). Sophisticated supply chain processes may improve competitiveness through their ability to provide quality products, ensure standards are met, enable traceability, and generally demonstrate reliability (Penny, 2003).

At the time of writing, advanced information systems are in place only for the cattle-beef supply chain while the sheep meat industry makes limited use of information technology. This suggests room for improvement. The first step is an assessment of the current situation. An understanding of the downstream information flows is a crucial component for the sheep meat supply chain, and it is this information flow that is addressed in this research.

Research Method

Being an exploratory study, the primary concerns in this research were the identification of stakeholders in the sheep meat supply chain, the information they sought and supplied, the media used for its distribution and storage, and, ultimately, the identification of redundancies and inefficiencies in information flows. We aimed to not only understand *what* was happening, but also *why* it was happening; that is, to understand the motivators or reasons for what was happening. Hence, a case research methodology in line with recommendations of Benbasat, Goldstein, and Mead (1987) seemed appropriate. Data collection and analysis followed procedures introduced by Creswell (2003).

Informants included representatives of organisations directly involved in the supply chain and others with an oversight function. Informants directly involved in the supply chain included a sheep farmer, stock agent, meat processor, a meat wholesaler/retailer, supermarket butcher, and an independent retail butcher. Those with an oversight function included the director of the Meat industry Association and a field representative of a Food & Safety Authority. The interview with the director of the Meat Industry Association provided us with background knowledge with which we could prepare for further interviews. Furthermore, this informant was able to provide a high-level view of the industry and what the future might hold.

Semi-structured interviews were designed to gather specific information while allowing for unexpected data to emerge. Interviews took between 30 and 60 minutes and were transcribed in full upon completion. Transcripts were analyzed following the generic steps suggested by Creswell (2003) for analysis and interpretation of qualitative data. Steps included organizing and preparing the data (transcribing interviews and typing field notes), deriving a general sense of the data, and coding for detailed analysis. These generic steps proved to be a valuable guide for analysis and significantly contributed to the outcome of the investigation.

Results

In this section, we first provide a brief summary of each of the stakeholders in the sheep meat supply chain followed by an analysis of the information flows.

Figure 1. Stakeholders in the sheep meat supply chain

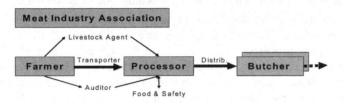

Stakeholders

The present investigation focuses on the domestic product and information flows of a meat processing plant and its suppliers, customers, inspectors, and associated livestock agents with the director of the national Meat Industry Association providing a broad, high-level perspective. The relationship among these stakeholders is shown in Figure 1. The primary product flow is simple: from farmer to processor (via a transporter or sometimes a spot market) and from processor to butcher (via refrigerated wagons). In this, as in many other supply chains, the retailer is considered the customer—the end of the chain. Relative to product flows, information flows are more complex and involve other players. These other players include livestock agents, food and safety officials, transporters, and auditors. We briefly describe each stakeholder before turning our attention to the information flows.

Farmer

The medium-sized commercial sheep farmer interviewed for this study raises sheep both for meat production and for sale as breeders. On the meat production side, he was not bound by supply contracts to any particular meat processor but sold to whoever paid the most at any particular time. In seeking to provide optimal growing conditions, the farmer shifted sheep between paddocks, monitored their health status, administered vaccinations and, where needed, treated them with remedies. Regulations require the farmer to keep a record of these activities in the form of remedy use records. This ensures transparency in the growing phase of the sheep and is regularly audited. Each meat processor provides its own booklets for this recording, and only by keeping these up-to-date will the farmer be able to sell sheep to a particular processing company. The farmer was displeased with this requirement and interpreted it as a strategy of meat processors to increase farmer dependency. The farmer tagged and kept individual record for each sheep. This, he acknowledged, was not normal process for sheep meat supply but related to the breeding side of his business.

The farmer did not consider meat-supply contracts to be beneficial to his business model since it would "cut [him] out of a lot of flexibility." Rather, he sold sheep to a meat processor either directly or through a livestock agent when necessary. The role of the stock agent was considered valuable because the agent had a better overview of the market. When sheep are ready for sale, a transporter takes the sheep, accompanied by the animal status declaration completed by the farmer, to the processor. Approximately 10 days later, the farmer receives a "killing sheet" in which the meat processor states the "yield" obtained from each sheep and any premiums granted. Having to wait 10 days for the killing sheet was not considered satisfactory by the farmer because the results could not be considered for interim selling decisions. The farmer communicated with other supply chain members mostly via telephone, fax, and post. Computer-mediated communication was not used because transmission rates in his rural location were low.

Stock Agent

The stock agent played a pivotal role in the livestock market, acting as an information intermediary between buyers and sellers who were geographically, industrially, and organizationally dispersed. From his perspective as a market insider, the stock agent observed that downstream information flows had improved in recent years. For example, while formerly the animal status declaration would often be incompletely or inaccurately completed because "farmers inherently dislike filling out forms," today no stock trading can be effected without accurate and complete forms. Hence, the reliability of information has improved. The stock agent opined that traceability and individual tagging of sheep would soon become a necessity.

Meat Processor

The meat processor in this study was a single-plant operator located in the lower North Island dedicated to the procurement, slaughtering, and exporting of sheep and beef meat, and capable of halal processes. Sheep were procured from farmers or on-spot markets. Fixed-term supply contracts were not considered a viable option due to the many unpredictable factors. In lieu of contracts, the company focused on establishing long-term relationships with farmers through reliable performance and loyalty schemes. Although no supply contracts specified desired quantities and quality, price sent a signal to farmers that is, as the meat processor commented, "to be honest, a very blunt signal." However, on the demand side, the processor entered into very prescriptive contracts with overseas customers. These contracts prescribed quantity, product specifications, and delivery dates.

The most important information flows to and from the meat processor are those related to health and safety. Upon delivery of a load of sheep, the transporter hands the animal status declaration to a Food & Safety Authority official who inspects the sheep and, if satisfied, staples a clearance form to the pen gate. A second inspection follows postmortem, after which a Food & Safety Authority official declares the product suitable for human consumption. Following slaughter, carcasses may be packed whole, disassembled into 10-15 pieces and put into cartons, or minced. Most output is subsequently frozen and shipped overseas, leaving only a small portion in the New Zealand domestic market.

Food & Safety Authority

The Food & Safety Authority official interviewed was one of a small team of officers located within the premises of the meat-processing plant. The role of the team was to monitor activities in the meat-processing plant to ensure that activities and processes complied with regulations. Responsibility started with the antemortem inspection of the animals in holding pens. This includes checking information on the animal status declaration and compliance with any withholding periods related to vaccinations or treatments administered to the animal. In reaching decisions to "pass" the animals antemortem, reliance is placed on the accuracy of information supplied by the farmer. Consequently, trust plays a major role in the approval process. Farmers found to provide false information are put on a suspect list, which leads to a separate verification process in future sheep sales and slaughter. Once a pen of animals is passed, a pen card is stamped with a "passed veterinary inspection" stamp.

Prior to slaughter, the Food & Safety Authority is provided with a killing sheet declaring which animals are to be processed. Postmortem inspection commences after the slaughter and dressing process are complete. Carcasses are inspected by a separate Food & Safety team and, when passed, are declared as "fit for human consumption." In the case of export, Food & Safety representatives issue an electronic certificate stating that the product meets legal and contractual requirements. In the case of meat destined for the domestic market, no further certification beyond the "fit for human consumption" declaration is required. All Food & Safety documents are stored in paper form for specified retention periods by either the Food & Safety officials or the meat processor.

Retail Butchers

Interviews were conducted with a meat wholesaler/retailer, a supermarket butcher, and a small independent butcher. Although the three butchers operated on different scales, they maintained similar processes in ordering, handling, and distributing meat to consumers. All three ordered product by telephone. This was considered "easy" and a means by which they could maintain the relationship with the processor. It also allowed for receipt of further product information. The requirement criteria of each outlet were known to the meat processor, who would allocate product to meet these criteria thereby reducing rejection rates. Identification tags attached to carcasses within the processing plant were not considered by any of the butchers. Rather, they relied on personal backdoor inspection of the carcass—the small independent butcher was not even able to interpret the information on the identification tag.

Retail butchers process carcasses to meet the requirements of consumers, adding labels with limited information beyond *packed on* and *use by* dates. Informants reported that consumers rarely requested information exceeding that provided on the labels. The few queries received usually related to preparation of the meat or suitability for particular dishes. The provision of more detailed information such as breed of cattle, region of origin, or feed regimes were not considered important by the average shopper and were not used to add value to the product.

All three butchers stated that they would not be able to reliably trace a particular piece of meat back to the carcass from which it was taken. So, although carcasses are uniquely identified via the meat processor's tag, traceability is lost as the butcher processes meat for sale from several carcasses at the same time. The most the butcher could state is that it came from one of a set of carcasses. While traceability is not a current concern, it is likely to become so in the future. Stakeholders seemed to consider that this "will be dealt with when we come to it."

Meat Industry Association

The Meat Industry Association (MIA) represents the national and international interests of New Zealand's meat processors and provides a strategic orientation for the industry as a whole. Its perception of the industry indicates a shift from the original "freezing business" to a "food business" with the introduction of automated processes employing robotics and information technology. The MIA envisions increased collaboration between farmers and processors in terms of shared market information and drafting of long-term contracts that might establish "farming on demand" where "[the meat processor] can be confident that the farmer will send ... raw material ... on the right day and of the right weight." Information and communication technology is considered a major enabler of these shifts in the industry. Dramatic change, particularly with respect to market responsiveness, is expected within the next 10 years.

Analysis of Information Flows

The downstream information flows in the supply chain included structured information flows carrying discrete information recorded on form sheets, and

Table 1. Overview of the structured information flows

Artefact	Content	Purpose	Origin	Recipient	Media
Animal Status Declaration	History: Feeding, vaccinations, diseases, treatments	Declares the health status of the sheep	Farmer	Food & Safety Authority	Paper with carbon copy
Animal Remedy Use Record	Date, stock class, treatments, product names, holding periods	Records treatments the sheep has received	Farmer	Meat Processor (via auditor)	Booklet
Carcass Tag	Lot-number, production date and time, sex, quality grading, body-fat, weight, barcode	Identifies the carcass lot	Meat Processor	Butcher, but it is not considered.	Paper
Quality Check-list	Date, delivery number, temp., observations	Records any deficiencies in storage temperatures	Super-market Butcher	Own use (super-market)	Paper
Product Label	Packed-by date, use-by date, product weight, price	Informs consumers of product freshness	Super-market Butcher	Consumer	Paper

unstructured verbal information flows. The structured downstream information included the animal status declaration, animal remedy use record, carcass tags, quality checklist, and product labels (Table 1).

Animal Status Declaration

The animal status declaration is a legal, paper-based form detailing the animal's history, treatments, feeding supplements, vaccinations, and remedies. It is prepared by the farmer and accompanies the sheep to the meat processor where it is examined and retained by the Food & Safety Authority.

Animal Remedy Use Records

The animal remedy use record is a collection of farm-specific data captured by the farmer on an ongoing basis and recorded in booklets. The record contains information on the translocation of sheep-mobs on different paddocks, medical treatments administered, and any "withholding dates" during which the sheep must not be consumed due to medical treatment. Each meat processor with whom the farmer deals requires an independent and different record to meet their quality audit.

Other Records

The killing sheet, which shows the slaughter schedule, is passed in paper form from the meat processor to the Food & Safety Authority. It enables the Authority to keep track of activities. A carcass tag is affixed to every carcass after slaughter. The tag contains an ID number and barcode that identifies the piece of meat and the processing plant. The product label affixed to the packaged meat by the butcher is another structured information flow that follows the product out of the chain to the consumer. Supermarket staff (but not the independent butcher) kept a quality checklist of the temperature and condition of the meat product.

Unstructured Information Flows

Unstructured information flows (Table 2) also play an important role in the supply chain. These included information exchanges between the farmer and livestock agent, and between the farmer and the meat processor. These exchanges were

Table 2. Overview of the unstructured information flows

Circumstance	Purpose	Media
Conversation between farmer and livestock agent	The farmer discusses with the livestock agent the quality of the sheep and the conditions under which they should be sold.	Telephone or face-to-face
Conversation between farmer and meat processor	The farmer discusses with the meat processor the quality of the sheep and the conditions under which they could be sold.	Telephone or face-to-face
Ordering process from butcher to meat processor	In the ordering process, the butcher receives information about the products available, confirms an order and receives additional information about the market-situation.	Telephone

made either by phone or in face-to-face encounters, and often included discussion of the quality and characteristics of the sheep to be traded. Another important unstructured information flow was the conversations between the butchers and the meat processors. Orders were completed over the telephone, and, at the same time, product information was communicated. The supermarket representative noted, "We get to know what is going on. The sales representative can tell ... straight away if the product is available or if it is not available—and other facts we need to know." In general, the unstructured information between the supply chain members was considered as important as structured information, since product is sold via "relationship marketing" (meat processor).

Discussion

The research suggests that information flows in the sheep meat supply chain do not follow the well-coordinated and integrated information flows described in manufacturing supply chains but rather form isolated transfers of information between adjacent partners in the chain.

The research identified six key participants in the sheep meat supply chain contributing to the downstream information flow: farmers, livestock agents, quality auditors, meat processors, the Food & Safety Authority, and butchers. The consumers of sheep meat are not considered to be part of the supply chain but are viewed as external entities. It is the retail butchers who are referred to as "customers" by other supply chain members (Meat processor, Stock agent). The terminology used suggests that participants do not see themselves as part of a distributed organizational structure with a common goal but rather as independent business entities seeking to satisfy the next entity in the chain. The meat processor dominates the chain. The processor is in a financially strong position with deep customer knowledge and, therefore, becomes the driver of change within the supply chain. The other members of the chain follow the processor's requirements, which are driven by overseas rather than domestic customers.

There was tension and lack of trust between farmer and processor, with the farmer voicing concerns over perceived abuse by the processor of his dominant position while the processor considered the farmers unreliable and opportunistic. In the case in question, both parties operated without a fixed supply contract. By contrast, the director of the Meat Industry Association suggested there was strong success in contract farming. These differences reflect current and potential future practice.

Downstream information flows in the supply chain were largely restricted to exchanges between adjacent members, with no information accompanying the product from the farm to the retailer. Unstructured information flows between adjacent stakeholders via telephone and face-to-face encounters were considered useful because they were fast, easy, and they helped to build relationships. Digitised information accumulated by the meat processor and the Food & Safety Authority were not shared with other members. Rather, butchers and consumers relied on the fact that the Food & Safety Authority inspected the product at the processing plant. Making more information available to the consumer was not considered to add value.

The research revealed several inefficiencies in information flows. For example, the farmer complained about the need to complete separate books of record for each meat processor and about the general use of paper-based information, which necessitated double handling and increased administration. Other potentially useful information was ignored. For example, the distributor and butcher did not consider possibly useful information on carcass tags affixed by the meat processor. In the final link in the chain, only pack and use-by dates were communicated to consumers.

The inefficiencies and redundancies provide room for improvement. Much of this could be achieved through the use of computer-based information systems. For example, software could help the farmer to integrate his livestock administration with the required quality documentation. This information could then be digitally transferred to the Food & Safety Authority which could assess the record before arrival of sheep at the meat processing plant.

The traceability of sheep meat could be advanced by assigning a personal identifier to all sheep with information recorded on electronic tags accompanying product throughout the supply chain. In this way, all members of the supply chain could access and add to information, enabling transparency and traceability while minimising redundancy and handling. Some of this information could be used to add value to the product, for example, identifying region of origin, breed, or particularly feeding regimes.

Examples such as the Scottish Borders TAG initiative for beef (Pettitt, 2001) and the Belgian poultry initiative (Viaene & Verbeke, 1998) show processes and information flows that meet the need for traceability. Both these supply chain initiatives were developed to restore consumer confidence following disease outbreaks. No such event has yet occurred in New Zealand. Any disease outbreak would be disastrous for the industry and the need for proactive implementation of improved information flows is indicated.

Conclusion

It is a fascinating business, we have seen more change in the last ten years than in the hundred years before... and information underpins everything. (MIA director)

Despite this positive and convincing comment by the Meat Industry Association representative, this study has shown that information flows are not yet used in an integrated way to support production and processing in New Zealand's sheep meat industry. Hence, despite recent improvements, even more dramatic changes are necessary in the near future if the industry is to remain competitive in international markets.

The investigation revealed several inefficiencies in the generation and transfer of information that need to be addressed. For example, sheep are not consistently identified on farms, and the farmer is required to keep duplicate records in order to meet the requirements of different processors. Furthermore, available information was not used to add value to the product, and no processes to assure traceability were identified. The lack of end-to-end information flows and lack of trust indicate low levels of integration among supply chain partners.

In addition to identifying issues in the current supply chain, the study suggested possible areas for improvement in information flows. Most important in this regard is the suggestion that the integration of information flows could become a starting point for re-conceptualising the supply chain. The development of a common information platform would not only facilitate the introduction of traceability but also bring the stakeholders closer together, which may ultimately lead to the generation of new business models and value propositions for customers.

Limitations and Future Research

The present research followed a rigorous method. However, concentration on a single supply chain limits the generalisability of findings. Future studies investigating information flows of sheep meat supply chains could include more chains and more representatives at each tier in the chain. This would provide data on a greater variety of business interactions and perspectives. In particular, the internal information handling of the meat processor warrants further investigation since the meat processor is the dominant stakeholder in the supply chain and any improvement initiatives would require support by that stakeholder group.

It would also be useful to investigate the information needs of the consumers. Knowledge of consumers' information requirements would provide the industry with incentives to use information to add value to the product. In this context, the information requirements of overseas customers should also be addressed in future research since it can be expected that their needs would drive any innovation in information flows.

Although New Zealand's sheep meat industry has seen many changes in its recent history, there are more to come. New Zealand is a strong competitor in international markets, being known for its "clean, green" image and quality product. In order to remain competitive, the industry has to overcome old structures, make use of new technologies, and be creative in their use. Once information exchanges improve, collaboration will improve. This seems to be universally applicable—whether the product is sheep meat or a manufactured good.

References

Bailey, W. C., Norina, L., & Cassavant, K. (2002). *The use of supply chain management to increase exports of agricultural products*. The United States Department of Agriculture. Retrieved March, 2003, from http://www.ams.usda.gov/tmd/SCM/SCM_Ag.pdf

Basnet, C., Corner, J., Wisner, J., & Tan, K. C. (2003). Benchmarking supply chain management practice in New Zealand. *Supply Chain Management: An International Journal, 8*(1), 57-64.

Benbasat, I., Goldstein, D., & Mead, M. (1987). The case research strategy in studies of information systems. *MIS Quarterly, 11*(3), 369-386.

Buhr, B. (2000). Information technology and changing supply chain behaviour: Discussion. *American Journal of Agricultural Economics, 82*(5), 1130-1132.

Creswell, J. W. (2003). *Research design: Qualitative, quantitative, and mixed methods approaches.* Thousand Oaks, CA: Sage Publications.

Dorp, K. J. (2003). Beef labelling: The emergence of transparency. *Supply Chain Management: An International Journal, 8*(1), 32-40.

Fallon, M. (2001). Traceability of poultry and poultry products. *Rev. sci. tech. Off. int. Epiz., 20*(2), 538-546.

Hobbs, J. E., & Young, L. M. (2000). Closer vertical co-ordination in agri-food supply chains: A conceptual framework and some preliminary evidence. *Supply Chain Management: An International Journal, 5*(3), 131-142.

Hoek, R. I. v. (1998). Logistics and virtual integration: Postponement, outsourcing and the flow of information. *International Journal of Physical Distribution & Logistics Management, 28*(7), 508-523.

Hull, B. (2002). A structure for supply-chain information flows and its application to the Alaskan crude oil supply chain. *Logistics Information Management, 15*(1), 8-23.

Jongen, W. M. F., & Meulenberg, M. T. G. (1998). *Innovation of food production systems.* Wageningen, The Netherlands: Wageningen Academic Publishers.

Kannan, V. R. (2002). Supplier selection and assessment: Their impact on business performance. *The Journal of Supply Chain Management, 38*(4), 11-21.

Lambert, D. M., & Cooper, M. C. (2000). Issues in supply chain management. *Industrial Marketing Management, 29*, 65-83.

Mariotti, J. L. (1999). The trust factor in supply chain management. *Supply Chain Management Review, 3*(1), 70-77.

Ministry of Agriculture and Forestry. (2002). *Situation and outlook for New Zealand agriculture and forestry.* Retrieved July 12, 2004, from http://maf.govt.nz/mafnet/rural-nz/statistics-and-forecasts/sonzaf/2002/httoc.htm

Mousavi, A., Sarhadi, M., Lenk, A., & Fawcett, S. (2002). Tracking and traceability in the meat processing industry: A solution. *British Food Journal, 104*(1), 7-19.

O'Keeffe, M. (1998). Establishing supply chain partnerships: Lessons from Australian agribusiness. *Supply Chain Management: An International Journal, 3*(1), 5-9.

Penny, G. M. (2003). *Supply chain (re)alignment in New Zealand's sheep meat and dairy industries: Knowledge, networks and learning at the farmer-processor site.* New Zealand: University of Auckland.

Pettitt, R. G. (2001). Traceability in the food animal industry and supermarket chains. *Rev. sci. tech. Off. int. Epiz., 20*(2), 548-597.

Sahin, F., & Robinson, E. P. (2002). Flow coordination and information sharing in supply chains: Review, implications, and directions for future research. *Decision Sciences, 33*(4), 505-536.

Salin, V. (2000). Information technology and cattle beef supply chains. *American Journal of Agricultural Economics, 82*(5), 1105-1111.

Sanders, N. R. (2002). IT applications in supply chain organizations: A link between competitive priorities and organizational benefits. *Journal of Business Logistics, 23*(1), 65-83.

Singh, J. (1996). The importance of information flow within the supply chain. *Logistics Information Management, 9*(4), 28-30.

Statistics New Zealand. (2000). *New Zealand Official Yearbook.* Wellington. Retrieved July 12, 2004, from http://www.stats.govt.nz/domino/external/Web/nzstories.nsf/092edeb76ed5aa6bcc256afe0081d84e/89bfc36cef20ede5cc256b1f0000b8dc?OpenDocument

Viaene, J., & Verbeke, W. (1998). Traceability as a key instrument towards supply chain and quality management in the Belgian poultry meat chain. *Supply Chain Management, 3*(3), 139-141.

Wilson, T. P., & Clarke, W. R. (1998). Food safety and traceability in the agricultural supply chain: Using the Internet to deliver traceability. *Supply Chain Management, 3*(3), 127-133.

Zhao, X., Xie, J., & Zhang, W. J. (2002). The impact of information sharing and co-ordination on supply chain performance. *Supply Chain Management: An International Journal, 7*(1), 24-40.

Chapter IV

Virtual Integration: Antecedents and Role in Governing Supply Chain Integration

Jeffrey C. F. Tai, National Central University, Taiwan

Eric T. G. Wang, National Central University, Taiwan

Kai Wang, Ming Chuan University, Taiwan

Abstract

The integration and coordination of strategic suppliers becomes increasingly important as the manufacturer relies on external transactions to build up collaborative advantages. By conceptualizing virtual integration as an efficient and effective vertical coordination mechanism, the study discussed in this chapter developed a model to examine the role virtual integration plays in improving manufacturing performance and the antecedent factors that can lead supply chain members to rely on virtual integration to govern supply chain integration. Based on the resource-based view and transaction costs theory, the suppliers' specific investments and environmental uncertainty are identified as critical antecedents to virtual integration. The results show that the suppliers' specific investments can significantly improve the manufacturers' achievement of manufacturing goals, thereby motivating the manufacturer to rely on virtual integration to better coordinate with the suppliers who made significant idiosyncratic investments for enhancing transaction value while controlling the potential hazards.

Introduction

There has been a relative shift from capacity to specialized subcontracting by large original equipment manufacturing (OEM) makers when they were facing increasingly fragmented and uncertain demand (Whitford & Zeitlin, 2004). With eroded operating margins and shortened product life cycles, modern manufacturers have increasingly leveraged outsourcing practices for the benefit of low-cost manufacturing, global logistics services, and accelerated product development. Moreover, other than fabrication services, suppliers have been more and more involved in the manufacturers' value chain activities to provide add-on values to buyers and to construct higher entry barriers against competing suppliers (Carter & Narasimhan, 1990). Although strategic sourcing has become an important instrument for realizing the ideal of "externalization of the core," careful management of such supply chain integration efforts are required to reap the expected profit (Narasimhan & Das, 1999; Nesheim, 2001).

The management of supply chain integration has been increasingly addressed in academic research as the practice of supply chain management continues to proliferate in industrial networks. Two themes predominantly examined by prior research were practices of supply chain integration and the impact of supply chain integration on performance improvement. For the former case, prior studies examined the scope, sophistication and focus of supply chain integration, which aimed at illuminating the essence of supply chain integration (Frohlich & Westbrook, 2001; Morash & Clinton, 1998; Narasimhan & Jayaram, 1998; Simatupang, Wright, & Sridharan, 2002). For the latter, supply chain integration was shown to be positively associated with manufacturing and operational performance improvements (Frohlich & Westbrook, 2001; Narasimhan & Jayaram, 1998). Although the fundamental importance of supply chain integration is widely accepted given the aforementioned studies, important questions remain open about how to manage supply chain integration. In particular, our knowledge is still weak concerning the kinds of mechanisms suppliers and customers use to govern supply chain integration under different transacting circumstances. Moreover, we know little about the causal linkages between governance mechanisms choices and resulting performance implications in the context of supply chain integration. Such questions motivated this research to focus on exploring the use of information and communication technology (ICT)-enabled coordination as an alternative governance mechanism to managing supply chain integration.

As outsourcing practices gradually proliferate in modern business environments, ICT-enabled interorganizational integration has also been increasingly adopted to facilitate the implementation of such practices (Malone, Yates, & Benjamon, 1987). Since the inception of electronic data interchange (EDI), the use of ICT-enabled coordination has evolved from electronic monopoly to electronic partnership, allowing the customer-supplier relationship to develop toward a more cooperative mode (Clemens, Reddi, & Row, 1993; Hart & Saunders, 1998). Furthermore, ICT is utilized to support communication and operation of a supply chain as if the OEM makers and their suppliers functioned as an extended enterprise, advancing ICT-enabled coordination toward a "virtual integration" mechanism (Chandrashekar & Schary, 1999; Magretta, 1998). The success of Dell's direct model, in particular, demonstrates that virtual integration indeed is a viable means to facilitating integration of physically separated units and permitting coexistence of centralization and decentralization within an operating system (Stapleton, Gentles, Ross, & Shubert, 2001; van Hoek, 1998). Therefore, instead of common ownership, ICT has become more and more emphasized in implementing supply chain integration (Frolich & Westbrook, 2001).

The research question of this study is to explore the role ICT-enabled coordination plays in managing supply chain integration. Drawing on both resource-based perspective (RBV) and transaction cost theory (TCT), ICT-enabled coordination is regarded as a governance mechanism to managing supply chain integration. The construct representing ICT-enabled coordination is construed as virtual integration, which captures the extent to which ICT is used by a manufacturer to coordinate with its suppliers. As such, the objectives of this study are to: (1) evaluate the effectiveness of virtual integration in governing supply chain integration, and (2) investigate the antecedents to which virtual integration is utilized in governing supply chain integration, thereby contributing to our knowledge as to the contingencies of utilizing virtual integration as a viable governance mechanism.

The remainder of the chapter is organized as follows. Next, we provide related supply chain integration literature, theoretical foundation and research framework. The following section develops the research hypotheses and model. Research method and measurement are then described, followed by data analysis. Finally, we provide concluding remarks and address the limitations of the study.

Conceptual Background and Research Framework

Supply Chain Integration: Ideal and Reality

The central theme of supply chain integration is the integration of relationships, activities, functions, processes, and locations of a firm within itself as well as with its customers, suppliers, and other channel members (Bowersox & Morash, 1989; Lambert & Cooper, 2000). For example, Narasimhan and Jayaram (1998) proposed that supply chain integration is the confluence of supplier integration, strategic integration, and customer integration. Frohlich and Westbrook (2001) showed that inward-facing, peripheral-facing, supplier-facing, customer-facing, and outward-facing strategies were commonly adopted in supply chain integration practices. Morash and Clinton (1998) suggested that the locus of supply chain integration could be intraorganizational process integration, interorganizational collaborative integration, and interorganizational operational integration. These studies all proposed that the more completed and sophisticated supply chain integration is, the greater the improvement in supply chain performance. However, they also pointed out that gaps exist between the rhetoric and reality of implementing supply chain integration.

Through a multimethod empirical study, Fawcett and Magnan (2002) found that few companies achieved complete forward and backward integration from their suppliers' supplier to their customers' customer. In most instances, true collaboration only occurs between the first-tier members and the focal manufacturer either upward or downward on its supply chain. The responsibility for managing members outside the first-tier circle is often handed off to the first-tier members of the focal company. This in turn results in limited execution and poor performance of the overall supply chain because the operation and information of the whole supply chain are not fully synchronized.

In addition, SCM practices such as linked information systems, integrative interorganizational processes, aligned goals, consistent measures, and shared risks as well as rewards are commonly agreed upon, yet several barriers still can prevent these practices from being widely adopted by supply chain members (Frohlich, 2002). For example, Wagner (2003) indicated that setting up intercompany communication and information systems, co-locating supplier personnel, sharing technology, or investing in physical assets would consume enormous amounts of manufacturer investment. Since firms' resources are inevitably limited, they can only integrate a small number of carefully selected suppliers. Moreover, supply chain integration involves considerable interorganizational changes. Serious commitments must exist among corresponding supply chain members or the necessary process changes cannot be fully materialized (Fawcett & Magnan, 2002). As a result, the reality is that most companies implement supply chain integration only in a limited and fragmented manner, with the result being that the expected benefits are unable to be realized.

Supplier-Specific Investments, Environmental Uncertainty and Coordination Requirements in Supply Chain Integration

The adoption of supply chain integration has much to do with individual member's role within a supply chain (Halley & Nollet, 2002). Usually, supply chain integration processes inevitably require idiosyncratic investments by either party of the supply chain members. The roles suppliers play are directly associated with the coordination efforts required in the supply chain integration processes. Large OEM manufacturers often segment their suppliers and trading partners into several categories by how much coordination effort is needed (Dyer, Cho, & Chu, 1998; Krause, 1997). The preferred suppliers play a central role in the value-creation process. They are usually logistical extensions of a large OEM maker's production system and may play the role of product and system design specialist, flow specialist, and relational specialist (Halley & Nollet, 2002). In such a transaction context, exchanges between OEM manufacturers and preferred suppliers often extend beyond assets and physical goods to include both information and knowledge (Giannakis & Croom, 2004; Simatupang et al., 2002). In contrast, regular suppliers only integrate with their manufacturers in a limited manner due to the commodity nature of the exchanges. As such, the considerations of supply chain integration not only hinge on the scope and sophistication of the implementation but also on the management of coordination problems associated with idiosyncratic investments made (Jap, 1999).

In addition, supply chain system dynamics caused by environmental uncertainty also bring about further coordination problems that require cooperation among supply chain parties (Lee, Padmanabhan, & Whang, 1997; Towill, 1996). The concept of the "information enriched supply chain" has been increasingly noticed and leads to many innovative supply chain integration practices to counter the negative impacts of bullwhip effects, deterministic chaos, and parallel interaction among supply chain parties (Mason-Jones & Towill, 1999a; Wilding, 1998). For example, the development of collaborative planning, forecasting, and replenishment (CPFR) initiatives aims to increase the agility and responsiveness of a supply chain through enhanced information visibility and transparency among supply chain parties (Raghunathan, 1999). In such a collaboration context, suppliers can receive forecasting and replenishment plans from customers to improve their production plans and reduce stock levels, whereas customers can benefit from increased sales as their suppliers can supply the right goods in the right place at the right time (Seifert, 2003). Nevertheless, the collaboration processes inevitably require suppliers' idiosyncratic investment and the sharing of sensitive cost and process information on the part of the customer, which accordingly changes the dependency and information structure of customers and suppliers and leads to further coordination issues and concerns (Buvik & Gronhaug, 2000; Lusch & Brown, 1996).

The aforementioned realities lead to the questions of what circumstances are suitable for supplier-manufacturer cooperation for supply chain performance improvement and how they manage the associated coordination problems. The fundamental assumption underlying a closely collaborative relationship is that this kind of relationship makes both the manufacturer and supplier better off than when there is no such relationship (Iyer & Bergen, 1997). If the joint profits achieved through collaboration are less than the sum of uncoordinated individual profits or the allocated profits are less than the profits attained by individual member without such coordination, then the coordinated efforts among supply chain parties would not last for the long run (Kim, 2000). Therefore, the decision as to whether or not to join a collaborative relationship and the stability of such collaborative relationship largely hinge on how the "pie" could be expanded and divided by the supply chain members (Jap, 1999; 2001). Due to the uncertain nature of exchanges and bounded rationality of decision makers, however, there is no such perfect solution that can once and for all effectively govern interfirm collaboration process ex ante and ex post (Williamson, 1975). Accordingly, the existence of flexible coordination mechanisms to support both pie expansion and the division process becomes an important governance design issue to supply chain integration (Jap, 1999; 2001).

Theoretical Foundation: Resource-Based View and Transaction Cost Theory

The governance of interfirm collaboration has been well studied in terms of resource-based view and transaction cost theory (Dyer & Singh, 1998; Rindfleisch & Heide, 1997; Tsang, 2000). Resource-based view (RBV) provides insights regarding value creation and dynamic efficiency of interfirm collaborative relationships, whereas transaction cost analysis (TCA) enriches our knowledge as to designing governance mechanisms with maximized value and minimized transaction costs. Both theoretical explanations are incorporated as the foundation for justifying the role virtual integration plays in supply chain integration and for identifying the relevant antecedents to virtual integration in the later part of the paper.

According to Penrose (1959), firms are rent-seeking institutions and tend to expand whenever profitable opportunities exist. Firms that are able to accumulate resources and capabilities that are rare, valuable, non-substitutable, and difficult to imitate will achieve a competitive advantage over competing firms (Barney, 1991; Dierickx & Cool, 1989; Rumelt, 1984). Amit and Schoemaker (1993) further argue that specialization of assets is "a necessary condition for rent" and "strategic assets by their very nature are specialized." Because firms must do something specialized or unique to develop a competitive advantage, a firm may choose to seek advantages by creating assets that are specialized in conjunction with the assets of an alliance partner (Klein, Crawford, & Alchian, 1978; Teece, 1987). As a result, productivity gains and relational rents in the value chain are possible when firms are purposely establishing idiosyncratic interfirm linkages (Dyer & Singh, 1998).

The key to creating relational rents is the presence of relational-specific assets, complementary resource endowments, knowledge-sharing routines, and effective governance (Dyer & Singh, 1998). Relational-specific assets include site-specific, physical asset-specific and human capital-specific investments (Williamson, 1985). Through relational-specific investments, relational rents are generated in terms of reduced inventory and transportation costs, enhanced product differentiation and quality, greater communication efficiency of transactors, and faster product development cycles (Asanuma, 1989; Clark & Fujimoto, 1991). Complementary resource endowments can create synergy among alliance parties because the combined resource endowments are more valuable, rare, and difficult to imitate than they have been before they are combined (Oliver, 1997). Interfirm knowledge-sharing routines are a pattern of interfirm interactions that permit the transfer, recombination, and creation of specialized knowledge (Grant, 1996). With superior institutionalized interfirm processes to facilitate knowledge exchanges, alliance partners can learn through collaboration and are more able to result in performance-enhancing innovations (Von Hippel, 1988).

Governance plays a key role in the creation of relational rents, but it also influences transaction costs as well as the willingness of alliances parties to engage in value creation initiatives (Dyer, 1996). According to Coase's (1937) theorem, in the absence of transaction costs, parties to an exchange will devise joint value-maximization exchanges regardless of their power differentials or resource endowments (Williamson, 1996). However, transaction costs are never really at zero in the real world; devising exchanges with maximized joint value inevitably involves minimizing transaction costs of the exchanges. Especially when considering the fact that transaction parties are self-interested, they would not involve the exchanges unless their own share of the joint value exceeds their previous profits. Even though they have been engaged in the exchanging process, transacting parties with disadvantageous ex post bargaining position would scale back investment, adapt less, and forgo activities, and hence reduce value creation of the exchanges (Grossman & Hart, 1986). Therefore, value claiming also matters in addition to value creation, and TCA complements RBV in that TCA provides detailed explanations regarding how transactors deal with value claiming problems associated with transaction costs through governance design (Ghosh & John, 1999; Williamson, 1991).

Theoretically, the design of governance mechanisms should consider securing specific investments, adaptation problems, and performance measurement issues (Rindfleisch & Heide, 1997). Securing specific investments is necessary for increasing joint value creation of an exchange, yet it also poses a dilemma that transaction parties may incur ex post bargaining costs and enforcement costs of contracts (Poppo & Zenger, 1998). TCA approaches this problem by devising forms of governance that possess sufficient safeguards to secure these valuable but vulnerable investments in order to get as close as possible to joint value maximization (Ghosh & John, 1999). Adaptation problems arise because transacting parties continuously encounter uncertainties that require them to change previously planned courses of action and decisions about the exchange. Given that uncertainty may bring transacting parties with opportunity costs of maladaptation or coordination costs of haggling, governance design should either facilitate fast abandonment of an exchange or facilitate faster revision of the exchange relationship (Young-Ybarra & Wiersema, 1999). Performance measurement problems happen when transacting parties have difficulties assessing the contractual compliance of each other due to bounded rationality and behavioral uncertainty (Rindfleisch & Heide, 1997). Because performance evaluation problems incur screen and selection costs ex ante as well as measurement costs and productivity losses issues ex post, governance design should either support alleviation of the problems resulting from bounded rationality and behavioral uncertainty or fall into the choice of vertical integration to avoid transaction costs (Heide & John, 1990; Williamson, 1985).

Based on both RBV and TCA, governance design of interfirm exchanges should, on the one hand, facilitate the creation of relational rents and, on the other hand, provide mechanisms to minimize the problems of safeguarding specific investments, adaptation, and performance evaluation difficulties. Additionally, both RBV and TCA point out that specific investments and uncertainty are critical antecedents to value creation and value claiming. Therefore, this study will incorporate both constructs as antecedent variables to examine the role virtual integration played in supply chain integration.

Governing Supply Chain Integration: Virtual Integration as Means to Enhancing Transaction Value and Economizing on Transaction Costs

Virtual integration uses technology and information to blur the traditional boundaries in the value chain between suppliers, manufacturers, and customers (Magretta, 1998). The firm begins by defining what it does best and focuses on that, and then partners with other companies for capital and labor-intensive services using the same quality and performance standards it uses. Instead of governing exchanges through common ownership, virtual integration coordinates a series of transactions based on open information-based partnerships that speed the flow of data, improve efficiency, add customer value, and provide benefits to the partners (Stapleton et al., 2001). Based on the principles of market orientation, core competence, collaboration, and information partnership, virtual integration provides benefits such as systems that become easier to form and expand, lower capitalization requirements, maximization of local control and autonomy, more streamlined decision making through fewer layers of corporate bureaucracy, and more agility in identifying and responding to local market growth opportunities (Stapleton et al., 2001).

The power of virtual integration originates from the ability of ICT to improve (inter)organizational information processing capabilities (Bensaou & Venkatraman, 1996). From the governance design viewpoint, virtual integration can improve value creation and reduce ex post transaction costs of interfirm exchanges. As to value creation, the utilization of ICT is complementary to the specific investments made by exchanging partners. Through its electronic communication and integration effects, ICT can play a role in helping to create and support a set of governance arrangements that enable exchanges of information and other goods to be carried out without large transaction costs (Clemons et al., 1993; Gurbaxani & Whang, 1991; Malone et al., 1987). For example, many innovative supply chain integration practices were introduced and implemented with interorganizational information systems, such as postponed manufacturing, vendor-managed inventory (VMI) and CPFR (Raghunathan, 1999; van Hoek, 1998; Waller, Johnson, & Davis, 1999). Additionally, ICT also has great potential in facilitating timely interfirm joint decision making, coordination, process control, and feedback, all of which are essential for implementing learning-by-monitoring mechanisms in a pragmatic collaboration context (Helper, Macduffie, & Sabel, 2000; Scott, 2000). As such, ICT-enabled virtual integration can facilitate interfirm knowledge sharing and, thus, create the benefits of enhancing transaction value through interfirm learning.

In addition, ICT has been argued to be able to reduce ex post transaction costs through alleviating relation-specific investments and accommodating adaptation problems. Regarding the former case, ICT-mediated transactions break the limitations imposed by time and distance and make large scale relation-specific investments less necessary. Even though ICT investments are required to substitute for idiosyncratic physical or site-specific assets, ICT assets are less likely to be relationship-specific than other investments designed to reduce coordination costs between firms (Brynjolfsson, 1993; Clemens et al., 1993). As a result, the threats of holdup and opportunism are alleviated through the coordination of virtual integration. As to adaptation problems, the communicative and integrative effects of ICT improve the coordination between transacting parties and facilitate greater modification flexibility of the exchanging relationships (Young-Ybarra &Wiersema, 1999). When the costs of haggling are too expensive to maintain the exchanging relationships, transacting parties can more easily exit the transacting relationships without the bonds of ownership and hostages of considerable specific assets (Williamson, 1985; Young-Ybarra & Wiersema, 1999). Accordingly, transaction adaptation problems can be addressed through efficient and flexible coordination enabled by ICT.

To examine the potential effects of ICT in governing supply chain integration, the construct "virtual integration" is developed to capture the extent to which the trading partners use ICT to implement two aspects of vertical coordination in the supply chain: collaborative operation execution and collaborative process planning and control (Buvik & Gronhaug, 2000; Buvik & John, 2000; Morash & Clinton, 1998). These two aspects of vertical coordination have been widely addressed in prior studies and are combined to frame the domain of virtual integration activities in this study (Narasimhan & Kim, 2001; Raghunathan, 1999). Collaborative operation execution refers to the extent to which ICT facilitates the common operations between supply chain partners, such as purchasing, production, and logistics operations, while collaborative process planning and control represents the degree to which ICT is used to support collaborative decision and performance control by the partners.

Conceptual Framework

This study aimed at investigating the antecedents and the role virtual integration plays in supply chain integration. Through the theoretical lens of RBV and TCT, virtual integration is reinterpreted to be a kind of governance mechanism. Whether manufacturers rely on virtual integration to govern their suppliers becomes a matter of governance mechanism choices. Therefore, based on the

Figure 1. Conceptual framework

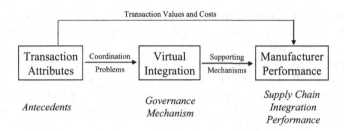

conceptual developments and theoretical background provided in the above subsections, the conceptual framework of the study is depicted in Figure 1.

The central themes of the above framework are threefold. First, the exchange attributes such as uncertainty and asset specificity are essential sources of transaction values and costs to supply chain integration. Hence, they are identified as one of the major sets of antecedents to the performance of supply chain integration, that is, manufacturer performance. Second, the exchange attributes can lead to numerous coordination problems, such as knowledge sharing, interfirm learning, safeguarding investments, and mutual adaptation. Such problems cause the supply chain parties to rely on virtual integration in governing the exchange relationships to achieve higher transaction value as well as reduce transaction costs. Finally, virtual integration can provide supporting mechanisms to supply chain integration, and accordingly lead to greater supply chain integration performance.

Research Hypotheses and Model

This section draws on resource-based view (RBV) and transaction cost theory (TCT) to develop hypotheses that link transaction attributes and manufacturer performance with virtual integration. The first group of hypotheses identifies the direct effects of environmental uncertainty on virtual integration and manufacturer's manufacturing goals achieved; the second group identifies the direct effects of suppliers' specific investments on virtual integration and manufacturers' manufacturing goals achieved; finally, the third group relates virtual integration to manufacturer's manufacturing goals achieved.

Effects of Environmental Uncertainty

The major challenge that environmental uncertainty imposes on a supply chain is the increased coordination costs (Bensaou & Venkatraman, 1996). As a manufacturer encounters demand volatility, a natural response to it is to raise stock levels or to change ordering patterns frequently (Pagell, Newman, Hanna, & Krause, 2000). These certainly would result in increased inventory and coordination costs for both manufacturers and suppliers (Lee et al., 1997). When taking into account industrial dynamics and time-varying behaviors of industrial organizations, the demand expressed at each subsequent stage upstream in the supply chain becomes even more cyclical and extreme in variation. Consequently, not only are coordination efforts increased, but also other serious cost and performance problems are incurred. For example, manufacturers and suppliers may incur excess raw materials costs or material shortages due to poor product planning and forecasting. Consequently, they are forced to spend additional manufacturing expenses caused by excess capacity, inefficient utilization, and overtime. Furthermore, excess warehousing expenses also arise as higher stock levels are required to serve as buffers to countering uncertainties (Towill, 1996).

H_1: *The greater the degree of environmental uncertainty faced by a manufacturer, the less is the extent to which its manufacturing goals are achieved.*

Several remedies have been proposed to increase information processing and coordination capabilities of a supply chain in response to poor supply chain performance caused by environmental uncertainty. For example, just-in-time (JIT) production practices, flexible manufacturing systems, logistical integration, postponed manufacturing, and total cycle-time compression across the supply chain are suggested as viable means to mitigate the influence of industrial dynamics (Mason-Jones & Towill, 1999b). However, many of these practices require the involvement of ICT to provide complementary information-processing capacities. In fact, electronic integration along the supply chain is increasingly important to firm performance in that "it is futile to spend millions of dollars to reduce the manufacturing cycle time by one day while leave untouched two to three-weeks of ordering time that dominates the total turnaround cycle" (van der Vorst, Beulens, de Wit, & van Beek, 1998). Similarly, van Hoek (1998) emphasized the important role of ICT-enabled integration in implementing manufacturing postponement for effective mass customization. Mason-Jones and Towill (1999b) also demonstrated the critical role of electronic integration in bypassing informational distortions and thereby improving supply chain visibility.

The proliferation of several well-known ICT-based integration programs has manifested themselves in their ability to cope with demand volatility. For example, the adoption of EDI has been proven useful in reducing the occurrence of erroneous ordering information and accelerating ordering processes, thus mitigating information distortions between trading firms (van der Vorst et al., 1998). The implementation of VMI and CPFR programs can also fulfill the idea of "substituting information for inventory," and thus improves resource utilization for both manufacturers and suppliers (Raghunathan, 1999; Waller et al., 1999). With the aid of ICT-enabled integration programs, virtually integrated firms can benefit from better common operations execution and joint planning and control without necessarily being governed under common ownership. By improving interfirm information processing and coordination, virtual integration can be seen as a strategy to reducing the influence of uncertain environments (Forster & Regan, 2001).

Lastly, environmental uncertainty causes information asymmetry to emerge and therefore creates opportunities for either transaction party to behave opportunistically. To reduce the increased transaction costs associated with higher environmental uncertainty, some forms of vertical coordination mechanism should exist (Buvik & Gronhaug, 2000). Since the proper use of ICT for supply chain coordination can enhance manufacturers' control capacity over suppliers and the changeability of supply chains in responding to environmental uncertainties, supply chain companies tend to have strong motivation to implement electronic integration mechanisms for more efficient mutual adaptations, especially when the environment is highly uncertain.

H_2: *The greater the degree of environmental uncertainty faced by a manufacturer, the greater is the extent to which it is virtually integrated with its supplier.*

Effects of Suppliers' Transaction-Specific Investments

The role of specific-investment made by suppliers is growing in importance as manufacturers increasingly externalize their core to seek collaborative advantages (Dyer, 1996; Nesheim, 2001). Traditionally, proponents of the resource-based view emphasized that a firm's competitive advantage originates from those resources and capabilities that are owned and controlled within the firm. However, this notion has been challenged in that internal co-specialized resources may become rigid and hamper performance when technological change is rapid (Poppo & Zenger, 1998). Evidence also suggests that more and more companies transact with external suppliers for tapping into a network of qualified suppliers, accessing competent personnel, and acquiring capacity in response to unexpected demand volatility (Jones et al., 1997). Therefore, external transactions are also regarded as extensions of a firm's strategic core as long as transacting parties make relation-specific investments and are able to combine resources in unique ways (Dyer & Singh, 1998). Furthermore, external transactions can also create the potential for gaining competitive advantages if transacting parties specialize their relationships through interfirm knowledge-sharing routines, complementary resource endowments and deploying effective governance mechanisms (Dyer & Singh, 1998).

Actually, numerous supply chain practices demonstrate the importance of a supplier's transaction-specific investments on improving supply chain performance. Early supplier involvement is the one frequently adopted by strategic suppliers in the automobile industry. As illustrated by Womack and Jones (1990), first-tier suppliers of Toyota usually invest in developing a variety of parts and present all the alternatives to Toyota before the carmaker decides on its own vehicle concepts. With the specific investments made by the early-involved suppliers, Toyota can solve problems in its product development process and hence reduce the time-to-market on new product introduction (Levy, 1997).

Another example is the global logistics system that is commonly implemented in the PC industry (Chen, 2002). With the PC industry's efforts towards reduction of lead time to market, coupled with lower production and inventory costs requested by customers, many subcontractors are forced to upgrade their positions within the global production system. They have gradually taken over the essential functions of coordinating the global supply chain originally played by their OEM customers, and, in turn, have participated in cross-border supply chain management, logistics operations, and after-sales services. Because these subcontractors had no prior experience in setting up a global-scale and quick-response production and logistics networks, they have had to incur huge initial sunk costs in order to meet the contractual requirements of their customers. Owing to specific investments made by the suppliers to accommodate their customers' requests, the OEM makers reduce the need to handle inventory and transportation costs, and hence can re-configure a leaner, more agile supply chain (Huang & Lo, 2003; van Hoek, 2001).

Both examples illustrate suppliers' contribution to overall supply chain performance improvements through their idiosyncratic investments. Therefore, this study proposes the following hypothesis:

H_3: The greater the degree of specific investments made by a supplier, the greater is the extent to which its customers' manufacturing goals are achieved.

Although suppliers' transaction-specific investments are rare, valuable, non-substitutable, and difficult to imitate strategic resources for manufacturers in creating relational rents and competitive advantages, when the "price" of using such a governance mode is being considered, interfirm cooperation is not necessarily the only choice for arranging exchanges with significant investments (Dyer & Singh, 1998; Williamson, 1991). In particular, transaction-specific investments can lead to information asymmetry and holdup problems, which in turn may incur considerable transaction costs (Alchian & Demsetz, 1972; Klein et al., 1978). To deal with these problems, transacting parties need to devise corresponding governance mechanisms to minimize information costs and to control opportunism (Kulkarni & Heriot, 1999; Stump & Heide, 1996).

Vertical coordination has been argued to permit ongoing adjustments and bargaining for transacting parties to split up transaction profits (Buvik & John, 2000). Through harmonized interaction patterns of vertical coordination, activity sets of transacting parties can be revised or shifted without formal reassignment of roles. Thereby, tightly coupled activities can be accomplished more smoothly without one party inadvertently stepping on the other's toes. Meanwhile, the information flow aspect of vertical coordination induces the "cheap talks" effect, or the tacit understanding among parties engaged in frequent interaction (Buvik & John, 2000). With cheap talks among transacting parties, the receiver is able to shift activities to accommodate changes occurring on the sender's side (Farrell & Gibbson, 1995). As such, transaction parties who need to make transaction-specific investments can retrieve information and learn from the other parties more effectively through the mechanism of vertical coordination (Hult, Ketchen, & Slater, 2004). Consequently, transaction hazards resulting from idiosyncratic investments could be greatly minimized.

Nevertheless, vertical coordination incurs coordination costs. Considering the impact of supply chain dynamics, without accurate information processing capacities vertical coordination can waste large amounts of communication and maladaptation costs in the coordination process. In addition, transaction parties need to closely cooperate and transfer knowledge with each other when idiosyncratic investments are involved in an exchange (Germain, Droge, & Christensen, 2001). Because interorganizational information systems can enhance information processing capability and support interorganizational learning requirements, transacting parties may rely on ICT-enabled integration mechanism to vertically coordinate with each other (Huber, 1991; Malone et al., 1987). Therefore,

H₄: The greater the degree of supplier's specific investments, the greater is the extent to which manufacturer is virtually integrated with this supplier.

Virtual Integration and Manufacturing Performance

As pointed out by prior studies, today's buyer-supplier relationship is character-ized by the very nature of interdependence (Turner, LeMay, Hartley, & Wood, 2000). Once a supplier fails to perform, the buyer's performance may be adversely affected (Shin, Collier, & Wilson, 2000). The major advantage virtual integration can bring about for managing supply chains is enhanced visibility (Allem, 2000). With seamless information channels connected to suppliers, manufacturers can track variations in suppliers' production, product quality, inventory levels, and delivery capability more easily. And, by receiving such information in a more timely fashion, manufacturers are able to plan and adjust their own operations more rapidly and thereby achieve greater adaptability to any expected events caused by suppliers. By providing suppliers with timely infor-mation regarding changes in their own plans, manufacturers also make suppliers more responsive in making timely adjustments to such changes.

On the other hand, virtual integration is also critical to the implementation of certain manufacturing practices that are regarded as important to increasing manufacturing flexibility. For example, van Hoek (1998) empirically demon-strates the important role of ICT in facilitating postponed manufacturing; Koufteros, Vonderembse, and Doll (2001) put great emphasis on the role of concurrent work-flow and early involvement in implementing concurrent engi-neering, which may also benefit considerably from proper use of ICT. Thus, this study suggests that a manufacturer's manufacturing changeability to environ-mental uncertainty should be significantly affected by the extent to which its production and supply chain operations are electronically linked with suppliers.

Implementing virtual integration can also help manufacturers achieve low-cost advantage in terms of efficient resource utilization in production and supply chain operations (Christopher & Towill, 2000). Through the enabling effect of ICT, supply chain costs can be lowered, speed of feedback and error correction increased, agility of supply chain operations improved, and relationships between trading partners enhanced. As such, existing bottlenecks in the supply chain may be removed and variability of production flows leveled. According to "the theory of swift, even flow," improvements in procurement-production processes should in turn lead to better manufacturing performance such as reduced production cost (Schmenner & Swink, 1998). Also, with electronically integrated interfirm processes, the performance of manufacturers' production function and supply chain operation can be greatly improved due to the elimination of waste in time, inventory, and transportation (Mason-Jones & Towill, 1999b).

Figure 2. Research model

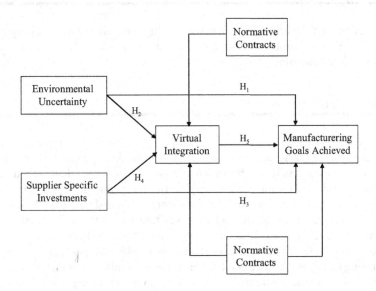

H_5: *The greater the manufacturer's reliance on virtual integration to manage its supplier, the greater is the extent to which manufacturer's manufacturing goals are achieved.*

Based on the above hypotheses, the research model of the study is depicted in Figure 2. Note that we also incorporate normative contracts and buyer power as control variables in the research model. Normative contracts reflect the transacting parties' social consensus or norms as to how to interact or deal with each other in the transacting process (Macneil, 1978). Interfirm relational behaviors such as cooperation are usually governed by normative contracts. Normative contracts may affect virtual integration and supply chain performance through its effects on interfirm relational behaviors, and hence is included in the research model (Lusch & Brown, 1996). In addition, power structure is argued to have profound impact on the results of profit division (Watson, 2001). It can also lead to different interfirm relational behaviors if power imbalance exists (Anderson & Weitz, 1989). As a result, this study includes both constructs as control variables to eliminate potential confounding impacts on the dependent variables.

Method

This section first describes the survey procedure and discusses sampling and data collection methods. It then explains how the research constructs are operationalized and measured.

Survey Procedure

A cross-sectional mail survey was administrated for collecting data from randomly selected large and medium-sized manufacturing firms in Taiwan. A draft survey was developed based on measures that were identified in the literature as suitable for the current study. After compiling the English version of the questionnaire, the draft survey items were first translated into Chinese by a bilingual research associate and then verified and refined for translation accuracy by one MIS professor and two senior PhD students. The Chinese version of the draft was then pretested by two senior IS managers and two senior purchasing managers for face and content validity, resulting in wording modifications of several survey items. The final version of the survey was distributed to the senior purchasing managers of 980 manufacturing firms randomly selected from the directory of the 2001 Top 5000 largest firms in Taiwan published by China Credit Information Services, Ltd. This directory contains comprehensive and authoritative data regarding the larger companies in Taiwan.

The low response rates typical in Taiwan and the resource constraints led us to adopt the single-informant approach for the survey, even though a multifunction, multi-respondent design is more effective for mitigating the threats of method variance and informant bias. This limitation, however, can be partially alleviated by choosing an informant who is the most knowledgeable about the research issues in a company (Huber & Power, 1985). Since the purchasing function plays a critical boundary-spanning role across trading companies (Stanley & Wisner, 2001) and its senior managers should also have a firm grasp of the conditions in sales and manufacturing, it is believed that senior purchasing mangers should be the most knowledgeable and reliable single informant within a company to respond to our survey. This conjecture was confirmed by the senior managers we interviewed during the pretesting phase of the survey instrument.

Sample

Through the procedures described above, 154 surveys were returned, with 145 having completed data usable for subsequent analysis, yielding an effective response rate of 14.79%. Table 1 presents the characteristics of the responding

Table 1. Demographic characteristics of the responding firms (n = 145)

	Percentage of Firms
Total Assets (NT$)	
Less than $0.8 Billion	1.4
$0.8 Billion - $1.2 Billion	12.4
$1.3 Billion - $2 Billion	20.0
$2.1 Billion - $4 Billion	30.3
$4.1 Billion - $8 Billion	12.4
Over $8 Billion	23.4
Number of Employees	
Less than 100	4.1
101 - 500	44.8
501 - 1000	17.2
Over 3000	33.8
Industry	
Automobile	7.6
Chemical	5.5
Computer & electronics	55.2
Machine & tool	6.2
Molds	8.3
Textile	6.2
Others	11.0

firms. Although the response rate is not high and may be somewhat lower than that of typical mail surveys conducted in UK and U.S., given the fact that many companies in Taiwan are more conservative in answering surveys, our response rate is in fact higher than that of similar studies conducted in Taiwan, which according to our experience is typically around 10%. In addition, we believe that demonstrating a lack of response bias is more important than a high response rate. To ensure the representativeness of the responding firms, two statistical analyses were conducted (Armstrong & Overton, 1977). First, we compared the responding and nonresponding firms in terms of company assets and number of employees; no significant differences between the two groups were found based on the independent sample t test ($p = 0.003$ and 0.007, respectively). Then, the respondents were further divided into two halves based on the dates of return. The comparison on company assets and employee numbers of the two groups again showed no significant differences based on the results of χ^2 test ($p = 0.556$ and 0.558, respectively). Accordingly, the non-response bias should not be a problem in this study.

Measures

Multi-item scales were used for measuring the four research constructs and two control variables, all designed to use five-point scale (see the Appendix for the scale items).

Environmental Uncertainty (EU)

As discussed earlier, demand volatility is the primary source of environmental uncertainty encountered by supply chain companies. Demand volatility, resulting from bullwhip effect and clockspeed amplification, leads to unpredictability of market demand. Four items about demand unpredictability have been enclosed in the survey to measure environmental uncertainty: sales volume, purchase volume, product specification or features, and required service supports. These four items were selectively adapted from Artz and Brush (2000) and Cannon et al. (2000), and constitute the formative scale of the construct (Chin, 1998).

Supplier's Specific Investments (SSI)

According to Williamson (1996), transaction-specific investments encompass site specificity, physical specificity, dedicated specificity, human specificity and time specificity. The operationalization of this construct aims at assessing the magnitude of investments made by suppliers. Therefore, eight items adapted from Artz and Brush (2000), Joshi and Stump (1999), and Buvik and Gronhaug (2000) were encompassed, forming a formative scale of the construct.

Virtual Integration (VI)

This construct attempts to capture the extent to which ICT-enabled integration mechanisms are implemented and relied on by trading partners in a supply chain to support common operation execution and joint process planning and control. Based on past works on supply chain interaction, this study developed measurement items corresponding to ICT-based interfirm integration activities including order processing, market information sharing, production capacity coordination, inventory level coordination, and support for logistics integration, material or component design, conflict resolution, and quality control (Frohlich & Westbrook, 2001; Morash & Clinton, 1998; Narasimhan & Kim, 2001).

Manufacturing Goals Achieved (MG)

To date, there is still no consensus regarding how supply chain performance should be properly operationalized though numerous approaches have been proposed (Beamon, 1996). This study, however, took a dyadic view to assess manufacturer's manufacturing goals achieved to evaluate the impact of transaction attributes and virtual integration. Such an approach has been suggested by several SCM studies, and it can reflect that the ultimate benefits of supply chain integration come from buying firms and suppliers (Krause, 1999; Narasimhan & Jayaram, 1998). Based on these works, this study evaluated the extent of improvements in the quality, dependability, and manufacturing flexibility of the buying firm. These aspects of manufacturer performance link to the supply base of a manufacturing firm in that they influence strategic outsourcing decisions and management of suppliers in pursuit of these manufacturing goals (Narasimhan & Jayaram, 1998).

Normative Contracts (NC)

This construct assesses manufacturer's and supplier's reliance on informal agreements to govern their transaction relationship in the aspects of role specification, planning, adjustment processes, monitoring procedures, incentive system, and means of enforcement (Heide, 1994). Measurement items were adapted from Lusch and Brown (1996) and Heide (1994).

Buyer Power (BP)

This construct attempts to capture manufacturer's power relative to supplier to reflect the degree of buyer's dominance in a dyadic transacting relationship (Cox, 2001). The measures assess the degree of supplier's dependence on the manufacturer for providing product specification and design, market information and technical support. Operationalized items were primarily adapted from Cox (2001) and Boyle and Dwyer (1995).

Analysis

Data analysis was conducted in two parts: measurement validation and hypothesis testing. For measurement validation, the measures were examined by exploratory factor analysis (EFA) and the Cronbach reliability test to ensure the measurement properties of the scales were sufficiently satisfied. Then, a structural equation model was constructed for hypothesis testing. The software packages used to perform the above statistical analyses were SPSS for Windows 8.0 and EQS for Windows 5.3.

Measurement Analysis

Because the formative nature of the scales and the limitation of sample size, exploratory factor analysis (EFA), instead of confirmatory factor analysis, was carried out individually for each construct to assess the underlying factor structure of the measurement items. The measurement items were divided into two groups for factor analysis with a varimax rotation. The threshold employed for judging the significance of factor loadings was 0.50 (Hair, Anderson, Tatham, & Black, 1992). Subjective methods used to determine the number of latent

Table 2. EFA results of the independent variables

	EU	SSI	NC	BP	Mean	S.D.
EU1	0.693				2.7034	1.1188
EU2	0.845				2.4759	1.0677
EU3	0.845				2.0483	1.0430
EU4	0.786				2.2069	1.0344
SSI1		0.805			3.0759	1.1431
SSI2		0.690			3.0759	1.0677
SSI3		0.825			3.3517	1.0771
SSI4		0.854			3.2966	1.0873
SSI5		0.861			3.3172	1.0455
SSI6		0.842			3.1724	1.0297
SSI7		0.856			3.3172	0.9768
SSI8		0.818			3.3931	0.9810
NC1			0.861		3.9931	0.7407
NC2			0.907		4.0207	0.7019
NC3			0.890		4.0276	0.6967
NC4			0.764		3.8069	0.7197
NC5			0.807		3.8897	0.7083
NC6			0.595		3.6690	0.7911
NC7			0.776		3.9034	0.7846
NC8			0.825		3.9310	0.7787
BP1				0.695	3.3379	1.0221
BP2				0.710	3.3034	0.9812
BP3				0.732	2.7103	1.0403
Eigenvalue	2.620	5.743	5.344	1.855		
% of Var.	65.607	71.784	66.797	61.817		

Notes: EU—Environmental uncertainty; SSI—Supplier's specific investments; NORM—Normative contracts; BPWR—Buyer power

Table 3. EFA results of the dependent variables

	VI	QTY	SP	MF	Mean	S.D.
VI1	0.852				3.2569	1.1015
VI2	0.878				3.2778	1.0932
VI3	0.827				3.2222	1.0474
VI4	0.885				3.2986	1.0844
VI5	0.883				3.2083	1.1023
VI6	0.876				3.1944	1.0792
VI7	0.889				3.1667	1.0774
VI8	0.870				3.1181	1.1374
VI9	0.853				3.1250	1.1023
QTY1		0.786			3.7862	0.7187
QTY2		0.783			3.7379	0.6974
QTY3		0.858			3.6552	0.6910
QTY4		0.772			3.7931	0.6656
QTY5		0.770			3.8552	0.6453
SP1			0.738		3.8069	0.7002
SP2			0.735		3.7862	0.6891
SP3			0.751		3.5517	0.8244
SP4			0.735		3.5310	0.7822
MF1				0.841	3.7448	0.7147
MF2				0.856	3.6966	0.7667
MF3				0.748	3.7379	0.7073
Eigenvalue	6.946	3.563	2.856	2.534		
% of Var.	77.182	71.262	71.409	84.466		

Notes: VI—Virtual integration; QTY—Quality; SP—Supplier performance; MF—Manufacturing flexibility

variables included latent root criterion, scree test, and percentage of variance explained. The results showed that items for measuring site specificity (SSI1), legal remedies (NC6), standard of operational procedures (NC8), and purchasing price (NC9) failed to load on the same factor as the other items, and thus were dropped out from the subsequent analyses. In so doing, a clear factor structure was obtained for all the items as shown in Table 2 and Table 3, demonstrating convergent validity and thereby undimensionality of all the scales (O'Leary-Kelly & Vokurka, 1998). In addition, all the scales explained more than 50% of the data variances and thus were considered capturing sufficient data variations and thus of acceptable quality (Heck, 1998).

Given the unidimensionality of the scales, Cronbach's alpha was then used to determine an unbiased estimate of measurement reliability (Nunnally, 1978), which indicates the degree of internal consistency among the measurement items and is inversely related to the degree to which a measure is contaminated by random errors (Bollen, 1989). The value of coefficient alpha higher than the threshold level of 0.70 was deemed to provide satisfactory reliability, which was satisfied by all the scales as shown in Table 4 except for Buyer Power (BP). The

Table 4. The intercorrelations, means, standard deviations and reliability of the composite scores

Construct	EU	SSI	NC	BP	VI	QTY	SP	MF
EU	(0.820)							
SSI	0.190**	(0.942)						
NC	-0.125	0.274***	(0.925)					
BP	0.149	0.487***	0.114	(0.691)				
VI	-0.042	0.378***	0.232***	0.371***	(0.963)			
QTY	-0.049	0.305***	0.181**	0.210**	0.259***	(0.899)		
SP	-0.008	0.263***	0.201**	0.121	0.288***	0.577***	(0.862)	
MF	-0.041	0.272***	0.223***	0.114	0.194**	0.558***	0.609***	(0.908)
Mean	2.359	3.250	3.905	3.117	3.208	3.766	3.669	3.726
S.D.	0.859	0.888	0.600	0.798	0.959	0.577	0.632	0.671

*Notes: EU—Environmental uncertainty; SSI—Supplier's specific investments; NC—Normative contracts; BP: Buyer power; VI—Virtual integration; QTY—Quality; SP—Supplier performance; MF—Manufacturing flexibility; *** $p<0.01$, **$p<0.05$, Cronbach's alphas are in parentheses*

reason for lower reliability of BP may result from the fact that only three items were employed to measure this construct.

For subsequent analysis, a composite score for each of the measures was obtained by averaging their corresponding items and used as the indicant of the underlying construct. The intercorrelations, means, and standard deviations of the composite scores are shown in Table 4. Further, according to the test recommended by Gaski (1986), the level of discriminant validity can be demonstrated by showing that the correlation between any pair of scales is lower than the reliability of both the scales. Since Table 4 demonstrates this pattern, discriminant validity among the research variables clearly holds. Overall, it was then concluded that all the scales were acceptably reliable and valid.

Hypotheses Testing

The structural equation modeling approach was applied to test the proposed hypotheses. Since a full structural equation model including both the measurement model and the structural model is too complicated with our sample size and because the scales are largely formative in nature, a model in which each construct was measured with a single indicant (i.e., the composite score) was

Figure 3. Structural equation model with path estimates

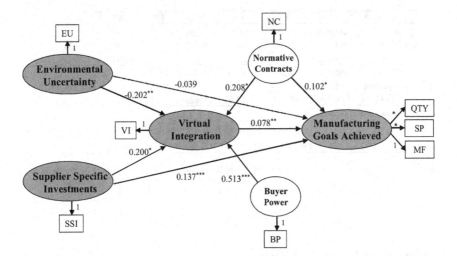

constructed, as depicted in Figure 3. To avoid clutter, all the error terms were omitted in the figure. After this simplification, the model satisfied the typical requirements of five-to-one ratio and sample size larger than 100 for structural equation analysis (Bentler & Chou, 1987). Even though all the constructs were represented by a single indicant, the measurement errors can still be estimated. The measurement errors of each scale were estimated as the product of $(1-\alpha)$ and the variance of the composite score (Joreskog & Sorbom, 1982). Also, all the path coefficients from error variance to construct were constrained to unity for model identification. Further, as quality (QTY), dependability (SP), and manufacturing flexibility (MF) are three dimensions of manufacturing goals achieved, the composite score of the three constructs were used as indicators of this higher order factor. The results of model estimation using EQS are shown in Table 5.

As shown in Table 5, all the overall model fit indexes indicate an excellent fit of the model, and the estimates of the structural parameters can then be used for hypothesis testing. Of the five structural paths (hypotheses) analyzed, four are significant with one-tailed test ($p < 0.01$). Meanwhile, the explained variance (R^2) of the two endogenous variables are all relatively high ($R^2 > 0.204$), indicating that most of the endogenous variables are well explained by the factors proposed in the study. The following subsection provides a more detailed discussion of the findings.

Table 5. The results of model estimation

Construct		EU	SSI	NC	BP	VI	R^2
Manufacturing Goals Achieved (MG)	estimate	-0.039	0.137***	0.102*		0.078**	
	S.E.	0.055	0.053	0.072		0.043	0.204
	z value	-0.713	2.598	1.420		1.813	
Virtual Integration (VI)	estimate	-0.202**	0.200*	0.208*	0.513**		
	S.E.	0.113	0.133	0.146	0.189		0.264
	z value	-1.795	1.501	1.426	2.718		

Overall model fit indexes:

χ^2(df: 11) =7.586; p = 0.750; NFI = 0.972; NNFI = 1.036;

CFI = 1.000; IFI = 1.013; GFI = 0.987; AGFI = 0.958; RMR = 0.012

Notes: EU—Environmental uncertainty; SSI—Supplier's specific investments; NC—Normative contracts; BP—Buyer power; VI—Virtual integration; *** p<0.01, ** p<0.05, *p<0.1, one-tail test

Findings and Implications

As shown in Table 5, environmental uncertainty has an insignificant negative effect on the manufacturing goals achieved. Although such result does not support H_1, the statistical effect is consistent with our proposition yet. Meanwhile, further investigation finds that the factor score of environmental uncertainty reported by the responding firms was relatively low, which may decrease the degree of negative impact of uncertainty imposed on manufacturing performance (Pagell & Krause, 1999). The same problem may also cause environmental uncertainty to have a significant negative effect on manufacturer's reliance on virtual integration, which is in opposition to our proposition suggested in H_2.

In fact, transaction cost economics suggests that either market or hybrid mode are alternative governance structures for managing transactions under low uncertainty, whereas market and firm are alternative governance structures under the condition of high uncertainty (Williamson, 1991). The necessity of vertical coordination mechanism as a means for facilitating mutual adaptation by transacting parties is contingent on other factors such as asset specificity or behavioral uncertainty (Anderson & Buvik, 2001). Without considering the initial conditions of transaction parties and boundary conditions associated with adaptation requirements, empirical results concerning the effects of environmental uncertainty on vertical coordination mechanisms are often inconclusive (John & Weitz, 1988; Klein, 1989). In other words, our empirical result regarding H_2 might indicate that adaptation is not so much a critical problem under conditions of low uncertainty and medium asset specificity (cf. Table 4). Hybrid

Table 6. Research hypotheses and empirical support obtained

Hypothesis	Supported?
(H_1) Environmental Uncertainty $\xrightarrow{(-)}$ Manufacturing Goals Achieved	No
(H_2) Environmental Uncertainty $\xrightarrow{(+)}$ Virtual Integration	No
(H_3) Supplier's Specific Investments $\xrightarrow{(+)}$ Manufacturing Goals Achieved	Yes
(H_4) Supplier Specific Investments $\xrightarrow{(+)}$ Virtual Integration	Yes
(H_5) Virtual Integration $\xrightarrow{(+)}$ Manufacturing Goals Achieved	Yes

governance mechanisms such as normative contracts or long-term relationship might suffice for providing adaptation capabilities for both transacting parties (Macneil, 1978). In contrast, vertical coordination mechanisms such as virtual integration might be too costly a governance mechanism for providing adaptation capability in this situation, and, thus, are negatively associated with environment uncertainty in this study.

The second set of hypotheses deriving from supplier's transaction-specific assets receives greater support from our empirical data. Supplier's transaction-specific investment is shown to have significantly positive effects on both manufacturing goals achieved (H_3) and virtual integration (H_4). Support for H_3 confirms this study's conjecture that transaction-specific investments made by a supplier is essential to improving supply chain performance in general and manufacturer performance in specific. Support for H_4, however, validates our proposition that manufacturer and supplier would rely on virtual integration as a viable vertical coordination mechanism when the exchange requires higher levels of the supplier's transaction specific investments. Because the supplier's transaction-specific investments require closer coordination and cooperation with the manufacturer to realize its potential value, the manufacturer needs to control and monitor its suppliers' performance when the supplier holds asymmetric information derived from its transaction-specific investments. The significantly positive effect exhibited in H_4 also corroborates the resource-based and transaction-cost theory in that enhancing transaction value while controlling opportunism are both important considerations in an exchange relationship.

Further, virtual integration, as hypothesized by H_5, is indeed significantly and positively associated with the achievement of manufacturing goals, indicating that ICT-enabled integration is a useful mechanism for the manufacturer to enhance its manufacturing flexibility, manufacturing quality and dependability. By taking H_4 and H_5 together, we can see the important role of virtual integration in mediating the effect of supplier's specific investments on manufacturing goals achieved; that is, supplier's specific investments tend to motivate the manufacturer to electronically integrate with suppliers that have made such idiosyncratic investments, which once again can enhance manufacturing goals achieved. Actually, this also demonstrates the fact that formal coordination mechanisms enabled by ICT can be beneficial to supply chain integration, resulting in greater mutual adaptability between trading partners when there is strong need to learn from each trading partner and to control potential hazards under the condition of specific investments involved. Another implication of the above result is that although most studies emphasize uncertainty reduction as the primary reason for implementing ICT-enabled coordination mechanisms, this study demonstrates that learning and control requirements are also important considerations to implementing virtual integration (Mason-Jones & Towill, 1999a, 1999b; Towill, 1996).

Finally, although this study did not hypothesize the substantial relationships of normative contracts and buyer power on the other variables in the research model, the empirical results shown in Table 5 exhibit that both variables do have significantly positive effects on virtual integration and manufacturing goals achieved. Particularly, when the effects of normative contracts on both virtual integration and manufacturing goals achieved are controlled, virtual integration still has significant positive impact on manufacturing goals achieved, indicating that virtual integration indeed is influential to manufacturing performance even in a relational exchanging relationship (Lambert, Knemeyer, & Gardner, 2004). Virtual integration is also affected by buyer power and normative contracts in addition to supplier specific investments. These facts reveal that power and social relationships might be other critical antecedents to implementation of virtual integration (Hart & Saunders, 1998). Nevertheless, power is criticized to be an ambiguous concept and is somewhat connected with the concept of asset specificity (Williamson, 1996). Normative contracts often exist in a long-term exchanging relationship, and its development relies on repeated or enduring transaction relationships (Lambe, Spekman, & Hunt, 2000; Macneil, 1978). To validate the relative explanatory power of transaction costs/resource-based, power, and social relationships factors on virtual integration more precisely, further research should explicitly delineate the interrelationships among these factors and incorporate other contingency variables of the transaction relationship, that is, previous relationships, as control variables to exclude potential confounding effects.

Conclusion

By conceptualizing virtual integration as a vertical coordination mechanism, this study contributes to the literature by demonstrating the pivotal role that virtual integration plays in effecting the achievement of manufacturing goals in supply chain integration. First, the supplier's idiosyncratic investments significantly affect manufacturer's manufacturing goals achieved. Since the supplier's specific investments are critical to the manufacturer's own performance, manufacturers are motivated to effectively manage their suppliers who made considerable idiosyncratic investments. Second, the value of idiosyncratic investments is highly dependent on the cooperation and coordinated efforts made by transacting parties. To facilitate mutual adaptation while controlling potential hazards, the manufacturer can rely on virtual integration to integrate its strategic suppliers that make significant idiosyncratic investments. Third, the manufacturers' manufacturing goals can be greatly achieved owing to the fact that virtual integration can facilitate exploring and exploitation of supplier's specific investments through learning-by-monitoring mechanisms embedded in the interorganizational information systems. In addition, as virtual integration brings complementary collaboration between supplier and manufacturer, manufacturing goals can be much more easily attained.

As to managerial implications, this study contributes to our understanding that ICT-enabled collaboration can also be regarded as alternative governance mechanism, that is, virtual integration. With ICT-enabled collaborative operation execution and process planning and control, virtual integration supports both value creation and transaction cost reduction. Therefore, virtual integration is particularly an effective and useful governance mechanism for integrating supply chain under the condition of significant asset specificity.

Although the empirical results are largely supportive to the effects of asset specificity as indicated by TCT and RBV, the hypothesized effects of environmental uncertainty not only do not receive empirical support but also exhibit unexpected results in that environmental uncertainty and virtual integration are significantly and negatively associated. Such an unexpected effect is opposed to the majority of SCM and IOS literature that suggests that environmental uncertainty would result in greater information-processing requirements and hence lead to a greater level of ICT-mediated coordination (Mason-Jones, 1999a; Towill, 1996). Since many other interfirm factors that have been shown to influence interorganizational information systems adoption are not included in this study (for example, trust, commitment and dependence), potential confounding effects may exist (Kumar & Crook, 1999; Kurnia & Johnston, 2000). Therefore, further studies are suggested to incorporate contingency variables of interorganizational relationship to further explore the substantial relationship between environmental uncertainty and virtual integration (Ramamurthy, Premkumar, & Crum, 1999).

Finally, this study has several methodological limitations that may undermine the validity of the results. First, because the study adopted a single-informant approach based on the manufacturer's perspective, respondent bias is possible. Second, the study used perceptual measures, which might not accurately reflect the objective or real relationships among the theoretical constructs examined. Given the proposition that it is the perceptions of managers that largely determine their actions and decisions, such a limitation might not be so serious. Still, further development and validation of the measures utilized here are needed. Fourth, the response rate of the survey appeared to be somewhat lower than the usual cases. Even though the possibility of non-response bias had been checked and ruled out at least statistically, the representativeness of the sample, and thus the generalizability of the results, could still be limited, especially as the data were collected only from manufacturing firms in Taiwan.

References

Alchian, A., & Demsetz, H. (1972). Production, information costs and economic organization. *American Economic Review*, 62, 777-95.

Allem, S. (2000). Full pipeline visibility of Compaq's supply chain. *Taiweb*, 46-55. Retrieved April 10, 2002, from http://taiweb.compaq.com.tw

Amit, R., & Schoemaker, P. (1993). Strategic assets and organizational rent. *Strategic Management Journal*, *14*, 33-46.

Anderson, E., & Weitz, B. (1989). Determinants of continuity in conventional industrial channel dyads. *Marketing Science*, *8*(4), 310-23.

Anderson, O., & Buvik, A. (2001). Inter-firm coordination: International versus domestic buyer-seller relationships. *Omega*, *29*, 207-19.

Armstrong, J. S., & Overton, T. S. (1977). Estimating non-responses bias in mail surveys. *Journal of Marketing Research*, *14*, 396-402.

Artz, K. W., & Brush T. H. (2000). Asset specificity, uncertainty and relational norms: An examination of coordination costs in collaborative strategic alliances. *Journal of Economic Behavior & Organization*, *41*, 337-62.

Asanuma, B. (1989). Manufacturer-supplier relationships in Japan and the concept of relation-specific skill. *Journal of the Japanese and International Economies*, *3*, 1-30.

Barney, J. (1991). Firm resources and sustained competitive advantage. *Journal of Management, 17*(1), 99-120.

Beamon, B. M. (1996, October 2-3). Performance measures in supply chain management. In *Proceedings of the 1996 Conference on Agile and Intelligent Manufacturing Systems*, Troy, NY.

Bensaou, M., & Venkatraman, N. (1996). Interorganizational relationships and information technology: A conceptual synthesis and a research agenda. *European Journal of Information Systems, 5*, 84-91.

Bentler, P. M., & Chou C.P. (1987). Practical issues in structural modeling. *Sociological Methods and Research, 16*, 78-117.

Bollen, K. A. (1989). *Structural equations with latent variables*. New York: Wiley.

Bowersox, D. J., & Morash, E. A. (1989). The integration of marketing flows in channels of distribution. *European Journal of Marketing, 23*(2), 58-67.

Boyle, B. A., & Dwyer, F. R. (1995). Power, bureaucracy, influence, and performance: Their relationships in industrial distribution channel. *Journal of Business Research, 32*, 189-200.

Brynjolfsson, E. (1993). Information assets, technology, and organization. *Management Science, 40*(12), 1645-1662.

Buvik, A., & Gronhaug, K. (2000). Inter-firm dependence, environmental uncertainty and vertical coordination in industrial buyer-seller relationships. *OMEGA, 28*, 445-54.

Buvik, A., & John, G. (2000). When does vertical coordination improve industrial purchasing relationships. *Journal of Marketing, 64*, 52-64.

Cannon, J. P., Achrol, R. S., & Gundlach, G. T. (2000). Contracts, norms, and plural form governance. *Academy of Marketing Science, 28*(2), 180-195.

Carter, J. R., & Narasimhan, R. (1990). Purchasing in the international marketplace: Implications for operations. *Journal of Purchasing and Materials Management, 26*(3), 2-11.

Chandrashekar, A., & Schary, P. B. (1999). Toward the virtual supply chain: The convergence of IT and organization. *The International Journal of Logistics Management, 10*(2), 27-39.

Chen, S. H. (2002). Global production networks and information technology: The case of Taiwan. *Industry and Innovation, 9*(3), 249-65.

Chin, W. W. (1998). Issues and opinion on structural equation modeling. *MIS Quarterly, 21*(1), vii-xvi.

Christopher, M., & Towill, D.R. (2000). Supply chain migration from lean and functional to agile and customised. *Supply Chain Management, 5*(4), 206-13.

Clark, K. B., & Fujimoto, T. (1991). *Product development performance.* Boston: Harvard Business School Press.

Clemens, E. K., Reddi, S. P., & Row, M. (1993). The impact of information technology on the organization of economic activity: The move to the middle hypothesis. *Journal of Management Information Systems, 10*(2), 9-35.

Coase, R. H, (1937). The nature of the firm. *Economica* NS, *4*(16), 386-405.

Cox, A. (2001). Understanding buyer and supplier power: A framework for procurement and supply competence. *The Journal of Supply Chain Management, 37*(2), 8-15.

Dierickx, I., & Cool, K. (1989). Asset stock accumulation and sustainability of competitive advantage. *Management Science, 35*(12), 1504-1511.

Dyer, J. H. (1996). Does governance matter? Keiretsu alliances and asset specificity as sources of Japanese competitive advantage. *Organization Science, 7,* 649-66.

Dyer, J. H., Cho, D. S., & Chu, W. (1998). Strategic supplier segmentation: The next 'best practice' in supply chain management. *California Management Review, 40*(2), 57-77.

Dyer, J. H., & Singh, H. (1998). Relational view: Cooperative strategy and sources of interorganizational competitive advantage. *Academy of Management Review, 23*(4), 660-79.

Farrell, J., & Gibbson, R. (1995). Cheap talk about specific investments. *Journal of Law, Economics and Organization, 11,* 313-34.

Fawcett, S. E., & Magnan, G. M. (2002). The rhetoric and reality of supply chain integration. *International Journal of Physical Distribution & Logistics, 32*(5), 339-61.

Forster, P. W., & Regan, A. C. (2001). Electronic integration in the air cargo industry: An information processing model of on-time performance. *Transportation Journal,* 46-61.

Frohlich, M. T. (2002). e-Integration in the supply chain: Barriers and performance. *Decision Sciences, 33*(4), 537-56.

Frohlich, M. T., & Westbrook, R. (2001). Arcs of integration: An international study of supply chain strategies. *Journal of Operations Management, 19,* 185-200.

Gaski, J. F. (1986). Interrelations among a channel entity's power sources: Impact of the exercise of reward and coercion on expert, referent, and legitimate power sources. *Journal of Marketing Research, XIII,* 62-77.

Germain, R., Droge, C., & Christensen, W. (2001). The mediating role of operations knowledge in the relationship of context with performance. *Journal of Operations Management, 19,* 453-69.

Ghosh, M., & John, G. (1999). Governance value analysis and marketing strategy. *Journal of Marketing, 63*, 131-45.

Giannakis, M., & Croom, S. R. (2004, Spring). Toward the development of a supply chain management paradigm: A conceptual framework. *The Journal of Supply Chain Management,* 27-37.

Grant, R. (1996). Prospering in dynamically-competitive environments: Organizational capability as knowledge integration. *Organization Science, 7*, 375-87.

Grossman, S., & Hart, O. (1986). The costs and benefits of ownership: A theory of vertical and lateral integration. *Journal of Political Economy, 94*, 691-719.

Gurbaxani, V., & Whang, S. (1991). The impact of information systems on organizations and markets. *Communications of the ACM, 34*(1), 59-73.

Hair, Jr., J. F., Anderson, R. E., Tatham, R. L., & Black, W. C. (1992). *Multivariate data analysis with readings* (3rd ed.) New York: Macmillan.

Halley, A., & Nollet, J. (2002, Summer). The supply chain: The weak link for some preferred suppliers? *The Journal of Supply Chain Management,* 39-47.

Hart, P. J., & Saunders, C. S. (1998). Emerging electronic partnerships: Antecedents and dimensions of EDI use from the supplier's perspective. *Journal of Management Information Systems, 14*(4), 87-111.

Heck, R. H. (1998). Factor analysis: Exploratory and confirmatory approaches. In G. Marcoulides (Ed.), *Modern methods for business research* (pp. 177-215). Mahwah, NJ: Lawrence Erlbaum.

Heide, J. B. (1994). Inter-organizational governance in marketing channels: Theoretical perspectives on forms and antecedents. *Journal of Marketing, 58*, 71-85.

Heide, J. B., & John, G. (1990). Alliances in industrial purchasing: The determinants of joint action in buyer-seller relationships. *Journal of Marketing Research, 27*, 24-36.

Helper, S., Macduffie, J. P., & Sabel, C. (2000). Pragmatic collaborations: Advancing knowledge while controlling opportunism. *Industrial and Corporate Change, 9*(3), 443-88.

Huang, C. W., & Lo, C. P. (2003). Using postpond manufacturing to reconfigure the supply chain in the desktop personal computer industry: The case of Taiwan. *International Journal of Management, 20*(2), 241-56.

Huber, G. P. (1991). Organizational learning: The contributing processes and the literatures. *Organization Science, 2*(1), 88-115.

Huber, G. P., & Power, D. J. (1985). Retrospective reports of strategy-level managers: Guidelines for increasing their accuracy. *Strategic Management Journal, 6,* 171-80.

Hult, G. T. M., Ketchen, Jr., D. J., & Slater, S. F. (2004). Information processing, knowledge development, and strategic supply chain performance. *Academy of Management Journal, 47*(2), 241-53.

Iyer, A. V., & Bergen, M. E. (1997). Quick response in manufacturer retailer channels. *Management Science, 43*(4), 559-70.

Jap, S. D. (1999). Pie-expansion efforts: Collaboration processes in buyer-supplier relationships. *Journal of Marketing Research, 36,* 461-75.

Jap, S.D. (2001). Pie sharing in complex collaboration contexts. *Journal of Marketing Research, 38,* 86-99.

John, G., & Weitz, B. (1988). Forward integration into distribution: An empirical test of transaction cost analysis. *Journal of Law, Economics and Organization, 4,* 337-55.

Jones, C., Hesterly, W. S., & Borgatti, S. P. (1997). A general theory of network governance: Exchange conditions and social mechanisms. *Academy of Management Journal, 22*(4), 991-945.

Joreskog, K. G., & Sorbom, D. (1982). Recent developments in structural equation modeling. *Journal of Marketing Research, 19,* 404-416.

Joshi, A.W., & Stump, R.L. (1999). Determinants of commitment and opportunism: integrating and extending insights from transaction cost analysis and relational exchange theory. *Canadian Journal of Administrative Science, 16*(4), 334-52.

Kim, B. (2000). Coordinating an innovation in supply chain management. *European Journal of Operational Research, 123,* 568-84.

Klein, B., Crawford, R., & Alchian, A. (1978). Vertical integration, appropriate rents, and the comparative contracting process. *Journal of Law and Economics, 21,* 297-326.

Klein, S. (1989). A transaction cost explanation of vertical control in international markets. *Journal of Academy of Marketing Science, 17,* 253-60.

Koufteros, X., Vonderembse, M., & Doll, W. (2001). Concurrent engineering and its consequences. *Journal of Operations Management, 19,* 97-115.

Krause, D.R. (1997, Spring). Supplier development: Current practices and outcomes. *International Journal of Purchasing and Materials Management,* 12-19.

Krause, D.R. (1999). The antecedents of buying firms' efforts to improve suppliers. *Journal of Operations Management, 17,* 205-24.

Kulkarni, S.P., & Heriot, K. C. (1999). Transaction costs and information costs as determinants of the organizational form: A conceptual synthesis. *American Business Review*, 43-52.

Kumar, R. L., & Crook, C. W. (1999). A multi-disciplinary framework for the management of interorganizational systems. *The DATA BASE for Advances in Information Systems*, *30*(1), 22-37.

Kurnia, S., & Johnston, R. B. (2000). The need for a processual view of interorganizational systems adoption. *Journal of Strategic Information Systems*, *9*, 295-319.

Lambe, C. J., Spekman, R. E., & Hunt, S. D. (2000). Interimistic relational exchange: Conceptualization and propositional development. *Journal of the Academy of Marketing Science*, *28*(2), 212-25.

Lambert, D. M., & Cooper, M. C. (2000). Issues in supply chain management. *Industrial Marketing Management,* *29*, 65-83.

Lambert, D. M., Knemeyer, A. M., & Gardner, J. T. (2004). Supply chain partnerships: Model validation and implementation. *Journal of Business Logistics*, *25*(2), 21-42.

Lee, H. L., Padmanabhan, V., & Whang, S. (1997). Information distortion in a supply chain: The bullwhip effect. *Management Science*, *43*(4), 546-58.

Levy, D. L. (1997). Lean production in an international supply chain. *Sloan Management Review*, 94-102.

Lusch, R. F., & Brown, J. R. (1996). Interdependency, contracting, and relational behavior in marketing channels. *Journal of Marketing*, *60*, 19-38.

Macneil, I. R. (1978). Contracts: Adjustment of long-term contract relations under classical, neoclassical, and relational contract law. *Northwestern University Law Review*, *72*, 854-905.

Magretta, J. (1998). The power of virtual integration: An interview with Dell Computer's Michael Dell. *Harvard Business Review*, *76*, 72-84.

Malone, T., Yates, J., & Benjamin, R. (1987). Electronic markets and electronic hierarchies: Effects of information technology on market structure and corporate strategies. *Communications of the ACM*, *30*(6), 484-97.

Mason-Jones, R., & Towill, D. R. (1999a). Information enrichment: Design the supply chain for competitive advantage. *Supply Chain Management*, *2*(4), 137-48.

Mason-Jones, R., & Towill, D. R. (1999b). Total cycle time compression and the agile supply chain. *International Journal of Production Economics*, *62*, 61-73.

Morash, E. A., & Clinton, S. R. (1998). Supply chain integration: Customer value through collaborative closeness versus operational excellence. *Journal of Marketing Theory and Practice*, 6(4), 104-20.

Narasimhan, R., & Das, A. (1999). An empirical investigation of the contribution of strategic sourcing to manufacturing flexibilities and performance. *Decision Sciences*, 30(3), 683-718.

Narasimhan, R., & Jayaram, J. (1998). Causal linkages in supply chain management: An exploratory study of North American manufacturing firms. *Decision Sciences*, 29(3), 579-605.

Narasimhan, R., & Kim, S. W. (2001). Information system utilization strategy for supply chain integration. *Journal of Business Logistics*, 22(2), 51-75.

Nesheim, T. (2001). Externalization of the core: Antecedents of collaborative relationships with suppliers. *European Journal of Purchasing & Supply Management*, 7, 217-25.

Nunnally, J. C. (1978). *Psychometric theory* (2nd ed.), New York: McGraw-Hill.

O'Leary-Kelly, S. W., & Vokurka, R. J. (1998). The empirical assessment of construct validity. *Journal of Operations Management*, 16, 387-405.

Oliver, C. (1997). Sustainable competitive advantage: Combining institutional and resource-based views. *Strategic Management Journal*, 18, 697-714.

Pagell, M., & Krause, D. R. (1999). A multiple-method study of environmental uncertainty and manufacturing flexibility. *Journal of Operations Management*, 17, 307-25.

Pagell, M., Newman, W. R., Hanna, M. D., & Krause, D. R. (2000). Uncertainty, flexibility, and buffers: Three case studies. *Production and Inventory Management Journal*, 35-43.

Penrose, E. T. (1959). *The theory of the growth of the firm*, Oxford, UK: Blackwell.

Poppo, L., & Zenger, T. (1998). Testing alternative theories of the firm: Transaction cost, knowledge-based and measurement explanations of make-or-buy decisions in information services. *Strategic Management Journal*, 19(9), 853-77.

Raghunathan, S. (1999). Interorganizational collaborative forecasting and replenishment systems and supply chain implications. *Decision Sciences*, 30(4), 1053-1071.

Ramamurthy, K., Premkumar, G., & Crum, M. R. (1999). Organizational and interorganizational determinants of EDI diffusion and organizational performance—A causal model. *Journal of Organizational Computing and Electronic Commerce*, 9(4), 253-85.

Rindfleisch, A., & Heide, J. B. (1997). Transaction cost analysis: Past, present and future applications. *Journal of Marketing, 61*, 30-54.

Rumelt, R. P. (1984). Towards a strategic theory of the firm. In R. B. Lamb (Ed.), *Competitive strategic management* (pp. 556-571). Englewood Cliffs, NJ: Prentice Hall.

Schmenner, R. W., & Swink, M. L. (1998). On theory in operations management. *Journal of Operations Management, 17*, 97-113.

Scott, J. E. (2000). Facilitating interorganizational learning with information technology. *Journal of Management Information Systems, 17*(2), 81-113.

Seifert, D. (2003). *Collaborative planning, forecasting, and replenishment.* New York: AMACOM.

Shin, H., Collier, D. A., & Wilson, D. D. (2000). Supply management orientation and supplier/buyer performance. *Journal of Operations Management, 18*, 317-33.

Simatupang, T. M., Wright, A. C., & Sridharan, R. (2002). The knowledge of coordination for supply chain integration. *Business Process Management Journal, 8*(3), 289-308.

Stanley, L. L., & Wisner, J. D. (2001). Service quality along the supply chain: Implications for purchasing. *Journal of Operations Management, 19*, 287-306.

Stapleton, D., Gentles, P., Ross, J., & Shubert, K. (2001). The location-centric shift from marketplace to marketplace: Transaction cost-inspired propositions of virtual integration via an e-commerce model. *Advances in Competitiveness Research, 9*(1), 10-41.

Stump, R. L., & Heide, J. B. (1996). Controlling supplier opportunism in industrial relationships. *Journal of Marketing Research, 33,* 431-41.

Teece, D. (1987). Profiting from technological innovation: Implications for integration, collaboration, licensing, and public policy. In D. Teece (Ed.), *The competitive challenge.* New York: Harper & Row.

Towill, D. R. (1996). Time compression and supply chain management-A guided tour. *Supply Chain Management, 1*(1), 15-27.

Turner, G. B., LeMay, S. A., Hartley, M., & Wood, C. M. (2000). Interdependence and cooperation industrial buyer-supplier relationships. *Journal of Marketing Theory and Practice*, 16-24.

Tsang, E. W. K. (2000). Transaction cost and resource-based explanations of joint ventures: A comparison and synthesis. *Organization Studies, 21*(1), 215-42.

van der Vorst, J. G. A. J., Beulens, A. J. M., de Wit, W., & van Beek, P. (1998). Supply chain management in food chains: Improving performance by reducing uncertainty. *International Transactions in Operational Research*, *5*(6), 487-499.

Van Hoek, R. I. (1998). Logistics and virtual integration postponement, outsourcing and the flow of information. *International Journal of Physical Distribution & Logistics Management*, *28*(7), 508-523.

Van Hoek, R. I. (2001). The discovery of postponement: A literature review and directions for research. *Journal of Operations Management*, *19*, 161-184.

Von Hippel, E. (1988). *The sources of innovation*. New York: Oxford University Press.

Wagner, S.M. (2003). Intensity and managerial scope of supplier integration. *The Journal of Supply Chain Management*, 4-15.

Waller, M., Johnson, M. E., & Davis, T. (1999). Vendor-managed inventory in the retail supply chain. *Journal of Business Logistics, 20*(1), 183-203.

Watson, G. (2001). Subregimes of power and integrated supply chain management. *The Journal of Supply Chain Management*, 36-41.

Whitford, J., & Zeitlin, J. (2004). Governing decentralized production: Institutions, public policy, and the prospects for inter-firm collaboration in US manufacturing. *Industry and Innovation*, *11*(1/2), 11-44.

Wilding, R. D. (1998). The supply chain complexity triangle-Uncertainty generation in the supply chain. *International Journal of Physical Distribution & Logistics Management*, *28*(8), 599-616.

Williamson, O. E. (1975). *Markets and hierarchies: Analysis and antitrust implications*. New York: The Free Press.

Williamson, O. E. (1985). *The economic institutions of capitalism*. New York: Free Press.

Williamson, O. E. (1991). Comparative economic organization: The analysis of discrete structural alternatives. *Administrative Science Quarterly, 36*, 269-296.

Williamson, O. E. (1996). *The mechanisms of governance*. New York: Oxford University Press.

Womack, J. P., & Jones, D. T. (1990). *The machine that changed the world: The story of lean production*. New York: Harper Perennial.

Young-Ybarra, C., & Wiersema, M. (1999). Strategic flexibility in information technology alliances: The influence of transaction cost economics and social exchange theory. *Organization Science, 10*(4), 439-59.

Appendix

Survey Items

All survey items are five-point rating scales anchored as follows:

- Environmental Uncertainty, Supplier Specific Investments, Virtual Integration, Manufacturing Goals Achieved: 1, very low; 5, very high
- Normative Contracts, Buyer Power: 1, strongly disagree; 5, strongly agree

Environmental Uncertainty

Evaluate the following aspects of environment facing your company:

- (EU1) The unpredictability of your company's sales volume
- (EU2) The unpredictability of volume purchased from your primary supplier
- (EU3) The unpredictability of product specification or features from your primary supplier
- (EU4) The unpredictability of service supports required from your primary supplier

Supplier's Transaction-specific Investments

Evaluate the extent to which your primary supplier has made the following specific investments to your company:

- (SSI1) Plant proximal to your company
- (SSI2) Tooling and equipments
- (SSI3) Logistics and warehouse facilities
- (SSI4) Adjustments of manufacturing process to fit your company's specification of technology and standard
- (SSI5) Technology investments to produce components demand by your company

- (SSI6) Business processes reengineering to improve the performance of the trading
- (SSI7) Significant time and money on training to work with your company
- (SSI8) Significant time and money on product and process qualification approved by your company
- (SSI9) Significant time and money on timeliness of the trading

Normative Contracts

Evaluate the extent to which your primary supplier and your company rely on the following shared norms to regulate each other's trading behavior:

- (NC1) Role played
- (NC2) Responsibility
- (NC3) Behavior
- (NC4) Dealing with unexpected events
- (NC5) Dealing with conflicts
- (NC6) Legal remedies
- (NC7) Performance evaluation
- (NC8) Standard of operational procedures
- (NC9) Purchasing price
- (NC10) Purchasing volume
- (NC11) Purchasing duration

Buyer Power

Evaluate the extent to which you agree with the following statements about the relationship between your company and your primary supplier:

- (BP1) Your primary supplier needs your company to provide suggestion on product specification and design
- (BP2) Your primary supplier needs your company to provide market information
- (BP3) Your primary supplier needs your company to provide technical support

Virtual Integration

Evaluate the extent to which your company and your primary supplier rely on the supply chain information system to coordinate on the following:

- (VI1) Issuing purchasing order
- (VI2) Tracing purchasing order
- (VI3) Exchanging price and market information periodically
- (VI4) Quality control on the purchased goods
- (VI5) Cooperating on new material and component testing
- (VI6) Dealing with complains and solving conflicts
- (VI7) Coordinating production plan
- (VI8) Coordinating Inventory
- (VI9) Coordinating Logistics

Supply Chain Performance

Evaluate the extent of improvements in the quality, dependability and manufacturing flexibility of buying firm after launching and operation of the supply chain information system:

- (QTY1) Product features
- (QTY2) Product reliability
- (QTY3) Product durability
- (QTY4) Product performance
- (QTY5) Conformance to the product specification
- (SP1) Speed of delivery
- (SP2) Reliability of delivery
- (SP3) Inventory costs
- (SP4) Shortage costs
- (MF1) Process flexibility
- (MF2) Volume flexibility
- (MF3) Mix flexibility

Section II:

The Participants' Role in Supply Chain Management

Chapter V

Trust and Transparency in Netchains:
A Contradiction?

Gert Jan Hofstede, Wageningen University, The Netherlands

Abstract

This chapter analyses the effects of increased transparency in supply netchains. The term netchain refers to both chain and network aspects. Three levels of transparency are distinguished: history transparency (e.g., tracking and tracing), operations transparency (e.g., collaborative logistics planning), and strategy transparency (e.g., joint innovation). Using an example in the Dutch egg sector, the chapter shows how the role of the individual company changes in a netchain and discusses the implications. Though technology push makes transparency feasible and economically attractive, social-psychological barriers exist that should be taken seriously. A brief review of cases from several continents shows that these barriers vary across cultures, depending on prevailing attitudes towards relationships and authority. Transparency may run counter to tradition, to trust, and to entrepreneurial freedom in the netchain, but it also offers opportunities for creating netchains that are profitable to all participants. To grasp these requires vision on behalf of those involved.

Introduction

Over the last decades, the relations between partners in a trade network have changed. This change was driven by technology, notably the arrival first of electronic data interchange (EDI) and then of the World Wide Web and e-business. The expectation of efficiency gains was a strong motivator for companies to adopt the new technologies. But the changes are not limited to efficiency gains. They also affect trade networks' social and political dynamics. In the food industry, for instance, they lead to heavy requirements for data collection by primary producers, and possibly to increased dependency of producers on factories or retailers.

It was Thorelli (1986) who introduced networks as a subject for organisation-theoretical research. Relations and power balances in trade networks have shifted due to technological advances. These changes have recently grown into an important area of study. A specialised academic journal, based in the Netherlands, has seen the light of day: the *Journal on Chain and Network Science*. The Dutch government has stimulated joint research efforts by business and research institutions to enhance knowledge about cooperation in the e-age. In this chapter, we shall discuss those efforts and their results, giving particular attention to the requirement for transparency in business networks and the consequences of this requirement for relationships between the actors in the network. Transparency has quickly become of great importance in the meat and egg sectors due to the recent food scares in Europe (Beulens, 2003). In plant sectors, fear of consuming genetically modified plant material has been a driver for transparency. Thus, much of the experience has been collected in the food and agribusiness industry.

Figure 1. Egg networks in The Netherlands (Arrows indicate flow of goods or services)

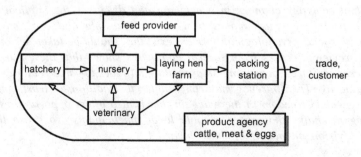

A business network in this sector could look like Figure 1. This network will serve as an illustration in this chapter. There are one or two companies of each type in the network. Hens move from hatchery through nursery to laying hen factory; eggs move from there through packing station to customer. Feed providers and veterinarians provide feed and medical services, respectively. The product agency is responsible for both public relations and good conduct of the sector. It also mediates with legislators and it lobbies on the sector's behalf. A number of parallel networks of similar composition exist in the Netherlands.

The Dutch agribusiness sector is at the forefront of network integration. Yet the concepts discussed in this chapter are by no means limited to the agribusiness sector. On the contrary, other sectors in which integration between actors has not yet taken such a flight, for example, health care or building and construction, could benefit from the experiences of the agribusiness sector.

Network integration frequently coincides with the adoption of business-to-business (b2b) e-business. An important aspect of e-business is that it requires formal standards of communication between organisations in a network. These standards, in their turn, change relationships in many ways, both at the level of operations and at strategic level. The role of stakeholders outside the network, such as government and customers, also changes.

History has shown that it takes many years for new technologies to become agents of social and institutional change. The telephone, the car, and the Internet are cases in point. It can be expected that transparent networks will also take many years to reach their full impact on business and society. What kind of an impact will that be? Will it stifle entrepreneurial freedom and hamper innovation? Will it reduce the smaller stakeholders in a netchain to slavery? Or will it lead to wider horizons, joint innovation, and mutual benefits? What research is needed to find out more about these matters? And how can enterprises proactively influence the impact that networks will have on them?

In the chapter, we articulate these questions further and begin to answer them. For this, we first introduce the main concepts of the field. Then we discuss network integration, its drivers, and its consequences from an institutional point of view. A discussion about the implications for research and for practice and some concluding propositions terminate the chapter.

Central Concepts

Chains, Networks, Netchains

Companies are necessarily connected to their suppliers and to their customers, who are usually companies too. Most companies are also linked to competitors and to service providers. Thorelli (1986, p. 38) remarks, "Probably the most salient part of the environment of any firm is other firms". Since then, abstract notions have been pinpointed to discuss the ties between companies (often called "actors").

The notion of chains, notably supply chains, has become important since the early 1990s. The concept and the literature were technology-driven at first. Logistical savings and improved planning have been important organisational drivers. By and large, supply chain integration has become widespread. For many sectors, it has become an economic necessity.

"Network" is a concept that originates from the social and organisational sciences. The Web metaphor has recently been a powerful driver. According to the Web metaphor, people as well as organisations are supposed to be part of volatile, opportunistic networks. Virtual X, Y, or Z is a buzzword.

Often, "chains and networks" is used as if it were one word, as in the name of the *Journal on Chain and Network Science*. This is because chains and networks are two sides of the same coin. The word "chain" emphasises the streams of goods, money, and information that flow between the participating actors. The word "network" emphasises the nonlinear character of almost any set of connected firms. Most authors also use it to signify the social relationships that exist between the actors.

Recently, the concept *netchain* was coined (Lazzarini, Chaddad, & Cook, 2001) to reconcile the two terms. The authors define a netchain as "a set of networks comprised of horizontal ties between firms within a particular industry or group, which are sequentially arranged based on vertical ties between firms in different layers" (p. 7).

Tracking and Tracing

The notion of chain brought to the fore the related notion of flows through that chain: goods flow from producer to consumer, money flows in the reverse sense, and information could flow both ways. In a situation where farmers directly sell at markets or to village stores, knowing about the provenance or destination of products is no problem. But in industrial agribusiness chains, information does not necessarily flow all the way. A customer often has trouble determining from where his meat or fruit came. This lack of insight could be dangerous to public health. In Figure 1, for instance, customers usually do not know from what farm their egg came, and if they would fall ill after eating the egg, how could the netchain make sure that all eggs that might also be contaminated are removed from the shops? A technological solution was proposed and became popular during the last decade—tracking and tracing.

Tracing is finding out the flow of products through a food chain after the fact. Tracking is following products through the chain to see what happens to them. Tracking and tracing are particularly useful in food scares, that is, when customers fall ill after consuming food products. It enables the chain as a whole to find out from where the contamination originated and where the products that are dangerous to public health have gone. This allows the chain to warn all the relevant stakeholders about the danger, so that the consequences remain limited. Tracking and tracing are now operational in much of agribusiness. As of January 1, 2005, the General Food Law (van der Meulen & van der Velden, 2004) obliges all food companies in the European Union to keep track of from whom they bought their food and to whom they sold it.

Transparency

Recently, the notion of transparency has come into fashion (Hofstede, 2002). It takes a wider stance than just tracking and tracing. It connotes honesty, and claims that anybody can see through what we produce and how we do it. Transparency is aimed not only at businesses in the netchain but also at other stakeholders, for instance, government bodies or firms' shareholders. The public at large, both as customers and as citizens, also comes into focus here.

A definition of transparency (Hofstede, Spaans, & Beulens, 2004, p. 290) is, "Transparency of a netchain is the extent to which all the netchain's stakeholders have a shared understanding of, and access to, the product-related information that they request, without loss, noise, delay and distortion." In this definition, *product-related information* is meant in the widest sense and can include, for example, information about raw materials, production processes, labour circumstances, environmental impacts, or even cost prices. It can serve various aims, for example, preserving identity, food safety, or adding value. Furthermore, the words *shared understanding* merit attention. Without sharing or at least seamless translation of language, meaning, and standards, there cannot be transparency.

Though hyped, the quest for transparency is not new. It is at the heart of accounting. Accounting aims at making the central financial figures of companies transparent so that these companies are shown to abide by the law. A cynic might find that accounting is in fact institutionalised distrust, since there is no other reason for accounting than believing that the target organisations would not be honest without it. Even worse, accounting does not help, as recent scandals of, for example, Enron and Worldcom have shown. Thus, accounting and transparency could be claimed to boil down to hiding the essentials.

As a buzzword, "transparency" is used for various purposes. Three aspects can frequently be found, depending on whether transparency is aimed at the past, present, or future. I shall label them history, operations, and strategy transparency.

History transparency is needed to track and trace products. Its main driver has been the need to contain calamities. It should enable the netchain to respond quickly and effectively as soon as defective products cause any damage. In the case of agri-food netchains, this usually means consumers fall ill after consuming a product, but it might also mean defective products are intercepted before reaching consumers. In such a case, the cause of the problem must be traced, and any other products that have become dangerous for public health have to be destroyed.

Some preconditions hold for history transparency. Standards are needed for product identification, and agreements are needed about procedures, for example, keeping batches separate and cleaning equipment, so that contamination does not spread. And all parties have to record their manipulations with the products, using the same or at least compatible identification systems, so that the identity of small product units can be preserved through the netchain. In the egg case of Figure 1, achieving history transparency was one of the aims. Because of this, the actors needed to agree on batch size and on not mixing batches, which turned out to be tough going. Once agreements of this kind have been reached, no communication is needed in the daily processes of the actors in the netchain. The data can be kept in a central repository (see, for example, Wilson & Clarke, 1998) encrypted by keys, and need only be accessed in case of emergency. In the food sector, history transparency is more and more being enforced by law or by retailers, such as Ahold or Carrefour, who anticipate future regulations.

A netchain can use history transparency as a marketing device. Netchains incur costs when they introduce history transparency, but such transparency could be made to increase the products' value. Customers may be willing to pay more if they know the quality and provenance of the products. For instance, high-quality meat chains provide a view of the   living conditions of their animals through Webcams in shops (www.petersfarm.com). A more common quality indicator is branding or certification. Sauvée (2000) discusses a case of branding in the French tomato sector, showing that reputation is the driving force for a brand.

Operations transparency deals with information exchange between business partners that enables them to coordinate their operations. It includes collaborative planning and logistics, as well as much of the communication in what is usually termed supply chain management. Compared to history transparency, it relies less on formal identification systems and information-technological infra-structure, although these certainly are very helpful in most cases. But its main use may be to help netchain partners signal exceptional circumstances in advance, for example, a lapse in the supply or an unexpected price change. Such signalling is likely to be at least partly voluntary.

Strategy transparency looks into the future. It involves sharing not only operational, but also strategic information. It might also involve cooperative innovation. It can be formalised, as in the case of joint ventures or licensing of patents. Or it could be informal. Uzzi (1997) presents a simple case of strategy transparency:

A typical example (...) was described by a manufacturer who stated that he passes on critical information about "hot selling items" to his embedded ties before the other firms in the market know about it, giving his close ties an advantage in meeting the future demand. (p. 46)

History transparency is usually imposed on a netchain from the outside. The other two are usually voluntary, and are not always distinct. Rather, they involve different levels in the organisation. Strategy transparency takes place between managers or R&D personnel, while operational transparency is part of the routine of logistics and inventory planners.

Trust

Since the advent of the Web, quite a bit of literature about trust and its importance in the age of electronic communication has seen the light of day. From this literature it is apparent that trust is not the same thing to everyone. In this context, Checkland and Holwell (1998) present a useful distinction of two strands of research in information systems (IS). The "hard" tradition conceptualises organisations as social entities that set up and seek to achieve goals. In this light, interorganisational trust is instrumental. It is only needed for achieving the organisation's goals. The "soft" tradition sees organisations as social entities that seek to manage relationships. This perspective is the one adopted here. It puts trust centre stage. It implies that narrow, instrumental definitions of trust are not sufficient to comprehend interorganisational ties that are needed for netchains to function. It also implies that information systems should look to the social sciences to define trust.

Rousseau, Sitkin, Burt, and Camerer (1998) show that economists, psychologists, and sociologists tend to work with widely different conceptions of trust. We shall adopt the compromise definition presented by Rousseau et al. (1998, p. 395): "Trust is a psychological state comprising the intention to accept vulnerability based upon positive expectations of the intentions or behaviour of another." The keyword in this definition is *vulnerability*. Trusting people means that you do not need to take the trouble of checking on them, accepting the chance that they might cheat on you. Trust without vulnerability is gratuitous. This implies trust can only increase gradually through being tested in situations of reciprocal interdependency and not broken. As Julos Beaucarne (1975) put it in a poem, "On ne bâtit pas de vieilles amities" (One cannot make old friends). Once broken, trust is very hard to mend.

From an economic perspective, the definition above means trusting somebody is a way to save transaction costs. To a psychologist, it means trusting somebody makes one feel more secure, so one can give one's attention to other things. A sociologist might infer that the trusted person is a likely candidate for a network of friends or business relations. These three perspectives basically point in the same direction: trust is very valuable.

Uzzi (1997) presents a very enlightening empirical investigation into the relationship between the economic and social scientific aspects of trust. In the New York better-dress sector, he found that close relationships of trust between netchain partners indeed conform to the three advantages postulated from the three perspectives. He uses the term *embedded ties* for durable business relationships based on mutual trust. Embedded relationships were found to be timesaving because "there was an absence of monitoring devices designed to catch a thief" (p. 43). They involved complex coadaptation and allowed for allocative efficiency gains, economies of time and risk reduction. Uzzi found that in a way, one can "make old friends" through what he calls third-party referral. If a friend introduces two members of his embedded network to one another, that considerably speeds up the building of trust between the new acquaintances.

Uzzi (1997) contrasts embedded ties with *arm's length* business relations. The latter are not based on trust but on market-conform contracts without obligations beyond the individual contract. The paradox of embeddedness, as he calls it, is that "the same processes by which embeddedness creates a requisite fit with the current environment can paradoxically reduce an organisation's ability to adapt" (p. 57). A case in point is the exit of an important partner in the embedded network or the entry of powerful, arm's length players that work strictly according to one-shot deals. Therefore, Uzzi concludes, organisations would be wise to not rely on either type of relationship alone but choose their mix depending on their business environment.

The cultural dimension of individualism versus collectivism can inform Uzzi's dichotomy (Hofstede, 2001). In individualist societies, the expectation is for business relationships to be arm's length and, accordingly, for economic rationality to govern business life. Obviously this is not always really so, as Uzzi's (1997) New York case study reveals. At the other end of the spectrum, in collectivist societies, the expectation is for relationships to be embedded. Within an in-group people are "family," and they are supposed to support one another through thick and thin. This is why it takes more time for business relationships to develop in collectivist countries than it does in individualist ones (Hofstede & Hofstede, 2005).

The recent debate on trust has been spurred by the advent of the Web with its "virtual teams" in which neither the boss nor other team members are physically present to check on one another. But trust is obviously much older than the Web as a point of attention for organisational sciences and practices. It is, for instance, central to the well-known notion of situational management developed by Kenneth Blanchard (Blanchard & Johnson, 1978). Situational management holds that if a manager trusts an employee to be both able and willing to perform a task, that manager should not check on the employee but leave him alone. Why? Because checking on the employee would mean to him that he is *not* being trusted. Nor has trust been neglected in economics. In 1982, Fried wrote, "So powerful a tool is trust that we pursue it for its own sake; we prefer to do things cooperatively when we might have relied on fear or interest or worked alone" (p. 8).

In conclusion, people who trust one another do not need to tell each other anything just to show what they did. They only tell one another what they know the other needs to know. So we see that in sharp contrast to transparency, trust implies hiding *all but* the essentials. It also follows from the definition that any *voluntary* action or communication by a netchain actor to help one of the other actors is trust building. For instance, if a supplier voluntarily warns a buyer of a lapse in supply, that action builds trust with the buyer. The buyer will tend to reciprocate and will rely on the supplier to warn him again if needed. Thus, a virtuous cycle ensues. If the warning is not perceived to be voluntary but obligatory, no trust is built.

Netchain Integration

Netchain integration can be viewed from a process, an institutional, or a performance perspective (Trienekens, 1999). Transparency has historically been connected to tracking and tracing and to the process perspective. This perspective is important for history- and operations transparency. The performance aspect is central to economic theory. In this chapter, we stress the institutional aspect, integrating institutional economics with a social-scientific perspective.

Drivers and Consequences

The technological advances of the last decades have dramatically changed the nature of transaction costs for business-to-business trade. Electronic data interchange (EDI) replaced paper administration, building on data definition standards for the seamless integration of business order administrations. Creating these standards is costly, but once standards and EDI systems are in place, economies of scale are strong. Tracking and tracing systems extend this trend. Designing them is costly, but economies of scale are reached once they are in place.

In addition to this technology push, there are external forces that drive netchain integration. A very important force is the market. In the food and agribusiness, as in other sectors, retailers are big players. Their customers have a choice of competitors to go to, and most of them rely heavily on marketing and on product innovations in order to lure customers into their shops. A closer integration of the retailers with their suppliers could make them more flexible in their dealings with customers, for example, for planning year-round availability of fresh produce.

Another external driver towards integration is government policy, itself influenced by food scares. Both national and supranational governmental bodies impose restrictions and obligations on food netchains. The French and the British no doubt remember "la guerre du boeuf" that raged a few years ago at the time of the BSE ("Mad cow disease") crisis. More and more, governments and their executive bodies require netchains as wholes to implement safety standards, such as Hazard Analysis Critical Control Points (HACCP) or EUREP-GAP Euro-Retailer Produce Working Group—Good Agricultural Practices (EUREP-GAP, see www.eurep.org). As we saw, integration can be limited to history transparency of product flow data, it can involve daily operations, or it can even involve strategic cooperation.

The drawback of netchain integration is that opting out of a business relation becomes costly. It frequently means changing standards, procedures, and/or computer infrastructure. Also, if an actor opts out, he loses the capacities or expertise for which he relied on other netchain actors (Uzzi, 1997).

Big players in a network can try to use electronic systems as an exit barrier to tie smaller partners to them. Open standards are a means to limit the cost of exit and entry. Frequently, big players try to enforce proprietary standards whereas smaller ones develop and spread open standards.

An Egg Netchain

In 2001, aided by a subsidy from the KLICT foundation that promotes public/ private partnerships and network building (www.klict.org) and cooperating with two universities and two consulting firms, eight small and medium-sized enter- prises (SMEs) in the Dutch egg sector (see Figure 1) decided to try to form a "virtual organisation." The stated aim was to enhance cooperation in a virtual network while maintaining the independence of the actors and their freedom to entertain other business relations. Preventing food scares was one of the objectives, but achieving economic benefits through better responsiveness to the market was an important motivator.

The actors knew one another very well from community life in their rural area, but they were not used to coordinating their businesses. They worked with yearly arrangements about quantities and price, keeping dependency to a minimum. In Uzzi's (1997) terms the ties were embedded. However, the egg sector is historically much less fashion-prone than the dress sector. As a consequence, the intricate cooperation patterns aimed at responding to market fluctuation expectations that Uzzi found had not developed in the egg sector. Instead, this is a cost market. The actors rather had the feeling of having one pie to share among them, and the fear that if they revealed vital information, others might use that to cut themselves a larger slice. As a result, the firms' willingness to share confidential knowledge turned out to vary widely. Having every participant sign a secrecy declaration and appointing a mediator helped build trust. The project yielded a "Memorandum of Understanding and Principles" of largely symbolic value, and most participants decided to join in a follow-up project. No actual tracking and tracing system or other operational transparency medium was delivered.

The project report (Mevissen, 2002) mentions some critical success factors: involve people with decision-making authority to keep momentum, and keep the project team constant to enhance trust. This latter result points to the fact that trust builds among people, not organisations. A netchain thus consists of three levels: the netchain as a whole, constituting organisations, and the people in those organisations who actually cooperate.

Business-related communication increased from yearly superficial talks to weekly alerts about expectations and trends, thus lifting operational and strategy transparency to a much higher level. The participants also became aware that, despite their modest size, together they accounted for about 30% of the Dutch egg production. This made them realise that as a network they might wield some power against competitors or against the big retailers. A final noteworthy result is that the participants realised that staying independent while forming a network was *not* possible. Even though they were free to do business on the side, the investment in infrastructure, data definition, and agreements bound them together and made exiting costly.

To sum up, while tangible results were not impressive, trust building was significant, and so was the acquisition by participants of a sense of agency at the level of the netchain.

Institutional Mechanisms and Transparency

The concept of transparency pertains to only the information aspect of a netchain. The information flow in a netchain is dependent on the organisation of that netchain as a whole. The three archetypal mechanisms for network governance are presented in Figure 2. Powell (1990) and Diederen (2004, p. 44) inspired the figure. The three network mechanisms have different information exchange patterns associated with them.

In a market, the actors have no obligations to each other apart from exchanging things against an agreed price. In Uzzi's (1997) words, a market requires no

Figure 2. The spectrum of institutional mechanisms (Hofstede, Spaans & Beulens, 2004, p. 286 [From "The Emerging World of Chains and Networks"]; Copyright, RBI Reed Business Information, reprinted with permission)

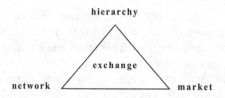

Note: The corners of the triangle depict ideal types while the surface connotes the various mixes of institutional mechanisms that can occur in a netchain.

more than arm's length ties. Information has its price, and withholding it can be made to have its price—for example, by law. According to economic theory, withholding information is detrimental to a market because it inhibits pricing.

In a hierarchy, the boss and inferior—in economic parlance, the *principal* and *agent*—have asymmetric relationships (Eisenhardt, 1989). The principal has paid the agent to provide some service, but may want to check on him if he does not trust the agent's ability or willingness to perform the task—here we see Blanchard's situational management at work (Blanchard & Johnson, 1978). The principal then needs to know about the agent's behaviour, but the agent does not need to know about the principal. In netchains, certification is a mechanism for checking whether agents keep their contractual arrangements.

Markets and hierarchies have long been the dominant institutional mechanisms in the literature, notably transaction cost economics (Williamson, 1998) and agency theory (Eisenhardt, 1989). Both rely on neoclassical economical rationality of the participating actors. But since authors such as Thorelli (1986) and Ring and Van de Ven (1992), networks have received increasing attention. Ring and Van de Ven distinguish two forms of networks: "recurrent contracting" and "relational contracting." The former consist of arm's length ties and behave like a market with habitual partners. In Figure 2, they would be located halfway from the bottom axis. The latter are networks in the ideal-type sense, located at the bottom left of Figure 2. We shall call them "fully embedded networks."

Fully embedded networks contain only what Uzzi (1997) calls embedded ties. In a fully embedded network, norms about how friends behave with regard to one another regulate behaviour, not economics alone. Actors will provide one another with goods or information, anticipating one another's needs, knowing that some time they will receive something in return if they need it. Fully embedded networks have low transaction costs because no checking is needed. Implicit trust takes the place of checking. This implies that it takes a lot of investment to create them, though not in the financial sense. It takes common understanding of the practices in the network, and this in turn may take a lot of time. And such networks are, as Giddens (1997) would say, high-trust systems, and building trust takes years.

In reality, netchains harbour a varied mixture of these exchange mechanisms. They could be located anywhere in Figure 2, except opposite the network pole. They might be part hierarchy if one actor holds more power than the others. They might be part market if arm's length ties prevail. The institutional mechanism that prevails in a netchain is likely to affect the type and degree of transparency that is economically efficient. This relation is moderated by market conditions, as the comparison between the Dutch egg case and Uzzi's (1997) New York dress case shows.

The Institutional Bottleneck

We shall now discuss in institutional terms the situation of a sector with both arm's length and embedded ties that considers achieving greater network integration. In terms of Figure 2, this means moving from the right-hand "market" corner of the triangle towards the left-hand "network" corner. It also means relying more heavily on informal arrangements than on the small print of contracts, and on long-term relationships rather than one-shot transactions. Practice in the Netherlands reveals that talks between would-be netchain partners tend to become strained once critical information has to be shared. Such information, for example, on profit margins, is necessary in order to determine how to divide the benefits, the costs of investments, but especially the costs of risks. Actors sacrifice economic manoeuvreing room by providing strategic data and committing themselves formally to their netchain partners. Such explicit netchain integration runs counter to the usual gradual building of trust that coincides with a slow movement from right to left in the institutional triangle of Figure 2.

Hierarchy changes the pattern. Netchain building can proceed faster if a dominant partner is present who can act as a "netchain leader." The agricultural smallholders in developing countries who supply to major retailers are a case in point (Engel, 2002). But in this case, participation is hardly voluntary, and those who feel they had no alternative but to join might not be very loyal to the netchain. In the egg case, the partners were clear about not wishing a dominant partner in.

When netchain formation is an engineered process and not a spontaneous one, the trust-building phase is critical. Several of the projects in the history of KLICT confirmed this. In institutional terms, this phase occurs at the transition from a market to a network. Therefore, we labelled it the institutional bottleneck. It involves changing the mindset of the actors from seeing themselves as independent companies in a market to being participants in a netchain. If this bottleneck is not passed, the project will fail.

Discussion

Do Trust and Transparency Contradict...

History transparency can be and has been enforced through tracking and tracing systems. To the extent that it is imposed upon the netchain, it is not trust building. Primary producers in the agricultural sector cannot but comply, but they essentially perceive added data logging chores without any benefit other than staying in business. In embedded netchains, history transparency may even damage trust because the data collection activities required for tracking and tracing may signify to actors that they are being checked on, and therefore not trusted.

...Or Don't They?

Yet the establishment of history transparency in a netchain can also be used as a stepping-stone for achieving trust-building forms of transparency. The act of showing the intent to share information builds trust itself. Managers have to meet in order to agree on the scope of history transparency, and they can use these contacts as a starting point for becoming better acquainted. What contacts about history transparency can also do for them is sensitise them to the aggregation level of the netchain in which they operate. This can help them get past the institutional bottleneck. If they achieve agency at the level of the netchain, they create a situation whereby all netchain actors can profit. As the egg case shows, creating a group of people from all participating organisations who trust one another and believe in the netchain is important. Such a team can help break down the walls around the individual organisations. These people, if committed to the team, can convince others in their respective organisations that there are benefits to reap from netchain integration.

So, to avoid the contradiction between trust and transparency, giving primacy to trust is important—at least in the Dutch context, as the egg case demonstrates. In the egg project, the motivation was opportunity rather than enforcement, so that providing one another with confidential data was an act of trust. In the same vein, the project was not merely negatively motivated; the aim was not limited to preventing food scares, but included creating better market value.

How to Lead a Netchain Across the World

Creating a netchain is an act of vision and of persuasion. One cannot force partners into the netchain; if one could, the collaboration would more aptly be called vertical integration. So there is always a measure of freedom, and no single organization is boss. Yet at the same time, leadership is required for making a netchain work. How to organize this? Hofstede (2004) argues that participants are likely to organize a netchain according to a model of leadership that is familiar to them. Hofstede, Schepers, Spaans, Trienekens, and Beulens (2004) assembled 20 case studies from around the world, and they confirm this suggestion.

When it comes to organizing collaboration between organizations, locally suitable leadership models are used.

The Dutch are culturally strongly co-operation-oriented ("feminine") rather than competition-oriented ("masculine"), compared with most countries (Hofstede & Hofstede, 2005). This means that relentless pursuit of self-interest, either by an individual or by a firm, is ill perceived in the Netherlands. It suggests that the Dutch would be more prone to make and keep informal deals among companies, and less likely to create open competition, than, for instance, the British and the Americans. These latter are culturally similar to the Dutch in other regards, for example, both are egalitarian societies. But they widely differ on the masculinity-femininity dimension. Rademakers (1999) compared the Dutch and the British potato sectors and indeed found more cooperation in The Netherlands compared to either spot markets or hierarchical integration in the UK. This confirms the expectation based on cultural difference.

In an Anglo context, one would expect competition to be more prevalent. Indeed, competition in free markets is one of the central tenets of neoclassical economic theory with its Anglo roots. Under neoclassical assumptions, cooperation in a highly embedded netchain may lead to the suspicion that the netchain will try to enforce market dominance against competitors. Thorelli (1986) mentions a case of cooperation among U.S. hospitals and their suppliers that was motivated purely by cost considerations but saw itself faced with a civil antitrust suit.

Other dimensions of culture also affect netchain governance, as indicated by the cases in Hofstede, Trienekens, and Beulens (2004). In Thailand, a country with a hierarchical, long-term oriented culture, government played a "parental," future-directed role in improving transparency about pesticide use on crops, both for export and for local consumption. In Italy, where protecting traditional local food products is highly valued, a transparency initiative in quality wines produced by small growers was successful even though it forced traders to disclose their source price. In Ghana, which has a short-term oriented culture, not government but fair trade-oriented private initiative was the motor for change towards a netchain with transparency that added value. In the Jepara wood trade in Indonesia, which was in the hands of very small companies in a collectivist society, business relationships were family relationships and transparency was not an issue. In all these cases, the relation between trust and transparency was different.

Summing up, we can conclude that national law and national culture affect the type and level of institutional arrangement in a netchain. Since most netchains are cross-national, this is an important area of study. In Hofstede, Schepers, Spaans, Trienekens, and Beulens (2004), a chapter is devoted to discussing the dynamics of trust and transparency across cultures.

Trust by Accident

The above might convey a culture-dependent picture of the relation between trust and transparency. But reality is so varied that one cannot draw simplistic predictions based on culture. A case described by Storer in Hofstede, Schepers, Spaans, Trienekens, and Beulens (2004) demonstrates this. It is about a Japanese fast food chain and its Australian supplier. From a cultural viewpoint, one would not expect these to be very closely integrated across the cultural gap. But four years ago, a food scare happened. Customers in Japan found bits of plastic in their pasta sauce. The sauce, including meat and onions, came from the Australian producer. They were alerted by the Japanese, and soon a Japanese delegation was in Australia, double-checking production. After two very strained weeks in which nothing was found, the Japanese decided to have another look at the plastic and found out that it was, in fact, onion peel. It turned out that Australians were used to onions with much harder peels than were Japanese. In the initial panic, nobody had taken the trouble to check on the bits of "plastic."

After the Australians and the Japanese had been through such an ordeal together, and had seen so much of one another's companies, they were both eager and willing to work on their mutual relationship. Four years later, this chain is very transparent, well organized, and ahead of competitors. Nothing works better for creating collaboration than having been through a hard time together.

Research Agenda

The area of netchains offers huge challenges to the social and economic sciences. Three levels of aggregation are involved in a netchain. They are the individual, the organisation, and the netchain. With some simplification, one could say that these three levels have been the domains of social psychology, economy, and sociology, respectively. But all three have to be simultaneously addressed in the study of netchains. In a netchain, individuals interact who are supposed to represent organisations that together form a new unit of agency.

Economics has grown branches towards sociology recently, with, for example, institutional economics (Menard, 2000) and the work of some authors discussed here (Lazzarini et al., 2001; Thorelli, 1986; Uzzi, 1997; Williamson, 1998). Economics has also grown branches towards psychology, for example, behavioural economics. But the integration is still weak, and the contribution from social psychology almost nonexistent.

Netchains could be the research arena that unites the different strands of research. Longitudinal empirical studies will be best suited to gather the rich understanding that is needed to complement disciplinary research. But some laboratory research can complement this. One promising research method in this area is simulation gaming, combining model-based settings abstracted from real life with actual human behaviour (e.g., Hofstede, Kramer, Meijer, & Wijdemans, 2003; Meijer & Hofstede, 2003; www.netchaingame.org).

What Can Businesses Do?

Various forces drive network integration. Technology push combined with concerns of governments about safety issues has led and will lead to history transparency. Business incentives to achieve benefits of scale and logistic savings lead to operations transparency. A concern for long-term relationships can lead to strategy transparency.

But what do these forms of transparency imply for the role of entrepreneurs? Network integration creates dependencies and, with them, obligations to one's partners and high costs of exit. This could stifle creativity and innovation. Entrepreneurs could be made powerless by a web of obligations that ensnares them! In the Dutch egg case, fear of being trapped did play a role. This fear had better be taken seriously, for it is likely to potentially affect the viability of netchains and the quality of their products and services. One way of avoiding being trapped is to adopt or create open standards wherever possible, for instance, for exchanging business-to-business messages with large buyers.

Transparency often begins with a request for history transparency issued by government or by powerful netchain stakeholders close to the customer. Such a beginning is likely to arouse defensive reactions among other stakeholders, because it entails transaction costs without obvious benefits, and loss of independence. But entrepreneurs should not leave it at this. They should take the obligation as an opportunity. They can use the momentum to achieve more profitable and forward-looking forms of transparency as well. If they cooperate with their close neighbours, the new unit will be in a better position to compete with other netchains. With luck, they might be turning "Big Brother" into big business.

Conclusion

This chapter has developed a number of propositions, based on existing theory from various disciplines that are relevant to netchain theory, as well as on some empirical evidence from the Dutch egg sector.

- **Proposition 1:** Trust and transparency in netchains can be contradictory, because trust emphasizes showing only the essentials and transparency may be construed as the art of hiding the essentials. This is the case if transparency is imposed from outside the netchain, or if the netchain is in fact institutionally a hierarchy and the leader imposes the transparency.

- **Proposition 2:** Three types of transparency can be distinguished: history, operations, and strategy transparency. They have different drivers and consequences. The latter two are usually voluntary and therefore trust-building.

- **Proposition 3:** When studying the behaviour of netchains, it is important to distinguish three levels of aggregation: the netchain, the participating organisations, and the people in those organisations who actually make the netchain run.

- **Proposition 4:** Even though history transparency is frequently imposed, it can serve a netchain by bringing the stakeholders together and creating a platform for achieving other forms of network integration, notably operations and strategy transparency.

- **Proposition 5:** Netchain integration differs across social settings. Basic cultural parameters, as well as our nature as social beings, come into play here. What some may call "being ensnared," others may perceive as "being connected." Contingency factors, for example, the nature of a sector, the presence of large or small actors in the sector, determine which institutional arrangements are economically viable. Social psychological factors co-determine which arrangements are acceptable to stakeholders. Where economic viability and acceptability do not coincide, social unrest can be expected.

- **Proposition 6:** This chapter is an example of work in the field of interdisciplinary research called "chain and network studies." Obviously, this field is just emerging. But in our era of globally expanding economic activity, it is an important field. No single discipline suffices. Contributions from economics, technology, social psychology and cultural anthropology will be needed to advance.

Acknowledgments

Thanks go to two anonymous reviewers for valuable remarks to an earlier version of this chapter.

References

Beaucarne, J. (1975). *Chandeleur '75.* RCA: LP disk.

Beulens, A. J. M. (2003). Transparency requirements in supply chains and networks: Yet another challenge for the business and ICT community. In D. Ehrenberg & H.-J. Kaftan (Eds.), *Herausforderungen der Wirtschaftsinformatik in der Informationsgesellschaft* (pp. 213-234). *Leipzig, Germany: Gutenbergplatz.*

Blanchard, K., & Johnson S. (1978). *The one-minute manager.* New York: Fontana/Collins.

Camps, T., Diederen, P. J. M., Hofstede, G. J., & Vos B. (Eds.). (2004). *The emerging world of chains and networks, Bridging theory and Practice.* The Hague: Reed Business Information.

Checkland, P., & Holwell, S. (1998). *Information, systems, and information systems: Making sense of the field.* Chichester, UK: Wiley.

Diederen, P. J. M. (2004). Co-ordination mechanisms in chains and networks. In T. Camps, P. Diederen, G. J. Hofstede, & B. Vos (Eds.), *The emerging world of chains and networks, bridging theory and practice* (pp. 33-47). The Hague: Reed Business Information.

Eisenhardt, K. M (1989). Agency theory: An assessment and review. *Academy of Management review, 14*(1), 57-74.

Engel, P. (2002). Global chains: Chain gangs or development opportunities? In E. Van Amerongen, C. Van der Harg, R. Kruse. & S. Pegge (Eds.), *The Challenge of Global Chains, Proceedings of Symp. Mercurius* (pp. 17-25). Wageningen: Wageningen Academic Publishers.

Fried, C. (1982). *Contract as promise.* Cambridge, MA: Harvard University Press.

Giddens, A. (1997). *Sociology* (3rd ed.). Cambridge, UK: Polity Press.

Hofstede, G. (2001). *Culture's consequences: International differences in work-related values* (2nd ed.). Beverly Hills, CA: Sage Publications.

Hofstede, G. J. (2002). Transparency in netchains. In E. Van Amerongen, C. Van der Harg, R. Kruse, & S. Pegge (Eds.), *The challenge of global chains, Proceedings of Symp Mercurius* (pp. 73-89). Wageningen: Wageningen Academic Publishers.

Hofstede, G. J. (2004). Globalisation, culture and netchains. In H. Bremmers, O. Omta, J.H. Trienekens, & E. Wubben (Eds.), *Dynamics in food chains. Proceedings of the 6th International Conference on Chain Manage-*

ment in Agribusiness and the Food Industry (pp. 427-434). Wageningen: Wageningen Pers.

Hofstede, G., & Hofstede, G. J. (2005). *Cultures and organizations, software of the mind: Intercultural cooperation and its importance for survival* (2nd ed). London: McGraw-Hill.

Hofstede, G. J., Kramer, M., Meijer, S. A., & Wijdemans, J. (2003). A chain game for distributed Trading and Negotiation. *Production Planning & Control, 14*(2), 111-121.

Hofstede, G. J., Schepers, H., Spaans, L., Trienekens, J., & Beulens, A. J. M. (Eds.). (2004). *Hide or confide: The dilemma of transparency.* The Hague: Reed Business Information.

Hofstede, G. J., Spaans, L., & Beulens, A. J. M. (2004). Transparency: Perceptions, practices and promises. In T. Camps, P. Diederen, G. J. Hofstede, & B. Vos (Eds.). (2004). *The emerging world of chains and networks, Bridging theory and practice* (pp. 285-310). The Hague: Reed Business Information.

Lazzarini, S. G., Chaddad, F. R., & Cook, M. L. (2001). Integrating supply chain and network analyses: The study of netchains. *Journal on Chain and Network Science, 1*(1), 7-22.

Meijer, S. A., & Hofstede G. J. (2003). The trust and tracing game. In J. O. Riis, R. Smeds, & A. Nicholson (Eds.), *Proceedings of the 7th International Workshop of the IFIP WG 5.7 Special Interest Group on Experimental Interactive Learning in Industrial Management*, Aalborg, Denmark (pp. 101-116).

Ménard, C. (2003). The economics of hybrid organizations. *Journal of Institutional and Theoretical Economics, 160*(3), 3435-376.

Meulen, B. M. J. van der, & Velde, M. van der. (2004). *Food safety law in the European Union, An introduction.* Wageningen: Wageningen Academic Publishers.

Mevissen, I. M. J. (2002). *Onafhankelijke MKB in een virtuele organisatie* (in Dutch). Retrieved January 1, 2005, from http://www.klict.org

Powell, W. W. (1990). Neither market nor hierarchy: Network forms of organization. *Research in Organizational Behavior, 12*, 295-336.

Rademakers, M. F. L. (1999). *Managing inter-firm cooperation in different institutional environments: A comparison of the Dutch and UK potato industries.* Doctoral dissertation, Erasmus University, Rotterdam.

Ring, P. S., & Van de Ven, A. H. (1992). Structuring co-operative relationships between organizations. *Strategic Management Journal, 13*, 483-498.

Rousseau, D. M., Sitkin, S. B., Burt, R. S., & Camerer, C. (1998). Not so different after all: A cross-discipline view of trust. *Academy of Management Review,* 23(3), 393-404.

Sauvée, L. (2000). Managing a brand in the tomato sector: Authority and enforcement mechanisms in a collective organization. *Acta Hort. (ISHS),* 536, 537-544.

Smith, P. B., & Bond, M. (1993). *Social psychology across cultures.* New York: Harvester Wheatsheaf.

Thorelli, H. B. (1986). Networks: Between markets and hierarchies. *Strategic Management Journal, 7,* 37-51.

Trienekens, J. (1999). *Managing processes in chains: A research framework.* Doctoral dissertation, Wageningen University.

Uzzi, B. (1997). Social structure and competition in interfirm networks: The paradox of embeddedness. *Administrative Science Quarterly, 42,* 35-67.

Williamson, O. E. (1998). Transaction cost economics: How it works, where it is headed. *The Economist, 146*(1), 23-58.

Wilson, T. P., & Clarke W. R. (1998). Food safety and traceability in the agricultural supply chain: Using the Internet to deliver traceability. *Supply Chain Management, 3*(3), 127-133.

Chapter VI

Integration of Global Supply Chain Management with Small and Medium Suppliers

Asghar Sabbaghi, Indiana University South Bend, USA

Ganesh Vaidyanathan, Indiana University South Bend, USA

Abstract

The purpose of this chapter is to develop a conceptual insight and an integrated framework to global supply chain management through strategic aspects of business philosophy as it pertains to the small- to mid-sized supplier. Primary consideration is given to characteristics of the integrated supply chain and the necessity of adaptation in managing the supply chain in order to attain competitive advantage. A review of the current literature and an analysis of the supply chain in changing global markets emphasize the relative importance of strategically managing the supply chain process given the limited resources of the small- to mid-sized firm. It is argued that managing the supply chain through the development of market specific strategies allows the small to mid-sized firm to be anticipatory as opposed to being reactive in its strategic planning, which can greatly benefit customer satisfaction levels and thus enhance the performance of the firm.

Introduction

Supply chain management (SCM) as a strategy for competitive advantage has gained prominence in both large and small organizations. An understanding of the supply chain management concept from the perspective of suppliers and, in particular, small and medium enterprises (SMEs) is crucial to the study of vertical integration of global SCM. This understanding will better formulate internal business strategies of suppliers by supporting both the objectives of the supply chain and their own businesses. About 80% of the supply chain members are SMEs, and a major impact and savings may well be found with the SMEs within the supply chain (Smeltzer, 2002). By taking advantage of their position and criticality in the supply chain, SMEs can add value and contribute to the vertical integration essential in the supply chain. This creates advantages not just for themselves, but also for other members within their supply chain.

By some definitions, a supply chain is a network of facilities that performs the functions of procurement of material, transformation of material to intermediate and finished products, and distribution of finished products to customers (Lee & Billington, 1995). The supply opportunity analysis technique (SOAT) moves away from a reactive to a proactive mode by taking (determining) the suppliers' perspective (Bhattacharya, Coleman, & Brace, 1995). When customers demand customized products, products often become increasingly complex. In addition, the development and manufacturing of such products demand even greater resources that need to be shared by the supply chain members. In addition, the development and manufacturing of such products by the original equipment manufacturing (OEM) partners require supply chain members to increasingly share available resources as virtual partners (Rota, Thierry, & Bel, 2002). To the suppliers, these virtual partnerships can provide both opportunities of growth and threats of becoming obsolete from the supply chain. A supplier is usually involved with multiple customers and therefore in several supply chains. The supplier receives both firm orders and forecast orders. To be successful, the supplier needs to negotiate these firm orders and the forecast orders with its suppliers. To deliver customized products with short delivery times and high due-date observance, to plan for the supplier's own raw material requirements, it is important for the customer to effectively share information (Rota et al., 2002).

The transformation from reactive to proactive procurement parallels a transformation in relationships between suppliers and buyers. Suppliers have developed partnerships with customer firms. This partnership has turned into collaborative relationships or strategic alliances (Burt, Dobler, & Starling, 2003). The rising cost of product development, globalization, and shorter product lead times have been cited as important reasons for supplier collaboration (Bruce, Fiona, & Dominic, 1995; Helper, 1991; Lamming, 1993). The involvement by partners has a positive impact on strategic purchasing, and strategic purchasing has a positive impact on a firm's financial performance (Masella & Rangone, 2000). Even though there are many benefits from this collaborative or alliance network between suppliers and customers, there are obstacles. Trust plays a critical role in such collaborative or alliance relationships between suppliers and customers (Burt et al., 2003). However, such collaborations and alliances enable information flow across the supply chain.

To answer questions such as why a supplier was not treated according to its capabilities or why did engineering think it had capabilities when it did not, the characteristics of the suppler has to be clearly articulated (Nellore, 2001). Developing visions for suppliers can help OEMs to create clear expectations and thus better the core capabilities of the buyer and supplier firms (Nellore, 2001). OEMs also increase supplier involvement in product development and the share of inbound just-in-time (JIT) deliveries. However, while suppliers increase their outsourcing and globalization of production and product development activities, OEMs do not (von Corswant & Fredriksson, 2002). By outsourcing certain activities to specialized suppliers, companies can focus on those products and activities that they are distinctively good at (Venkatesan, 1992). This specialization, enabling a reduction of the capital base, implies improved return on invested capital (Quinn & Hilmer, 1994) and the possibility to benefit from economies of scale. However, outsourcing means that important activities are placed outside the boundaries of the firm (Richardson, 1972). In addition, coordination of these activities demands vast resources, and many companies therefore strive to reduce their supply bases (Cousins, 1999). A cooperative strategy between OEMs and suppliers is needed to ensure efficient coordination of these activities. Information flow enables such cooperative strategies.

A significant portion of product nonconformance costs can be directly attributed to variation in supplier processes. To mitigate the effects of variation in the near term it may be tactically prudent to assess tolerances to influential supplier processes. Such tolerance allocation strategies tend to be adversarial in nature, since the cost associated with a nonconforming product is principally borne by suppliers via scrap and repair costs, not to mention costs associated with safety stock increases, and so on. However, a more appropriate long-term strategy for reducing nonconformance costs is to consider ways to achieve a reduction of variation in supplier processes (Plante, 2000). Variance reduction of a supplier's processes requires knowledge of what influences the process variation so that appropriate improvement action can be undertaken in an informed manner. Gaining such knowledge requires that organizations invest in and commit to continuous learning (Plante, 2000). Companies such as Raytheon finds that 50% to 70% of its product costs are represented by outside purchases, with a majority of the material dollars spent on a few key parts provided by a few key suppliers. To address this conundrum, the Raytheon Six Sigma with Suppliers process was created, providing a set of tools and resources to help reduce supplier costs. The Raytheon Six Sigma with suppliers process has six steps (visualize, commit, prioritize, characterize, improve, and achieve), including an intense two-day workshop, which requires a heavy involvement and commitment by the supplier. Information flow between suppliers and customers can enable acquisition and use of this process knowledge to reduce supplier costs.

Measures related to quality, cost, delivery, and flexibility have been used to evaluate how well the suppliers are performing. Companies track supplier performance over time to detect problems early. It is imperative for even small businesses to establish performance measures (Knechtges & Watts, 2000). Performance cannot be measured solely by past or current levels of sales and profitability but should also include quantitative indicators of how the firm will do in the future. A recent study showed that in a supply chain, the supplier management practices adopted by first-tier suppliers affected second-tier suppliers' performance. Second-tier suppliers' performance consequently influenced both first-tier suppliers' quality and delivery performance (Park & Hartley, 2002). As performances of suppliers are evaluated regularly and frequently, these problems can be mitigated easily and at an earlier stage. The implementation of a successful supplier performance measurement system not only clarifies supplier understanding of performance expectations, consequences for poor performance, and rewards for performance excellence, but it also provides documentation of actual supplier performance. Supplier performance metrics can be used for a wide range of continuous improvement efforts. For example, they can be the basis for a establishing a proactive supplier development process, or making critical decisions when rationalizing the supply base, or even for determining how to distribute costs over several suppliers to better manage risk. Information flow of performance plays a critical part for maintaining supplier relationships. Supplier process, performance, strategy, and relationships can be made effective and efficient using information technology. Given the symbiotic relationship existing between supplier and customer, all participants of the global supply chain need to be educated and trained to facilitate IT adoption (Kirby & Turner, 1993).

In the next section, we present the characteristics, opportunities and challenges for SME companies and suppliers in general. Based on that discussion, we illustrate a conceptual framework consisting of five dimensions for suppliers in the third section. The remaining sections expand these five dimensions. The final section presents a summary and conclusions of the five dimensions.

Small- to Medium-Sized Companies: Their Characteristics, Opportunities, and Challenges

Small and medium enterprises (SMEs) have played a significant role in the global supply chain management in various countries and in the landscape of global business competition (Chapman, Ettkin, & Helms, 2000). As reported by the U.S. Small Business Administration (USSBA, 1999), SMEs are an integral part of the renewal process that pervades and defines market and economies. New and small firms play a critical role in experimental and innovation that leads to technological changes and productivity growth. With the emergence of the new technologies, new products, new services, new markets, and new management concepts, the pattern of competitive advantage for companies—particularly for small- to medium-sized organizations—has changed and has subsequently led to new opportunities and new challenges. There is no universally accepted definition of a small and medium enterprise (SME). In the literature, the definition of SME varies based on the number of employees, ownership of the shares capital investment, or financial turnover, among others (Reed, 1998; Taylor & Adair, 1994).

In order to better understand the strategic roles of SMEs in the global business, it is important to recognize their inherent characteristics. SMEs are often independently owned and operated and closely controlled by the owners/managers who are the principal investors and decision makers having entrepreneurial behavior. The attitude and expression of values (cultural and personal) of owners can play a significant role in the adoption of new technology and strategy development (Stansfield & Grant, 2003). The decision maker, often an entrepreneur or small network of associates, formulates attitudes based on perception of its environment. The entrepreneur's attitudes influence his/her own behavior, such as decision making, and thereby have a direct impact on the SME's capability. They also influence an employee's attitudes and behaviors and thus affect the internal environment through the organizational culture factor, and further indirectly affect the SME's capability through that mechanism.

SMEs are also characterized by an absence of standardization and formal working relationships, having a flat organizational structure. Thus, they have a more organic organizational structure when compared to a more bureaucratic structure in large firms (Ghobadian & Gallear, 1996). These characteristics make SMEs more flexible to environmental changes (Levy, 1998; Storey & Gressy, 1995) as well as incurring lower overhead expenses and thus are perceived more innovative. Consequently, they have the potential of playing a significant role in global competition. In particular, SMEs who possess/exhibit entrepreneurial behavior can use the new information technologies as the strategic tools to generate new products and services, and as driving force behind new processes, new forms of business organization, new scope for consumers, and new market opportunities and supply chain management.

The characteristics of an SME can determine the strategic opportunities and challenges available to these companies, particularly in the area of supply chain management. The entrepreneurial behavior of SMEs differentiates them from larger companies in supply chain management, particularly in a cross-cultural dimension and global market. While SMEs' managers are more sales oriented, they do not have a well-developed overall strategic plan. According to Dodge and Robbins (1992), 64% of SMEs that failed did not have a business plan. SME managers tend to rely on their tacit knowledge rather than systematic techniques in supply chain management planning activities, such as vendor selection (Park & Krishnan, 2001). The competitiveness of an SME is defined by its flexibility to environmental changes and dependent on its owner/manager (OECD, 1993), since the adoption of a strategic planning approach is affected by its ownership structure (O'Regan & Ghobadian, 2002). However, they may have limited resources required for efficient supply chain management and find themselves encountering more barriers due to increased competition at national and international levels, particularly when they do not have the resources to meet the demands of their trading partners in the supply chain. SMEs that are subsidiaries of larger organizations may be able to access resources from their parent organizations (O'Regan & Ghobadian, 2002) and be able to overcome these challenges of limited resources. However, they are typically responsible for their local strategies and limited flexibility in their national and international strategies. Furthermore, as managers of SMEs are usually holding multiple roles as entrepreneur, and owner/manager, the management focus tends to be operational rather than strategic. However, in order to take advantage of supply chain management as a means for competitive advantage and succeed, these companies need to take a strategic approach of supply chain management. In particular, SMEs are challenged to balance their short-term operational focus with long-term strategies and technological innovations. This in turn requires greater financial and technical resources. The lack of resources required for effectiveness and efficiency is another major challenge for SMEs in adopting appropriate strategies for their supply chain management, particularly in their quest for global competition.

Table 1. Strategic supplier typology

	Low Collaboration	High Collaboration
Low Technology	**Commodity Supplier** • Spot market supplier • Low cost, low price priorities • Little or no differentiation	**Collaboration Specialist** • Detailed control parts supplier • Uses a closed network in each industry • Can be in many industries to maintain customer product information
High Collaboration	**Technology Specialist** • Proprietary parts supplier • Innovation in product technology used to produce high barriers to entry • First mover advantages • Uses design capabilities for competitive advantage	**Problem-solving Supplier** • Black box supplier • High differentiation • Cost less important • Small runs, high process and labor flexibility

Small to medium suppliers are less resourceful and often play niche roles within the supply chain as a commodity supplier, collaboration specialist, technology specialist, and problem-solving supplier (Kaufman, Wood, & Theyel, 2000) as shown in Table 1. The supplier topology divides along two dimensions: technology and collaboration. By dividing these dimensions into high and low categories, Kaufman et al. (2000) create four distinct supplier strategies. The top left quadrant defines suppliers who use standard technologies and relate to customers through standard market contracts. These suppliers compete on the basis of low cost. These suppliers can be replaced since switching costs are low. These commodity suppliers design and sell parts to their customers as specified by their customers. The top right quadrant describes collaboration specialists. These suppliers use standard technologies that meet customer specifications and delivery schedules. However, these firms develop enhanced collaborative techniques to fulfill current and to anticipate future customer needs. These suppliers use vendor managed inventory (VMI) strategy. The collaboration essentially requires accurate and timely information. They reduce the customers' internal monitoring or administrative costs.

The suppliers in the lower right quadrant are the problem-solver suppliers. They help their customers to avoid costly investments in specific resources. They employ both advanced technologies and collaborative methods in promoting innovative design and manufacture of supplied parts. The bottom left quadrant defines the technology specialists. They supply proprietary parts using advanced technologies. However, they have weak relationships with customers and the customers benefit from acquiring high technology parts without having to invest in resources. These different suppliers can also be classified as subcontractors who are connected to their customers through supply networks and play coordinating roles between both domestic and foreign players (Andersen & Christensen, 2005).

The common theme in this four dimensional topology is information technology (IT). Information technology is perceived as a critical enabler for efficient exchange of information between the SMEs and the members of supply chain management, and to improve organizational performance and enhance competitive advantage. However, due to resource constraints, SMEs place lower priority on IT investments. Thus, SMEs differ from large companies in their supply chain management practices and technology. Large companies have a greater scope of operation and thus are more likely to be involved in diverse markets. They can spread costly new systems over large units of production, and have internal technical development and maintenance capabilities (Smeltzer, 2001). SME managers and, in particular, small business entrepreneurs, tend to lack or not value many of the basic skills needed to adopt and implement networked processes. They are not operationally inclined or concerned with issues of managing their supply base methodically. They are keen to sell more. Larger firms have invested time and money in implementing their enterprise resource planning (ERP) and e-commerce strategies, including e-procurement and online selling, integrating with these firms can be frustrating. SMEs must develop the business planning skills to identify, select, and implement the supporting technology. Particularly, SMEs must adopt an integrated system such as ERP, e-commerce, and e-procurement systems to support their supply chain management and be able to "pull through" from downstream customers.

In the context of Porter's framework of competitive advantage strategies, and given the characteristics, opportunities, and challenges facing SMEs, the competitive success of these companies may not critically depend on price leadership or differentiation strategies but on how they are unique and critical to their trading partners (Quayle, 2002). In this context, SMEs could focus on meeting ultimate customers' needs, strive to supply quality products/services, and add value to meet the demands of their supply chains. Thus, it is essential that SMEs can link their business strategies to that of the supply chain. The organic organizational structure of SMEs should enable them to develop strategic alliances with their trading partners in the supply chain so that they are able to leverage the skills and expertise of supply chain partners to gain strategic advantage for the whole chain.

Conceptual Framework

Forrester (1958) viewed a supply chain as part of industrial dynamics, alternatively known as system dynamics and management system dynamics; it is broadly defined as the application of feedback thinking and control engineering concepts to the study of economic, business, and organizational systems. System dynamics is concerned with problem solving in living systems that bring together machines, people, and organizations. It links together the system theory and the control theory so that we are able to generate added insight into system dynamic behavior and, particularly, into the underlying causal relationships in the context of global performance of the system and internal control. In this context, supply chain is defined as a system of business enterprises that link together to satisfy customer demands and to provide value to the end customer in terms of product and services. We can discern a distinct generic procedure as part of the production/operation process in a supply chain that is called an echelon. In their most basic form, materials/goods flow from one echelon to the next until they reach the end customer. In reality, however, supply chains do not exist in isolation, but form part of a network of supply chains satisfying different demands.

Figure 1 describes a framework for suppliers in the global integrated supply chain. The four major dimensions of the framework include strategy, process,

Figure 1. Integration framework for supplier network

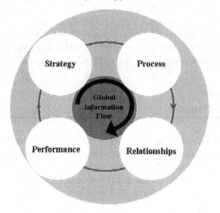

partnership, and performance. These dimensions are enabled by the fifth dimension, global information flow. The ultimate goal in supply chain management is to create value for the end customers and the firms in the supply chain network. To accomplish this, firms in the supply chain network must integrate all their supply chain process activities both internally and with other firms in the network. This integrated supply chain process needs a supply chain strategy. The strategic fit requires the firm to achieve a balance between its responsiveness and its efficiency in its supply chain that best meets the requirements of its competitive strategy. The supply chain performance of the firm with respect to its supply chain strategy is in terms of its responsiveness and efficiency (Chopra & Meindl, 2004). Furthermore, to create value for the supply chain network, it is critical that suppliers and customers develop strong relationships and partnerships based on a strategic perspective. Good supplier relationships are a key ingredient necessary for developing an integrated supply chain network (Wisner, Leong, & Tan, 2005). Good supplier and customer relationships and a great supply chain strategy are not enough to create value in an efficient, integrated supply chain process. The supportive role of information technology is essential along with the use of information technology to measure the supply chain performance. This provides the firm with the ability to make decisions about supply chain improvements. It is generally accepted in the literature that today's forward thinking managers use an integrated approach to managing their business by using quantitative and technological tools to bring together multiple facets of the business including, but not limited to, procurement, inventory management, manufacturing, logistics, distribution, and sales. It has been argued that the next century's paradigm for addressing challenges from increasingly demanding customers and global competition will rely on the effective use of information sharing and inventory control to streamline operations and coordinate activities throughout the supply chain. The conceptual integrated framework of the supply chain network brings collaboration and information sharing to fruition. The collaboration and information sharing results in reduced supply chain costs, greater flexibility to respond to market changes, less safety stock, higher quality, reduced time to market, and better utilization of resources (Wisner et al., 2005).

Integrated Process

According to the Global Supply Chain Forum, supply chain management is defined as the integration of key business processes from end user through original suppliers that provides products, services, and information that add value for customers and other stakeholders (Croxton, Garcia-Dastugue, & Lambert, 2001). This definition identifies eight key processes as the core of supply chain

Figure 2. Integrated supply chain process

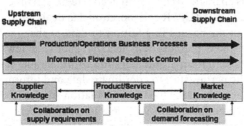

management. The eight processes include: (1) customer relationship management, (2) customer service management, (3) demand management, (4) order
fulfillment management, (5) manufacturing flow management, (6) supplier
relationship management, (7) product development and commercialization, and
(8) returns management. These processes transcend the length of the supply
chain cutting through firms and functional silos alike. These processes also
provide a framework for various aspects of strategic and tactical issues present
in the supply chain processes. The integration of such processes would allow
successful management of the supply chain for the suppliers as well.

Figure 2 shows a relatively simple and generic supply chain that links a company
with its suppliers upstream and its distributors and customers downstream.
Upstream supply chain includes the organization's first-tier suppliers and their
suppliers. Such a relationship can be extended in several tiers all the way to the
origin of material. Downstream supply chain includes all the processes involved
in delivering the product or service to the final customers. Thus, there are
physical flows in the form of raw materials, work-in-process inventories, and
finished products/services, between supply chain echelons, from suppliers/
vendors to manufacturers to distributors and retailers, and to consumers. Supply
chain also includes the movement of information and money, and the procedures
that support the movement of a product/service. Managing these physical and
informational flows effectively and efficiently requires an integration approach
that promotes organizational relationship and fosters the sharing of strategic and
technological efforts (Sabbaghi & Sabbaghi, 2004).

An effective supply chain management has required an integrated approach and
collaboration among the various tiers of suppliers and retailers, and has led to
information sharing relations. In 1995, a pilot project between Wal-Mart,
Warner-Lambert, Benchmarking Partners, SAP, and Manugistics led to the

concept of collaborative planning, forecasting and replenishment (CPFR) (Cooke, 1998). Skoett-Larsen, Thernoe, and Anderson (2003) have defined three levels of CPFR: (1) basic CPFR collaboration that only involves few business processes and a limited integration with trading partners, (2) developed CPFR collaboration that is characterized by increased integration in several collaboration areas, and (3) advanced CPFR collaboration that deals with synchronization of dialogue between the parties in addition to data exchange. While in basic CPFR, the supply chain partners will usually choose a few key processes relevant to precisely their form of collaboration with customers and suppliers, in developed CPFR the parties start to coordinate data and information exchange by making agreements about the type of information sharing and exchanges. In advanced CPFR, the collaboration will be expanded to coordinate processes within forecasting, replenishment, and planning. The planning processes may in turn be decomposed into collaboration on production planning, product development, transport planning, and market activities.

CPFR is a set of norms and procedures created by the Voluntary Inter-industry Commerce Standards (VICS) Association to drive companies toward common business planning procedures and to search for efficiency in the supply chain while establishing standards to facilitate the physical and informational flow. The CPER model is part of the integration mechanism among these processes and a valuable technological innovation tool to support the implementation of various types of transactions among the supply chain companies. These norms would provide the foundations for companies in the supply chain to collaborate in sharing data and information, in forecasting and ordering, in better production and distribution, and to achieve a global optimum of cost and services. Successful collaboration and implementation of CPFR norms would enhance the partnership in a supply chain. This would lead to lower costs, improved product or service quality, better customer service, quicker project results, reduced cycle time/lead time, and improved value to customers. Furthermore, managing business processes requires both internal and external knowledge about the company's operations and its strategies, as the development of effective behavior standards influences operational processes among the partners in the supply chain. Thus, given the constant need for innovation in organizational processes and corresponding information technology, CPFR can be viewed as a tool for competitive advantage in the supply chain.

The effective competitiveness of supply chain between supplier and customer partly depends on the effectiveness and efficiency of the flow of order and information between various parties in the supply chain. Participating organizations need to adopt an appropriate business model and culture that facilitate inter-organizational integration, sharing of skills and knowledge, and enable change in response to market forces. The challenge at the front end, before the order, is to have relationships with suppliers over time using as much electronic technology as possible to be able to source product availability in real time, to meet the customers' requirements. At the back end, the challenge is to understand and identify the best way to integrate with all their suppliers. This requires system standardization that allows suppliers to easily connect into their IT systems to improve not only their data communication facilities but also improve their business processes and facilitate collaboration between partners. This can be supported by the use of an integrated enterprise-wide information system such as enterprise resource planning (ERP) system. Enterprises, particularly SMEs within a supply chain, must then be evaluated as to added value in this process provided to customers and by their working relationships and partnerships to improve their performance and competitiveness. Where material and component suppliers are regarded as partners in the activity of satisfying customers, the adversarial approach to supplier auditing is not appropriate. All aspects of the supplier's business process, from receiving and reviewing an order, through manufacture to delivery, needs to be reviewed by the auditor to ensure that they meet minimum acceptable standards and to identify opportunities to improve. The auditor acts as an independent observer in reviewing the SCM system. This method aims to identify opportunities for improvement in the customer-supplier relationship that will improve quality, delivery, and service (Saunders, 1994).

In a move to remain competitive, many OEMs have resorted to outsourcing a large amount of design and manufacturing work. In so doing, they have repositioned themselves as customer-focused market players instead of design and manufacturing experts. This repositioning has consequently led to an increased reliance on the Tier 1 suppliers. With increased reliance comes increased pressure. Because of these new market changes, today's suppliers are facing a significant shift in responsibilities: while their share of the design and development responsibilities has increased, there is a concomitant expectation that costs will decrease. Furthermore, suppliers have multiple OEMs and consequently need to respond to multiple process integration. There is an increased focus on suppliers becoming leaner, as well as a push for heightened investment in rigorous processes that focus on innovation in close collaboration with OEM customers. A significant factor contributing to the length of product development is the time and process required in responding to design changes. Communicating design changes in language relevant to or understood by both the manufacturer and supplier is difficult, time consuming, and expensive. Evaluating the impact of change, reaching agreement on options, and implementing the change can take months due to the back and forth communication between all parties involved in the project. This complex communication process involves exchanging and remastering design information in a variety of formats during product design, analysis, and change. This can be improved by using a collaboration tool that shares design intelligence between these departments, dramatically shortening the time to communicate change, evaluate tradeoffs, and make decisions. Engineering supply chain collaboration also results in early problem detection, saving time and money for all involved, and making it easy to tie and integrate processes from various OEMs and respond to them individually.

SMEs need to identify a number of factors that can impede external process integration along the supply chain, causing information distortion, longer cycle times, stock-outs, and the bullwhip effect, resulting in higher overall costs and reduced customer service capabilities (Wisner et al., 2005). Failing to see the big picture and acting only in regard to a single department within the firm or a single tier in the supply chain can create quality, cost delivery timing, and other service problems. To overcome this silo mentality, firms must strive to align their supply chain processes and strategy to the overall vision of the supply chain network. The inability to easily share information from all the members of the supply chain is a common process integration problem. Using information technology, one of the dimensions discussed in this chapter, can solve this problem. Successful process integration between the members of the supply chain requires trust. Trust and commitment may be improved by collaborating on a small scale, better communication, and going for a win-win situation. Lack of process knowledge within the firm and among partners can lead to the downfall of supply chain activities. Educating and training the employees can improve their process knowledge. Finally, reducing the length of supply chain, making demand data available to suppliers, improving order batching efficiency, reducing price fluctuations, and eliminating short gaming can improve the supply chain integrated process (Wisner et al., 2005).

Integrated Strategy

The integration of business processes in supply chain management from suppliers would add value first to original equipment manufacturers (OEM) and finally to their customers. This integrated strategic process is enhanced through the use of logistics management. According to the Council of Logistics Management (Cooper, Lambers, & Pagh, 1997), logistics management is defined as the process of planning, implementing, and controlling the efficient, cost-effective, flow and storage of raw materials, in-process inventory, finished goods, and related information flow from point-of-origin to point-of-consumption for the purpose of conforming to customer requirements.

The scope of the supply chain management expands further upstream to the source of supply and downstream to the point of consumption, involving the integrated strategic process. The need for integration of information systems, planning, and control activities exceeds the level of integration necessary in the management of logistics alone (Cooper et al., 1997).

Although not all efforts toward integration are successful, companies are increasingly using an integrated, strategic approach not only to manage the supply chain, but as a general philosophy in managing the business due to the perceived benefits of improved performance (Tan, 2001). In fact, one study completed in 1998 supports a positive impact to performance by correlating supplier performance and firm performance (Tan, Kannan, & Handfield, 1998). The study summarizes literature available to that point. The study also concludes that a company's customer relations and purchasing practices—as major components of supply chain management strategy—have a positive impact on the effectiveness of supply chain management as a whole. Furthermore, through empirical analysis, the same study lays a foundation for the premise that additional practices of concurrent engineering, customer focus, strategic alliances, and quality-driven production improve the strategic management of the supply chain management function as a whole (Tan et al., 1998).

However, in slight contrast to these findings, companies should be further interested in the firm's overall performance and their ability to attain competitive advantage, as opposed to merely positively impacting the supply chain management strategic process. Since the concept of supply chain management as a strategic tool for business planning is relatively new, there is less clear data on the effect of "overall" performance of the corporation given a successful supply chain management strategy. A statistical study on the impact of purchasing and supply chain management of activities relating to corporate success was published in 2002 (Ellram, Zsidisin, Siferd, & Stanly, 2002) that attempted to answer many of the questions concerning overall firm performance by stratifying companies into three categories using a number of different financial and benchmarking criteria. The results determined that above-average firms showed no increased use of supply chain management processes when compared to average and below-average firms and that below-average firms had higher perceptions of actually practicing this strategic process. The reasons for this are partially explained by realizing that firms with average and below-average performance levels may be facing market pressures and declining profitability and must seek ways to improve performance and lower costs. In other words, above-average performing firms may not seek the advantages of strategically managing the supply chain given the relative success of the corporation despite additional opportunities to increase the firm's performance.

These results heavily support many of the underlying principles developed later in this analysis when looking closer at the scarce resources available to the small firm and any attempts at using supply chain management as a replacement for corporate strategy, as some of the supply chain management literature suggests. Although many companies are moving toward such strategies due to the far-reaching effects of overall customer satisfaction, supply chain management should not be confused with, and cannot make up for, broader corporate strategy and the need for managing effective strategic processes in areas such as marketing, financing, and distribution, just to name a few (Ellram et al., 2002).

Small- to medium-sized firms are confronted with the issue of scarce resources to a greater extent than are larger corporations. In fact, often in such companies, it is the same individual(s) developing the strategic initiative, which means focusing too heavily on any one strategic area, inclusive of supply chain management, may actually lead the company to greater risk. Product and technology life cycles have shortened significantly and competitive product introductions make life cycle demand difficult to predict. At the same time, the vulnerability of supply chains to disturbance or disruption has increased, not only to the effect of external events such as wars, strikes or terrorist attacks, but also to the impact of changes in business strategy. Many companies have experienced a change in their supply chain risk profile as a result of changes in their business models, for example, the adoption of "lean" practices, the move to outsourcing, and a general tendency to reduce the size of the supplier base. A research study (Christopher & Lee, 2004) suggests that one key element in any strategy designed to mitigate supply chain risk is improved "end-to-end" visibility. It is argued that supply chain "confidence" will increase in proportion to the quality of supply chain information. Rather, it is the balance of strategic planning and execution within these organizations that is the common denominator among successful firms of small- to mid-size. Consequently, it is the successful management of the supply chain for any firm in context of its overall business strategy that can provide it with a competitive advantage, but doing so with a poor business strategy or a weak marketing plan is not likely to provide the firm an advantage in the marketplace.

It is clear that the uncertainty of global market conditions leave companies on the edge with respect to their strategic thought process in all aspects of strategic planning; yet it is the responsibility and opportunity of the enterprise to interpret, comprehend, and even predict circumstances relevant to the global market that determines its effectiveness. Global supply chain management provides a key element to understanding these conditions of uncertainty and is one of the primary reasons that the strategy is being so well accepted across organizations of all types and sizes. However, some unique problems and opportunities arise for smaller companies who are able to redefine, adapt, and redesign the supply chain. Managing each defining component of the supply chain is difficult for the small to mid-sized entity due to scarce resources. However, given the knowledge base and the in-depth understanding of the supply chain processes by limited individuals in the smaller firm, it seems reasonable to change and make necessary adjustments to the supply chain management processes.

For the smaller corporation, supply chain performance is based on the flexibility of the management strategy practiced by the entity to reduce the level of risk provided by factors of global market uncertainty. A company's performance in the marketplace has been specifically linked to flexibilities involving volume, product launch, and target markets (Vickery, Calantone, & Droge, 1999). This empirical study looks at the furniture trade and is extremely relevant given the trend toward overseas production and a declining U.S. market for producers. It reveals that companies able to adapt to changing market conditions performed more favorably in terms of financial measures and marketability by exhibiting performance in areas of volume flexibility and product launch flexibility over all others. Volume flexibility is the ability to increase or decrease aggregate production of a good or service, and launch flexibility refers to the ability to introduce new products, as well as variations of existing products, involving the entire supply chain. Both provide excellent examples of ways small companies should be able to pursue competitive advantages, given their ability to control these processes initiating with the need to do so. In other words, they do not require direction from other "functional" departments, but rather respond to immediate needs of the market as opposed to reacting too late. Clearly, flexibility can be used as a strategic tool for the smaller enterprise.

Partnerships

Partnerships are business relationships based on mutual trust and openness as companies share risks and rewards leading to such an advantage (Muskin, 2000). The ability of a firm to extend beyond traditional corporate boundaries by working with partners will increase efficiencies and success.

Traditionally, in the market economy, products and services are produced to meet the forecasted demand. Firms in a supply chain are tightly integrated and focused on high-volume, maximum utilization of working capital, and cost efficiency in their supply of products/services. The optimum competitive decision is often accepted as achieving economies of scale and/or economies of scope. Productive processes are arranged so as to optimize the utilization of production and distribution capacity. In this economy, sharing technology and expertise with customers or suppliers was considered risky and thus unacceptable. There has been much emphasis on in-sourcing and vertical integration in supply chain strategies and little emphasis on outsourcing and cooperative and strategic buyer-supplier partnership (Sabbaghi & Sabbaghi, 2004). For example, in the computer industry, companies such as IBM or Digital Equipment Corporation tended to provide most of the key elements of their own computer systems, from operating system and application software to the peripherals and electronic hardware, rather than sourcing bundles of subsystem modules acquired from third parties. Products and computer systems typically exhibited closed, integral architectures, and there was little or no interchangeability across different companies' systems, keeping existing customers hostage. Each company maintained technological competencies across many elements in the chain and emphasized the value of its overall systems-and-service package, determined to stave off competitors who might offer better performance on one or another piece of the package.

The supply chain strategy in the market economy has been designed to "push" products to the customer based on forecasted demand. It focuses on supporting a tightly integrated enterprise geared toward mass production of goods at the lowest possible price. The production processes across the supply chain are synchronized for efficient utilization of all resources. Information technology, however, acts as an enabler for operational optimization across the supply chain by offering better forecasts that are customer driven in addition to robustly synchronizing the sourcing, production, and processes across the supply chain to achieve optimal performance, even if the forecasts are not perfect. For example, in car manufacturing, cars are traditionally manufactured to match forecasted demand that lacks much customer input.

However, in the new information economy, also called the Internet economy or the Web economy, the focus is exclusively on customer needs. To this end, the firms collaborate in a network of trading partners, each specializing in one or more core competencies (be it shipping, manufacturing, marketing, billing, order entry, or procurement services) and divesting itself of non-core activities beyond those associated with sourcing, manufacturing, or distributing products/services. In this network economy, information technologies, digital networking, and communication infrastructures provide a global platform over which people and organizations interact, communicate, collaborate, and search for information. The Internet has created more sophisticated customers who demand innovative, personalized products/services delivered at their convenience. It has also expanded the very definition of the word "customer," so that it now includes employees, distributors, suppliers, business partners, and shareholders. As a result of these changes, a company's competitive position in this Internet economy depends on its ability to deliver customized, relevant, highly responsive service to every participant in these networks of economic relationships. This new economy has led to the rapid emergence of business networks and new business models within and outside the firm to satisfy the strategic need for competitive flexibility. In this new economy, the supply chain is geared toward the customer "pulling" products customized to their specific needs, and the firm's resources are organized to meet the unpredictable demand patterns of the customer. Therefore, the benefits of supply chain management integration promote organizational relationships that in turn foster the sharing of information technology and strategic efforts.

Partnership in supply chain management, in this network economy, has led to the development of various cooperative arrangements among various supplier and retailers. Jagdev and Thoben (2001) identify three types of collaboration and partnership between independent companies:

1. supply chain type of collaboration based on long-term collaboration where the participating companies in the supply chain must operate synchronously to meet customer demands;

2. extended enterprise type of collaboration, most integrated form of collaboration, where the information and decision systems and respective production processes are integrated; and

3. virtual enterprise type of collaboration, as a short-term collaboration where the participating companies, without system integration, are loosely related to bundle their competencies to meet customer demand.

The type of partnership would determine the effective strategies that SMEs may consider and the perceived value added in the supply chain. For example, in vendor-managed inventory system, the responsibility of stock management is handed over to the supplier (Hvolby & Trienekens, 2002). This would make it possible for the supplier to adjust production and distribution planning to changes in consumer demand. In this system, SMEs as the suppliers would be able to access the retailer's information systems to view stock levels and future requirements. On the other hand, advanced planning systems (APSs) make it possible to include suppliers and customer relations in the planning procedure to optimize the whole supply chain on a real-time basis (Kennerly & Neely, 2001). They would support collaborative planning among several partners in a network by shared access to information about known and expected material requirements and resources (Hvolby & Trienekens, 2002).

Quantity flexibility (QF) contract is an arrangement between supplier and retailer that responds effectively to the demand fluctuations over time and divides the risk of excess capacity. A retailer in this model is committed to purchasing a percentage of its forecasted demand. However, the supplier is committed to delivering more than the forecast. For example, if they agree to a 25% of QF contract, the retailer is committed to purchase 75% of the forecast while the supplier is committed to delivering up to 125% of the forecast should the retailer need more than forecast. If demand turns out to be low, the supplier is protected by the lower limit, whereas if demand turns out to be high, the retailer can take advantage of that upside by knowing that the supplier has some additional capacity. Thus, both supplier and retailer can be better off in a QF contract.

As another type of arrangement, revenue-sharing contracts between suppliers and retailers, for example, in the video rental industry, would allow retailers to increase their stock of newly released movies, thereby substantially improving the availability of popular movies. Under a typical revenue-sharing contract, a supplier charges a retailer a wholesale price per unit plus a percentage of the revenue the retailer generates from the unit. This revenue-sharing model has been practiced for quite some time in the distribution of films to theaters, where the studio charges the theater a small up-front fee and then takes a certain fraction of the box-office revenues. Cachon and Lariviere (2005) examined the revenue-sharing contract model in supply chain management where the partnership between supplier and retailer would improve the performance of any supply chain toward a global optimization. They have cited Blockbuster, a video rental chain, as a successful case to illustrate the effectiveness of revenue-sharing strategy in collaborative supply chain management.

Traditionally, video rental stores have to spend typically $60 to purchase a tape from a distributor and then rent that tape to customers for $3 to $4. However, demand for new releases drops dramatically after the first few weeks, and video retailers have a hard time making any money on the rentals. Consequently, they can only afford to buy a few cassettes to accommodate that initial surge in demand. Customers consistently complained about the poor availability of new release videos. Blockbuster decided in 1998 to enter into revenue-sharing agreements with the major studios. The rental company agreed to pay its suppliers 30 to 45% of its rental income in exchange for a reduction in the initial price per tape from $60 to $8. The introduction of revenue-sharing model at Blockbuster coincided with a significant improvement in performance in the supply chain. It has been reported that Blockbuster's market share of video rentals increased from 24% in 1997 to 40% in 2002 after a revenue-sharing contract was adopted (Warren & Peers, 2002). The increase in the industry's total profit due to revenue-sharing strategy has been estimated at 7% (Moretimer, 2000). However, there are some limitations and drawbacks in revenue-sharing model. The first is that it is administratively burdensome compared with the straightforward wholesale price-only contract. Revenue sharing takes an organizational effort to set up the deal and follow its progress. If profits are only increasing by a very small percentage so that the revenue sharing does not cover the extra administrative expenses, then there is no incentive for the retailer to enter into a revenue-sharing contract. The second limitation, according to Cachon and Lariviere (2005), is when the retailer actions influence demand. Specifically, it is assumed that the retailer can increase demand by exerting costly effort, and that this effort is non-contractible. If a retailer is taking in only a small fraction of the generated revenue, this may not be sufficient incentive to improve sales. On the other hand, a supplier wants the retailer to buy the right quantity and to sell at a higher rate. The model may help to make sure the retailer buys the right quantity, but it may hurt its sales effort.

Collaborative computer-based information systems have become a major trend in today's business (Grossman, 2004). SCM evolved with the aim of integrating disparate functions like forecasting, purchasing, manufacturing, distribution, sales, and marketing into a harmonious ecosystem that would envelop the company's suppliers and customers. SCM promised to align all participants to act in unison to serve the end customer. Collaboration would enable managers to stop optimizing their individual silos to work together with partners—both internal and external—to achieve efficiency and effectiveness across the value chain. A truly collaborative partnership would encompass multiple customers and suppliers. OEMs would regularly communicate product availability, supply plans, and product content changes to distributors and other channel partners. Based on upstream forecasts and product changes, the channel partners would communicate demand requirements to manufacturing service providers. In this fashion, members of the outsourced supply chain would be assured of accurate, up-to-date information to help them make decisions that elicit common, supply chainwide benefits. While collaborating, there is distinction between big and small companies; it is between big, aggressive, large muscled organizations and agile, flexible, adaptable organizations that can survive in an environment of rapid change, constant uncertainty, and disruptive technologies.

Involving suppliers early and giving them influence over design is associated with greater contributions of suppliers to cost reduction, quality improvement, and design for manufacturability (Liker, Kamath, & Wasti, 1998). Increasing competitive parity in the areas of cost and quality has forced global manufacturers to seek other sources of competitive advantage, with new product development rapidly becoming the focal point in the quest for sustained growth and profitability. The essence of today's new product development strategies is the simultaneous development of the new product and the accompanying manufacturing process such that quality is enhanced, costs reduced, and lead times shortened. The implementation of the integrated product development (IPD) process has come to depend on the use of multifunctional teams. Supplier involvement promotes better resource utilization, the development and sharing of technological expertise, and network effectiveness (Birou & Fawcett, 1994). Evaluation and monitoring of performance metrics are key aspects of the integration process, partnerships, and strategy. In the next section, we will discuss how customers evaluate suppliers' performance, how SMEs respond to their customers' evaluation actions, and the impact of these performance evaluations.

Performance

Buying firm respondents who reported their firms' supplier development efforts to be satisfactory were more likely to have a proactive philosophy regarding suppliers' performance, put more effort and resources into their supplier development efforts, and exhibit a greater willingness to share information with their suppliers than their counterparts, who were generally dissatisfied with their firms' supplier development results (Krause & Ellram, 1997).

On its Global Procurement Web site (http://ch0107.whirlpool.com/SRM/ generalhelp.htm), Whirlpool provides a list of requirements for potential companies wanting to become a Whirlpool supplier. All Whirlpool suppliers are required to pass a supplier quality audit. These requirements are based on ISO 9000, QS 9000, and ANSI/ASQC Q90-94 standards. They are to ensure the best cost, quality, manufacturing efficiency, and continuous innovation in design and manufacturing. All Whirlpool suppliers are to meet the Integrated Supply Management (ISM) guidelines as a common process for doing business using electronic communication. Whirlpool is also committed to establishing and maintaining a capable, qualified, competitive, and diverse supply base providing minority-owned, disadvantaged, and small businesses. Whirlpool also provides each supplier with the plan year's forecast, profit plan volume, and cost to be used later for total cost productivity targets.

Information provided by the supplier performance will be used to assess efficiency in the supply chain (Wisner et al., 2005). FedEx not only has performance scorecards for its suppliers but also has developed a Web-based "reverse scorecard" that allows suppliers to provide constructive performance feedback to enhance the customer-supplier relationship.

A supplier's service level is, in general, insufficient for the manufacturer to warrant the desired service level at the customer end. The method by which the supplier achieves its service level to the manufacturer also affects the customer-service level. Procedures and metrics must be in place to collect and report performances of the eight processes that were discussed earlier in the integrated process section of this chapter. To assure that the integrated process is supporting the integrated strategy and the working relationships of partners, performance is continuously measured using metrics for each of the eight processes. These performance measures need to be both internal and external. As process integration improves across the supply chain, the overall performance will improve. Over time, under-performing suppliers and unsuitable customers will be eliminated. Suppliers can then concentrate on establishing beneficial relationships and forming strategic alliances to create a win-win situation.

Figure 3. Supply chain performance factors

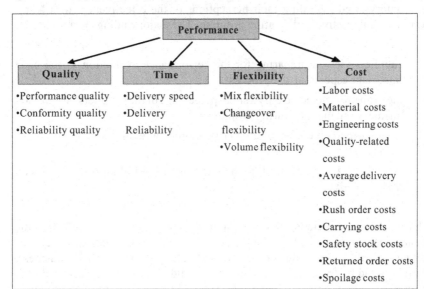

As shown in Figure 3, evaluating and responding to the results of supply chain performance metrics and measurements have a huge impact on business performances. Four generic performance factors have been identified by Bozarth and Handfield (2005) as relevant to the supply chain management. These factors include quality, time, flexibility, and cost, as illustrated in Figure 3. Performance quality includes the basic operations characteristics of the product or service, conformance quality questions whether the product was made or service was performed to specifications, and reliability quality explores whether the product or service will perform consistently over a period of time and without failing or high maintenance costs. Time has two basic characteristics: speed and reliability. Delivery speed refers to how quickly the supply chain can fulfill a requirement, while delivery reliability refers to the ability to deliver products or services when promised. The ability to produce a wide range of products and services is the mix flexibility, while changeover flexibility questions the ability to provide a new product with minimal delay, and volume flexibility is the ability to produce whatever volume the customer needs. Cost categories include labor costs, material costs, engineering costs, quality-related costs, average delivery costs, rush order costs, carrying costs, safety stock costs, returned order costs, and spoilage costs (Bozarth & Handfield, 2005; Wisner et al., 2005).

In a study by Purdy, Astad, and Safayeni (1994), automotive supply organizations were interviewed regarding their perceptions of the effectiveness of a North American automotive certification program. The major findings were that:

- suppliers viewed preparing for the performance evaluation as the most important aspects of the process;
- the evaluators detected only a small percentage of the suppliers' significant business and manufacturing problems;
- suppliers perceived an overemphasis on procedures and documentation on the part of the evaluators; and
- suppliers felt that the performance evaluation did not accurately reflect their effectiveness.

The same study concluded that the supplier evaluation program reflected the management style of the large bureaucratic customer organization, which was not necessarily appropriate for the size and nature of the supplier's business. Further, good performance on the evaluation did not directly correspond with further business contracts (Lyn et al., 1994). In today's world, definition of quality revolves around customer satisfaction, quality of product and service, timely delivery, and cost/price (Mehta, 2004).

Information Technology

Information technology (IT) offers huge potential for large suppliers as well as SMEs to achieve effective SCM mechanisms. In today's global marketplace, organizations are faced with ever-changing customer requirements and intensifying competition. To succeed, companies are looking at streamlining their supply chain through the successful deployment of Information Technology. Supply chain management expands the notion of integration beyond a single company to encompass all related trading partners in the supply chain. Suppliers, customers, third-party logistics providers, distribution centers, and relevant government agencies share the information and plans necessary to make the chain more efficient and competitive.

Manufacturers increasingly rely on IT to streamline their business processes. By integrating business processes across the supply chains, companies can quickly move information and materials to their trading partners and respond quickly to market changes. Internet technology is considered to be the most promising network infrastructure for supply chain connectivity. By having an integrated network infrastructure, companies can now manage their operations anywhere by accessing information using the Internet. Most companies are positioning IT as one of the key components for enhancing supply chain management, and they want to be updated regularly on new technologies that they can apply in their work.

Achieving integration in the global supply requires an enormous commitment by all members of the supply chain. In order to exploit competitive advantages by forming strategic alliances and partnerships and facilitating these relationships, companies must exchange information through increased communication and cooperation. The level of integration companies strive for now and in the future can only be possible through significant advances in information technology, which, in the past, has been costly and available only to larger companies with budgets that could support such endeavors. It has been argued that this helps explain the trend toward vertical integration as opposed to increasing horizontal communication efforts between suppliers, manufacturers, distributors, and customers. Information flow and sharing are essential in all components of supply chain. Supply chain information flow integrates all the facets of logistics as well (Vaidyanathan, 2005).

Although companies utilize technological tools such as electronic data interchange (EDI), and enterprise resource planning (ERP), there are still many issues arising from incompatible systems (interoperability) that drive inefficiencies. Additionally, as new technology develops, such as wireless networks, which still lack standard protocols, the problem does not appear to be going away too fast. This can be a major issue for the small- to mid-sized company, given budget restraints and the aggressive nature of larger budget companies to incorporate new technologies and information systems. Therefore, despite companies feeling they are actively sharing information with their supply chain partners, there continues to be inefficiencies and waste throughout the supply chain. The problem is further intensified when looking at partnerships on a global scale due to the traditional issues of cultural barriers and communication differences.

Internet technology has been increasingly used to enhance global supply chain through electronic commerce functionalities. Many Internet-based systems have been designed and developed for SCM to interconnect suppliers and customers. A four-phase migration model with technical, security, and financial requirements as a plan for the migration of the procurement process onto the Internet has been proposed by Yen and Ng (2003). The first part of the migration is the digitization of data in a local area network (LAN) to manage the information storage and retrieval within the company. The second phase is deployment of communication infrastructures such as EDI. The third phase is the installation of electronic commerce front-end system to implement procurement business processes such as Web sites and search engines. The fourth phase is the integration of vertical portal, that is, information processing with third-party service providers for financial transactions and logistics.

Small- and medium-sized enterprises are different than large enterprises in three primary ways that hinder e-commerce adoption (Smeltzer, 2002). SMEs seldom have mature technology. They usually emphasize product development and survival rather than supply chain integration. The large enterprises have costlier, mature integration software as well as internal technical development and maintenance capability (Smeltzer, 2002). Some of the large companies have integrated SMEs in their supply chain. As a $41 billion retailer, Sears has successfully connected every one of its 7000 suppliers by using a targeted technology, a proven process, and dedicated resources provided by a supply chain integration service (Smeltzer, 2002). The question confronting these suppliers is often not whether they should use SCM systems, but rather how they can take advantage of these systems and benefit from their use (Subramani, 2004).

Suppliers use IT for many reasons that include: requests for quotation (RFQ) received electronically by suppliers, support documents such as detailed part drawings and quality specifications accessed online, electronic transmission of purchase orders, shipment notifications, scheduling delivery windows at warehouse loading docks, electronic payment, electronic notification of changes, and inventory alerts based on preset triggers to communicate stocking levels of products in warehouses (Subramani, 2004).

Internet technology with its communication infrastructure has enhanced SCM initiatives. Companies are taking advantage of this technology and moving their procurement functions such as sourcing, negotiating with suppliers, payment, and other transactions onto the Internet. Such electronic procurement (e-procurement) results in control, flexibility, and cost savings. This provides suppliers with the ability to become proactive in doing their business. By implementing the supply chain onto the Internet, both suppliers and the customers will face both challenges and opportunities. Such challenges and opportunities include careful planning of the ways that people integrate changes and the benefits that the Internet can bring to the business, such as reduction in overall costs, respectively (Srinivasan, Reeve, & Singh, 2000). A large academic bookseller, Co-op Bookshop, launched electronic commerce and faced difficulties when competing globally. The lesson learned from this launch is that a company should study the existing customers and markets before it deploys e-commerce on the Internet (Loebbecke, Powell, & Gallagher, 1999).

E-procurement is more than putting purchasing decisions online; its functions also include linking suppliers and buyers into the purchasing network and rethinking of business processes such as transactions (Fisher, 2000a). With efficient information, such product information is structured by electronic catalogs with which e-procurement can form a good basis in order to attract more buyers to the shopping site (Avery, 2000a). Shell Services International launched its e-procurement service as a cost-cutting driver, and its electronic catalogs contain a broad list of suppliers ranging from huge contract partners to small chemical producers with which Shell has pre-negotiated discounts and service contracts. When a purchasing order is received, it will be automatically forwarded to the appropriate suppliers (Fisher, 2000b). E-procurement could reduce costs and cycle time by fostering a better relationship between buyers and sellers with a vertical supply chain Avery (2000b). The introduction of an e-procurement system in Texas Instruments has reduced the number of transactions in which purchasing was involved and replaced the internally based catalog system, saving a significant amount of cost (Atkinson, 2000a). The Texas-based Burlington Northern Santa Fe Railway planned to apply e-procurement for strategic sourcing and SCM, as it believed that collaboration with its suppliers could be facilitated in order to achieve full contract discount pricing (Atkinson, 2000b).

Yen and Ng (2003) classified the impact of electronic commerce in the procurement process into buyer and seller, and then further divided it into individual and inter-organizational categories. Individual and inter-organization classifications represent the internal efficiency and external impact, respectively. With *sourcing*, buyers can search for quick and complete information of materials from suppliers' online electronic catalogs while purchasing is enhanced. During *quotation* and *negotiation*, sending inquiries with the electronic and automated inquiry forms to suppliers can save time, and, in return, suppliers could direct the forms with quick and customizable responses, facilitating communication between buyers and sellers. With automated, synthesized, and modifiable *order placement*, cost and time are saved while purchase records can be viewed in a quick and timely fashion. Suppliers can benefit from efficient and error-free profiling management and more accurate demand forecasts in order to improve overall profitability. Again, communications between buyers and sellers can be enhanced while time is saved. Electronic *transactions* can take place without the need for physical forms of payment that are restricted by geographical and currency barriers. Suppliers can benefit from secure real-time collection of payment while the risk of unsuccessful receipt of payment is lowered, resulting in improved profitability. With *delivery*, uncertainty of receiving time is reduced by separated logistics and shipment, while information flow or communication between suppliers and logistic third parties is facilitated.

Electronic data interchange (EDI) is a way of conducting inter-organizational transactions electronically (O'Callaghan & Turner, 1995). The key components of EDI are: the electronic transfer of data, the use of standards, and the exchange of data with minimal human intervention. An event in a customer company's operational processes, for example, a purchase order, may trigger a computer application that generates an electronic message which is sent to, received, and processed by another computer application in a supplier's company. This message will trigger another event in the receiving supplier organization, for example, the delivery of products. Enabled by standardization of the message exchange, this communication takes place without human intervention. The organizations involved have to agree on contents, grammar, and organizational actions resulting from the message exchange. SMEs can improve their competitiveness by integrating their systems with their suppliers or other trading partners. Existing approaches to integration like EDI might help SMEs to overcome part of the integration problems, but they have their limitations (Themistocleous & Chen, 2004).

The Dutch coordination center for EDI reported that around 25.000 out of a potential 400.000 companies in the Netherlands are currently using EDI. The number of users has grown by 10.000 companies since 1994, but despite this relatively high growth in the number of EDI users, the current number still falls short of expectations (van Heck & Ribbers, 1995). In the U.S., for instance, Oakie (1997) reports that only 100,000 out of a potential 1.9 million companies are currently participating in EDI. Therefore, the adoption and implementation of EDI is still not prevalent. There are different reasons for this apathy to the adoption of EDI. One of the difficulties in EDI adoption is that its full benefit can be reached only if enough critical mass is achieved. To transact EDI messages, one needs to have partners who also are willing to adopt EDI. The other reason is that some EDI implementations are costly. One of the critical factors is the availability of EDI standards. The use of commercially available standards reduces the development costs and time and decreases the risk linked to the new EDI application (Krcmar, Bjÿrn-Andersen, & O'Callaghan, 1995). SMEs will adopt EDI if EDI message formats are available, if they decrease the risk linked to the new EDI standards, and if they reduce the development cost and time (van Heck & Ribbers, 1995). As more competitors and trading partners become EDI-capable, small firms are more inclined to adopt EDI in order to maintain their own competitive position (van Heck & Ribbers, 1995).

Another medium of e-procurement is the use of electronic business-to-business (B2B) commerce marketplaces. While there are many advantages to the use of B2B marketplaces, there are many disadvantages as well. The potential decrease in product quality is a big issue for B2B participants. Expectations will vary from one buyer to another, and the definition of quality will vary across suppliers. B2B may not be of interest to suppliers since the forced price reduction of supplies by new suppliers trying to gain a share of the market will hurt the supplier's margins and strain their ability to stay in the market (http://www.primetechnologywatch.org.uk).

Rovere (1996) argues that the role of SMEs should be investigated with regard to innovation and regional development studies with a focus on industrial districts. This argument is based upon the increasing importance of flexible organizations in today's economic environment, with the main elements of the flexible specialization model being networks of small firms, flexibility of equipment, and human resources. Rovere further argues that these ideas must be thoroughly considered in defining an IT diffusion policy for SMEs. The relatively inexpensive availability of IT products and services serves to create many new business opportunities for SMEs. If flexible production capabilities do indeed lie within the environs of networked SMEs, IT increases in importance to ensure the platform to allow for efficient information flow within and outside of SME networks.

Another problem posed to the SSM for the SMEs is integration. Enterprise resource planning (ERP) systems are an integrated software solution to manage a company's resources and to integrate all business functions, such as planning, inventory/materials management, sales and distribution, finance, human resources, and services. The complexity of ERP systems and the non-flexible nature of ERP solutions, combined with their high cost of implementation have impeded many companies' quest for integration. The major problem with ERP is integration, as ERP packages are not designed to tie up other autonomous applications (Cingil, Dogac, & Azgin, 2000). As a result, autonomous and heterogeneous applications coexist in companies with ERP systems, and integration problems have not been addressed. Therefore, the use of ERP systems no longer supports or leads to competitive advantages for organizations, especially SMEs (Themistocleous & Chen, 2004).

According to the United Nations report on e-commerce and development (avaliable at http://www.unctad.org/en/docs/ecdr2004ch2_en.pdf), SMEs in Latin America have recognized the need to increase their capacity to differentiate their products and services, and to link electronically with their customers and suppliers. However, none of the enterprises surveyed had advanced beyond the first stage of information and communications technology (ICT) adoption. For example, while most of them were on a local area network (LAN) and some of them used the Internet for looking up information, none used EDI or an Intranet, and very few communicated with clients via electronic mail, preferring to use the telephone or fax.

According to a study conducted by the World Wide Worx (http://www.theworx.biz/download/Exec%20Summary%20%20SME%20Survey%202003.doc), investment in information technology is having a major impact on the competitiveness of small and medium businesses in South Africa. Among the key findings of the survey was that SMEs are spending a higher proportion of their turnover on IT each year. In 2001, 47% of SMEs spent more than 1% of turnover on IT; in 2002,

48%; and in 2003, 49% expect to spend more than 1% of their turnover on IT. According to a Canadian net impact study (http://www.netimpactstudy.com/ca/pdf/release_final.pdf), 50.2% of Canadian SMEs are currently using or implementing the Internet. The same study concludes that a firm with $10M in revenues, with a 20% gross margin and 10% net margin, can achieve increases in net profit of up to 154% in a "best case" scenario, that is, if these average changes in revenues and costs were realized together.

In a recent survey, Deloitte Research undertook an exploratory study of IT purchasing by SMEs (available at http://www.deloitte.com/dtt/research/0,1015,sid%253D16418%2536cid%253D632D63293,00.html) in an effort to understand decision making in different stages of the information technology purchase process. The resulting study identifies the key factors impacting technology purchase decisions by small and medium enterprise owners. In particular, it found that: SMEs need information and help to manage their IT growing pains; price isn't necessarily the bottom line when considering IT purchases; and vendor Web sites and reputations are extremely important in the minds of SME decision makers when looking for information and making purchase decisions.

Various forms of SCM applications are arising among the enabling technologies. Prominent vendors in SCM applications market include i2 Technologies, SAP, Oracle, and Invensys, which produce a range of hardware and software components that span communication, optimization, and modeling systems.

SMEs are becoming increasingly dependent on information technology to operate efficiently, serve customers effectively, and work with partners and suppliers more collaboratively. Faced with all the challenges and opportunities of competing in a fast-paced environment, growing companies must be especially confident that their networks can support business evolution. Building an effective network foundation is integral to, and an operational insurance policy for, achieving e-business transformation. It is vital that SMEs focus their attention on the critical success factors that drive growth in their particular market. They cannot afford to expend precious time re-architecting, re-learning, and managing networks. Network infrastructures should be the invisible plumbing that enables the transport of company information and communications and enables efficient processes.

Conclusion

The subject of global supply chain management is an important new frontier for businesses choosing to participate in the new global economy. The inherent processes range from raw material supplier to end-user and involve literally all functions in between. Consequently, the integration of these processes is crucial to achieving supply chain management success, which is only facilitated by adequate information exchange between partners within the supply chain—a task not easy to accomplish due to issues of interoperability. Yet, the ability for companies to successfully implement strategic relationships relies on their ability to develop or maintain an effective partnership strategy, as it is not always necessary to enter into full-scale partnerships with all suppliers perceived to be partners within the chain. Additionally, in today's uncertain global economy and associated issues of security and trust, many companies continue to re-evaluate their partnerships and foster those relationships that are more likely to lead to a competitive advantage. The literature emphasizes the importance of trust in developing such partnerships, as firms will attempt to reduce risk by not entering into partnerships lacking trust. However, the need to leverage the resources of the supply base and revenue sharing cannot be overlooked, and companies will pursue such relationships. In a changing world, the subject of truth and ethics is important when discussing supply chain management strategy.

Most discussions of supply chain management are presented in abstract terms and in ways that apply to product and service organizations alike. However, most small companies, and even larger corporations, focus on niche markets. Niche markets are where managers will correctly argue that profits are created and realized; therefore, the goal of many organizations is to develop business and market strategies to exploit these opportunities in the market. Similarly, as this chapter has detailed, it has been shown that an affective supply chain management strategy can benefit these very initiatives.

More specifically, the smaller firm in the supplier role has unique opportunities to develop business, market, and supply chain management strategies that are unique from those of the larger established companies. Realizing that the "buying" company within the supply chain—or end-user—is actively pursuing competitive advantage through marketing of its unique product or service, the small company is often better positioned to adapt to the needs of the customer. More precisely, the level of information available to key members of the smaller supplying organization and its integrated partners provide market opportunities that may not exist to larger corporations.

Supply chain management strategies, because of the unique circumstances of specific markets, can not be characterized as "one size fits all." In fact, global supply chain strategies are contingent upon market characteristics and business strategy, which seek to attain higher-level customer responsiveness at less total cost to the supply chain as a whole. Nowhere are the unique characteristics more prevalent than in the small- to mid-sized corporations, as each of these types of corporations seeks competitive advantage through management of the supply chain and, more specifically, management of the supply chain for a specific niche market.

Moreover, there are some unique obstacles and challenges in managing the supply chain given the scarce resources of the small- to mid-sized supplying company. More specifically, because of the involvement of so few within the supply chain management process in the smaller firm, there is greater responsibility for those individuals to manage this very important strategic process given the unique opportunities to exploit niche markets. The ability of a small firm to offer flexibility in terms of volume and product differentiation provides the competitive advantage businesses of all size pursue. Supply chain management strategy, then, is applicable to all sized firms and has unique characteristics for smaller entities. To maximize the Internet and supply chain management, SMEs must be included. The SMEs need to have the information technology capability to fully integrate into the supply chain. Only then will the supply chain management be effective to save time, decrease costs, improve relationships, and maximize overall responsiveness.

References

Andersen, P.H., & Christensen, P.R. (2005). Bridges over troubled water: Suppliers as connective nodes in global supply networks. *Journal of Business Research, 58*(9), 1261-1273.

Atkinson, W. (2000a, September 21). Railway's shift to strategic sourcing and SCM paves pathway for e-procurement. *Purchasing*.

Atkinson, W. (2000b, September 21). Print firm uses e-buying to strengthen its supply chain. *Purchasing*.

Avery, S. (2000a, September 21). E-procurement: A wealth of information for buyers. *Purchasing*.

Avery, S. (2000b, September 21). E-procurement is one tool to reduce costs, cycle time. *Purchasing*.

Bhattacharya, A. K., Coleman, J. L., & Brace, G. (1995). Re-positioning the suppler: An SME perspective. *Production Planning and Control, 6*, 218-226.

Birou, L. M., & Fawcett, S. E. (1994). Supplier involvement in integrated product development: A comparison of U.S. and European practices. *International Journal of Physical Distribution and Logistics Management, 24*(5).

Bozarth, C. C., & Handfield, R. B. (2005). *Introduction to operations and supply chain management*. Upper Saddle River, NJ: Pearson Prentice Hall.

Bruce, M. L., Fiona, L. D., & Dominic, W. (1995). Success factors in collaborative product development. *R&D Management, 25*(1), 33-44.

Burt, D. N., Dobler, D. W., & Starling, S. L. (2003). *World class supply management: The key to supply chain management.* Boston: McGraw-Hill.

Cachon, G., & Lariviere, M. (2005). Supply chain coordination with revenue sharing contracts. *Management Science, 51*(1), 30-44.

Chapman, C., Ettkin, S., & Helms, M. M. (2000). Do small businesses need supply chain management? *IIE Solutions, 32*(8), 31.

Chopra, S., & Meindl, P. (2004). *Supply chain management: Strategy, planning, and operation.* Upper Saddle River, NJ: Pearson Prentice-Hall.

Christopher, M., & Lee, H. (2004). Mitigating supply chain risk through improved confidence. *International Journal of Physical Distribution & Logistics Management, 34*(5), 388-396.

Cingil, I., Dogac, A., & Azgin, A. (2000). A broader approach to personalization. *Communications of the ACM, 43*(8), 136-141.

Cooke, J. A. (1998, December). VMI: Very mixed impact? *Logistics Management Distribution Report, 37*(12).

Cooper, M. C., Lambers, D. M., & Pagh, J. D. (1997). Supply chain management: More than a new name for logistics. *The International Journal of Logistics Management, 8*(1), 1-8.

Cousins, P. D. (1999). Supply base rationalization: Myth or reality? *European Journal of Purchasing& Supply Management, 5*(3-4), 143-55.

Croxton, K. I., Garcia-Dastugue, S. J., & Lambert, D. M. (2001). The supply chain management processes. *The International Journal of Logistics Management, 12*(2), 13-36.

Dodge, H. R., & Robbins, J. E. (1992). Empirical investigation of the organizational life cycle. *Journal of Small Business Management, 30*(1), 8-30.

Ellram, L. M., Zsidisin, G. A., Siferd, S. P., & Stanly, M. J. (2002). The impact of purchasing and supply management activities on corporate success. *The Journal of Supply Chain Management, 38*(1), 4-17.

Fisher, A. (2000a, Winter). It's a small world after all. *Financial Times,* 6-7.

Fisher, A. (2000b, Winter). Playing catch up. *Financial Times,* 22-23.

Forrester, J. W. (1958). Industrial dynamics: A major breakthrough for decision makers. *Harvard Business Review, 36*(4), 37-66.

Forrester, J. W. (1961). *Industrial dynamics.* Cambridge, MA: MIT Press.

Ghobadian, A., & Gallear, D. N. (1996). Total quality management in SMEs. *Omega, 24*(1), 83-106.

Grossman, M. (2004, September). The role of trust and collaboration in the Internet-enabled supply chain. *Journal of American Academy of Business,* 391-396.

Helper, S. (1991). How much has really changed between U.S. automakers and their suppliers? *Sloan Management Review, 33*(3), 114-135.

Hoyt, D. (2000). Lucent Technologies: Global supply chain management. *Graduate School of Business, Stanford University, GS-01.*

Hvolby, H.-H., & Trienekens, J. (2002). Supply chain planning opportunities for small and medium sized companies. *Computers in Industry,* 3-8.

Jagdev, H. S., & Thoben, K. D. (2001). Anatomy of enterprise collaborations. *Production Planning & Control, 12*(5), 437-451.

Kaufman, A., Wood, C.H., & Theyel, G. (2000). Collaboration and technology linkages: A strategic supplier typology. *Strategic Management Journal, 21*(6), 649-663.

Kennerly, M., & Neely, A. (2001). Enterprise resource planning: Analyzing and impact. *Integrated Manufacturing System, 12*(2), 103-113.

Kirby, D. A., & Turner, M. J. S. (1993). IT and the small retail business. *International Journal of Retail and Distribution Management, 21*(7), 20-27.

Knechtges, J. P., & Watts, C. A. (2000). Supply chain management for small business: How to avoid being part of the food chain. *Hospital Material Management Quarterly, 22*(1), 29-35.

Krause, D. R., & Ellram, L. M. (1997). Success factors in supplier development. *International Journal of Physical Distribution and Logistics Management, 27*(1), 39-52.

Krcmarc, H., Bjørn-Andersen, N., & O'Callaghan, R. (1995). *EDI in Europe: How it works in practice.* Chichester, UK: John Wiley & Sons Ltd.

Lambert, M.D., & Cooper, M.C. (2000). Issues in supply chain management. *Industrial Marketing Management, 29,* 65-83.

Lamming, R. (1993). *Beyond partnership: Strategies for innovation and lean supply.* Hertfordshire, UK: Prentice Hall International.

Lee, H., & Amaral, J. (2002). Continuous and sustainable improvement through supply chain performance management. *Stanford Global Supply Chain Management Forum SGSCMF-W.*

Lee, H. L., & Billington, C. (1995). The evolution of supply chain management models and practice at Hewlett-Packard. *Interfaces, 25,* 42-63.

Levy, M. (1998). SME flexibility and the role of information systems. *Small Business Economics, 11*(2), 183-96.

Liker, J. K., Kamath, R. R, & Wasti, S. N. (1998). Supplier involvement in design: A comparative survey of automotive suppliers in the USA, UK and Japan. *International Journal of Quality Science, 3*(3), 214-238.

Loebbecke, C., Powell, P., & Gallagher, C. (1999). Electronic commerce in the book trade. *Journal of Information Technology, 14*(3), 295-301.

Magretta, J., & Rollins, K. (1998). The power of virtual integration: An interview with Dell Computer's Michael Dell. *Harvard Business Review, 76*(2), 72-83.

Manrody, K. B., Holcomb, M. C., & Thompson, R. H. (1997, Fall). What's missing in supply chain management? *Supply Chain Management Review,* 80-86.

Masella, C., & Rangone, A. (2000). A contingent approach to the design of vendor selection systems for different types of co-operative customer/ supplier relationships. *International Journal of Operations and Production Management, 20*(1), 70-84.

Mehta, J. (2004). Supply chain management in a global economy. *Total Quality Management, 15*(5-6), 841-848.

Moretimer, J. H. (2000). *The effects of revenue-sharing contract on welfare in vertically separated markets: Evidence from the video rental industry.* Working Paper, University of California at Los Angeles.

Muskin, J. B. (2000). Interorganizational ethics: Standards of behavior. *Journal of Business Ethics, 24*(4), 283-297.

Nellore, R. (2001, Winter). The impact of supplier visions on product development. *The Journal of Supply Chain Management,* 27-36.

Oakie, S. (1997, February). Making money on the Internet: The myths, the facts, the truth. *EC World,* 12-13.

O'Callaghan, R., & Turner, J. A. (1995). Electronic data interchange: Concept and issues. In H. H. Krcmarc, N. Bjørn-Andersen, & R. O'Callaghan (Eds.), *EDI in Europe: How it works in practice.* Chichester, UK: John Wiley & Sons.

OECD (1993). *Small and medium-sized enterprises: Technology and competitiveness.* Organization for Economic Co-operation and Development, Paris, France.

O'Regan, N., & Ghobadian, A. (2002). Effective strategic planning in small and medium sized firms. *Management Decision, 40*(7), 663-671.

Park, D., & Krishnan, H. A. (2001). Supplier selection practices among small firms in the United States: Testing three models. *Journal of Small Business Management,* 259-272.

Park, S., & Hartley, J. L. (2002, Spring). Exploring the effect of supplier management on performance in the Korean automotive supply chain. *The Journal of Supply Chain Management,* 46-52.

Plante, R. (2000). Allocation of variance reduction targets under the influence of supplier interaction. *International Journal of Production Research*, *38*(12), 2815-2827.

Purdy, L., Astad, U., & Safayeni, F. (1994). Perceived effectiveness of the automotive supplier evaluation process. *International Journal of Operations and Production Management*, *14*(6), 91-103.

Qin, Z., & Yang, J. (2004, September). Analysis of a revenue-sharing contract in supply chain management, *Working paper*.

Quayle, M. (2002). Supplier development and supply chain management in small and medium size enterprises. *International Journal of Technology Management*, *23*(1-3), 172-188.

Quinn, J. B., & Hilmer, F. G. (1994, summer). Strategic outsourcing. *Sloan Management Review*, 43-55.

Reddy, R., & Reddy, S. (2001). *Supply chains to virtual integration*. New York: McGraw-Hill.

Reed, D.M. (1998). Using the business excellence model in small service business. *British Quality Foundation*.

Richardson, G. B. (1972, September). The organization of industry. *The Economic Journal*, 883-896.

Rota, K., Thierry, C., & Bel, G. (2002). Supply chain management: A supplier perspective. *Production Planning and Control*, *13*(4), 370-380.

Rovere, R. L. (1996). IT diffusion in small and medium-sized enterprises: Elements for policy definition. *Information Technology for Development*, *7*(4), 169-181.

Sabbaghi, A., & Sabbaghi, N. (2004). Global supply-chain strategy and global competitiveness. *International Business & Economics Research Journal*, *3*(7), 63-76.

Saunders, A. (1994). Supplier audits as part of a supplier partnership. *The TQM Magazine*, *6*(2), 41-42.

Skoett-Larsen, T., Thernoe, C., & Anderson, C. (2003). Supply chain collaboration. *International Journal of Physical Distribution & Logistics Management*, *33*(6), 531-549.

Smeltzer, L. R. (2002). *The five immutable laws of universal supply chain connectivity*. Retrieved from http://itresearch.forbes.com/detail/RES/991155741_679.html

Srinivasan, M. M., Reeve, J. M., & Singh, M. P. (2000). E-business in the supply chain. In *Proceedings of International Conference on Advances in Infrastructure for Electronic Business Science, and Education on the Internet*, Italy.

Stansfield, M., & Grant, K. (2003). An investigation into issues influencing the use of the Internet and electronic commerce among small-medium sized enterprises. *Journal of Electronic Commerce Research, 4*(1), 15-33.

Storey, D. J., & Gressy, R. (1995). *Small business risk: A firm and bank perspective.* Working paper, SME Center, Warwick Business School, Coventry, UK.

Subramani, M. (2004). Benefits from IT use in supply chain relationships. *MIS Quarterly, 28*(1), 45-73.

Tan, K. C. (2001). A framework of supply chain management literature. *European Journal of Purchasing and Supply Management, 7*, 39-48.

Tan, K. C., Kanan, V. J., & Handfield, R. B. (1998). Supply chain management: Supplier performance and firm performance. *International Journal of Purchasing and Materials Management, 34*(3), 2-9.

Taylor, W. A., & Adair, R. G. (1994). Evolution of quality awards and self-assessment practices in Europe: A case for considering organization size. *Total Quality Management, 5*(4), 227-237.

Themistocleous, M., & Chen, H. (2004). Investigating the integration of SMEs' information systems: An exploratory case study. *International Journal of Information Technology and Management, 3*(2-4), 208-234.

USSBA (1999). *Ecommerce: Small business venture online.* U.S. Small Business Administration, July. Retrieved from www.sba.gov/library/reportsroom.html

Vaidyanathan, G. (2005). A framework for evaluating third-party logistics. *Communications of the ACM, 48*(1), 89-94.

Van Heck, E., & Ribbers, P. M. (1995). The adoption and impact of EDI in Dutch SMEs. In *Proceedings of the 32nd Hawaii International Conference on System Sciences* (pp. 1-9).

Venkatesan, R. (1992, November-December). Sourcing: To make or not to make. *Harvard Business Review*, 98-107.

Vickery, S., Calantone, R., & Droge, C. (1999). Supply chain flexibility: An empirical study. *Journal of Supply Chain Management, 35*(3), 16-24.

Von Corswant, F., & Fredriksson, P. (2002). Sourcing trends in the car industry: A survey of car manufacturers' and suppliers' strategies and relations. *International Journal of Operations & Production Management, 22*(7-8), 741-758.

Wang, Y., Li, J., & Shen, Z. (2004). Channel performance under consignment contract with revenue sharing. *Management Science, 50*(1), 34-47.

Warren, A., & Peers, M. (2002, June 11). Video retailers have day in court—Plaintiffs say supply deals between Blockbuster Inc. and Studios Video violates the law. *Wall Street Journal.*

Wisner, J. D., Leong, G. K., & Tan, K. (2005). *Principles of supply chain management: A balanced approach.* Stanford, CT: Thomson South-Western.

Yen, B. P. C., & Ng, E. O. S. (2003). The impact of electronic commerce on procurement. *Journal of Organizational Computing and Electronic Commerce, 13*(3-4), 167-189.

Chapter VII

Strategic Alliances of Information Technology Among Supply Chain Channel Members

H. Y. Sonya Hsu, Southern Illinois University, USA

Stephen C. Shih, Southern Illinois University, USA

Abstract

This chapter explores novel ways of improving flexibility, responsiveness, and competitiveness via strategic information technology (IT) alliances among channel members in a supply chain network. To gain competitiveness, firms have to constantly update their operational strategies and information technologies through collaborative efforts of a "network" of supply chain members rather than the efforts of an individual firm. In sum, the foci of this chapter are: (1) an overview of supply chain management (SCM) issues and problems, (2) supply chain coordination and integration, (3) the latest IT applications for improved supply chain performance and coordination, and (4) strategic IT alliances. This chapter concludes with a discussion of business implications and recommendations of future research.

Introduction

Supply chain management (SCM), characterized by interorganizational coordination (Hill & Scudder, 2002), deals with how each company in a supply chain coordinates and cooperates with its business partners. Along the supply chain, most business activities are integrated for effectively supplying products and services to customers via a continuous, seamless flow. Drawing on the concepts of value chain and value system (Porter, 1985), SCM inherits the viewpoint of "process." In a value system, simply a series of integrated processes is insufficient to support a supply chain and offer fully synchronized operations of all supply chain partners (Williamson, Harrison, & Jordan, 2004).

Recently, it has been realized that information technology (IT) plays an important role in supporting systematic integration and synchronization by providing automatic information flows throughout the entire supply chain. More and more SCM researchers have emphasized the need to embrace the enabling information technologies and explore the essential capabilities of effective information management for supply chain integration (Dai & Kauffman, 2002a). Kopczak and Johnson (2003) stated that the synchronization in a value system required a sophisticated information system (IS) to foster real-time information processing and sharing, coordination, and decision making by the entire supply chain. In line with Kopczak and Johnson's research, other researchers (Dai & Kauffman, 2002b; Gunasekaran & Ngai, 2004) have utilized a systematic study to classify the landscape of emerging online business-to-business (B2B) marketplaces.

In addition, Internet technology is then conceived as an enabling tool for effective integration of the information-intensive SCM processes via ubiquitous availability of timely information (Boyson, Corsi, & Verbraeck, 2003). Information transfer via Internet facilitates more interactive partnerships in multi-directions as opposed to the traditionally linear movement of information within a supply chain (Boyson et al., 2003). This information sharing from multiple directions has boosted the power of process integration and synchronization as well as effective collaboration among the supply chain members.

The remainder of this chapter is organized as follows. First, an overview of issues and problems existing in SCM (such as free-riding phenomenon, negative externalities, and bullwhip effects) is presented. Next, it describes the importance of supply chain coordination and integration, followed by a discussion of the latest IT applications that improve supply chain performance and coordination. The following sections focus on (1) the importance of supply chain portal (SCP) in term of e-collaboration between firms, and (2) the "spillover" effect of IT investments.

With these two foci, the authors attempt to classify the differences between supply chain management systems (SCMS) and SCP in terms of major functions, applications, performance matrices, and the like. Two forms of strategic IT alliances for effective SC coordination are then discussed in detail, including technology similarity or geographic proximity. A typology of competitive advantage positions in terms of alliances and spillovers is also presented. In In addition, the researchers intend to emphasize a new selection of IT, namely, SCP, and a different perspective of SCM, namely, a "spillover" effect of IT investments and a strategic alliance of IT. Last but not least, this chapter attempts to find an innovative way to improve a company's flexibility and responsiveness in terms of competitiveness. Finally, the last section concludes this chapter by discussing a number of business implications and recommendations for future research.

Supply Chain Coordination
Problems and Issues

Free-Riding Phenomenon

A noticeable "free-riding" phenomenon has become more prevalent in a multichannel supply chain (Wu, Ray, Geng, & Whinston, 2004). With the occurrences of free riding, a channel member may acquire relevant sales data from one upstream member but actually purchase the products or receive the services from other vendors, possibly at a lower price. In other words, one channel member carries out the final sale transactions, while another channel member debuts the activities that are required to sell the products/services. In practice, a number of advanced information technologies, particularly the Internet, have increased supply chain channel members' caliber to access a wide range of handy information at a much modest cost. Without doubt, companies that sell their products through multiple-channel sales and distribution are often concerned about the free-riding phenomena for fear that the downstream retailers would have less incentive to promote their products.

Another problem with the free-riding phenomenon is likely to arise when additional efforts made by one channel member bring about increasing revenue that is shared by other channel members in a supply chain. As a consequence, a member may be inclined to work less and enjoy a free ride of improved financial rewards realized by other member(s) in the supply chain. One way to alleviate this problem is to implement an incentive program to motivate the channel members to bring forth adequate contributions in order to receive the comparable compensation. On top of that, a monitoring system should be constructed to measure the effort of each member and to ensure the financial gains of each individual member match their contributions.

Negative Externalities

An effect of externality occurs in a supply chain when a business decision or action results in costs or benefits to members other than the member actually making the decision or carrying out the action. In other words, the decision maker does not bear all of the costs or reap all of the gains from the action. On the other hand, the spillover costs, or negative externalities, may be imposed on a certain channel member without compensation from other parties. For example, a delivery delay caused by the vendor will spill superfluous production costs or excessive inventories over to the manufacturer or other downstream member(s) in a supply chain. Mostly, inferior decisions or deficient data can cause subsequent spillovers on invoices and shipment notices, which will, in turn, lead to incorrect shipments, delays, and costly reductions.

The Bullwhip Effect

In a supply chain, demands can be distorted by members attempting to achieve local optimization. This phenomenon of information distortion on demands is referred as the "bullwhip" or "whiplash" effect (Lee & Padmanabhan, 1997). This phenomenon may occur in many echelons where the variability of demand increases at each stage of the supply chain (Kopczak & Johnson, 2003). In reality, the bullwhip effect may exist in various industries at different levels of a supply chain network. This effect can also cause unnecessary costs and excessive inventories in production, distribution, logistics, and intermediaries.

Supply Chain
Coordination and Integration

Horizontal vs. Vertical Coordination

In earlier SCM studies, the adoption of IT was mainly on the use of advanced planning systems to reduce uncertainty of the demand side and to optimize flows (Kumar, 2001). Integrated supply chains strive to achieve not only "horizontal coordination" but also "vertical coordination" (Kumar, 2001, p. 61). Horizontal coordination refers to communication and process synchronization within an industry, while vertical coordination is across industry or firms. Vertical coordination can be further explored from the aspect of transaction costs in a supply chain (Williamson, 1995). With vertical coordination, the possible costs (e.g., the investment costs, spillover costs, or "free-rider" costs) should be properly applied to all the business transactions for each participating channel member in a supply chain during the movement of a product and/or a service, business transactions. Enhanced by the "transaction costs" point of view, Jap, Bercovitz, and Nickerson (2005) argued that the level of expected cooperative exchange norms (i.e., joint transaction-specific investments) could be beneficial to interorganizational performance.

In addition, Williamson (1993) further indicated that the partnership entails the willingness to realize some risks, which imply the uncertainties between part-ners. To resolve the uncertainties among members, the "trust" relationship may evolve over time under a certain governance structure (Kogut, 1988) and information-sharing mechanism for safeguarding against potential risks or certainties. Upstream members are often characterized as "power asymme-tries" (Subramani & Venkatraman, 2003, p. 46) compared to downstream members. The investment costs among supply chain members may be shared under contractual agreements or long-term alliances. The former is a "close, fast-developing, short-lived exchange" relationship (Lambe, Spekman, & Hunt, 2000, p. 213), whereas the latter are equity based or strategic resources alliances (Colwell & Vibert, 2005). As far as effective information sharing goes, both horizontal cooperation and vertical cooperation would require a well-structured information communication technology (ICT) platform to carry out such an operation (Kumar, 2001).

Positive Externality: IT Investment Spillover Effect

In contrast to negative externality, there is a positive externality (or beneficial externality) existing in a supply chain, especially the spillover effect in IT investments. The effect of spillovers from a channel member's IT investments is well documented in the literature (Harhoff, 1996; Lambertini, Lotti, & Santarelli, 2004; Mahajan & Vakharia, 2004; Owen-Smith & Powell, 2004; Rosenkopf & Almeida, 2003). Typically, the spillover costs in IT investment exist in a supply chain when there is a more powerful upstream member who covers some or the majority of costs. As a result, spillovers were mainly studied from a perspective of upstream supply chain.

Utilizing mathematical modeling, Mahajan and Vakharia (2004) developed two strategies that underpinned the IT investment decisions from the supplier perspective: (1) myopic strategy, making the IT investment solely on maximizing its own gain, and (2) global strategy, resulting in gains accruing to the entire value chain. According to their research results, the "global strategy" is a comparably better decision than the "myopic strategy." Furthermore, the "global strategy," with or without a distributor's own investments in IT accruing to the entire supply chain, was tested with better results as well. Based on their results, it is apparent that some free riders may exist among the IT investments from the upstream members, such as distributors and other downstream members. However, overall spillovers or positive externalities can still offer a competitive advantage to a firm or a supply chain in a marketplace at times.

Another aspect of spillover is related to R&D investments. According to Harhoff (1996), the R&D investment can be specific to a firm's product and production methods. As a result of the supplier's R&D contribution, the outputs in the downstream can be greatly expanded and enhanced (Harhoff, 1996). Additionally, on the supplier's side, the demand is shifted to a higher level, and its R&D expenditure is furnished with a higher profit gross. In a sense, a higher profit gross indicates a higher return on investment that is one of important performance metrics for evaluating the outputs of IT investment (Gunasekaran & Ngai, 2004). About a 1% upsurge in IT investments in manufacturing industries will trim down the labor intensity of their suppliers by about 0.01%. In time, investments in IT appear to have spilled over through the supply chain. Other research data show that increasing IT investments in manufacturing industries by 1% will boost the supplier investments by 0.6%, and customer investments by 0.3% (Gorman, 2005).

In sum, the spillovers from the upstream supply chain can add value to the entire supply chain. To reap the global benefits of positive externalities, a control over spillovers (Lambertini et al., 2004) or intentional spillovers (Harhoff, 1996) may be necessary. However, according to the results of empirical studies by Lambertini et al., the extent to which the firms can endogenously control the spillovers is low. Instead, the tight cooperation between the firms can embrace a higher level of spillovers because of increasing information sharing across the firms.

Information Sharing and Integration in a Coordinative Environment

To a great extent, effective information sharing is indispensable due to the efficiency required from each channel member in a supply chain. Defined by Ganeshan, Jack, Magazine, and Stephens (1999, p. 851), information sharing "specifies schemes for coordination" that apply to the efficient operation in a supply chain. Srinivasan and Yeh (1991) supported that some state-of-the-art information-sharing technologies, such as electronic data interchange (EDI), could significantly improve the suppliers' shipment performance in a just-in-time environment. Furthermore, the research showed that performance of the production and logistics can be dramatically enhanced by accurate and timely information through the facilitation of EDI.

Going beyond information sharing, Kulp, Cohen, Hau, and Ofek (2004) emphasized "information integration," which is similar to Lee and Padmanabhan's (1997) concept of "decentralization" in a supply chain. To better support SCM, Kulp et al. combined the methods of vendor-managed inventory (VMI), new products/services, and reverse logistic systems, along with effective information integration and sharing on customer needs, inventory levels, and so forth. In their research, the task of information integration was empirically tested with significances to improve the supply chain performance at different levels. To further assess other supply chain performance measures, information sharing was associated with higher manufacture performance, while collaboration of new products/services was positively related to intermediate performance. The uncertainty resulting from fluctuating customer demands will, in turn, require seamless information integration for better decision making in a more timely fashion.

IT for Improving Relationship-Specific Investments

Williamson (1995), a transaction cost economist, has pointed out that relationship-specific investments have notably contributed to value creation in a supply chain. The relationship-specific investments can be specifically interpreted as customized business processes catering to the requirements of a particular buyer (Subramani, 2004). According to Subramani and Venkatraman's (2003) field study, the companies that possess intangible, relationship-specific assets are usually capable of imposing an enhanced value creation over those competitors operating without such assets. In light of supplier investments, Subramani (2004) identified two types of intangible asset specificity—business-process specificity and domain-knowledge specificity. Business-process specificity refers to the development of relationship-specific routines or standard operating procedures for efficient task execution. On the other hand, domain-knowledge specificity arises from an understanding of cause-effect relationships that facilitate effective actions and provide resolutions of ambiguities in task planning and execution. By emphasizing IT-mediated buyer-supplier interactions, a firm creates and retains value of domain-knowledge based on the combination of transactions-cost and resource-based views (Subramani, 2004).

The investments of IT within a firm create a resource-based view, whereas the transactions-cost view occurs when the investment "spills over" its supply chain members. Spilling over the IT investments from suppliers to their distributors (Mahajan & Vakharia, 2004) is one field of research, whereas the IT investments from a R&D perspective is another important area of research (Harhoff, 1996; Lambertini, Lotti, & Santarelli, 2004; Rosenkopf & Almeida, 2003). Having conducted a case study involving the ship repair industry, Chryssolouris, Makris, Xanthakis, and Mourtzis (2004) demonstrated how modern IT could promote effective communications among different partners and enable seamless information flows within value-added chains. The IT investments can lead to enormous benefits from an efficient product life cycle, a shorter lead-time, better product quality, or simply cost reductions.

IT in Supply Chain Management

According to Kumar (2001), three factors have contributed to the needs of effective supply chain management. On the demand side, more sophisticated customers are increasingly demanding a customized value from the supply chain. On the other hand, suppliers are increasingly embracing IT to obtain a forward-looking perspective of the entire supply chain and, in turn, to optimize the processes for meeting the demands. Finally, on both the demand and supply sides, the emergence of global markets has stretched a supply chain to a longer distance. These longer chains—along with the accumulated demands of variability, uncertainties, costs, distances, and time lags—make SCM vulnerable yet in great need of advanced information technologies.

From an enterprise-centric perspective, SCM is considered an extension of enterprise resource planning (ERP) (Kumar, 2001) and has evolved into numerous interwoven information-intensive networks focusing on improving the coordinating and collaborative relationships among supply chain members. Along the line, the trend of a modern supply chain is to fulfill uncertain demands with an array of variety and desired product quality in a timely fashion at the least possible cost (Kumar 2001). If the products and/or services can be delivered by a supply chain with sufficient value at a lower cost than other competitive supply chains, then it has a competitive advantage. Kumar (2001) stated that an innovative use of IT could dramatically increase the competitive advantage via changing the cost and value equation in a supply chain. In the following sections, a number of cutting-edge SC coordination practices and information technologies are described.

EDI, ECR, CPFR, and VMI

Electronic data interchange (EDI) was once used just for transferring information (Hill & Scudder, 2002). Lately, many SCM practitioners have increasingly embraced a number of emerging SCM practices, such as efficient consumer response (ECR), collaborative planning, forecasting and replenishment (CPFR), and cross docking, to facilitate improved coordination among channel members. Launching in the United States, the ECR movement was initiated in 1993 as a result of modern consumers who are more sophisticated and increasingly demand higher quality, more product variety, and better services for less money and less lead-time. ECR responds to tailor products through continuous improvements, focusing on both the demand and supply sides.

CPFR, first adopted by companies like Wal-Mart, Pillsbury, and Procter and Gamble, is an emerging SCM initiative that pursues greater profits through improved operational efficiencies and better collaboration and information sharing between trading partners. By embracing the CPFR technology, Wal-Mart's retailing is able to establish a solid information-rich relationship with most of its customers and suppliers (Gottfredson, Puryear, & Phillips, 2005), which has dramatically strengthen its coordinative capability with its business partners and greatly enhanced its fundamental economies of scale in distribution (Moore, 1993). Different levels of coordination have led to a lower inventory level and lower operating costs, successfully sustaining Wal-Mart's dominance and superior bargaining power.

In supply chain operations, inaccuracy in the information flow may significantly hold up inventory levels and undercut production rates. Addressing this issue, the participating supply chain members need to acquire necessary information about sales forecasting and replenishment to improve the deficient product throughputs. To satisfy this need, CPFR can be used as a novel way of sharing and disseminating information in a supply chain network. With CPFR, participating supply chain partners are required to collaborate and share information throughout the entire design and production life cycle, from planning to execution (Esper & Williams, 2003).

Addressing the bullwhip effect mentioned previously, Lee and Padmanabhan (1997) analyzed the sources of the bullwhip effect and called for cooperation and coordination among members to lessen its negative effects. For example, by using CPFR with the philosophy of vendor-managed inventory (VMI), channel members can share forecast and demand information and further streamline replenishment, which leads to significant reduction of the bullwhip effect (Kopczak & Johnson, 2003). To achieve better coordination and diminish the phenomenon of demand distortion, more and more companies have started sharing point-of-sales (POS) information throughout the supply chain (Steckel, Gupta, & Banerji, 2004).

Cross Docking

Between 1972 and 1992, Wal-Mart went from $44 million in sales to $44 billion, partially because this retailing giant has been capable of optimizing its distribution and logistics (Hammer, 2004) by adopting the so-called "cross docking" technique. Cross docking refers to a logistic process whereby the goods transported to a distribution center from the suppliers are immediately transferred to the stores (Hammer, 2004). In other words, cross docking is a process of taking a finished good from the manufacturing plant and delivering it directly to the customer with little or no handling in between. Simply put, the cross-docking process means receiving goods at one door and shipping them out through the other door almost immediately, without ever putting them in storage. As a result, the step of filling a warehouse with inventory before shipping it out can be virtually eliminated. In practice, implementation of the cross docking process requires seamless coordination of products transportations among different suppliers, distribution centers, and retail stores in a timely fashion.

Internet Technology for SC Coordination

The Internet and its associated technologies (e.g., intranet and extranet) provide enormous opportunities for companies to make significant improvements in managing and optimizing their supply chains through efficient and effective information flows (Boyson et al., 2003). Shared information enabled by the Internet helps break down functional barriers. Further, Internet technology can help supply chain members to develop a common understanding of the marketplace (Boyson, Corsi, Dresner, & Harrington, 1999). With effective use of the Internet, the entire network of a supply chain allies as a whole instead of just a single member or chain to compete in the marketplace. As an example, Dell responds to supply-demand imbalance by changing its price options or price bundling to steer demand by making the most of Internet. Dell's marketing scheme—Sell What You Have—would not exist without Internet technology (Kopczak & Johnson, 2003) because price elasticity can be managed easier online. For example, the price changes at the Dell site can be seen by all participating members. As a result, there is no need for Dell to inform any of its channel members via paper invoices that slow down the business processes.

Stretching the use of the Internet, Johnson and Whang (2002) divided Internet-enabled e-business and e-supply chain technologies into three categories: e-commerce, e-procurement, and e-collaboration. According to their definitions, e-commerce helps a network of supply chain partners identify and respond quickly to changing customer demands captured over the Internet. E-procurement allows companies to use the Internet for procuring direct or indirect materials as well as handling value-added services like transportation, warehousing, customs clearing, payment, quality validation, and documentation. E-collaboration facilitates coordination of various decisions and activities beyond transactional operations among partners, suppliers, and customers over the Internet.

Internet-Enabled Supply Chain Portal for Heterogeneous IT Environment

Transmitting information electronically reduces errors and increases reuses of information. However, each supply chain member may not adopt the same standards and/or systems to communicate with each other during the business processes. Addressing this issue, a Web-based supply chain portal (SCP) is one of Internet technologies that can be used to solve the problems associated with different standards and systems in SCM. Examining recent business practices, the SCP has actually taken SCM in an electronic form to a new level. Managed and designed by an organization, a SCP can support any business processes in supply chain management (Boyson et al., 1999). The portal is also capable of supporting collaboration among business partners on related business processes. In practice, the collaborative partners are not limited to suppliers and sellers/retailers but can also include customers downstream in a supply chain. On the demand side, a typical SCP solution facilitates an e-commerce, front-end interface for promoting products or services and processing transactions. On the supply side, a portal streamlines and coordinates internal business transactions and interorganizational operations in a real-time mode (McCormack & Johnson, 2001).

A portal can manage many peer-to-peer relations as well as simplify numerous business processes (McCormack & Johnson, 2001). Unifying supply chain partners in a single portal will make the transactions easier for the buyers and, in the meantime, more efficient for the suppliers despite different standards and communication technologies throughout the whole supply chain. With the use of SCP, any authorized partner in a supply chain can bypass excessive security procedures, such as log-on access, and immediately retrieve the relevant information (McCormack & Johnson, 2001). With SCP, the user's access privilege in a portal depends upon his or her level of security clearance.

Meanwhile, information on a portal can be updated in real-time from multiple sources.

In terms of the functionality and practicality of SCP, McCormack and Johnson (2001) summarized that the SCP can be adapted to:

- provide a unified format and middleware platform;
- use real-time messaging to assure supply chain operations within optimal inventory level parameters;
- personalize portal views based on user requirements and security/access classifications;
- distribute field-based data gathered from scanners, PDA devices, and other information appliances to multiple users; and
- construct a seamless grid of information on key operational performance areas.

Supply Chain Management Systems

Evidence provided by Subramani (2004) showed that IT-enabled electronic integration technologies, such as supply chain management systems (SCMS), could create and retain greater value for each channel member in a supply chain. According to Subramani, there are two major functions of SCMS: automating and informating. These functions are further distinguished in two different perspectives, namely, exploitation and exploration. Exploitation is the extension or elaboration of old certainties, whereas exploration is the method of pursuing new possibilities (Subramani, 2004). More precisely, exploitation refers to using the system to perform structured, repetitive tasks, while exploration is meant to use SCMS for unstructured tasks that may seek or create new business processes and/or opportunity (Subramani, 2004). In general, exploitation can be a supplement to exploratory uses of SCMS.

Derived from several research studies, Table 1 summarizes the differences between SCMS and SCP in several categories including major functions, functionalities (Johnson & Whang, 2002), communication, channels, applications (Boyson et al., 1999), performance metrics (Otto & Kotzab, 2003), and their drawbacks. Performance metrics in an organization perspective are represented by transaction costs, time to network, flexibility, and density of relationships (Otto & Kotzab, 2003). The density of relationships is then evaluated by the density of a relation based on the distance of "social, technological, cultural, geographical, and time" (Otto & Kotzab, 2003, p. 315).

Table 1. Comparison of SCMS and SCP

	SCMS	SCP
Major functions	Automation Information sharing	Information sharing Knowledge sharing Interoperation
Functionalities	e-Procurement e-Commerce	e-Procurement e-Commerce e-Collaboration
Communication	Hierarchical Sequential Difficult to update	Open Multi-directional Easy to update
Channels	Business-to-business Business-to-consumer (limited)	Business-to-business Business-to-consumer Consumer-to-consumer (limited)
Applications	EDI VMI CPFAR ECR	Search engine KM repository Data mart Data warehouse Index/category filter Information push Information mining
Performance Metrics • Transaction cost • Time to network • Flexibility • Density of relationship	 High Long Easily change Low density	 Low Short More easily change High density
Drawbacks	Disconnection Broken channel links Lack of interoperation	Vulnerable to malicious attacks Trust & commitment issue among trading partners

IT Alliances for
Effective SC Coordination

Transitioning from controlled spillovers to strategic alliances of IT investments reveals a new, promising aspect of knowledge sharing for seamless coordination among supply chain members. Essentially, IT alliances between channel members are formed to search for "new capabilities" and interdependencies within limited social networks (Rosenkopf & Almeida, 2003, p. 753). These limited social networks are the clusters close to each other in some way. Alliances of IT-related R&D facilitate the growth and/or profit of a supply chain because alliances offer great accessibility to essential business and SCM-related knowledge. In a study of the semiconductor industry, Rosenkopf and Almeida (2003) illustrated overall knowledge flows across supply chain networks, while the firms allied and worked together as networks of networks. Further strategic IT alliances can be formed by either technology similarity or geographic proximity among participating members.

Technology Similarity

When firms form alliances, they are more likely to cooperate with other companies that have similar technologies. In other words, the firms that maintain similar positions in constructing their technological landscapes will build their allied relationships upon the knowledge stock of the firms' core competencies. For example, common patent citations are used to form alliances in a semiconductor industry (Stuart & Podolny, 1996). Using a secondary data analysis, Kalaignanam, Shandar, and Varadarajan (2005) provided some insights about information technology industry. They found that the alliance scope contributed to financial gain in large firms, while the alliance type (scale or link alliance) contributed to financial gain in small firms. Evidently, the sizes of firms matter to the IT alliances strategically.

Geographical Similarity

Silicon Valley is a good example of strategic alliances in a geographical cluster. Having conducted a social network analysis, Owen-Smith and Powell (2004) documented alliances as knowledge flows among the firms within the Boston region. According to the analysis results, the local links can be formal, that is, a strategic alliance, or informal, such as a social network that recognizes each other via professional courtesies in a region. Rosenkopf and Almeida (2003) suggested that geographic proximity should reduce costs and increase the frequency of personal contacts in a regional network. The more frequent contacts occur among firms, the better alliances they can organize. Therefore, the knowledge can easily flow among the allied members while geographic local searches can be reciprocally stimulated. The local searches, then, reinforce the organizational and/or regional establishment in terms of technology alliances.

Owen-Smith and Powell (2004) suggested that the spillovers resulting from proprietary alliances were a combination of the institutional commitments and members' practices in the network. Specifically, they made an attempt to capture any possible links by utilizing social network analyses. Between information spillovers and the strengths of regional networks, Owen-Smith and Powell found that contractual linkages along with physical proximity represented relatively strong alliances (Figure 1).

Figure 1. Strong vs. weak alliances among upstream vs. downstream channels (Rosenkopf & Almeida, 2003; Lancioni et al., 2003b; van der Vorst et al., 2002; van der Vorst, Beulens, & van Beek, 2000)

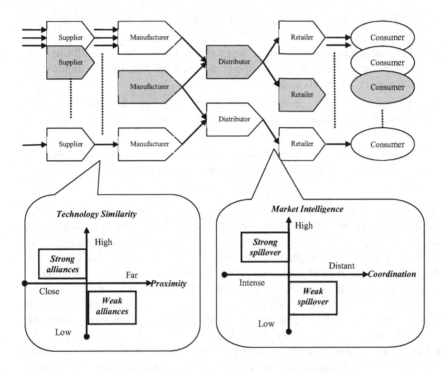

The strengths of alliances are embedded in a mechanism of a rich ecology and a regional labor market. Similarly, while studying technology-based alliances, Stuart (2000) also found that strong alliance increased innovation rates in the semiconductor industry. However, he discovered that those affiliations depended strongly on partner characteristics in terms of IT alliances. Also, Colwell and Vibert's (2005) study illustrated that firms were likely to be satisfied to collaborate with those with whom they had engaged in a satisfying partnership previously. Therefore, commitment and trust are embedded in a longer term of partnership.

One typology, developed by Tapscott, Ticoll, and Lowy (2000), and further interpreted by van der Vorst, van Dongen, Nouguier, and Hilhorst (2002), defines four different types of e-business initiatives based on economic control and value integration. This typology represents the value-added IT alliances into four categories:

- E-marketplaces that facilitate the exchange bring together sellers and buyers.
- Information chains that provide the transparency of information through the value chain and focus on the demand-driven information for monitoring customers' demands and behaviors.
- Virtual enterprises (or alliances) that play a role as a broker who leads a network of community to collect knowledge for every participating member.
- Value chains or "extended enterprises" (van der Vorst et al., 2002) that are represented as a form of "supply chain integration" (p. 133).

According to van der Vorst et al. (2002), "virtual enterprises" and "value chains" are different in terms of economic control. Every member in virtual enterprises has been empowered to access, create, and update the knowledge in the network, whereas "value chains" are controlled by a hierarchy that dominates the supply chain. Jap and Anderson (2003) have illustrated goal congruence as a powerful governance tool in alliances. In reality, the breadth and intensity of the relationship between alliances will either grow or discontinue over time (Dyer, 1997). For example, opportunists in a supply chain may eventually be dropped out of the cooperation for lacking commitment or contribution. The alliances may grow if the IT investments have added benefits to each channel member throughout the supply chain in addition to the harmonious relationships among the allies. Two potential benefits—short-term operational efficiency and longer-term new knowledge creation (Clark, 1989; Malhotra & Gosain, 2005)— may be generated in allied relationships.

To configure supply chain capacity, Malhotra and Gosain (2005) presented "structure" and "cognitive" impacts for alliances in electronic business (p. 31). The structural impact is the adoption of standardized interfaces for linking potential partners in a timely fashion, while the cognitive impact stands for the uses of new knowledge to reduce managers' cognitive loads (Malhotra & Gosain, 2005). The quick coordination between partners increases the capacity to create market intelligence that, in turn, enhances decision-making processes. Figure 1 presents such a model demonstrating that coordination and market intelligence may result from the IT alliances in the upstream.

Despite the importance of technology similarity and proximity, economical control, or value integration, Toyota has switched to a system of "dynamic learning capability" to encourage suppliers' involvement, promote knowledge sharing, and prevent free riders in its supply chain (Kim & Im, 2002). Doz (1996) explored alliances as a learning process that could occur in several dimensions, such as environment, tasks, processes, skills, and partner goals. The "dynamic learning capability" has led a whole supply chain to its competitive advantage. The value-added functions are distributed across the participating members who are interactively coordinated. The interactive coordination is indeed facilitated by a knowledge-sharing network known as "virtual enterprises," as mentioned above. According to Kim and Im (2002), the knowledge-sharing network facilitates a supply chain in three ways: (1) saving in procurement and transaction costs; (2) alleviating the bullwhip effect and lowering inventory; and (3) allying the R&D support and co-engineering.

In light of Otto and Kotzab's (2003) performance metrics (i.e., time to network, flexibility, and density of relationship), this chapter intends to incorporate the performance metrics to the downstream spillovers that are created from the upstream investments. Figure 1 shows such an effort. Future research is required to investigate how the spillover effect (resulting from either strong alliances or weak alliances) can add value and benefits to the supply chain as a whole. The researchers classify the possible spillovers outcomes with two determinants—market intelligence and coordination. The downstream spillover effect depicted in Figure 1 can be interpreted by a "technology similarity" that may make possible more knowledge sharing while "proximate" alliances lead to a better coordination in a supply chain. The knowledge sharing and coordination can also be explained by Malhotra and Gosain's (2005) "structure" and "cognitive" impacts.

The transaction costs may decrease or the values may increase while the spillover effect (mainly resulting from the IT investments in the upstream) moves to the downstream. Derived from value chain (Porter, 1985), transaction cost (Williamson, 1993, 1995), resource-based view (Barney, 2002) principles, and resource-advantage theory, Table 2 summaries a typology of competitive advantage positions in terms of alliances and spillovers.

Table 2. The typology of competitive advantage positions in terms of alliances and spillovers in a supply chain

	Downstream Weak Spillovers	Downstream Strong Spillovers
Upstream Weak Alliances	1. Money Pit	3. Competitive Advantage without Sustainability
Upstream Strong Alliances	2. Possible ROI in a Longer Term	4. Competitive Advantage with Sustainability

The four arrows in the table represent the emergent competitive advantage positions that synchronize with the market changes. These four positions of the typology are described in detail next.

Position 4: Competitive Advantage with Sustainability

Strong alliances in the upstream supply chain are likely to engage more sturdy spillovers that will lead to a more sustainable competitive advantage. Prior to reaching this phase of affiliation, the alliances between upstream members may have previously formed their partnership with satisfaction (Colwell & Vibert, 2005). The partners have learned from each other on how to work with each other (Jordan, 2004; Kim & Im, 2002). Therefore, they can team up with great ease, comfort, and trust. The more satisfied the partnership is, the more likely the firms are to ally repeatedly. While robust alliances can support stronger spillovers and sustain a better position in competitive advantage as a whole, the long-term relationships may collapse because of economic situation, market changes, consolidations, or conflicts of new alliances. The strength of upstream alliance diminishes and this sustainability could retreat to the third position.

Position 3: Competitive Advantage Without Sustainability

This position is characterized by the mixture of strong downstream spillovers and weak upstream alliances. The strong spillovers may support the supply chain with a competitive advantage; however, they may not be able to provide sufficient sustainability in competitive advantage. The argument here is that the competitive advantage may have been generated from the strong spillovers derived simply from weak resources, namely, less innovative technology, lack of coordination, or short of investment effort. From the perspective of resource-advantage (R-A) theory, this position is similar to Hunt's (2000) "Cell 6" of competitive position matrix. In Hunt's research, the competitive position matrix contributing to the thrust of R-A theory represents nine possible competitive positions based on the combinations of a firm's resource-produce value and relative costs for producing such value. The "Cell 6" represents an "effectiveness" advantage because "their parity costs produce superior value" (Hunt, 2000, p. 139). Simply put, Position 3 can be effective but not sufficient to sustain a competitive advantage over time. It is possible that it would recede to Position 1 or move to Position 4, depending on the fact that alliances become stronger or spillovers become weaker. To assume pessimistically, Position 3 is more likely moving towards to Position 1.

Position 2: Possible Return on Investment (ROI)

In this position, the ROI will take a longer time to evolve to stronger spillovers that will show beneficial impact to the supply chain. Jap et al. (2005) presented the "overshooting the target" situation to illustrate the long-haul investment in partnerships. Some R&D alliances may range from three to 10 years. Therefore, commitment and trust need to be established in addition to a governance structure. With strong upstream alliances, the downstream spillovers should be increasingly strengthened to move forward to Position 4. Nevertheless, there always are some possibilities that R&D may not be able to completely follow through. If that is the case, Position 2 can then turn into Position 1. However, with strong alliances or previous satisfying cooperation experiences, the spillovers in the downstream will eventually come around and cause the state of competitive advantage to move towards Position 3.

Position 1: Money Pit

This position represents a combination of weak alliances and weak spillovers that is likely to dangle the firms over the precipice of a potential money pit. Jordan (2004) has stressed that alliance success depends on the combination of a high level of cooperation and knowledge/information sharing. If the allies fail to learn or share from one another, then the supply chain's ability to compete may be compromised (Jordan, 2004; Kim & Im, 2002). Therefore, the investments may not realize a return. However, as the allied partners' learning experience becomes more satisfying, futile partnerships will eventually evolve to partnerships that are more favorable. Therefore, it is possible that Position 1 can swing towards Position 2. In this case, stronger downstream spillovers may come about due to increasing coordination and knowledge sharing.

Conclusion

As there are multiple channels, there are multiple combinations in grouping a supply chain (refer to the gray shaded areas in Figure 1). In other words, the reconfigurations continuously evolve as long as there is a change of trading partners in a supply chain or one of the trading partners changes the way of dealing with businesses. For example, if Wal-Mart switches to CPFR, then all of its distribution partners must change their business processes accordingly.

For most firms, their IT investments still remain in the upstream of the supply chain for better performance, more efficient throughput, shorter lead time, and improved customer satisfaction. Nevertheless, as IT improves the upper channels, it will be highly likely to enhance the performance for the entire chain because of the "spillover" effect. Hence, the spillover effect has been recognized as a viable enabler to turn the supply chain into a sustainable competitive advantage as a whole.

Furthermore, there is an increasing emphasis on the R&D investments in a supply chain in terms of strategic alliances in IT investment. In most cases, similarities in technology and geographic proximity are the two ultimate factors for forming such IT alliances. In reality, IT investments can be very costly. If a firm can strategically plan out the investments and properly spread out the costs among the trading partners, it can acquire a better marginal benefit and return on investment.

Since the late 1990s, Internet technology has introduced different aspects of innovative processes, such as mass customization, real-time inventory management, and, most importantly, the diminishing of intermediaries (Porter, 2001). Not only does the Internet move businesses from "brick and motor" to "click and play," it also facilitates the companies to fundamentally reengineer their businesses. Internet technology makes business processes among suppliers, customers, intermediaries (if they exist), and business partners more efficient and effective because of its real-time, ubiquitous capabilities. Nowadays, Internet technology has changed the landscape of SCM in almost every aspect, including business process integration, coordination, collaboration, and information/knowledge sharing.

Several issues on strategic alliances of IT among supply chain channel members have been illustrated in this chapter. However, there are a number of limitations needing to be addressed in future research. First, in extension of the typology of van der Vorst et al. (2002), Gunasekaran and Ngai (2004) introduced a framework for the development of IT for effective SCM. The framework includes such integral components as strategic planning of IT, virtual enterprise, e-commerce, IT infrastructure, knowledge management, and IT management and implementation. Making it more complete, it is suggested that the framework should include the study of organizational issues related to IT establishment as one of the future research activities.

As far as strategic alliances of IT investments are concerned, another important area of future research is to investigate how the spillovers can be properly incorporated into a firm's strategic planning needs (Mahajan & Vakharia, 2004). From a longer term perspective, a firm's R&D investment introduces a firm's specific capabilities. In line with a firm's investment in R&D, there are two important issues that ought to be in the spotlight for future research: (1) how the knowledge-sharing network can enhance its "dynamic learning capability" (Kim & Im, 2002), and (2) how the knowledge-sharing network fits into the landscape of the whole supply chain in a rapidly changing business environment.

In Mahajan and Vakharia's (2004) article, it was mentioned that the accruing benefits from each channel member may help increase efficiency and productivity of the entire supply chain. To assist investors in figuring out more financial measures beyond just ROI, some performance metrics should be in place. In light of this need, Otto and Kotzab (2003) offered a complete list of performance metrics of SCM, along with associated problems and suggested solutions. Furthermore, to prevent the free-riding phenomenon in a supply chain, the "fee-for-use" of IT was tested by the mathematical models developed by Mahajan and Vakharia (2004, p.681). Extending from Mahajan and Vakharia's research, examination of how much or how often to subsidize or charge the participating members in a supply chain is recommended.

References

Barney, J. (2002). *Gaining and sustaining competitive advantage.* Upper Saddle River, NJ: Prentice Hall.

Boyson, S., Corsi, T., Dresner, M., & Harrington, L. (1999). *Logistics and the extended enterprise.* New York: John Wiley & Sons.

Boyson, S., Corsi, T., & Verbraeck, A. (2003). The e-supply chain portal: A core business model. *Transportation Research*, Part E 39, 175-192.

Chryssolouris H, G., Makris, S., Xanthakis, V., & Mourtzis, D. (2004). Towards the Internet-based supply chain management for the ship repair industry. *International Journal Computer Integrated Manufacturing, 17*(1), 45-57.

Clark, K. B. (1989). Project scope and project performance: The effect of parts strategy and supplier involvement on product development. *Management Science,* 35, 1247-1263.

Colwell, S. R., & Vibert, C. (2005, June 16-18). Antecedents to partner satisfaction in non-equity based contractual alliance forms. In proceedings of *INFORMS Marketing Science Conference*, Atlanta, GA.

Dai, Q., & Kauffman, R. J. (2002a). B2B e-commerce revisited: Leading perspectives on the key issues and research directions. *Electronic Markets, 12*(2), 67-84.

Dai, Q., & Kauffman, R. J (2002b). Business models for Internet-based B2B electronic markets. *International Journal of Electronic Commerce, 6*(4), 41-73.

Doz, Y. (1996). The evolution of cooperation in strategic alliances: Initial conditions or learning processes? *Strategic Management Journal, 17*(7), 55-83.

Dyer, J. (1997). Effective interfirm collaboration: How transactors minimize transaction costs and maximize transaction value. *Strategic Management Journal, 18*(2), 535-556.

Esper, T.L., & Williams, L. (2003). The value of collaborative transportation management (CTM): Its relationship to CPFR and information technology. *Transportation Journal, 42*(4), 55-65.

Ganeshan, R., Jack, E., Magazine, M. J., & Stephens, P. (1999). In S. Tayur, R. Ganeshan, & M. Magazine (Eds.), *Quantitative Models for Supply Chain Management* (pp. 839-849). Boston: Kluwer Academic.

Gorman, L. (2005). Information technology spillover. *National Bureau of Economic Research.* Retrieved July 23, 2005, from http://www.nber.org/digest/may03/w9272.html.

Gottfredson, M., Puryear, R., & Phillips, S. (2005). Strategic sourcing from periphery to the core. *Harvard Business Review, 83*(2), 132-140.

Gunasekaran, A., & Ngai, E. W. T. (2004). Information systems in supply chain integration and management. *European Journal of Operational Research, 159*(2), 269-296.

Hammer, M. (2004). Deep change. *Harvard Business Review, 82*(4), 84-93.

Harhoff, D. (1996). Strategic spillovers and incentives for research and development. *Management Science, 42*(6), 907-925.

Hill, C. A., & Scudder, G. D. (2002). The use of electronic data interchange for supply chain coordination in the food industry. *Journal of Operations Management, 20*(4), 375-388.

Hunt, S. (2000). *A general theory of competition.* Thousand Oaks, CA: Sage Publications.

Jap, S., Bercovitz, J., & Nickerson, J. (2005, June 16-18). The antecedents and performance implications of cooperative exchange norms. In proceedings of the *INFORMS Marketing Science Conference,* Atlanta, GA.

Jap, S. D., & Anderson, E. (2003). Safeguarding interorganizational performance and continuity under ex post opportunism. *Management Science, 49*(12), 1684-1702.

Jordan, J. (2004). Controlling knowledge flows in international alliances. *European Business Journal, 16*(2), 70-77.

Johnson, M.E. & Whang, S. (2002). E-business and supply chain management: An overview and framework. *Production and Operations Management, 11*(4), 413-423.

Kalaignanam, K., Shankar, V., & Varadarajan, R. (2005, June 16-18). Value creation in asymmetrical alliances: Insights from the information technology industry. In proceedings of the *Informs Marketing Science Conference*, Atlanta, GA.

Kim, K. C., & Im, Il (2002, January 7-10). The effects of electronic supply chain design (e-SCD) on coordination and knowledge sharing: An empirical investigation. In *Proceedings of the 35th Hawaii International Conference on System Sciences*, Big Island.

Kogut, B. (1988). A study of the life cycle of joint ventures. In F. J. Contractor & P. Lorange (Eds.), *Cooperative strategies in international business* (pp. 205-226). Lexington, MA: Lexington Books.

Kopczak, L. R., & Johnson, M. E., (2003). The supply-chain management effect. *MIT Sloan Management Review*, *44*(3), 27-34.

Kulp, S., Cohen, L., Lee, H,, & Ofek, E. (2004). Manufacturer benefits from information integration with retail customers. *Management Science*, *50*(4), 431-445.

Kumar, K. (2001). Technology for supporting supply chain management: Introduction. *Communications of the ACM*, *44*(6), 58-61

Lambe, C. J., Spekman, R. E., & Hunt, S. D. (2000). Intermistic relational exchange: Conceptualization and propositional development. *Journal of the Academy of Marketing Science*, *28*(2), 212-225.

Lambertini, L., Lotti, F., & Santarelli, E. (2004). Infra-industry spillovers and R&D cooperation: Theory and evidence. *Economic Innovative New Technology*, *13*(4), 311-328.

Lancioni, R. A., Smith, M. F., & Schau, H. J. (2003). Strategic Internet application trends in supply chain management. *Industrial Marketing Management*, *32*(3), 211-218.

Lee, H. L., & Padmanabhan, V. (1997). Information distortion in a supply chain: The bullwhip effect. *Management Science*, *43*(4), 546-559.

Mahajan, J., & Vakharia, A. (2004). Determining firm-level IT investments to facilitate value chain activities: Should spillovers accruing to value chain members be incorporated? *European Journal of Operational Research*, *156*(3), 665-683.

Malhotra, A., & Gosain, S. (2005). Absorptive capacity configurations in supply chains: Gearing for partner-enable market knowledge creation. *MIS Quarterly*, *29*(1), 145-187.

McCormack, K., & Johnson, B. (2001). Business process orientation, supply chain management, and the E-corporation. *IIE Solutions*, *33*(10), 33-37.

Moore, J. F. (1993). The evolution of Wal-Mart: Savvy expansion and leadership. *Harvard Business Review, 71*(3), 75-83.

Otto, A., & Kotzab, H. (2003). Does supply chain management really pay? Six perspectives to measure the performance of managing a supply chain. *European Journal of Operational Research, 144*(2), 306-321.

Owen-Smith, J., & Powell, W. W. (2004). Knowledge networks as channels and conduits: The effects of spillovers in the Boston biotechnology community. *Organization Science, 15*(1), 5-21.

Porter, M. (1985). *Competitive Advantage.* New York: Free Press.

Porter, M. (2001). Strategy and the Internet. *Harvard Business Review, 79*(3), 63-78.

Rosenkopf, L., & Almeida, P. (2003). Overcoming local search through alliances and mobility. *Management Science, 49*(6), 751-766.

Srinivasan, R., & Yeh, A. (2001). Beyond EDI: Impact of continuous replenishment program (CRP) between a manufacturer and its retailers. *Information Systems Research, 12*(4), 406-420.

Steckel, J. H., Gupta, S., & Banerji, A. (2004). Supply chain decision making: Will shorter cycle times and shared point-of-sale information necessarily help? *Management Science, 50*(4), 458-464.

Stuart, T. (2000). Interorganizational alliances and the performance of firms: A study of growth and innovation rates in a high technology industry. *Strategic Management Journal, 21*(2), 791-811.

Stuart, T., & Podolny, J. (1996). Local search and the evolution of technological capabilities. *Strategic Management Journal, 17*(7), 21-38.

Subramani, M. (2004). How do suppliers benefit from information technology use in supply chain relationships? *MIS Quarterly, 28*(1), 45-74.

Subramani, M. R., & Venkatraman, N. (2003). Safeguarding investments in asymmetric interorganizational relationships: Theory and evidence. *Academy of Management Journal, 46*(1), 46-63.

Tapscott, D., Ticoll, D., & Lowy, A. (2000) *Digital capital.* Boston: Harvard Business School Press.

van der Vorst, J. G. A. J., Beulens, A. J. M., & van Beek, P. (2000). Modeling and simulation multi-echelon food systems. *European Journal of Operational Research, 122*(2), 354-366.

van der Vorst, J. G. A. J., van Dongen, J., Nouguier, S., & Hilhorst, R. (2002). E-business initiatives in food supply chains: Definition and typology of electronic business models. *International Journal of Logistics: Research and Applications, 5*(2), 119-138.

Williamson, E. A., Harrison, D. K., & Jordan, M. (2004). Information systems development within supply chain management. *International Journal of Information Management, 24*(5), 375-386.

Williamson, O. E. (1993). Calculativeness, trust, and economic organization. *Journal of Law and Economics*, 36, 453-486.

Williamson, O. E. (1995). Transaction cost economics and organization theory. In O. E. Williamson (Ed.), *Organization theory: From Chester Barnard to the present and beyond.* New York: Oxford University Press.

Wu, D., Ray, G., Geng, X., & Whinston, A. (2004). Implications of reduced search dost and free riding in e-commerce. *Marketing Science, 23*(2), 255-262.

Section III:

Implementation of Channel Integration

Chapter VIII

A Process Model of Inter-Organisational SCM Initiatives Adoption

Yu Ni Ham, University of Melbourne, Australia

Robert B. Johnston, University of Melbourne, Australia

Abstract

While the benefits of adopting interorganisational supply chain management (IOSCM) initiatives, such as efficient consumer response (ECR) and collaborative, planning, forecasting, and replenishment (CPFR), have been widely reported within industry, their adoption has been slow and below industry expectations. There is a lack of theory within the literature to explain this problem in IOSCM initiatives adoption. Employing an inductive case-study approach to theory building, broadly in the tradition of grounded theory, this chapter develops a process model that captures the complexity of intra-industry interactions in the course of IOSCM adoption and argues for a normative path that necessarily has to be taken to achieve the increasing levels of integration envisioned in IOSCM initiatives. The model proposes that three sets of requirements have to be met to achieve a certain level of integration: supply chain integration, interorganisational structures, and relationship intimacy. However, to achieve the higher levels of integration implicit in initiatives such as CPFR, it is necessary to have mastered capabilities at lower levels of integration demanded by earlier initiatives. We argue that this path dependence constitutes a major barrier to the adoption of more advanced IOSCM initiatives.

Introduction

Over the last two decades, the practice of supply chain reengineering among supply chain partners has become an important strategy to increase the capabilities of whole supply chains to survive and compete more effectively in a highly competitive and volatile marketplace (Clark & Stoddard, 1996). Supply chain reengineering is the process of transforming and synchronising supply-chain-related activities between groups of organisations along a traditional value chain to increase channel efficiency and effectiveness (Humphreys, Lai, & Sculli, 2001). Reengineering efforts often involve the adoption of various initiatives or programs that embody innovations in supply chain management thinking and processes. These initiatives, which we refer to in this chapter as *interorganisational supply chain management (IOSCM) initiatives,* are aimed at increasing the levels of cross-organisational interoperability and integration, such that greater visibility, velocity, and reduced variability along the supply chain can be achieved. Successful adoption of IOSCM initiatives promises reductions in overall supply chain costs and an increase in the quality of customer service (Clark, 1994). Some examples of such initiatives include just-in-time, quick response, efficient consumer response (ECR), and, more recently, collaborative planning forecasting and replenishment (CPFR). IOSCM initiatives usually also involve, concurrently, the implementation of various types of interorganisational systems (IOS) (Johnston & Vitale, 1988) to facilitate the electronic exchange of information across organisational boundaries. Examples of related IOS include Electronic Data Interchange (EDI); data synchronisation hubs, such as EANNet or UCCNet; and more sophisticated collaboration hubs such as GlobalNetXchange.

Although the benefits of supply chain synchronisation and collaboration are reasonably clear, many have found that the path to achieving the envisioned extents of integration within highly competitive environments is not an easy one (Crum & Palmatier, 2004). This is evident in the large proportion of organisations that have piloted initiatives with major trading partners but have failed or faced delays in formally implementing and scaling-up these initiatives (Frankel, Goldsby,

& Whipple, 2002; Neuman & Samuels, 1996). Adoption of supply chain initiatives often involves concerted effort among two or more organisations and is, therefore, complicated by the need to synchronise information, activities, and business mindsets across organisational boundaries (Borchert, 2002; Forger, 2002). Due to the interorganisational nature of supply chain initiatives, their adoption and, in particular, their lack of adoption have the potential to impact operational routines and relationship structures, not only among firms within a supply network, but possibly interactions at the industry level as well. This potential impact provides the necessary motivation here to understand why adoption has been problematic and the sort of challenges organisations face in their attempts to jointly adopt these initiatives with other organisations along the supply chain.

Much of the prior research on IOSCM initiatives adoption has taken a factors approach (Ramanathan & Rose, 2003) to identifying the conditions necessary for initiation and implementation of particular initiatives, most often EDI, usually at the organisational and dyadic levels, within a single epoch. There are currently very few studies attempting to understand the adoption of more sophisticated forms of IOSCM initiatives. Existing studies have explored how trust and the willingness to cooperate (Li & Williams, 1999), mutuality of benefits (Kurnia & Johnston, 2001), risks and costs as well as asymmetries in technical, organizational, and cultural systems are contributing factors in hindering adoption efforts (Barratt & Oliveira, 2000; Borchert, 2002; Svensson, 2002). These studies assume that innovation adoption will most likely occur if the necessary and sufficient conditions relating to the characteristics of the technology, capabilities of adopting organisations, and the forces in the external environment are present (Kurnia & Johnston, 2002). However, innovation is generally perceived to be a static end-state and its adoption follows a simple linear path. There is little emphasis on understanding the context and nature of change that can occur over time beyond the organisational level (Ramanathan & Rose, 2003).

Despite the recognition that supply chain cooperation and collaboration is a necessary condition in adopting highly integrative supply chain initiatives (Holmes & Srivastava, 1999; Horvath, 2001; Kurnia & Johnston, 2000a), few studies go on to explore how firms go about achieving the appropriate level of collaboration that is required to adopt these initiatives. This is due to the lack of theoretical frameworks about how groups of organisations interact to jointly adopt interorganisational supply chain management initiatives. The importance of developing theoretical frameworks that consider the complex emergent process of innovation development and adoption, especially those innovations that span organisational boundaries and involve concerted actions of multiple actors in its adoption, is now widely recognised within the information systems (IS) and IOS community (Li & Williams, 1999), however, such theories are still in limited supply.

Several authors (Damsgaard & Lyytinen, 1998; Kurnia & Johnston, 2000b, 2000c) have argued for interorganisational systems innovation adoption to be understood as an ongoing process. These authors have also suggested that investigations need to be conducted at multiple levels of analysis and argued for the broadening of the level of analysis beyond the organisational unit to include its immediate supply chain environment in order to understand the influences of intra-industry dynamics on adoption. Processual approaches to understanding innovation adoption also naturally assume a broadening of the temporal unit of analysis beyond a single epoch to include historical developmental events that might have led to the current adoption scenario. Development of such models requires researchers to investigate the multidirectional interactions and emergent characteristics of a phenomenon; thus, the use of more in-depth interpretive approaches for data collection, such as longitudinal case studies, ensures that the changes over time can be captured (Van de Ven & Huber, 1990).

This chapter seeks to address the limited theories within literature that can be used to explain difficulties in IOSCM initiatives adoption by developing a process model that captures the complexity of intra-industry interactions in the course of adopting increasingly more sophisticated IOSCM initiatives. In addressing this question, our specific focus is on the collaborative interactions and arrangements among groups of organisations in achieving greater levels of supply chain integration. The main objective is, therefore, to describe and illustrate a model that provides a new perspective to explain the sources of complexity faced by groups of organisations in adopting highly integrative supply chain management initiatives. The model aims to address limited understanding about how prior IOSCM adoption experiences provide the necessary prerequisites to adopt subsequently more complex initiatives. The concepts of interorganisational relationship development in a supply chain context and processual theories of interorganisational systems adoption are integrated to provide understanding of this process.

The model presented was derived from extensive empirical research using longitudinal exploratory case studies conducted within the context of CPFR adoption among leading players in the Australian Grocery Retail Industry. Employing an inductive approach to theory building, broadly in the tradition of grounded theory, findings suggest that supply chain initiatives are difficult to implement because their embedded vision of integration inherently poses three sources of complexity: (1) organisations are required to integrate systems, policies, and processes across organisational boundaries; (2) new forms of interorganisational structures are required to sustain new routines and cross-organisational interactions; and (3) it is necessary to build closer more intimate interorganisational relationships such that trust and commitment are established and sensitive information can be exchanged. The research finds that the difficulties in achieving greater levels of supply chain integration is due to organisations having to also achieve lower levels of integration, interorganisational structures, and relationship intimacy. A main contribution of this chapter is to conceptualise the three sources of complexity and their relationships in a process model highlighting a normative path that necessarily has to be taken to achieve greater levels of supply chain sophistication and integration. The model also clarifies the preconditions that exist at each step of this path.

The following section presents the methodology and grounded analysis of a case study of IOSCM initiative adoption in the Australian Grocery Industry. The outcome of this section is a grounded conceptual model of IOSCM adoption. The next section then develops this model by introducing dimensions to each of the major constructs, the outcome being an exposition of the varying levels of complexity inherent in different types IOSCM initiatives. That section concludes by proposing a process model of IOSCM initiatives adoption that provides a new understanding of the complexity organisations face in adopting highly integrative IOSCM initiatives. In conclusion, we apply the new understanding proposed in our process model to answer the question that motivated this research, and discuss the limitations and significance of this model to theory and practice. Some directions for future research are also suggested.

Case Study of IOSCM Initiatives Adoption in the Australian Grocery Industry

Sources of Data

Case studies were conducted within a network consisting of one major grocery retailer and five large consumer packaged goods manufacturers to explore the adoption of the emerging supply chain management concept of CPFR in the context of the Australian Grocery Industry. Table 1 shows the profiles of the organisations involved. Company names were changed and their geographic location was withheld to ensure anonymity in our case discussion. We have included the approximate global annual sales and number of categories and brands to indicate the size of the company and its product portfolio, respectively. Also, the table indicates the status of CPFR adoption at the time the interviews were conducted.

Manufacturers selected are all global leaders in their product range and are relatively large organisations. This is to ensure that the influence of power due to organisational size differences between retailer and manufacturer is moder-

Table 1. Profile of case organisations and participants interviewed

Company Code	Company Type	Global Annual Sales (US$)	SKUs or No. of Categories/ No. of Brands	Interviewee participants	Status of CPFR adoption
R-A	Retailer	$25-30 b	60,000 SKUs	Supply Chain Manager, CPFR Program Manager	Piloted CPFR manually with M-B and M-C; Rolling out to more manufacturers; Scaling-up to more categories; Implementing necessary IOS for CPFR collaboration with retailer
M-B	Manufacturer	$40-45 b	4 / 31	Customer Supply Chain Managers, Supply Chain Analyst, Channel Manager	Piloted CPFR manually with R-A; Scaling-up to more categories; Implementing necessary IOS for CPFR collaboration with retailer
M-C	Manufacturer	$45-50 b	22 / 80-85	Logistics Manager, IT Manager	Piloted CPFR manually with R-A; Rolling out to more categories; Implementing necessary IOS for CPFR collaboration with retailer
M-D	Manufacturer	$35-40 b	5 / 140-150	Supply Chain Development Managers	Preliminary trials with manual CPFR several years ago; Have not proceeded to formally pilot with R-A; Currently, in the process of getting sign-off to implement necessary IT for CPFR process; Implementing advanced planning and forecasting systems
M-E	Manufacturer	$85-90 b	10 / 110-120	Customer Logistics Manager	In the process of getting sign-off on CPFR project from top level mgmt;
M-F	Manufacturer	$ 6-7 b	1 / 50-60	Customer Supply Chain Manager	In the process of getting sign-off on CPFR project from top level mgmt

ated. All the manufacturers have existing links with the major retailer, but variations exist in the individual relationships with the retailer and also in the extent of prior cooperative activities. Several of the manufacturers have piloted CPFR with the retailer, and although some have decided to scaleup the initiative, others are still in the process of negotiations and decision making. These varied characteristics, therefore, make these manufacturers ideal cases for comparison in our attempt to illustrate the inherent technological, organisational, interorganisational, and relationship requirements necessary for adoption of the emerging CPFR concept.

The case studies were generally exploratory in nature, with the aim being to investigate the barriers and requirements faced by retailer-supplier dyads in the process of adopting and implementing supply chain initiatives—in particular, the CPFR initiative across organisational boundaries. The unit of analysis includes the collaborative arrangements between pairs of organisations, focusing on their joint activities and the nature of their relationship. However, interrelated data at various other levels of analysis were also sought. This included the examination of the individual experiences of supply chain managers, project managers, users, consultants, as well as the wider institutional context in which these organisational relationships were embedded (Pettigrew, 1990; Van de Ven & Huber, 1990).

Primary data were obtained through semi-structured interviews (Flick, 1998) conducted with customer supply chain managers, program managers, and supply chain analysts involved in the CPFR Project at different points in the project over a period of three years. The researchers were involved from close to the very start of the project and therefore had access to the pre-adoption and also the emergent adoption experiences. Additional data was obtained through participant observations in formal and informal meetings. In many cases, several follow-up interviews and informal meetings, sometimes with representatives from both retailer and supplier organisations present, were carried out in person and via electronic mail with the participants. Recorded interviews were transcribed verbatim shortly after each visit. Where interviews were not tape-recorded, either because the participants requested it or because the investigators felt that recording would hamper the candidness of the participants, notes were taken and a summary of the interview e-mailed to the relevant participants for feedback and confirmation.

Secondary sources of data were essential in providing relevant information on existing related initiatives, such as ECR, and the adoption experiences of these initiatives in other parts of the world leading up to CPFR. These sources of data include available formal promotional documentation on the various initiatives, proprietary consulting reports, grocery industry reports, trade journals (e.g., newspapers and business magazines), organisational documents, and corporate presentations, as well as press releases from the corporate Web site and from newspapers. The most important of these documents included a 1998 publication by the Merchandising Issues Committee of the Voluntary Inter-Industry Commerce Standards (VICS) organisation, an industry standards body, of a seminal document establishing a set of voluntary guidelines that serves as a road map for distributors, suppliers, and third-party providers of software and logistics to guide implementation efforts within the industry. This document describes the CPFR vision and its envisioned processes, along with suggestions about the technological and organisational changes necessary to operationalise the vision. Several companion documents have also been published by another industry body called Efficient Consumer Response Associations (ECRA). These documents supplement the original guidelines with adoption experiences in other parts of the world, namely, Europe, United States, Canada, and Australia. Also, they provide information on how earlier ECR initiatives are related to CPFR. The VICS organisation also maintains a Web portal dedicated to providing information about advances in the CPFR initiative (www.cpfr.org).

Data Collection and Analysis

Data collection, analysis, and theory building followed an approach that is qualitative (Eisenhardt, 1998; Miles & Huberman, 1994) and inductive, broadly in the tradition of grounded theory (Strauss & Corbin, 1998). The features central to the grounded theory approach include the method of constant comparative analysis, theoretical sampling, theoretical sensitivity, and theoretical saturation (Glaser & Strauss, 1967). This involved a process of textual analysis of transcripts and field notes for the identification of major categories and their causal relationships, using coding techniques of open coding, axial coding, and selective coding (Sarker, Lau, & Sahay, 2001; Strauss & Corbin, 1998). Broadly speaking, open coding helps analysts break down large chunks of data (e.g., an interview transcript) into more manageable parts (e.g., lines, paragraphs, or phrases) that can then be examined closely, compared, and differentiated, and developed into groups of categories in terms of their properties and dimensions. Through axial coding and selective coding, data is reassembled through statements about the nature of relationships among various categories. These statements are also commonly referred to as "hypotheses" or "propositions." Such techniques have been argued to produce rich descriptions of the phenomenon under study and theoretical models that are largely grounded in the data (Orlikowski, 1993; Sarker et al., 2001).

In our research, analysis of data collected from the first pair of organisations provided a set of preliminary concepts. Subsequent case sites were selected with the aim of refining emerging categories, providing the necessary data to inductively strengthen weak connections between categories, and deductively testing relationships that have already emerged (Sarker et al., 2001; Strauss & Corbin, 1998). Due to the long period of time immersed and interacting with the data, and by drawing on the literature and personal experiences, a theoretical sensitivity necessary to distinguish and assign meaning to what is significant in the data was developed. The constant self-reflection required throughout the theory-building process ensured that the researchers were conscious about not imposing a theoretical bias that does not actually correspond to the patterns in the data.

In the following section, an overview of the CPFR vision and aim is provided, followed by a discussion of the grounded analysis. The section concludes by presenting a conceptual model of IOSCM adoption that has emerged from the grounded analysis.

Establishing a Grounded Conceptual Model of IOSCM Initiatives Adoption

In this section, we describe and present the outcome of our grounded analysis on the case studies to establish a conceptual model of IOSCM adoption. We found evidence in our case studies to suggest that organisations and their partners faced three sources of complexity that complicate the adoption of an IOSCM initiative called CPFR. The following subsections will briefly describe the CPFR vision and then proceed to describe the sources of complexity and their relationships with each other.

Overview of the CPFR Vision and Aim

Established in 1997, collaborative planning, forecasting, and replenishment (CPFR) was developed to address the limitations that were present in earlier grocery industry initiatives in handling consumer demand variability. CPFR has been seen within industry as evolving from efficient consumer response (ECR) and, more specifically, from continuous replenishment program (CRP) (Barratt & Oliveira, 2000). CPFR envisions two or more organisations exchanging market information to jointly develop a market-specific business plan that describes the product to be sold, the way it will be merchandised and promoted in the marketplace, and the time frame in which this happens (VICS, 1998). Developed as a nine-step guideline for retailers and their manufacturers, the primary activities in CPFR suggest that organisations jointly develop a front-end agreement on terms of collaboration, targets, and performance metrics, create a joint business plan, jointly develop a sales forecast, identify exceptions in the forecast, jointly address and resolve the exceptions, generate an order forecast, and execute the order. By sharing promotion schedules, point-of-sales data and inventory data, a single shared forecast of consumer demand, at the detail of a product, is developed. The retailer and manufacturer can then base all internal planning activities relating to that particular product on the shared demand forecast. CPFR aims to increase visibility of demand information along the supply chain and leverage a collaboration-oriented relationship between retailer and manufacturer, to increase the flexibility of the supply chain in planning for and responding to volatile demand. Some benefits of CPFR include: more predictable order cycles, reduced costs, more receiver-friendly loads, smaller shipments, daily download of information, more frequent deliveries, accuracy of information, shorter production runs, improved timeliness of information, increased customer service, fewer out-of-stock scenarios, faster inventory turns, availability of real-time information, reduced overstocks, and reduced inventory holding (Barratt & Oliveira, 2001).

Major Sources of Complexity in the Adoption of CPFR

Analysis of the case studies suggests that efforts to achieve certain interorganisational requirements create potential barriers in the process of implementing and routinising the CPFR processes among participating organisations. Drawing on instances from our case study data, this subsection identifies three sets of requirements for adoption, which had been identified as major recurring themes from the open and axial coding process in our grounded analysis, and discusses how they pose sources of complexity that could potentially create difficulties in adoption efforts.

Synchronising Processes, Policies and Systems Across Organisational Boundaries

Joint planning and forecasting process: The major focus of the CPFR vision is how organisations can jointly develop a business plan and a single shared forecast of consumer demand for short- to medium- term business activities, in particular, product promotions. Where planning and forecasting processes were previously independent processes, within the CPFR vision, retailer and manufacturer organisations leverage their unique vantage points of the marketplace to jointly improve demand planning capabilities through an iterative exchange of data and business intelligence, with the outcome being the development of a single shared forecast of consumer demand at the point of sale. This shared-demand plan then becomes the foundation for all internal planning activities and is integrated with complementary processes, such as new product or market development, production, and replenishment, related to that particular product between the retailer and the manufacturer. This implies a shift in corporate thinking and supply chain focus from market area-specific planning to customer-specific planning (VICS, 1998). Such a shift in corporate thinking was reflected in our manufacturer cases, whereby all were in the process of restructuring their organisations to be more "customer facing." Boundary spanning positions were established and these were directly accountable to the retailer as a human interface between the manufacturer and retailer organisation.

Policies: The nature of the planning and forecasting process in CPFR has implications for existing inventory replenishment policies and retailer and manufacturer order cycles (VICS, 1998). Where traditional practices emphasize maintaining safety stock to cope with demand uncertainty and retailer's short-order cycles, CPFR takes a more consumer demand-driven approach by leveraging the availability of POS-level and store-level inventory data that is now shared between the retailer and the manufacturer to develop a single shared forecast and demand plan. Earlier practices generated forecasts using historical data and aggregated data of stock levels at warehouse and main distribution centres. Also, by extending the retailer's short order cycles to align with a manufacturer's longer order cycles, manufacturers can use the demand plan generated to manage production as a "make-to-order" process for particular products. This level of synchronisation between retailer and manufacturer organisations works to reduce uncertainty and, therefore, reduces the need to hold safety stock and to improve customer service.

Performance metrics: Due to the interorganisational nature of CPFR activities, a shared set of process-oriented performance metrics need to be established between partnering organisations to monitor the ongoing performance of the CPFR processes and to identify any areas for further improvement. Traditional forms of performance metrics tend to be focused on functional-level performance, such as sales forecast accuracy, stock levels, profitability, inventory turns, or quantity of orders or goods sold. Such metrics encourage competitive behaviour among internal departments and across organisations resulting in detrimental practices, such as forward buying practices. In CPFR, the focus is on the performance of the interorganisational collaboration. Process-oriented metrics monitor order forecast accuracy, order fill rates to each inventory holding location, cycle time for each process activity and process cost. These metrics are coupled with result-oriented measures such as out-of-stocks on the store shelf, inventory turns consolidated across the supply chain, total supply chain cycle time, sales forecast accuracy, profitability, and return on assets (VICS, 1998). However, the outcomes of these metrics cannot be generated without partnering organisations sharing the necessary process and results measurement information on a regular basis. Some organisations, such as M-B, are in the process of developing supply chain scorecards with trading partners to more proactively monitor partnership performance.

Interorganisational information systems: Although the retailer in our case study had piloted CPFR manually with manufacturers M-B and M-C separately, this was very time consuming and resource intensive. To scale up CPFR across more categories and with more trading partners, it is necessary to implement various interorganisational systems that will enable real-time information that is of a standardised format to be electronically exchanged and collaborated on between organisations. The implementation of collaboration platforms, for example, electronic hubs that provide collaboration applications services, such as WorldWideRetailExchange (www.worldwideretailexchange.org) and GlobalNetXChange (www.gnx.com), facilitate automation of certain parts of the CPFR process, especially the exceptions reporting process that is a major part of joint planning and forecasting. The promotional schedules and sales forecast data that feed into these collaboration hubs are derived from promotions planning, forecasting systems, and inventory management systems in the individual organisations. Therefore, these organisational-level information systems also need to be able to interface with the collaboration engine on the collaboration hub such that close to real-time consumer information can be uploaded and processed data can be downloaded for analysis.

In our case studies, we found that the lack of forecasting systems at manufacturer M-D created some delays in implementing CPFR with the retailer. This is because the retailer also did not have a forecasting system in place during the time of the interview. In CPFR, at least one organisation in the partnership is required to have a forecasting system installed to generate the necessary sales and order forecasts. On the other hand, manufacturers M-B and M-C could scale up the CPFR process because they have forecasting systems in place in their own companies that are able to generate promotional sales forecasts from information provided to them by the retailer. In another example, R-A and M-B had to upgrade their existing EDI capabilities in a separate project to share electronic versions of order information with each other.

Changing Existing Structures to Support Routine Cross-Organisational Interactions

The process synchronisation described above has implications for existing organisational structures and the structures between organisations. Where traditionally organisations tended to interact only on a transactional basis, CPFR requires extensive routine interactions between teams of people working on processes that span organisational boundaries. This means that organisations need to find new ways of dividing work that occurs beyond traditional functional and organisational boundaries. Retailers and suppliers might need to shift resources that are focused on functional alignments to process-driven roles (VICS, 1998). This is because the focus on activities has changed from "reactive expediting" or problem solving to one oriented towards synchronised planning. Potential impacts of this are that: the distribution and customer service staff may need to be moved into demand and supply planning roles; forecast analysts may have to shift from marketing to customer-specific support; and merchandising, marketing, and sales staff roles will focus more on consumer-oriented micro-marketing and micro-merchandising (VICS, 1998). Therefore, existing roles might be altered and new roles might need to be created to support new areas of responsibility.

For example, the need to align trading partner goals and medium-term strategies is a routine responsibility in the CPFR vision. In order to address and manage ongoing issues of establishing trust and interdependent processes in a traditionally competitive grocery industry environment, the importance of boundary-spanning, executive-level roles that are positioned to manage the relationship between their parent organisations with a specific customer has been recognised in many adopting organisations. In our case studies, some of supply chain managers interviewed had their roles created literally less than three months, and some less than a year, prior to the interview. Their new roles, which are focused predominantly on customer supply chain management and development, were created as part of a restructuring exercise in their organisations to become more "customer facing." Their objectives are to represent their parent organization, to maintain a communication channel between their organisation and the customer organisation for which they are accountable, and to identify new ways to work together with the customer to improve customer service levels. This includes finding ways to facilitate integration of trading partner processes with their own company. These executives also normally manage a team of people that is routinely involved at the tactical and operational levels as the interface between customer and suppliers. Roles such as supply chain analysts and co-managed inventory (CMI) personnel are involved daily in the development of sales forecasts and order forecasts with the merchandising team at the retailer. Organisations who do not have these appropriate boundary-spanning resources at the tactical and operational levels to support the level of routine analysis and interaction necessary, as in the case of manufacturer M-C and M-F, were found to face some barriers in adopting CPFR.

Generally in CPFR, in the retail environment, supply/demand decisions may involve a team composed of a merchandise or category manager working with inventory management, store operations, and logistics. In the supply environment, this responsibility may fall on a team that includes customer service, sales, marketing, distribution, and production. Also, IT teams from both organisations may have to be involved in managing the information technology integration activities and to work with the other process teams to interface interorganisational systems. The success of CPFR depends on the accountability of individuals or teams within these roles and their capabilities to make and carry out customer-specific decisions in a dynamic environment (VICS, 1998).

The new roles and responsibilities also have implications for staffing. Staff in these positions must have a broad understanding of supply chain functions embedded in their interorganisational CPFR process. A lack of understanding indicates the need for training or, alternatively, hiring staff with the appropriate knowledge of supply and demand processes.

Building Closer, More Intimate Trading Partner Relationships

The level of synchronisation and interactivity in the CPFR vision, as described in the earlier paragraphs, cannot be achieved and sustained in an adversarial relationship environment. The CPFR processes require trading partners to share and exchange sensitive business information and resources and commit willingly to work together in reengineering existing business activities towards reducing total supply chain costs and, ultimately, improving consumer satisfaction at the stores. This has implications for the way companies perceive their role in relation to their customers and suppliers along a supply chain. CPFR requires a shift in corporate and supply chain focus from market area-specific planning to customer-specific planning. A shift in perspective from "win-lose" attitudes and interactions to a "win-win" mentality is necessary to achieve optimal supply chain performance and foster the necessary environment for interorganisational synchronisation. In the CPFR approach, companies have to look across supply chain processes to see where their information or competencies can help the value chain and thus benefit the end consumer and associated supply chain partners. This outlook acknowledges that nobody wins until the consumer is satisfied (VICS, 1998).

However, such attitudes can only be fostered if there is sufficient trust and belief among trading partners that the other(s) also shares a similar value system that is based on trust and sustained commitment to equitably share any risks and returns on supply chain improvement activities in the long run. This deep understanding and alignment of trading partner business "mindset" requires organisations to openly engage and frequently communicate with their trading partners. In our case studies, all of the manufacturers we interviewed have been invited to participate in the retailer's long-term planning activities. However, only M-B and M-C have actively engaged with the retailer to initiate and implement a pilot project to trial CPFR manually. Other manufacturers have engaged the retailer in earlier initiatives to foster greater collaboration between their organisations. Several manufacturers who have placed CMI personnel in the retailer organisation, as described above, have done so to foster greater interaction and collaboration through the tactical level with the retailer.

A Grounded Conceptual Model of IOSCM Adoption

As part of the selective coding process, where the aim was to explicate the "story" from the data, the data was revisited to confirm that the themes we have identified were indeed the major categories and to examine how they are related to each other. The outcome of this final step in the grounded analysis points to a model consisting of an abstraction of the major categories, which are also called constructs, and their causal relationships to each other (Strauss & Corbin, 1998).

Major Constructs

Three major constructs were identified: supply chain (SC) integration, interorganisational structure, and relationship intimacy. SC integration is used to describe the *pattern of interdependence* between the information systems, policies, and activities of a given firm on those of another firm. Interorganisational structure describes the *pattern of interactivity* between organisational units required to support interdependent activities. According to Kumar and Van Dissel (1996), "structure" in interorganisational relationships can be understood as "the ways in which interorganisational work is divided among the partnering organisations by assigning specific roles to them" (p. 284). Relationship intimacy describes the *pattern of mutuality* in the relationships between participating organisation. Extending the concept of intimacy, within psychology (Moss & Schwebel, 1993), from between individuals to between organisations, intimacy can be determined by the pattern of mutuality—or exchange/sharing—in business understanding and commitment, and reciprocity in the exchange of informational and physical resources, risks, and rewards between participating organisations.

Causal Relationships

It was also observed from our grounded analysis that these three major constructs are interrelated. The pattern of interdependence required in integrating planning, forecasting, and replenishment systems, policies, and activities across organisational boundaries requires an interorganisational structure to be formulated that takes into account the pattern of interactivity among the various

Figure 1. Conceptual model of IOSCM initiatives adoption

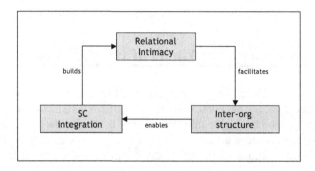

functions in the retailer organisation and in the manufacturer organisations. Such structures are necessary to sustain the routine collaboration necessary in the development of joint promotional plans and sales forecasts. The pattern of interdependence and interactivity in the CPFR processes requires organisations to alter their perception of the role they play in the larger context of their supply chain. As described above, a business attitude that is focused on mutuality and reciprocity is necessary to facilitate the sharing of information and complementary resources in sustaining the routine interactions and to reduce risks of potential opportunistic behaviour that might be associated with the level of interdependence envisioned. The figure below illustrates the major constructs and their causal relationships in our conceptual model of IOSCM initiatives adoption.

In summary, the model depicts three interrelated primary requirements in IOSCM initiatives adoption: relational intimacy, interorganisational structure, and supply chain integration. These requirements interrelate to suggest a basic process of IOSCM initiatives adoption. The model proposes that relationship intimacy facilitates the necessary interorganisational structures that have to be in place to enable the nature of supply chain integration envisioned in particular IOSCM initiatives. The final relationship in the model between SC integration and relationship intimacy suggests that the process of adoption does not end when integration efforts are achieved. This causal relationship proposes that the outcome of SC integration activities might serve to build greater relationship intimacy between existing partners due to the learning that is inherently embedded in the processes to becoming more integrated with another, for example, the learning that takes place in having to understand a partner's business processes during a process-mapping exercise.

The resulting circularity of the causal links discovered from the case study has interesting implications. It suggests that the completion of one cycle of the process prepares the partnership for future integration activities that might be more complex and more ambitious. On the other hand, this implies that one cycle has to be completed before the next cycle can happen. This, as we shall argue in the next section, can prove to be a much more difficult task than previously identified in the literature. We use the conceptual model established here as a basis for developing a theory to explain the difficulties organisations face in adopting increasingly complex IOSCM initiatives.

Developing a Process Model of IOSCM Initiatives Adoption

It has been argued within the innovations literature that to develop realistic theories of adoption, it is necessary to differentiate between types of innovations because not all innovations are alike and it is important to understand how underlying characteristics and requirements can influence their adoption (Damanpour, 1987). We find that the different types of interorganisational supply chain management initiatives that have been identified within the literature tend to have increasing demands in the way organisations integrate with each other (Brockman & Morgan, 1999; Ham, Johnston, & Riemer, 2003). Based on the understanding acquired in our grounded conceptual model, this implies that increasing demands on interorganisational structures and relationship intimacy could potentially be elicited as well. Therefore, in this section, we develop further the implication of the circular causality in the grounded conceptual model that was derived from the case studies by providing dimensions for each of the constructs in the grounded model. In terms of grounded theory development, these dimensions gives specification to the major constructs and provide the necessary range and variation to the theory being developed here (Strauss & Corbin, 1998). However, the dimensions established for each construct and the dependencies between dimensions of different constructs have been mainly derived from analysis of the supply chain management and IOS adoption literature and deductive arguments, based on our conceptual model. Armed with an understanding of the properties of major constructs, their dimensions, and their causal relationships, we conclude this section by proposing a process model of adoption that illustrates a path of increasing sophistication in IOSCM initiatives adoption.

Table 2. Different patterns and degrees of interdependence

Integrated Systems	Integrated Distribution	Integrated Business Planning	Integrated Business Development
Standardisation of communication protocols between computer-based information systems across organisations	Standardisation of materials handling procedures and synchronisation of distribution policies and processes across organisations	Standardisation and synchronisation of short to medium term planning activities, including promotions forecasting, across organisations	Standardisation and synchronisation of medium to long term planning and business development activities, including product design and development, across organisations

Supply Chain Integration:
Patterns and Degrees of Interdependence

As defined in the previous section, SC integration is used to describe the pattern of interdependence between the information systems, policies, and activities of a given firm on those of another firm. We propose that four different degrees of interdependence can be used to define and distinguish different underlying visions of integration in IOSCM initiatives. The degree of interdependence ranges from *integrated systems* to *integrated distribution, integrated business planning,* and *integrated business development*. IOSCM initiatives with underlying visions of integrated business development are the most difficult to achieve because this level of integration assumes the highest degree of interorganisational interdependence, including interdependence at the level of integrated systems, integrated distribution, and integrated business planning, to achieve full potential benefits. Table 2 describes the patterns of interdependence for each level of supply chain integration. The degree of interdependence increases from left to right.

Integrated Systems

Graham and Hardaker (2000) point out that one of the key mechanisms to facilitate supply chain integration is dynamic information. They emphasise that information flows affect an organisation's ability to synchronise operations that add value and innovativeness. To facilitate the flow of dynamic information across organisational boundaries, organisations must first be able to communicate data that is machine-processable at both ends. The vision of integrated systems involves the standardisation of data and communication protocols between computer-based information systems. Some examples of initiatives that introduce the concept of integrated systems include electronic data interchange (EDI) (Fearon & Philip, 1999), universal product numbering, EAN barcoding, and automatic identification (Johnston, 1999). More recent examples of interorganisational information systems, such as data synchronisation hubs, collaboration hubs (Sparks & Wagner, 2003), and electronic marketplaces, are also included here.

Integrated Distribution

The ability to efficiently replenish to meet consumer demands is an important strategy to ensure the right goods can be delivered at the right time to the right places in the right quantities (ECR, 1995). Initiatives that envision the integration of distribution activities focus on improving coordination in the flow of materials from upstream to downstream through the standardisation and synchronisation of materials handling procedures and distribution policies and processes across organisations. Such activities require the integration of inventory replenishment information systems with the distribution and logistics information systems. The outcomes of such integration reduce costs associated with product handling and non-value adding processes along the supply chain. Some examples of initiatives that envision the integration of materials handling and logistics operations include just-in-time delivery and those parts of ECR that focus on streamlining distribution processes such as continuous replenishment (ECR, 1995), including cross-docking and direct-store-delivery.

Integrated Business Planning

Typically, replenishment activities are complicated by changing patterns of consumer demands, promotional marketing activities, and certain strategic buying practices, such as the practice of forward buying (Kurnia & Johnston, 2000a). These initiatives require organisations to integrate previously disparate and disconnected materials planning, forecasting, and replenishment cycles between organisations into a single, unified, replenishment loop that, ideally, extends the whole supply chain from raw material supplier to point of sale (KSA, 1993; VICS, 1998). By standardising and synchronising the way organisations and their trading partners coordinate short- to medium-term planning and forecasting activities for replenishment, it is possible to reduce the need to hold high levels of buffer stock to cope with demand and supply uncertainties. This process is facilitated by interorganisational systems that enable the sharing and processing of real-time information (e.g., consumer demand at the point of sale) between trading partners so that a jointly developed demand plan and order forecast can be communicated to the appropriate integrated replenishment, distribution, and production systems (McCarthy & Golicic, 2002; Raghunathan, 1999; VICS, 1998). This improves the overall effectiveness of short- to medium-term business activities such as product promotions and new product introductions. Examples of initiatives that envision integration of business planning activities include collaborative planning, forecasting, and replenishment (CPFR). Earlier less advanced initiatives include vendor managed inventory (VMI) (Kurnia & Johnston, 2000b) and joint or co-managed inventory (JMI) (VICS, 1998).

Integrated Business Development

Integration at the business development level aims to create a sustainable advantage by leveraging the unique perspectives and intelligence that retailer and manufacturer organisations have of the marketplace to respond to emerging consumer demands and competitive pressures. These initiatives envision trading partners integrating medium- to long-term business planning and product development systems, policies, and processes to facilitate joint research and design, production, marketing, and distribution of whole new categories of products (ECR-Europe, 1997; Parker, 2000). Interorganisational systems that facilitate interactive joint planning and product development activities are necessary. Also, these systems have to be integrated with the materials planning, forecasting, and distribution systems and activities to streamline the sourcing, production, and replenishment of new products. Some visible examples of integrated business development activities include the integrated design and development of new products, such as those in the textile, automotive, aerospace, and, to some extent, in the grocery industries (ECR-Europe, 1997).

Interorganisational Structures:
Patterns and Degrees of Interactivity

As defined in the previous section, interorganisational (IO) structure describes the pattern of interactivity (i.e., the way work is divided and performed between organisational units) required to support envisioned integrated activities on a routine basis. We propose that different degrees of interdependence require

Table 3. Subsystem functions that form the basis for inter-organisational structures

Infrastructure	Operations	Tactical	Strategic
IT function, Sales order entry function, Purchase order entry function	Despatch and receiving functions at warehouses and distribution centres, distribution and logistics functions	Materials planning functions, Promotions planning function, Order and sales forecasting functions, replenishment functions	Strategic business development and planning functions, Product development function

different degrees of interorganisational interactivity ranging from between *infrastructure* to between *operations, tactical,* and *strategic* organisational subsystems. Building from the previous section, integrated business development activities would require the highest degrees of interactivity such that the strategic, tactical, operations, and the infrastructure subsystems of partnering organisations are envisioned to be interacting on a routine basis. Table 3 summarises the different functions within the organisational subsystems that form the basis of interorganisational structures necessary to support routine interdependent activities.

Integrated Information Systems: Infrastructural Interactivity

The routine maintenance of integrated information systems across organisational boundaries is predominantly the responsibility of the infrastructure organisational subsystem. Therefore, resources and services of a team of IT personnel, potentially belonging to a team that includes members from participating organisations, are required to maintain the routine upgrading of appropriate messaging standards, transportation protocols, security protocols, controls, and interfaces between business applications to allow the output and input of messages in conformity with the chosen standard (Cannon, 1993). Although existing workflows are not necessarily impacted, data entry and processing roles have to now support the new standardised approach to constructing a sales or purchase order using the adopted data and form standards, such as in the case of EDI (Brousseau, 1994).

Integrated Distribution Activities: Operations Interactivity

Integration of distribution activities has routine implications for the operations organisational subsystem, which includes distribution and logistics functions. A streamlined distribution and logistics process requires partnering organisations to coordinate routine interactions between the logistics functions at the factories, warehouses, distribution centres, and stores, to dispatch, receive, and sort smaller batches of goods (for example, in the case of Continuous Replenishment Program [Kurnia & Johnston, 2000b]) that have standardised identification labels, such as EAN or UPC barcodes, and that are packed in standardised shipping containers, pallets or cases, depending on agrees upon specifications (ECR-C, 1995). The routine interactivity across the infrastructure levels is also required to maintain, upgrade, and monitor the ongoing quality of interfaces between the inventory, replenishment, and distribution systems, across organisational boundaries and with other internal organisational systems.

Integrated Business Planning Activities: Tactical Interactivity

A shift from traditionally isolated decision-making structures in planning, forecasting, and replenishment to one that is much more inclusive and interactive with trading partners is part of integrating business planning activities. On a routine basis, extensive interactivity is required between the tactical subsystems of organisations, including materials planning functions, promotions planning function, order and sales forecasting functions, and the replenishment function across partnering organisations. New roles might be necessary to support boundary-spanning activities that were never required previously. For example, in our CPFR case studies, some manufacturers have co-managed inventory (CMI) personnel spending several days within the retailer organisation and several days back at their parent organisation. Their main role is to manage inventory for that particular retail account and involves interacting with the buyers and re-buyers in the merchandising department at the retailer to collaborate on a promotional sales forecast, monitor changes in promotional activities, and to create an order forecast based on the agreed-upon sales forecast. Such roles are also relationship-building roles that encourage increased interactivity across higher levels of the organisations.

Integrated Business Development Activities: Strategic Interactivity

Initiatives envisioning the integration of business development activities along the supply chain require partnering organisations to routinely interact to maintain alignment in corporate mindsets and strategic objectives, and to ensure continued involvement in the business and product development planning processes. To achieve the former, that is, aligning corporate mindsets, it is critical to establish patterns of interactivity that aim to build and develop closer interorganisational relationships between supply chain partners everyday (Hutt, Stafford, Walker, & Reingen, 2000; Volkoff, Chan, & Newson, 1999). For example, as described in our case studies earlier, executive-level roles such as supply chain managers and customer development managers have been developed in various manufacturers to act as communication conduits between the retailer and their parent organisations. As they are normally engaged in long-term business planning activities with the retailer, managers in these roles relay strategic-level information between the trading partners, and are also responsible for engaging with the retailer in finding new ways to improve customer-service levels and new growth opportunities. Such roles lay the foundation for other routine activities at the strategic subsystems of the organisations, such as joint product design and development. In joint product design and development, routine interactivity is required between the strategic business planning functions and the product research, design, and development functions, across organisations. Other lower level organisational subsystems are also involved to operationalise the strategic and tactical plans developed. Extensive degrees of interactivity between partnering organisations allows these organisations to virtually operate as a single entity in making decisions and planning strategic moves.

Relationship Intimacy: Patterns and Degrees of Mutuality

As defined above, relationship intimacy describes the pattern of mutuality in interorganisational relationships. Intimacy generally indicates the level of closeness between organisations and can be determined by the level of shared business understanding, the extent of commitment (short-term or long-term), and the reciprocity in the exchange of informational and physical resources, risks, and rewards between participating organisations (Granovetter, 1973; Hausman, 2001; Moss & Schwebel, 1993). The significance of varying extents of relationship intimacy in different types of interorganisational relationships have been recognised within the business literature (Golicic, Foggin, & Mentzer, 2003; Himmelman, 2001; Lambert, Emmelhainz, & Gardner, 1996). These authors argue that variations in relationship magnitude—or intimacy—needs to be recognised as a distinct component of relationship structure and is antecedent to the type of relationship organisations pursue. Thus, adapting the terminologies and definitions suggested by Himmelman (1996), we propose that four degrees of mutuality ranging from *networking to coordination, cooperation,* and

Table 4. Different patterns and degrees of mutuality

Networking	Coordination	Cooperation	Collaboration
Exchanging information for mutual benefit	Exchanging information for mutual benefit and altering activities for a common purpose	Exchanging information, altering activities, and sharing resources for mutual benefit and to achieve a common purpose	Exchanging information, altering activities, sharing resources, and a willingness to enhance the capacity of another for mutual benefit and a common purpose

collaboration can be used to describe the sort of relationship intimacy required to facilitate the kind of interactivity and interdependence envisioned in various IOSCM initiatives. Again, building from previous sections, the degree of interdependence and interactivity at the level of integrated business development would require organisations to engage in highly mutual collaborative relationships, which subsume other patterns of mutuality. Table 4 summarises the descriptions of the different patterns and degrees of mutuality.

Networking is defined as exchanging information for mutual benefit; it does not require much ongoing commitment, reciprocity, or shared business understanding between organisations. There is little to no change in organisational structures, policies, or processes required at this degree of mutuality. Such a degree of mutuality is necessary to facilitate the minimal interorganisational structures required to support the low degrees of interdependence envisioned in integrating information systems across organisational boundaries (Holmes & Srivastava, 1999).

Coordination is defined as exchanging information for mutual benefit and altering activities for a common purpose; it requires some ongoing commitment, some reciprocity in sharing and exchanging information, but requires limited shared business understanding across organisations. There are some changes in organisational structures, policies, and processes that might be required to achieve some common objectives. Such a degree of mutuality is necessary to facilitate the extent of interorganisational structures required to support the medium degrees of interdependence envisioned in integrating distribution activities.

Table 5. Varying requirements of different IOSCM initiatives

Inter-organisational Supply Chain Management (IOSCM) initiatives	Level of supply chain integration	Extent of Inter-organisational structures	Degree of Relationship Intimacy
Market-based transactions; little or no synchronisation between transactional partners	*None*	*Transactional, market-mediated structures*	*Arm's-length*
Implementing industry standards. Initiatives includes EDI, EAN Barcoding, Standardisation of Pallet and Carton sizes	Integrated systems	Infrastructure	Networking
Quick Response (QR), Just-in-time (JIT), Vendor management inventory (VMI), Continuous Replenishment Program (CRP), Category Management	Integrated systems, Integrated Replenishment	Infrastructure, Operations	Coordination
Basic Collaborative Planning, Forecasting, and Replenishment (CPFR), Efficient Consumer Response (ECR)	Integrated systems, Integrated Replenishment, Integrated Planning	Infrastructure, Operations, Tactical	Cooperation
Advanced Collaborative Planning, Forecasting and Replenishment (CPFR), Collaborative Product Design and Development	Integrated systems, Integrated Replenishment, Integrated Planning, Integrated Business Development	Infrastructure, Operations, Tactical, Strategic	Collaboration

Cooperation is defined as exchanging information, altering activities, and sharing resources for mutual benefit and a common purpose; it requires significant amounts of ongoing commitment, high levels of reciprocity, and significant sharing of business understanding between organisations. There is the potential for quite significant levels of changes to organisational structure, policies, and processes required to achieve the expanded benefits of mutual action. Such a degree of mutuality is necessary to facilitate the significant extent of interorganisational structures required to support the high degrees of interdependence envisioned in integrating business planning activities.

Collaboration is defined as exchanging information, altering activities, sharing resources, and a willingness to enhance the capacity of another for mutual benefit and a common purpose; it requires the most considerable amount of ongoing commitment, high levels of reciprocity, and extensive sharing of business between organisations. By transforming existing organisational structures, policies, and processes to align with those of another organisation, collaboration can produce significant benefits from mutual action and virtual integration. Such degrees of mutuality are necessary to facilitate the extensive interorganisational structures required to support the very high degree of interdependence envisioned in integrating business development activities.

Increasing Levels of Complexity in IOSCM Initiatives

Thus far in the chapter, we have identified dimensions for each construct and argued that different patterns of interorganisational interdependence require different supporting patterns of interactivity, which, in turn, require different supporting patterns of mutuality. Some evidence was provided from the strategic management, SCM, and IOS adoption bodies of literature, and from our case study data to support this major proposition.

In summary, we can deduce from the arguments above that different IOSCM initiatives vary in complexity because different visions of interdependence require different degrees of interactivity, which, in turn, requires different degrees of mutuality. Additionally, it should also be noted that the degrees of interdependence, interactivity, and mutuality form Guttman-type scales of cumulatively increasing complexity (Kumar & Van Dissel, 1996; Gulati & Gargiulo, 1999). In other words, integration of business development activities subsumes integration of systems, integration of distribution activities, and integration of business planning activities. This is similar for interorganisational structures, where strategic interactivity subsumes patterns of interactivity across infrastructure, operations, and tactical subsystems. Finally, with relationship intimacy, a collaboration relationship subsumes the patterns of mutuality that exists in networking, coordination, and cooperation relationships.

Therefore, we can also infer that highly integrative IOSCM initiatives, which envision extensive interorganisational interdependence, are much more complex and difficult to adopt because of the need for more extensive interorganisational structures and higher degrees of relationship intimacy to achieve and sustain the level of supply chain integration envisioned. Table 2 shows how different IOSCM initiatives require, in a cumulative fashion, the different patterns of interdependence, interactivity and intimacy. The variation in complexity between IOSCM initiatives with low levels of integration to high levels of integration can be observed. Based on these arguments, the next section proposes a process model of IOSCM initiatives adoption.

A Process Model of IOSCM Initiatives Adoption

In the previous sections, we have presented a conceptual model of three sets of requirements in adopting IOSCM initiatives—supply chain integration, inter-organisational structures and relationship intimacy—that are dependent on each other in a circular causality, where each facilitates and enables the other in a cyclic fashion. We then argued that each construct has dimensions, and these provide a more detailed understanding about how different IOSCM initiatives have inherently different sets of requirements that potentially differentiate them in terms of adoption complexity. Hence, if one cycle around our conceptual model prepares organisations to adopt a particular degree of supply chain integration, then to get to higher degrees, organisations would have to go around a few times to build the necessary levels of intimacy and interorganisational structures to support higher degrees of interdependence. This implies that there is essentially a cyclic path to achieving greater levels of supply chain integration, which further implies that a path also exists in the adoption of IOSCM initiatives with increasingly more integrative vision.

Figure 2 presents a process model that illustrates the cyclic path to accomplishing greater levels of relationship intimacy (**R**), interorganisational structures (**O**), and SC integration (**I**). R-1 to R-4 represent increasing degrees of mutuality from networking to coordination, cooperation, and collaboration. O-1 to O-4 represent the degrees of interorganisational interactivity from infrastructure, operations, tactical to strategic. I-1 to I-4 represent the degrees of supply chain integration envisioned from integrated systems to integrated replenishment, integrated planning, and integrated business development.

Figure 2. Process model of IOSCM initiatives adoption

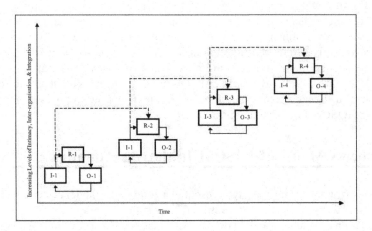

The process model in Figure 2 proposes that to achieve higher levels of integration, organisations and their trading partners must first achieve lower levels of integration. Through a process of learning and adaptation that is inherent in integration activities with another organisation (Doz, 1996; Holmqvist, 1999; Majchrzak, Rice, Malhotra, King, & Ba, 2000), groups of organisations can leverage established patterns of interdependence, interorganisational structures, and relationship intimacy in earlier integration activities to progress to the next level of integration (Li & Williams, 1999). However, as we move along the path, the complexity of each cycle increases due to increasingly demanding process requirements, which mean more demanding technological and physical infra-structures, and it becomes more difficult to complete.

Conclusion

The understanding of interorganisational innovation adoption as an emergent process has gained importance over the years. As the nature of business practice becomes ever more interorganisational, studies focusing on understanding how organisations jointly adopt a range of strategies and innovations to develop closer, more interdependent relationships with other organisations to gain complementary resources and achieve benefits from mutual action are in limited supply. Also, current research on interorganisational innovation adoption generally perceives innovation to be a static end-state and its adoption follows a simple linear path. There is little emphasis on understanding the context and emerging nature of change that can occur in innovations and in adopting these innovations over time. Such studies require the researchers to move away from quantitative, factor-based approaches to embrace a more qualitative and longitudinal, process-based perspective on innovation adoption and relationship development.

Therefore, one of the main contributions of this chapter is the reporting of the first longitudinal case study of CPFR adoption within an Australian grocery industry context. Another contribution is the application of an adapted grounded theory method of analysis to build a process model of IOSCM initiatives adoption. The model developed here highlights three sets of requirements—supply chain integration, interorganisational structures, and relationship intimacy—and their circular causal relationships to each other. We also argue that different degrees of integration are necessary for different IOSCM initiatives, with demands for interdependence, interactivity, and mutuality increasing cumulatively in IOSCM initiatives envisioning higher levels of integration. We then argue theoretically that there is essentially a necessary path in the progression towards adopting initiatives that are increasingly more integrative and complex. The need to tread this path explains why so few companies have progressed to the highest levels of integration.

Our theory of path dependence in the adoption of IOSCM initiatives has important implications for supply chain management practice. The path has implications for a planned incremental change approach to supply chain reengineering. Organisations that have jumped straight into the deep end of implementing highly integrative initiatives without the necessary foundation for a collaborative relationship, including the necessary interorganisational structure and integration strategy, will find themselves at risk of failure or face difficulties and delays in adoption and implementation. The model can be used as a conceptual tool to assess the current interorganisational situation and to help organisations and their trading partners plan out a possible path towards achieving greater supply chain integration.

Furthermore, the process model presented in this chapter is an important contribution to contemporary research on supply chain management because it is the first model to expand the temporal horizon of analysis to consider the process of progressing from one level of supply chain integration to the next. While previous models have only focused on understanding complexities of adopting one innovation at a particular snapshot of time, our model draws on the experiences of adoption studies across multiple related innovations to elicit the dynamics of supply chain integration over time. We bring together knowledge from multiple disciplines, including theories from sociology, psychology, behavioural studies, relationship marketing, strategic alliance management, supply chain management, and interorganisational systems adoption, to gain a rich understanding of both the technical and the deeply social aspects of supply chain integration.

There are, however, some limitations to this study. Although the grounded conceptual model developed is relatively abstracted and could potentially be generalisable across other industry contexts, the path model is slightly less generalisable due to the amount of industry-specific detail that it carries. However, it is not impossible to customise each of the main constructs in the conceptual model with industry-specific information to develop industry-specific IOSCM initiative adoption path models. We find that the model in this chapter is generally suitable for customer-supplier type relationships within manufacturing environments, for example, the auto industry and textile industry where the main components of supply chain management share similar traits and requirements for joint systems, distribution, planning, and business development. Therefore, this study encourages further research to apply the process understanding it established to study the development and adoption of interorganisational innovations in other industry contexts, for example, in the service industry or pharmaceutical industry, in order to evaluate, refine, and generalise further the theoretical arguments presented in this study.

In conclusion, the process model illustrates just how difficult it would be to try to take the fast path from an arm's length to a highly integrative relationship. The model emphasises that there are no shortcuts in developing an environment of trust and mutuality across organisational boundaries. The reality of the process of achieving true collaboration and virtual integration is that it requires time, cumulative learning, and long-term commitment.

Acknowledgments

The chapter has benefited from the constructive suggestions of the editors and anonymous reviewers. The authors would also like to thank Howard Evans, Peter Eng, and Miles MacFarlane for their continuous support and collaboration throughout the ongoing research process. And to all participants, we appreciate your willingness to share openly your experiences, without which this research would not have been possible.

References

Barratt, M., & Oliveira, A. (2000). *Exploring the enablers and inhibitors of collaborative planning, forecasting and replenishment (CPFR)* (Working Paper). Cranfield, UK: Cranfield Centre for Logistics and Transportation, Cranfield School of Management.

Barratt, M., & Oliveira, A. (2001). Exploring the experiences of collaborative planning initiatives. *International Journal of Physical Distribution & Logistics, 31*(4), 266-289.

Borchert, S. (2002). Implementation hurdles of ECR partnerships—The German food sector as an ECR case study. *International Journal of Retail & Distribution Management, 30*(7), 354-360.

Brockman, B. K., & Morgan, R. M. (1999). The evolution of managerial innovations in distribution: What prospects for ECR? *International Journal of Retail & Distribution Management, 27*(10), 397-408.

Brousseau, E. (1994). EDI and inter-firm relationships: Toward a standardization of coordination processes? *Information Economics and Policy, 6*(3-4), 319-347.

Cannon, E. (1993). *EDI guide: A step-by-step approach.* New York: Van Nostrand Reinhold.

Clark, T. H. (1994). *Linking the grocery channel: Technological innovation, organizational transformation, and channel performance.* Unpublished doctor of business administration thesis, Harvard University, Cambridge, MA.

Clark, T. H., & Stoddard, D. B. (1996). Interorganizational business process redesign: Merging technological and process innovation. *Journal of Management Information Systems, 13*(2), 9-28.

Crum, C., & Palmatier, G. E. (2004). Demand collaboration: What's holding us back? *Supply Chain Management Review, 8*(1), 54-62.

Damanpour, F. (1987). The adoption of technological, administrative, and ancillary innovations: Impact of organizational factors. *Journal of Management, 13*(4), 675.

Damsgaard, J., & Lyytinen, K. (1998). Contours of diffusion of electronic data interchange in Finland: Overcoming technological barriers and collaborating to make it happen. *Journal of Strategic Information Systems, 7*, 275-297.

Doz, Y. L. (1996). The evolution of cooperation in strategic alliances: Initial conditions or learning processes? *Strategic Management Journal, 17* (Special Issue: Evolutionary Perspectives on Strategy), 55-83.

ECR-C. (1995). *Road map to continuous replenishment*. Efficient consumer response, Canada. Retrieved from http://www.erc.ca

ECR-Europe. (1997). *Category management: Best practices report*. Efficient consumer response, Europe. Retrieved from http://www.ecrnet.org/

Eisenhardt, K. M. (1998). Building theories from case study research. *Academy of Management Review, 14*(4), 534-550.

Fearon, C., & Philip, G. (1999). An empirical study of the use of EDI in supermarket chains using a new conceptual framework. *Journal of Information Technology, 14*(1), 3.

Flick, U. (1998). *An introduction to qualitative research*. London: Sage Publications Ltd.

Forger, G. R. (2002). The problem with collaboration. *Supply Chain Management Review, 6*(2), S56-57.

Frankel, R., Goldsby, T. J., & Whipple, J. M. (2002). Grocery industry collaboration in the wake of ECR. *The International Journal of Logistics Management, 13*(1), 57-72.

Glaser, B. G., & Strauss, A. L. (1967). *The discovery of grounded theory: Strategies for qualitative research*. Chicago: Aldine.

Golicic, S. L., Foggin, J. H., & Mentzer, J. T. (2003). Relationship magnitude and its role in interorganizational relationship structure. *Journal of Business Logistics, 24*(1), 57-75.

Graham, G., & Hardaker, G. (2000). Supply-chain management across the Internet. *International Journal of Physical Distribution & Logistics Management, 30*(3/4), 286-295.

Granovetter, M. (1973). The strength of weak ties. *American Journal of Sociology, 78*(6), 1360-1380.

Gulati, R., & Gargiulo, M. (1999). Where do interorganizational networks come from? *American Journal of Sociology*, 177-231.

Ham, Y. N., Johnston, R. B., & Riemer, K. (2003, December 9-12). *Complexity and commitment in supply chain management initiatives*. Paper presented at the 3rd International Conference on E-business, Singapore.

Hausman, A. (2001). Variations in relationship strength and its impact on performance and satisfaction in business relationships. *Journal of Business & Industrial Marketing, 16*(7), 600-616.

Himmelman, A. T. (1996). Part two: Rationales and contexts for collaboration. In C. Huxham (Ed.), *Creating collaborative advantage* (pp. 19-43). London: Sage Publications Ltd.

Himmelman, A. T. (2001). On coalitions and the transformation of power relations: collaborative betterment and collaborative empowerment. *American Journal of Community Psychology, 29*(2), 277-284.

Holmes, T. L., & Srivastava, R. (1999). Effects of relationalism and readiness on EDI collaboration outcomes. *The Journal of Business & Industrial Marketing, 14*(5/6), 390-402.

Holmqvist, M. (1999). Learning in imaginary organizations: Creating interorganizational knowledge. *Journal of Organizational Change Management, 12*(5), 419-438.

Horvath, L. (2001). Collaboration: The key to value creation in supply chain management. *Supply Chain Management: An International Journal, 6*(5), 205-207.

Humphreys, P. K., Lai, M. K., & Sculli, D. (2001). An inter-organizational information system for supply chain management. *International Journal of Production Economics, 70,* 245-255.

Hutt, M. D., Stafford, E. R., Walker, B. A., & Reingen, P. H. (2000, Winter). Case study: Defining the social network of a strategic alliance. *Sloan Management Review,* 51-62.

Johnston, H. R., & Vitale, M. R. (1988, June). Creating competitive advantage with interorganizational information systems. *MIS Quarterly,* 153-165.

Johnston, R. B. (1999). Principles of digitally mediated replenishment of goods: Electronic commerce and supply chain reform. In S. M. Rahman & M. Raisinghani (Eds.), *Electronic commerce: Opportunities and challenges* (pp. 41-64). Hershey, PA: Idea Group Publishing.

KSA. (1993). *Efficient consumer response: Enhancing consumer value in the grocery industry* (Industry research). Washington, DC: Food Marketing Institute.

Kumar, K., & Van Dissel, H. G. (1996, September). Sustainable collaboration: Managing conflict and cooperation in interorganizational systems. *MIS Quarterly,* 279-300.

Kurnia, S., & Johnston, R. B. (2000a, July 2-5). *The issue of mutuality in ECR adoption: A case study.* Paper presented at the *8th European Conference on Information Systems,* Vienna, Austria.

Kurnia, S., & Johnston, R. B. (2000b). The need for a processual view of inter-organizational systems adoption. *Journal of Strategic Information Systems, 9,* 295-319.

Kurnia, S., & Johnston, R. B. (2000c, June 19-21). *Understanding the adoption of ECR: A broader perspective.* Paper presented at the 13th International Bled Electronic Commerce Conference, Bled, Slovenia.

Kurnia, S., & Johnston, R. B. (2001). Adoption of efficient consumer response: The issue of mutuality. *Supply Chain Management: An International Journal, 6*(5), 230-241.

Kurnia, S., & Johnston, R. B. (2002, January 7-10). *A review of approaches to EC-enabled IOS adoption studies.* Paper presented at the 35th Hawaii International Conference on System Science, Big Island.

Lambert, D., Emmelhainz, P., & Gardner, J. (1996). Classifying relationships. *Marketing Management, 5*(2), 28-29.

Li, F., & Williams, H. (1999, January 5-8). *New collaboration between firms: The role of interorganizational systems.* Paper presented at the 32nd Hawaii International Conference on System Sciences, Hawaii.

Majchrzak, A., Rice, R. E., Malhotra, A., King, N., & Ba, S. (2000). Technology adaptation: The case of a computer-supported inter-organizational virtual team. *MIS Quarterly, 24*(4), 569-600.

McCarthy, T. M., & Golicic, S. L. (2002). Implementing collaborative forecasting to improve supply chain performance. *International Journal of Physical Distribution & Logistics Management, 32*(6), 431-455.

Miles, M. B., & Huberman, A. M. (1994). *Qualitative data analysis.* Newbury Park, CA: Sage Publications.

Moss, B. F., & Schwebel, A. I. (1993). Defining Intimacy in Romantic Relationships. *Family Relations, 42*(1), 31-37.

Neuman, J., & Samuels, C. (1996). Supply chain integration: Vision or reality? *Supply Chain Management, 1*(2), 7-10.

Orlikowski, W. J. (1993). CASE tools as organizational change: Investigating incremental and radical changes in systems development. *MIS Quarterly, 17*(3), 309-340.

Parker, H. (2000). Interfirm collaboration and the new product development process. *Industrial Management & Data Systems, 100*(6), 266-260.

Pettigrew, A. M. (1990). Longitudinal field research on change: Theory and practice. *Organization Science, 1*(3), 267-292.

Raghunathan, S. (1999). Interorganizational collaborative forecasting and replenishment systems and supply chain implications. *Decision Sciences, 30*(4), 1053-1071.

Ramanathan, S., & Rose, J. (2003, January 6-9). *Rationalizing, probing, understanding: The evolution of the inter-organizational systems adoption field.* Paper presented at the 36th Hawaii International Conference on System Sciences.

Sarker, S., Lau, F., & Sahay, S. (2001). Using an adapted grounded theory approach for inductive theory building about virtual team development. *Database for Advances in Information Systems, 32*(1), 38-56.

Sparks, L., & Wagner, B. A. (2003). Retail exchanges: A research agenda. *Supply Chain Management, 8*(1), 17-27.

Strauss, A. L., & Corbin, J. (1998). *Basics of qualitative research: Techniques and procedures for developing grounded theory*. London: SAGE Publications.

Svensson, G. (2002). A firm's driving force to implement and incorporate a business philosophy into its current business activities: The case of ECR. *European Business Review, 14*(1), 20-30.

Van de Ven, A. H., & Huber, G. P. (1990). Longitudinal field research methods for studying processes of organizational change. *Organization Science, 1*(3), 213-219.

VICS. (1998). *Collaborative planning, forecasting and replenishment voluntary guidelines: Voluntary Interindustry Commerce Standards*. Retrieved from http://www.vics.org

Volkoff, O., Chan, Y. E., & Newson, E. F. P. (1999). Leading the development and implementation of collaborative interorganizational systems. *Information & Management, 35*(2), 63-76.

Chapter IX

Factors Affecting Inter-Organisational Information Management Systems Used to Coordinate Australian Food Processor Chains

Christine Storer, Curtin University of Technology, Australia

Abstract

It is agreed that good communication systems between organisations increase customer satisfaction and relationship behaviour and are important issues in chain collaboration and competition. However, less is known about the details of how information is used to manage relationships and coordinate customers and suppliers in chains. In earlier stages of the research, a dynamic model of interorganisational information management systems (IOIMS) and relationships was developed. This chapter presents an evaluation of this model based on a survey of Australian food processors and a green life industry case study and an evaluation of a revised version of this model. It was found that a strategic-oriented IOIMS were positively associated with IOIMS satisfaction that was, in turn, positively associated with perceived current outcomes (satisfaction with performance, perceived responsiveness, and strength of relationship trust). However, (attitudinal) commitment to develop long-term customer/supplier relationships was not significantly associated with the IOIMS, IOIMS satisfaction, or current outcomes. Results were moderated by the nature of the business environment—power/dependency, experience, and market uncertainty. These findings are discussed along with implications for management and suggestions for future research.

Introduction

There is support for the idea that suppliers' efforts to assist communication increases customer satisfaction, which, in turn, improves competitive advantage (Anderson & Narus, 1990; Keith, Jackson, & Crosby, 1990; Leuthesser & Kohli, 1995; Mohr, Fisher, & Nevin, 1996; Mohr & Nevin, 1990; Mohr & Sohi, 1995; Uzzi, 1997). However, very little research has been conducted on how information is exchanged through chains of collaborating organisations to achieve this (chain—a vertical sequence of at least three organisations, that is, focal firm, a customer, and a supplier). Of interest were studies that detailed how, when, and why information was exchanged to manage customers and suppliers and to increase competitive advantage. The empirical studies found that quantitatively collected data from chains of organisations did not look in detail at how information systems worked (Clare, Shadbolt, & Reid, 2002; Hardman, Darroch, & Ortmann, 2002; Lehtinen & Torkko, 2004; Matanda & Schroder, 2002; Spekman, Kamauff, & Myhr, 1998). Most published chain research has been based on case studies where generalisation of results can be problematic (e.g., Champion & Fearne, 2002; Chatfield & Bjorn-Andersen, 1997; Kola, Latvala, & Vertanen, 2002; Kornieliussen & Grønhaug, 2003; Lefebve, Cassivi, Lefebve, Léger, & Hadaya, 2003; Lindgreen, Trienekens, & Vellinga, 2004; Pratt, 2002; Simons, Francis, Bourlakis, & Fearne, 2003; Trienekens, 1999; Van der Vorst, 2000; Van Dorp, 2004). Even in the more substantial research into two organisations in a dyad (e.g., focal firm and customer), none were found that looked at information systems used to manage the relationship (e.g., Anderson & Weitz, 1992; Anderson & Narus, 1990; Clare et al., 2002; Claro, Zylbersztajn,

& Omta, 2004; Ellram, 1995; Forker, Ruch, & Hershauer, 1999; Ganesan, 1994; Heather, 2001; Karalis & Vlachos, 2004; Kornieliussen & Grønhaug, 2003; Lindgreen, 2001; McDermott, Lovatt, & Koslow, 2004; Miller, 2002; Sethuraman, Anderson, & Narus, 1988; Sparling & van Duren, 2002; Sweeney & Webb, 2002; Vlosky, Wilson, & Vlosky, 1997; Wilson & Vlosky, 1998). Some of these dyadic studies looked at the effect of implementing information communication technologies (Amanor-Boadu, Trienekens, & Willems, 2002; Wilson & Vlosky, 1998), obtaining information from buyers and suppliers (Claro et al., 2004), and information exchanged with buyers and sellers (Heather, 2001; Langton, 2004; Wilson, 2000). More dyadic studies were found that empirically evaluated associations between communication or information exchange and some of the factors that affect them, as indicated qualitatively in the chain studies. For example, the association with outcomes (Anderson & Narus, 1990), commitment (Anderson & Weitz, 1992), collaboration (Karalis & Vlachos, 2004; Siemieniuch, Waddell, & Sinclair, 1999), flexibility and joint action (Claro et al., 2004), trust, and dependence (Ganesan, 1994). Other dyadic studies looked more generally at the role of information and communication as a partnership success factor (Ellram, 1995), reason for entering an alliance (Sparling & van Duren, 2002), or a determinant of partnership advantage (Sethuraman et al., 1988).

In conclusion, there would seem to be a gap in the research on the role of information systems to manage interorganisational relationships in chains of organisations. This chapter presents a review of early phases of the research where a model was developed to explain how managerial and executive interorganisational information systems with customers and suppliers work. Suggestions are made to revise the model. Then, a detailed examination of a revised model is made to explain how the nature of interorganisational information systems were associated with the type of the relationships with customers and suppliers. In addition, the revised model was examined to look at the effect of the business environment. The implications for management and further research are explored.

Background Literature

Research Phase 1: Model Development

When the research was started in 1998, little research was found that explained how managerial and executive interorganisational information systems with customers and suppliers worked. As a result, a grounded theory approach was taken in the first phase of the research using literature reviews, informal in-depth interviews with experts internationally, and a case study network of five organisations involved in several Australian food chains ("netchain," Lazzarini, Chaddad, & Cook, 2001). In examining the vegetable, meat, and food netchains, a proposed model of interorganisational information management systems (IOIMS) was developed to explain how information was exchanged by organisations in a chain to manage customers and suppliers and to build the competitive advantage of the chain (Figure 1). The interorganizational information management system (IOIMS) has been defined as the information exchanged by organizations in a chain for the purpose of managing the relationships of the organisations in the chain. The IOIMS encompasses all aspects of the process of information exchange including the information communication technology tools used. While the IOIMS model has been described in more detail previously (Storer, 2001), the following describes key aspects relevant to this chapter.

In the model, it was suggested that (attitudinal) commitment to developing long-term customer/supplier relationships (future expected outcomes) would be

Figure 1. Model of inter-organisational information management systems in a chain context

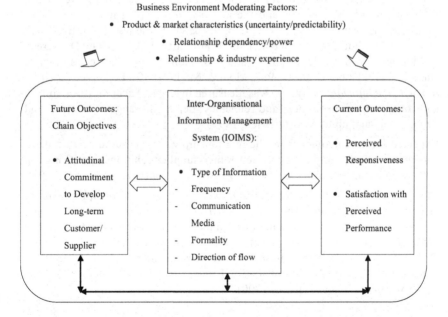

related to the nature of the interorganisational information management system (IOIMS) adopted in the chain which, in turn, would be related to perceived responsiveness, performance, and trust in the chain (current outcomes) (as suggested by Benedict & Margeridis, 1999; Bowersox & Closs, 1996; Stank, Emmelhainz, & Daugherty, 1996; Vijayasarathy & Robey, 1997).

Further, it was argued that the proposed associations in the model would be moderated by environmental factors such as product and market uncertainty, relationship dependency and power, and experience in the relationship and in the industry (as suggested by Ancona & Caldwell, 1992; Bensaou, 1999; Spekman et al., 1998).

To operationalise the model, the interorganisational information management system (IOIMS) was examined by asking participants about the *types of information* exchanged to manage the relationship (Mohr & Nevin, 1990). Specifically, participants were asked whether information was exchanged about performance feedback, problem resolution, new product developments, forecast supply and demand, and opportunities and threats. Based on the netchain case study, performance feedback was expanded to specifically cover product quality, on-time delivery, completeness of orders, flexibility to change orders, and invoice accuracy. For each type of information shared, details were sought regarding: the *frequency* it was shared on average in a year (absolute frequency) and adequacy of frequency, namely, was information exchanged as often as necessary (relative frequency); *communication media* used (phone, e-mail, EDI, etc.); the *direction* of flow (upstream, downstream, both directions); the *formality* of the process; and the key *people involved* in the exchanges (Anderson, Lodish, & Weitz, 1987; Bensaou & Venkatraman, 1995; Borgen & Ohren, 1999; Choo, 1996; Daft & Lengel, 1986; Daft & Lengel, 1996; Dansereau & Markham, 1987; Ellinger, Daugherty, & Plair, 1999; Farace, Monge, & Russell, 1977; Huber & Daft, 1987; Mohr & Nevin, 1990). Perceived *satisfaction with the information system* was measured in terms of accuracy, reliability, and completeness; usefulness and relevancy; depth and range of content; and being timely and up to date (O'Brien, 1999).

Expected future outcomes from the relationship were measured as attitudinal *commitment* to develop long-term customer-supplier relationships (Ganesan, 1994; Gundlach, Achrol, & Mentzer, 1995; Sharma, Young, & Wilkinson, 2001).

Current outcomes from the relationship were measured as perceptions of the customer/supplier's *performance, responsiveness and willingness to change,* and *trustworthiness* compared to others in the industry (Anderson et al., 1987; Anderson, Håkansson, & Johanson, 1994; Bensaou & Venkatraman, 1995; Doney & Cannon, 1997; Ganesan, 1994; Gassenheimer & Scandura, 1993; Gundlach et al., 1995; Kohli, Jaworski, & Kumar, 1993; Kumar, Stern, & Achrol, 1992; Womack, Jones, & Roos, 1990).

Moderating variables included uncertainty, dependency/power, and experience. *Uncertainty* was measured as: predictability of demand, production yield, quality, and quantity of supply; market competition; and changing consumer preferences (Ganesan, 1994; Kumar et al., 1992). Relationship *dependency and power* were measured as: availability of alternative customers and suppliers; importance to each other; influence; and ease of replacement (Ganesan, 1994; Kumar et al., 1992). *Experience* was measured in terms of the number of years working in the industry and with the organisation (Doney & Cannon, 1997; Ganesan, 1994).

To explore the dynamics of the interaction over time, the information satisfaction and relationship outcome variables were measured in terms of the current situation and how it had changed over the last five years. Comments were recorded about respondent's perceptions about the reasons for change. As a result of explanations about reasons given for change, two additional questions were added about perceptions of customers/suppliers *initiating new ideas* to improve the category/business or improving the organisation's *knowledge* of the industry.

Research Phase 2: Model Testing & Revision

The model has been tested in earlier phases of the research on a case study of nursery retail stores and wholesale nursery "green life" suppliers, as well as a survey of Australian food processors (see Storer, 2003; Storer, Soutar, Trienekens,

Figure 2. Comparison of Green Life case study (G) and Food Processor survey (F)

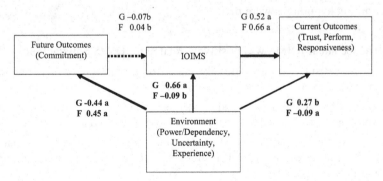

Structural Model Path Coefficients (a=significant; b=not significant)

Beulens, & Quaddus, 2004). These studies support some aspects of the model. The structural coefficient comparisons between the two studies have been shown in Figure 2, with G indicating the green life case study results and F the food processor survey results (a=significant, b=not significant).

Like the food processor survey, the green life case study found that the environment had a significant influence on expected future outcomes and that the IOIMS had a significant influence on perceived current outcomes. Both studies found that expected future outcomes were not significantly associated with the IOIMS. In addition, both studies found no significant (green life case study) or meaningful (food processor survey—coefficient 0.09 < 0.20) association between the environment and perceived current outcomes.

There was a difference between the two studies. Unlike the food processor survey, the green life case study found that the business environment had a significant association with the IOIMS. The difference may be due to the green life case study's small sample size (64) or the way the environment and IOIMS constructs were measured in each study.

In evaluating these results, it was concluded that the IOIMS construct was measuring two separate constructs. The social IOIMS subsystem measured satisfaction with the IOIMS and the technical IOIMS subsystem measured the processes used to manage information exchange. It was proposed that the nature of the technical IOIMS may be modelled as an antecedent to IOIMS satisfaction (social). In addition, it was proposed that the model may better show the moderating effects of the environment variables if the constructs were separated (power/dependency, uncertainty, and experience). Finally, with the commitment not being related to the IOIMS and current relationship outcomes (trust, performance, and responsiveness) as hypothesised, it was proposed that commitment results from the current relationship outcomes rather than being an antecedent. For structural equation modelling purposes, the model with these revisions has been shown in Figure 3.

The resulting hypotheses were that:

1. The technical IOIMS was positively related to IOIMS Satisfaction

2. IOIMS Satisfaction was positively related to Current Outcomes (perceived trust, performance, and responsiveness)

3. Current Outcomes (perceived trust, performance, and responsiveness) were positively related to Future Outcomes (attitudinal commitment)

4. The Environment (power/dependency, uncertainty, and experience) has a moderating effect on the IOIMS, IOIMS Satisfaction, Current Outcomes and Future Outcomes

Figure 3. Revised model of inter-organisational information management systems in a chain context

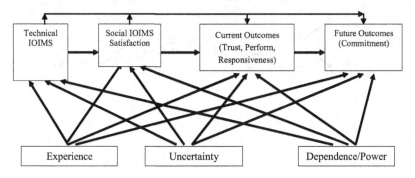

The purpose of this chapter is to test the revised model and provide insights into factors affecting information systems used to coordinate customers and suppliers in chains of organisations.

Methodology

This section outlines the methodology used to conduct the Australian food processor survey that has been used to test the revised model. Support for the research was received from a large Australian retail chain that provided introductions to major food processors in a number of food processing industries. A total of 45 food categories were covered and included dry, fresh, chilled, and frozen food products based on meat, dairy, fruit, vegetable, and cereals in the form of ingredients, as well as snacks, meals and drinks. Food processors varied from large multinational and national organisations to smaller regional suppliers.

In-depth interviews of 111 Australian food processor purchasing managers, sales/marketing managers, and general managers/owners in 42 companies were conducted between April and December 2002. Where possible, interviews were conducted face-to-face with phone interviews and self-completion used as a last resort (e-mailed or faxed back). Interviewees were asked to discuss two suppliers or two customers that were significant in terms of volume, value, or strategic intent (Figure 4). Some interviewees answered questions for several

Figure 4. Customers and suppliers discussed by food processors

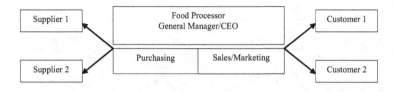

different product categories, for example, milk, cheese, and small goods. Relationships with 176 suppliers and 297 customers were discussed in the interviews.

Structural equation modelling (causal modelling) was used to test the revised model (Figure 3) so that there could be an analysis of the model's multiple constructs and their multiple indicators at the same time (Al-Gahtanl, 2001). Structural equation modelling allows the simultaneous assessment of the reliability and validity of the measures of the theoretical constructs and an estimation of the relationship among these constructs (Barclay, Higgins, & Thompson, 1995). As the model in this research was in the early stages of development there was high complexity and low theoretical information. As a result, analysis using partial least squares (PLS) graph was used instead of LISREL because LISREL required a stronger theoretical base (Barclay et al., 1995; Igbaria, Guimaraes, & Davis, 1995). PLS facilitates the testing of the psychometric properties of the scales used to measure a variable and estimating the parameters of a structural model—that is, the magnitude and direction of the relationships among the model variables (Igbaria et al., 1995). PLS does not depend on having multivariate normally distributed data (distribution free) and can be used with small samples (Igbaria et al., 1995).

Following procedures set out by Barclay et al. (1995), Igbaria et al. (1995), and Al-Gahtanl (2001), the model was analysed and interpreted in two stages: (1) the assessment of the reliability and validity of the measurement model; and (2) the assessment of the structural model. In stage one, the *measurement model* was assessed by examining: (a) individual item reliability; (b) internal consistency; and (c) discriminant validity. *Individual item reliability* was assessed by examining the loadings, or simple correlations, of the measures with their respective construct, which indicated the amount of variance in a measure due to the construct rather than error. Using Hair, Anderson, Tatham, and Black's

(1998) guidelines, loadings greater than 0.30 were considered "significant"; loadings greater than 0.40 were considered "more important"; and loadings 0.50 or greater were considered to be "very significant." *Internal consistency* was assessed using the measure of reliability developed by Fornell and Larcker (1981). Nunnally and Bernstein (1994) suggested that a value of 0.70 provides "modest" reliability applicable in early stages of research. *Discriminant validity* refers to the degree to which items differentiate between constructs or measure different concepts. The average variance shared between a construct and its measures (variance extracted or VE) should be greater than the variance shared between the construct and other constructs in the model (i.e., the squared correlation between two constructs). Another test of discriminant validity is that no item should load more highly on another construct (cross loading) than it does on the construct it intends to measure. Modest cross loadings (>0.50) may provide doubt about what construct is being captured by such items (Barclay et al., 1995). Following revision of the model based on the assessment of the reliability and validity of the measurement model, the second stage of the analysis was to assess the *structural model*. The structural model was assessed by examining the statistical significance of the loadings and of the path coefficients based on a jackknife analysis (which allows the testing of significance of parameter estimates from data not assumed to be multivariate normal). Following Chin (1998), standardized path coefficients should be at least 0.2 and ideally greater than 0.3 in order to be considered meaningful.

Before the model could be tested using PLS, the non-metric variables needed to be translated into metric scales where possible. Categorical "yes/no" responses were given about the ten types of information exchanged (IOIMS subsystems) and, for each of these ten subsystems, the formality, direction of information flow, and communication media used (face-to-face and phone being the most common). SIMCA correspondence analysis (Greenacre, 1986) was used to identify if there were any patterns or structures in the sets of nominal IOIMS variables. Correspondence analysis is an exploratory data analysis technique for multivariate categorical data (Hoffman & Franke, 1986). It is a form of principal component analysis (Soutar & McNeil, 1997). The correspondence analysis was run using increasing numbers of dimensions until the "quality" for each variable exceeded 500, thereby suggesting "the results obtained provide a good representation of that aspect of the data" (Soutar & McNeil, 1997, p. 34). A description of each dimension was made based on the variables that had the highest "absolute contributions" to that dimension.

Correspondence
Analysis Results

The correspondence analysis of the type of information, one-way communication, and two-way communication resulted in no patterns, as there was insufficient variation in responses. This indicated that these categorical responses
could not be translated into metric scales, and these variables were not able to
be used in subsequent model testing. Correspondence analysis for face-to-face
IOIMS, phone IOIMS, and formal and informal IOIMS each resulted in four
dimension solutions to produce the highest quality scores. Each of these
dimensions was used in the model testing. A description of the dimensions—
based on the variables with the highest absolute contributions—follows.

Face-to-Face IOIMS

In looking at the face-to-face IOIMS dimensions, more face-to-face oriented
communication systems made up the second and fourth dimensions. The second
face-to-face dimension related to the more frequent "negotiations" of prices and
resolving problems. The fourth face-to-face dimension related to less frequent
"strategic" systems for product quality, new product development, and opportunities and threats. The first face-to-face dimension was related to the more
frequently discussed "logistics" issues of timeliness of deliveries, order completeness, and flexibility to accept order changes where little face-to-face
communication was used. The third face-to-face dimension was related to less
frequently discussed invoice accuracy and forecast information systems where
less face-to-face communication was used.

Phone IOIMS

For the phone IOIMS, the first phone dimension was related to phone systems
used for "reliability" issues such as product quality, timeliness of deliveries,
invoice accuracy, and, to some extent, order completeness. The fourth phone
dimension was for phone "order reliability" systems to discuss the completeness
of orders and forecasts for future orders. The second and third phone dimensions
related to phone systems to develop the relationship. The second phone

dimension related to "relationship depth" where the phone was used to discuss the flexibility to accept order changes and negotiate prices, as well as future opportunities and threats. The third phone dimension related to "relationship future" where the phone was used to resolve problems, negotiate prices, and discuss new product development.

Formal IOIMS

With the formal IOIMS, formal dimension one related to not having formal systems for "current issues" such as resolving problems, product quality, timeliness of deliveries, order completeness, and flexibility to accept order changes. The second formal dimension was related to not having formal systems for discussion of "future" oriented issues of new product development, opportunities, and threats. The third formal dimension related to not having "formal forecasting" communication systems. The fourth formal dimension related to not having "formal price negotiation" communication systems.

Informal IOIMS

Informal dimension one related to not having informal systems for "tactical and operational" communication of problems, order completeness, and invoice accuracy. The second informal dimension related to not having "informal service quality" systems to discuss timeliness of deliveries, flexibility to change orders, and new product developments. The third informal dimension related to not having "informal strategic operational" systems to discuss problems, product quality, and forecasts. The fourth informal dimension related to not having "informal price negotiation" systems.

Partial Least Squares Graph (PLS) Analysis Results

The structural equation modelling program, partial least squares graph (PLS), was used to test the revised model. First, the results of assessing the measurement model have been presented, followed by the assessment of the structural model.

Measurement Model Assessment

In assessing the measurement model in terms of *internal item reliability,* all perceptions of the IOIMS satisfaction, current and future relationship outcomes construct variable loadings were over 0.5 and considered "very significant." The results for the IOIMS and environment (dependency, uncertainty, and experience) constructs were varied with one dependency variable, two experience variables, three uncertainty, and 31 IOIMS variables dropped with loadings of less than 0.30. In the case of the technical IOIMS construct, all that remained was a measure of "strategic" IOIMS where there were more face-to-face negotiations and more people involved in exchanging information about forecasts, new product developments, opportunities, and threats. Therefore, the technical IOIMS has been referred to as the "strategic IOIMS" in subsequent discussion.

After the model had been revised with the exclusion of low-loading variables, *internal consistency* of the constructs was assessed. The reliability of all reflective constructs exceeded 0.70 (strategic IOIMS was a formative measure so composite reliability was not applicable) and, therefore, they were considered satisfactory (Table 1).

Initial assessment of *discriminant validity* was satisfactory, as all variables loaded more strongly on their constructs than on other constructs. Of concern was that several variables had modest cross loadings greater than 0.50 on other constructs (IOIMS satisfaction and current relationship outcomes). However, given that these variables had high loadings with their constructs, they were retained in the model.

Table 1. Construct internal consistency

Construct	Number of Variables	Composite Reliability (reflective constructs)
Power/Dependence	4	0.83
Uncertainty	3	0.73
Experience	3	0.81
Technical 'Strategic' IOIMS	5	Not Applicable
IOIMS Satisfaction	10	0.93
Current Outcome	6	0.86
Commitment	2	0.80

Table 2. Construct discriminant validity correlations between constructs and variance extracted

Construct	Variance Explained (VE)	Correlations Between Constructs *						
		Power/ Depend	Uncert.	Exper.	Strategic IOIMS	IOIMS Satis	Current Outcome	Commit.
Dependence	0.55	**0.74**						
Uncertainty	**0.48**	0.04	**0.69**					
Experience	0.60	-0.01	0.05	**0.77**				
Tech. 'Strategic' IOIMS	N/A	-0.37	-0.25	-0.19	N/A			
IOIMS Satisfaction	0.57	0.01	-0.21	0.01	0.38	**0.75**		
Current Outcome	0.52	-0.04	-0.21	0.05	0.34	0.66	**0.72**	
Commitment	0.68	0.28	0.24	0.01	-0.05	0.02	0.11	**0.82**

* Diagonal elements in the 'correlations of constructs' matrix are the square roots of variance explained. For adequate discriminant validity, bold text diagonal elements should be greater than the corresponding off-diagonal elements.

Finally, in terms of discriminant validity, all constructs had a variance extracted (VE—variance shared between a construct and its measures) above the suggested 0.50 criteria (Table 2) except for the uncertainty construct, which was close at 0.48. However, all of the constructs had correlations less than the squares of the construct average variance extracted (bold diagonal in Table 2). In other words, the constructs correlated more highly with their indicator variables than with other constructs in the model.

In summary, the constructs in the measurement model were assessed as being adequate in terms of individual item reliability, internal consistency, and discriminant validity, although there might be discriminant validity problems with the environment construct. The next step was to assess the structural model propositions.

Structural Model Assessment

In *analysing the structural model,* Figure 5 shows the significant path coefficients (labelled a) between the constructs and the multiple R^2 below each construct. The effect of the current relationship outcomes construct (trust, performance, and responsiveness) on future relationship outcomes (commit-

Figure 5. Structural model—Path coefficients & R^2 (a=significant; b=not significant)

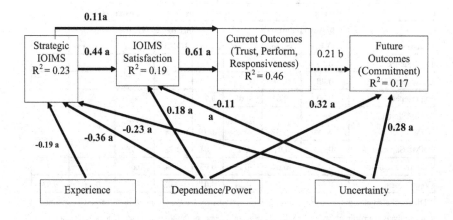

Table 3. Structural model path coefficients and multiple R^2

	Strategic Inter-Org Info Management System	Inter-Org Info Management System Satisfaction	Current Outcome	Future Outcome Commit
Dependency	**-0.36 a**	**0.18 a**	-0.01 b	**0.32 a**
Uncertainty	**-0.23 a**	**-0.11 a**	-0.06 b	**0.28 a**
Experience	**-0.19 a**	0.10 b	0.07 b	0.01 b
Strategic Inter-Org Info Manage System	**0.44 a**	**0.11 a**	0.11 b	
Inter-Org Info Manage System Satisfaction		**0.61 a**	-0.11 b	
Current Relationship Outcomes				0.21 b
Total	-0.78	0.61	0.72	0.82
Multiple R^2	0.23	0.19	0.46	0.17
Average R^2	0.15			
T Value: **a** > 1.97 (significant); b < 1.97 (not significant)				

ment) was not significant (t value $1.29 < 1.96$). Current relationship outcomes were not significantly affected by experience (t value 1.65), dependency (t value 0.20), or uncertainty (t value 1.77). In addition, experience did not have a significant moderating effect on IOIMS satisfaction (t value 1.81) or future outcomes (t value 0.08). Therefore, these aspects of the proposed model were not supported. The model was rerun with PLS after removing the nonsignificant paths with little change in the results.

There was support for the other aspects of the proposed model with an average of 15% of the variance in the constructs explained (strategic IOIMS 23%, IOIMS satisfaction 19%, perceived current relationship outcomes 46%, and future relationship outcomes 17%) and significant t values greater than 1.96 (Table 3).

Satisfaction with the IOIMS was positively associated with a "strategic-oriented IOIMS" where there were more face-to-face negotiations and more people involved in exchanging information about forecasts, new product developments, opportunities, and threats. A strategic IOIMS and satisfaction with the IOIMS were both positively associated with perceived current outcomes (satisfaction with performance, perceived responsiveness, and strength of relationship trust). However, commitment to develop long-term customer supplier relationships was not significantly associated with a strategic IOIMS, IOIMS satisfaction, or current relationship outcomes as hypothesised.

Factors affecting the relationships in the model constructs included respondent's experience and business environment power/dependency and market uncertainty. Dependency, market uncertainty, and experience were negatively associated with a strategic IOIMS. However, IOIMS satisfaction was negatively associated with uncertainty and positively associated with dependency. Dependency and market uncertainty were both positively associated with commitment.

Conclusion and Discussion

The review of literature identified a gap in research looking at the role of information systems to manage interorganisational relationships and to coordinate customers and suppliers in chains. A model was developed to identify aspects of the interorganisational information management system (IOIMS) to coordinate customers/suppliers and how it was associated with perceived current and future outcomes from the relationship (satisfaction with performance, perceived responsiveness, strength of relationship trust, and commitment to developing long-term customer/supplier relationships). In addition, the model looked at the effect of environmental factors (experience, market uncertainty, and power/dependency). Following on from previous testing of the model based on a survey of Australian food processors and an exploratory green life case study, the model was revised. Results of testing of the revised model were examined in this chapter.

In conclusion, the food processor survey presented and a previous exploratory green life case study provided some support for the model of IOIMS as originally proposed and the revised model. In all studies and models, satisfaction with the IOIMS was positively associated with perceived current outcomes (satisfaction with performance, perceived responsiveness, and strength of relationship trust). The revised model demonstrated an additional positive association between having a strategic IOIMS and IOIMS satisfaction. These findings were as hypothesised. It was expected that satisfaction with the IOIMS and perceptions of creation of knowledge and business improvement would be positively associated with current outcomes (greater perceived trust, performance, and responsiveness compared to others in the industry, as well as improvements in trust, performance, and responsiveness over time). Similarly, it was expected that the nature of the IOIMS would be positively associated with IOIMS satisfaction. What was interesting was that IOIMS satisfaction was associated with the more strategically oriented IOIMS where there were more face-to-face price negotiations and problem resolution, as well as more people involved in exchanging information about forecasts, new product developments, opportunities, and threats. This indicated that more sophisticated and developed IOIMS were important in developing IOIMS satisfaction. It may be that the management-control type IOIMS were seen as a prerequisite for business rather than as a value-added extra.

Managerial Implications

In terms of implications for management, the finding that the business environment was associated with commitment is not likely to be very surprising and will have been built into strategic planning processes. However, a key issue for management was the finding that increasing power/dependency was associated with greater IOIMS satisfaction, while increased uncertainty reduced satisfaction. This indicates that rewards of greater customer/supplier IOIMS satisfaction can be gained through management action to provide greater certainty in predictability of demand, production yield, quality, and quantity of supply. Anecdotal evidence collected during interviews indicated that many organisations had been addressing improvements in these areas. Uncertainty related to market competition and changing consumer preferences would be much harder, if not impossible, for management to influence.

Perhaps the main finding was that perceptions of customer/supplier trust, performance, and responsiveness were positively associated with users' satisfaction with an IOIMS and perceptions that it improved business and their knowledge. Therefore, if management is concerned about ensuring that the organisation is getting the best from customers/suppliers, it can monitor boundary-spanning staff's perceptions about these matters. Another key issue was the importance of relationships rather than technical-efficient IOIMS to satisfaction. This implies that a major managerial issue is ensuring that the culture of the organisation encourages the development of personal relationships between boundary-spanning staff and customers/suppliers. It can be encouraged through more social activities such as attendance of conferences, trade shows, and industry events. These "softer" skills can be emphasised in staff selection, training, and performance assessment processes. Management also needs to ensure that it allows time for relationships to develop by not rotating staff through boundary-spanning roles too quickly. A common complaint was that boundary-spanning staff in the customer/supplier organisation were changed too quickly. Some respondents commented that time was needed to understand each other's business and how to get the best response. Such comments may indicate that managing relationships with customers and suppliers is not based solely on explicit organisational rules and processes that can be quickly learned and passed on to successors. More detailed implicit knowledge may need to be gained that relies on personal experience, which cannot be passed on to subsequent boundary-spanning staff. Such implicit knowledge takes time and experience to gain.

Further Research

In terms of areas for future research, the aspects of the proposed model that were not supported need to be examined in more detail. What was not expected was that in all studies and models, expected future outcomes (commitment) were not significantly associated with either IOIMS satisfaction or current outcomes (performance, responsiveness, and trust). The moderating effects of the business environment variables may explain this finding. Both studies using the original model found that the business environment (power, dependency, and market uncertainty) had a significant influence on future expected outcomes or attitudinal commitment to develop long-term customer/supplier relationships. When these environment variables were separated out under the revised model, both power/dependency and market uncertainty had a significant positive association with commitment, while experience did not. This means that environments of greater dependence on customers/suppliers and market uncertainty were associated with greater commitment now and over time (future outcomes).

It had nothing to do with the experience of the respondent in the industry or with the organisation or his or her understanding of the organisation. With the average length of relationships with these customers and suppliers (22 years) being longer than found in three out of four other studies (Jonsson & Zineldin, 2003; Karalis & Vlachos, 2004; Langton, 2004), it may be that the food processors felt locked into these relationships. If so, the boundary-spanning staff (purchasing and sales) may not feel it has any say in who the company does business with and therefore there was no association between commitment and staff's perceptions of IOIMS satisfaction or current outcomes (performance, responsiveness, and trust). Many of the relationships discussed were with retailer supermarkets (35%), who Amanor-Boadu, Trienekens, and Willems (2002) note wield significant power in the agri-food sector through control of market access. In Australia, with three retail chains dominating the market, this power would be even more pronounced. Future research could be carried out to compare retailers and non-retailer relationships to explore this further.

Another explanation for the lack of an association between future expected outcomes (attitudes to commitment) and the IOIMS may be that the organisations do not have different systems in place to cater to different customers' or suppliers' needs, as there was little variation in the nature of the IOIMS—a situation one may expect in practice because of investments in systems and establishment of standards. As Anthony (1988) suggests, management control systems need to ensure responsibility centres, even if physically separated, and act consistently and in accordance with senior management wishes. This conclusion was supported anecdotally during data collection, with the same system used for all major customers and the same system used for all major suppliers, even for divisions in different states. Note that organisations had significantly different IOIMS for customers than those used for suppliers. Further analysis could be undertaken to investigate whether organisations have different IOIMS for different categories of customers and different IOIMS for different categories of suppliers. There was anecdotal evidence during data collection that adaptations were only made to systems with very important customers/suppliers where there were highly developed relationships. There-fore, in conducting this research, care will need to be taken to only analyse highly developed relationships. The adaptations may be in the form of restructuring boundary-spanning staff along product category or customer lines, exchanges of staff, or a greater range of staff involved. Note the adaptations may be done more for managerial processes than the more frequent operational or transac-tional processes.

In terms of the impact of the business environment variables, both studies found no meaningful effect on perceived current outcomes (performance, responsive-ness, and trust). This was contrary to expectations. The business environment (power/dependency and market uncertainty) was not strongly associated with perceptions of satisfaction with the IOIMS; creation of knowledge; business improvement; trust; performance; and responsiveness, nor with changes in trust, performance, and responsiveness over time. One explanation may be that the current outcome constructs were based on measuring aspects of a respondent's personal relationships with customer/supplier counterparts. Rather than measuring the organisation's perceived official position on these matters, respondents gave their opinions on whether they personally were satisfied, and so forth. Peters and Fletcher (2004) raise the concern that much of the interorganisational research has been based on personal psychological dimensions, but interactions are between groups of people and each individual is embedded in groups, organizations, and networks. Hardman, Darroch, and Ortmann (2002) measured trust based on both personal confidence and business confidence, but unfortunately did not report on whether respondents gave significantly different results to these two questions. From the personal relationship perspective, the business environment may have less of an influence, with the nature of the individuals involved being more important. Further studies could be done to collect data based on the official company position and personal opinions to see if this affects the results.

The impact of the business environment variables on IOIMS satisfaction was different in the two studies. Unlike the food processor survey, the green life case study found the business environment had a significant association with the IOIMS. These differences may be explained by the results of the revised model when the business environment constructs were separated out. In the food processor survey, the power/dependency and uncertainty affected IOIMS satisfaction in opposing ways. While increasing power/dependency was associated with greater IOIMS satisfaction, increased uncertainty reduced satisfaction. Possibly the increased uncertainty created more problems. Future research could be conducted to explore the interactions of these two business environment factors on the green life case study to see if the patterns were similar or if they reflect differences in the industries studied.

An alternative explanation for the differences in the studies may have to do with the way the data was collected. Additional variables used to measure the IOIMS in the food processor study resulted in a more reliable and valid assessment of it as a construct. This along with the larger sample size of the food processor study may mean the food processor study results were more accurate.

The other main finding from the revised model was the significant negative effect on strategic IOIMS of experience, power/dependence, and uncertainty. Strategic IOIMS were based on more face-to-face price negotiation and problem resolution, as well as more people involved in exchanging information about forecasts, new product developments, opportunities, and threats. It may be expected that less strategic information exchange would be required for respondents with greater experience in the industry and with the other organisation and with greater understanding of the other organisation. There may also be withholding of this type of information when in a dependency situation. However, it was expected that the exchange of strategic information would be critical in situations of uncertainty. The only explanation thought of was that perhaps the information exchange is dominated with dealing with day-to-day operational control management issues arising from the uncertainty. With the role of strategic IOIMS in IOIMS satisfaction, it is a concern that there seem to be so many forces affecting it negatively. Future research could look at factors that ameliorate these negative forces and promote the development of strategic IOIMS.

Many of the conclusions above have resulted in suggestions for further research. This should not come as a surprise given the gaps found in previous research. Any considering further work in this field that is an important element for future chain collaboration and competition are welcome to contact the author to discuss ideas and collaborate on research.

Acknowledgments

This research was supported by financial assistance from the Department of Agriculture in Western Australia. Personal assistance is greatly appreciated from: Professor Geoff Soutar, Professor Mohammed Quaddus, Professor Jacques Trienekens, and Professor Adrie Beulens. An earlier version of this chapter was presented as a paper at the Curtin Business School Doctoral Students Colloquium, September 2004.

References

Al-Gahtanl, S. (2001). The applicability of TAM outside North America: An empirical test in the United Kingdom. *Information Resources Management Journal, 4*(3), 37-46.

Amanor-Boadu, V., Trienekens, J. H., & Willems, S. (2002, June 6-8). *Information and communication technologies, strategic power and inter-organisational relationships*. Paper presented at the 5th International Conference on Chain and Network Management in Agribusiness and the Food Industry: Paradoxes in Food Chains and Networks, Noordwijk, The Netherlands.

Ancona, D. G., & Caldwell, D. F. (1992). Bridging the boundary: External activity and Performance in organizational teams. *Administrative Science Quarterly, 37*(4), 634-665.

Anderson, E., Lodish, L., & Weitz, B. (1987, February 1). Resource allocation behavior in conventional channels. *Journal of Marketing Research, 24,* 85-97.

Anderson, E., & Weitz, B. A. (1992, February 1). The use of pledges to build and sustain commitment in distribution channels. *Journal of Marketing Research, 29,* 18-34.

Anderson, J. C., Håkansson, H., & Johanson, J. (1994). Dyadic business relationships within a business network context. *Journal of Marketing, 58*(4), 1-15.

Anderson, J. C., & Narus, J. (1990, January). A model of distributor firm and manufacturer firm working partnerships. *Journal of Marketing, 54,* 42-58.

Anthony, R. N. (1988). *The management control function.* Boston: Harvard Business School Press.

Barclay, D., Higgins, R., & Thompson, R. (1995). The partial least squares approach to causal modeling: Personal computer adoption and use as an illustration. *Technology Studies, 2*(2), 285-309.

Benedict, C., & Margeridis, H. (1999, March). Chain reaction. *Charter,* 46-49.

Bensaou, M. (1999, Summer). Portfolios of buyer-supplier relationships. *Sloan Management Review, 40*(4), 35-44.

Bensaou, M., & Venkatraman, N. (1995, September). Configurations of inter-organizational relationships: A comparison between U.S. and Japanese automakers. *Management Science, 41*(9), 1471-1492.

Borgen, K., & Ohren, O. (1999, June 15-16). *The logistics of information in collaborative organisations.* Paper presented at the 11th NOFOMA - Annual International Conference on Nordic Logistics Research, Lund, Sweden.

Bowersox, D. J., & Closs, D. J. (1996). *Logistical management: The integrated supply chain process.* New York: McGraw-Hill.

Champion, S. C., & Fearne, A. P. (2002, June 6-8). *The communication vacuum in the wool supply chain—Insights from an exploratory study of the Australian apparel wool textile industry.* Paper presented at the 5th International Conference on Chain and Network Management in Agribusiness and the Food Industry: Paradoxes in Food Chains and Networks, Noordwijk, The Netherlands.

Chatfield, A. T., & Bjorn-Andersen, N. (1997). The impact of IOS-enabled business process change on business outcomes: Transformation of the value chain of Japan Airlines. *Journal of Management Information Systems, 14*(1), 13-40.

Chin, W. W. (1998). Issues and opinions on structural equation modeling. *Management Information Systems Quarterly, 22*(1), 7-16.

Choo, C. W. (1996). Towards an information model of organizations. In E. Auster & C. W. Choo (Eds.), *Managing information for the competitive edge* (pp. 7-40). New York: Neal-Schuman Publishers.

Clare, B., Shadbolt, N., & Reid, J. (2002, June 6-8). *Supply base relationships in the New Zealand red meat industry: A case study*. Paper presented at the 5th International Conference on Chain and Network Management in Agribusiness and the Food Industry: Paradoxes in Food Chains and Networks, Noordwijk, The Netherlands.

Claro, D. P., Zylbersztajn, D., & Omta, S. W. F. O. (2004). How to manage a long-term buyer-seller relationship successfully? The impact of network information on long-term buyer-seller relationships in the Dutch potted plant and flower industry. *Chain and Network Science, 4*(1), 7-24.

Daft, R. L., & Lengel, R. H. (1986, May). Organizational information requirements, media richness and structural design. *Management Science, 32*, 554-571.

Daft, R. L., & Lengel, R. H. (1996). Information richness: A new approach to managerial behavior and organizational design. In E. Auster & C. W. Choo (Eds.), *Managing information for the competitive edge* (pp. 171-215). New York: Neal-Schuman Publishers.

Dansereau, F., & Markham, S. E. (1987). Superior-subordinate communication: Multiple levels of analysis. In F. M. Jablin, L. L. Putnam, K. H. Roberts, & L. W. Porter (Eds.), *Handbook of organizational communication: An interdisciplinary perspective* (pp. 343-388). Newbury Park, CA: Sage Publications.

Doney, P. M., & Cannon, J. P. (1997, April 2). An examination of the nature of trust in buyer-seller relationships. *Journal of Marketing, 61*, 35-51.

Ellinger, A. E., Daugherty, P. J., & Plair, Q. J. (1999). Customer satisfaction and loyalty in supply chain: The role of communication. *Transportation Research Part E-Logistics & Transportation Review, 35*(2), 121-134.

Ellram, L. M. (1995). Partnering pitfalls and success factors. *International Journal of Purchasing and Materials Management, Spring, 31*(2), 36-44.

Farace, R., Monge, P., & Russell, H. (1977). *Communicating and organizing*. Reading, MA: Addison-Wesley.

Forker, L. B., Ruch, W. A., & Hershauer, J. C. (1999). Examining supplier improvement efforts from both sides. *Journal of Supply Chain Management, 35*(3), 40-50.

Fornell, C. R., & Larcker, D. F. (1981, February). Evaluating structural equation models with unobservable variables and measurement error. *Journal of Marketing Research, 18*, 39-50.

Ganesan, S. (1994, April 2). Determinants of long-term orientation in buyer-seller relationships. *Journal of Marketing, 58*, 1-19.

Gassenheimer, J. B., & Scandura, T. A. (1993, Spring). External and internal supplier influences: Buyer perceptions of channel outcomes. *Journal of the Academy of Marketing Science, 21*, 155-160.

Greenacre, M. J. (1986). SIMCA: A program to perform simple correspondence analysis. *American Statistician, 51*, 230-231.

Gundlach, G. T., Achrol, R. S., & Mentzer, J. T. (1995, January 1). The structure of commitment in exchange. *Journal of Marketing, 59*, 78-92.

Hair, J. F. J., Anderson, R. E., Tatham, R. L., & Black, W. C. (1998). *Multivariate data analysis* (5th ed.). Sydney, Australia: Prentice Hall.

Hardman, P. A., Darroch, M. A. G., & Ortmann, G. F. (2002, June 6-8). *Improving cooperation to make the South African fresh apple export value chain more competitive.* Paper presented at the 5th International Conference on Chain and Network Management in Agribusiness and the Food Industry: Paradoxes in Food Chains and Networks, Noordwijk, The Netherlands.

Heather, B. (2001). *Buyer-seller relations: Retail supplier relations in the horticultural industry.* Unpublished honours thesis, Curtin University of Technology, Bentley, Western Australia.

Hoffman, D. L., & Franke, G. R. (1986, August). Correspondence analysis: Graphical representation of categorical data in marketing research. *Journal of Marketing Research, 23*, 213-227.

Huber, G., & Daft, R. (1987). The information environment in organizations. In F. M. Jablin, L. L. Putnam, K. H. Roberts, & L. W. Porter (Eds.), *Handbook of organizational communication: An interdisciplinary perspective* (pp. 130-164). Newbury Park, CA: Sage Publications.

Igbaria, M., Guimaraes, T., & Davis, G. B. (1995). Testing the determinants of microcomputer usage via a structural equation model. *Journal of Management Information Systems, 11*(4), 87-114.

Jonsson, P., & Zineldin, M. (2003). Achieving high satisfaction in supplier-dealer working relationships. *Supply Chain Management: An International Journal, 8*(3), 224-240.

Karalis, V., & Vlachos, I. P. (2004, May 27-28). *Supplier-retailer collabora-tion in food networks: A typology and examination of moderating factors.* Paper presented at the 6th International Conference on Chain and Network Management in Agribusiness and the Food Industry: Dynamics in Chains and Networks, Ede, The Netherlands.

Keith, J., Jackson, D. J., & Crosby, L. (1990, July). Effects of alternative types of influence strategies under different channel dependence structures. *Journal of Marketing, 54*(3), 30-41.

Kohli, A. K., Jaworski, B. J., & Kumar, A. (1993). MARKOR: A measure of market orientation. *Journal of Marketing Research, 30*(4), 467-477.

Kola, J., Latvala, T., & Vertanen, A. (2002, June 6-8). *Quality information in the beef supply chain.* Paper presented at the 5th International Conference on Chain and Network Management in Agribusiness and the Food Industry: Paradoxes in Food Chains and Networks, Noordwijk, The Netherlands.

Kornieliussen, T., & Grønhaug, K. (2003). Quality perceptions in international distribution: An empirical investigation in a complete distribution channel. *Supply Chain Management: An International Journal, 8*(5), 467-475.

Kumar, N., Stern, L. W., & Achrol, R. S. (1992). Assessing reseller perfor-mance from the perspective of the supplier. *Journal of Marketing Research, 29*(2), 238-253.

Langton, N. (2004). *Investigating buyer-seller relationships within the cut flower export industry of Western Australia.* Unpublished honours thesis, Curtin University of Technology, Perth, Western Australia.

Lazzarini, S. G., Chaddad, F. R., & Cook, M., L. (2001). Integrating supply chain and network analyses: The study of netchains. *Chain and Network Science, 1*(1), 7-22.

Lefebve, E., Cassivi, L., Lefebve, L., Léger, P. M., & Hadaya, P. (2003). Supply chain management, electronic collaboration tools and organizational innovativeness. *Chain and Network Science, 3*(2), 81-94.

Lehtinen, U., & Torkko, M. (2004, May 27-28). *Outsourcing as a challenge for food firms.* Paper presented at the 6th International Conference on Chain and Network Management in Agribusiness and the Food Industry: Dynamics in Chains and Networks, Ede, The Netherlands.

Leuthesser, L., & Kohli, A. K. (1995). Rational behavior in business markets: Implications for relationship management. *Journal of Business Research, 34*(3), 221-233.

Lindgreen, A. (2001). In search of relationship quality, customer retention and shareholder value: Findings from an exploratory, qualitative multiple case study. *Chain and Network Science, 1*(1), 49-63.

Lindgreen, A., Trienekens, J. H., & Vellinga, K. (2004, May 27-28). *Contemporary marketing practice: A case study of the Dutch pork supply chain*. Paper presented at the 6th International Conference on Chain and Network Management in Agribusiness and the Food Industry: Dynamics in Chains and Networks, Ede, The Netherlands.

Matanda, M., & Schroder, B. (2002). Environmental factors, supply chain capabilities and business performance in horticultural marketing channels. *Chain and Network Science, 2*(1), 47-60.

McDermott, A., Lovatt, S. J., & Koslow, S. (2004, May 27-28). *Supply chain performance measures for producers and processors of premium beef cuts*. Paper presented at the 6th International Conference on Chain and Network Management in Agribusiness and the Food Industry: Dynamics in Chains and Networks, Ede, The Netherlands.

Miller, J. (2002). *Long-term buyer-seller relationships in the Western Australian nursery industry*. Unpublished honours thesis, Curtin University of Technology, Bentley, WA.

Mohr, J. J., Fisher, R. J., & Nevin, J. R. (1996, July 3). Collaborative communication in interfirm relationships: Moderating effects of integration and control. *Journal of Marketing, 60*, 103-115.

Mohr, J. J., & Nevin, J. R. (1990, October 4). Communication strategies in marketing channels: A theoretical perspective. *Journal of Marketing, 54*, 36-51.

Mohr, J. J., & Sohi, R. S. (1995). Communication flows in distribution channels: Impact on assessments of communication quality and satisfaction. *Journal of Retailing, 71*(4), 393-416.

Nunnally, J. C., & Bernstein, I. H. (1994). *Psychometric theory* (3rd ed.). New York: McGraw-Hill.

O'Brien, J. A. (1999). *Management information systems: Managing information technology in the internetworked enterprise* (4th ed.). Boston: Irwin/McGraw-Hill.

Peters, L. D., & Fletcher, K. P. (2004). Market-based approach to understanding communication and teamworking: A multi-disciplinary literature review. *Academy of Marketing Science Review, 2*. Retrieved from http://www.amsreview.org/articles/peters02-2004.pdf

Pratt, K. (2002). A case study: The power of managing knowledge in a worldwise enterprise. In R. F. Bellaver & J. M. Lusa (Eds.), *Knowledge management strategy and technology* (pp. 169-179). Boston: Artech House.

Sethuraman, R., Anderson, J. C., & Narus, J. A. (1988). Partnership advantage and its determinants in distributor and manufacturer working relationships. *Journal of Business Research, 17*(4), 327-347.

Sharma, N., Young, L., & Wilkinson, I. (2001, September 9-11). *The structure of relationship commitment in interfirm relationships.* Paper presented at the 17th Annual IMP Conference: Interactions, Relationships and Networks—Strategic Directions, Holmenkollen Park Hotel Rica, Oslo, Norway.

Siemieniuch, C. E., Waddell, F. N., & Sinclair, M. A. (1999). The role of "partnership" in supply chain management for fast-moving consumer goods: A case study. *International Journal of Logistics: Research Applications, 2*(1), 87-101.

Simons, D., Francis, M., Bourlakis, M., & Fearne, A. P. (2003). Identifying the determinants of value in the U.K. red meat industry: A value chain analysis approach. *Chain and Network Science, 3*(2), 109-121.

Soutar, G. N., & McNeil, M. M. (1997). Financial portfolios of Western Australian investors: A correspondence analysis. *International Journal of Business Studies, 5*(2), 33-44.

Sparling, D., & van Duren, E. (2002, June 6-8). *Strategic alliances in the Canadian biotechnology sector.* Paper presented at the 5th International Conference on Chain and Network Management in Agribusiness and the Food Industry: Paradoxes in Food Chains and Networks, Noordwijk, The Netherlands.

Spekman, R. E., Kamauff, J. W. J., & Myhr, N. (1998). An empirical investigation into supply chain management: A perspective on partnerships. *International Journal of Physical Distribution & Logistics Management, 28*(8).

Stank, T. P., Emmelhainz, M. A., & Daugherty, P. J. (1996, Fall). The impact of information on supplier performance. *Journal of Marketing Theory & Practice, 4*(4), 94-105.

Storer, C. E. (2001, June 25-28). Inter-organizational information feedback systems in agribusiness chains: A chain case study theoretical framework. Paper presented at the *2001 International Agribusiness Management Association World Food & Agribusiness Symposium*, Sydney Hilton, NSW.

Storer, C. E. (2003, November 7-8). *Modeling inter-organizational information management systems and relationships in perishable chains.* Paper presented at the Graduate School of Business Doctoral Conference 2003, Perth, Western Australia.

Storer, C. E., Soutar, G. N., Trienekens, J. H., Beulens, A. J., & Quaddus, M. A. (2004). Dynamic modelling of inter-organisational information management systems and relationships in food chains. *Chain and Network Science, 4*(1), 55-71.

Sweeney, J. C., & Webb, D. (2002). Relationship benefits: An exploration of buyer-supplier dyads. *Journal of Relationship Marketing, 1*(2), 77-91.

Trienekens, J. (1999). *Management of processes in chains: A research framework.* Unpublished PhD thesis, Wageningen Universeit, Wageningen, the Netherlands.

Uzzi, B. (1997). Social structure and competition in interfirm networks: The paradox of embeddedness. *Administrative Science Quarterly, 42*, 35-67.

Van der Vorst, J. G. A. J. (2000). *Effective food supply chains: Generating, modelling and evaluating supply chain scenarios.* Unpublished PhD thesis, Wageningen University, Wageningen, The Netherlands.

Van Dorp, C. A. (2004). *Reference-data modelling for tracking and tracing.* Unpublished PhD thesis, Wageningen Universiteit, The Netherlands.

Vijayasarathy, L. R., & Robey, D. (1997, December 5). The effect of EDI on market channel relationships in retailing. *Information and Management, 33*(2), 73-86.

Vlosky, R. P., Wilson, D. T., & Vlosky, R. B. (1997). Closing the interorganizational information systems relationship satisfaction gap. *Journal of Marketing Practice: Applied Marketing Science, 3*(3), 75-87.

Wilson, D. T., & Vlosky, R. P. (1998). Interorganizational information system technology and buyer-seller relationships. *Journal of Business and Industrial Marketing, 13*(3), 215-228.

Wilson, H. (2000). *Long-term buyer-seller relationships in the Western Australian wine industry.* Unpublished honours thesis, Curtin University of Technology, Bentley, Western Australia.

Womack, J. P., Jones, D. T., & Roos, D. (1990). *The machine that changed the world: Based on the Massachusetts Institute of Technology five-million dollar five-year study of the future of the automobile.* New York: Rawson Associates.

Chapter X

The Application of Soft Systems Methodology to Supply Chain Management

Ross Smith, Deakin University, Australia

David Mackay, Deakin University, Australia

Graeme Altmann, Deakin University, Australia

Lucas Merlo, Deakin University, Australia

Abstract

This chapter reflects upon techniques that might facilitate improved strategic decision making in a supply chain management (SCM) environment. In particular, it presents the integration of a selection of techniques adapted from an approach to systems-based problem solving that has emerged primarily in the UK over the last 20-30 years—the soft systems methodology (SSM). The results reported indicate that SSM techniques can complement existing SCM decision-making tools. In particular, this chapter outlines a framework for integrating some SSM techniques with approaches based upon the supply-chain operations reference-model (SCOR)

.

Introduction

Supply chain management (SCM) is a collaborative effort that combines many parties or processes in both the optimisation of the delivery of goods and services and optimisation of information flows. To the customer, optimisation means that the supplier knows what the customer needs and understands the timing of the delivery of goods and/or services. To the supplier, optimisation means that the right goods and/or services are available in the right quantities at the right time, when the customer needs them, without requiring the supplier to carry excess inventory or maintain excessive production capacity. Such collaborative efforts are necessarily founded upon negotiated, "whole-of-chain" strategies, often decided in an environment that brings together stakeholders across an entire product cycle.

In this chapter, we reflect upon techniques that might facilitate improved strategic decision making in an SCM workshop environment, in particular, integrating a selection of techniques adapted from an approach to systems-based problem solving that follows, in part, a socio-technical approach that has emerged primarily in the United Kingdom over the last 20 to 30 years—the soft systems methodology (SSM). A short timeframe action research approach, introducing a selection of SSM techniques in a workshop environment, has been applied. The results confirm and extend studies indicating that SSM techniques can complement existing SCM workshop approaches. In particular, this chapter outlines a framework for integrating some SSM techniques with approaches based upon the supply-chain operations reference (SCOR) model.

Background

Supply chain management is a collaboration based strategy to link cross-enterprise business operations to achieve a shared vision of market opportunity. It is a comprehensive arrangement that can span from raw material sourcing to end-consumer purchase" (John McConnell, as reported by Ferguson, 2000, p. 64)

As Ferguson (2000) notes, this definition introduces two important ideas. First, supply chain management (SCM) is collaborative, combining many parties and processes in a product cycle. Second, it suggests that SCM potentially covers an entire product cycle, from raw materials to the product sales point. Such collaborative efforts are necessarily founded upon negotiated, whole-supply-chain strategies, often decided in a workshop environment that brings together stakeholders across an entire product cycle.

It has been argued (Ferguson, 2000) that a company should implement SCM because of its powerful impact on short- and long-term goals—profit, market share, and customer satisfaction. To put the advantages in numeric terms, companies that have successfully implemented SCM have observed order-cycle times and inventory days of supply that are about 45% lower than their competition. Further, these companies have been observed to be able to meet their promised delivery dates 17% faster than their competition (Ferguson, 2000).

Despite this, a survey conducted by Deloitte Consulting has reported that while 91% of manufacturers in North America rate SCM as being very important or critical to the success of their company, only 2% of these manufacturers rank their supply chain as world-class (Elmuti, 2002). In support of this, the Bourton Group (quoted by O'Connell [1999]) revealed that in excess of 80% of manufacturing companies made the more effective management of their supply chains a number one priority. It has also been claimed by an industry expert that "the supply chain in the late 1990s is the one area where substantial gains in bottom-line profit performance can be made" (O'Connell, 1999, p. 40).

The role of technology as an enabler of SCM has facilitated the initial development of relationships between organisations, however, technology alone is not sufficient. Businesses are volatile and their operation is dependent upon a group of people cooperating along the chain. Researchers are now only in the early stages of understanding and modelling the social, cultural, and political dimensions of the supply chain and, in particular, understanding how the people-focused challenges of managing the supply chain might best be addressed. It remains an open question how supply chain managers might accommodate various stakeholder perspectives of supply chain problems: the cultural, social, and political forces at play; the diversity of individual skills and knowledge bases; and diverse individual value systems.

In this chapter, we reflect upon techniques that might facilitate improved strategic decision making in an SCM workshop environment, in particular, a selection of techniques adapted from an approach to systems-based problem solving that has emerged, primarily in the United Kingdom, over the last 20 to 30 years—the soft systems methodology (SSM).

SSM was developed at Lancaster University (UK) in the 1970s (Checkland & Scholes, 1990). It offers a means of dealing with problem situations that can potentially provide a path to improving or overcoming obstacles. Songkhla (1997) has observed that SSM can be characterised as an iterative methodology focusing and accommodating various stakeholders' perspectives in the design of change. Furthermore, Songkhla has argued that, unlike its predecessor (systems engineering), SSM does not seek one problem definition, but rather accommodates a variety of different perspectives to try to make sense of multiple problem situations.

Recent research (Smith, Mackay, Altmann, & Gencoglu, 2002), although preliminary in nature, has revealed that the use of some SSM techniques (rich pictures, root definitions, and conceptual modelling) within an SCM context shows promise. Building on this, the present study develops this stream of research further, investigating whether the wider spectrum of SSM techniques might be of value to supply chain managers in resolving strategic SCM issues in a workshop-based decision-making environment. Further, this study investigates the role SSM might play in complementing approaches that incorporate the widely used supply-chain operations reference (SCOR) model (Supply-Chain Council, 2005) for addressing the analysis and design of supply chain solutions.

In the next section of this chapter, SSM is introduced, together with a brief review of previous studies of the integration of a selection of SSM concepts and techniques with existing techniques used by practitioners who are supporting SCM decision-making activities within a workshop environment. The following section then outlines the short timeframe action-research approach that has been applied to investigate the introduction of a selection of SSM techniques in an SCM workshop environment. Results from the two-stage workshops conducted are then reported. Finally, some conclusions and possible future research directions are canvassed.

Using SSM to Facilitate
SCM Decision-Making Workshops

Soft System Methodology

In 1969, researchers at the Postgraduate Department of System Engineering of the University of Lancaster (UK) commenced a stream of research, continuing to this day, to investigate the application of systems concepts to the investigation of the sort of messy, ill-structured, organisational problems that managers of all kinds and at all levels face everyday.

Initially, they sought to explore whether it is possible to use well-established systems engineering approaches to address real-world managerial, rather than technical, problem situations. Systems engineering begins with a stated problem and applies systems concepts (e.g., input, output, communication, control, feedback) to design solutions to that problem. Such approaches have undoubtedly been highly successful in the delivery of production processes, chemicals, electrical systems, and the like. What the researchers found, however, was that system engineering concepts were unable to cope with the subtleties and immense complexity of management problems, characterised by conflicting appreciative settings and norms (Checkland, 1999). Systems engineering struggles to deal with situations where there are multiple conflicting perceptions of what the problem is and where ends and means are not related by simple causal relationships.

The Lancaster researchers moved away from working with the idea of an obvious problem that required a solution to working with the idea of a situation (a problem situation), which may be regarded as problematic by at least some people for multiple, different reasons.

The development of SSM might be characterised by four key understandings (Checkland, 1999):

- in all real-world problem situations, human beings in social roles seek or wish to take purposeful action;
- models of purposeful activity can only be built on the basis of a declared worldview;
- such models are not models of real-world action, but models that are relevant to discussion and argument about real-world action; and
- a problem-solving process inevitably consists of a learning cycle, in which models of human activity systems can be used to structure a debate about a change.

Of particular relevance is that the models of human activity that are constructed can be used to explore issues concerning what information systems might best be created to support real-world action.

This view of SSM as a cycle of inquiry and learning, leading to action to improve a problem situation, is illustrated in Figure 1 (Checkland, 1999). This cycle can be understood as follows:

- In real-world situations, humans interpret the world in different ways.
- As such, it should always be possible to have many models of a situation. SSM suggests that the best way to proceed is to make a handful of models representing pure ideas of purposeful activity, rather than being descriptions of part of the real world.

Figure 1. The inquiring/learning cycle of SSM (As presented by Checkland, 1999)

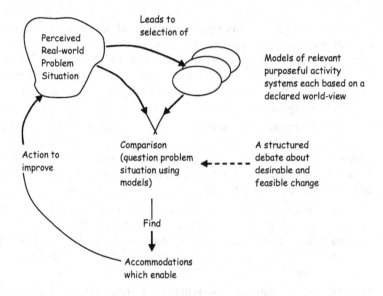

- These models can then be used as a source of questions to ask of the real situation and, in turn, provide new knowledge and insights concerning the problem situation. This can lead to further ideas and relevant models.

- Such an organised comparison of models and perceived real situations can lead to accommodations between the conflicting perspectives, enabling action to be taken that is arguably both desirable (in terms of the comparisons between models and perceived situations) and culturally feasible for a particular group of people with its particular history, relationships, culture, and aspirations.

SSM is, therefore, an organised learning system. By learning about organisational problems, plans for feasible desirable change emerge, and action can be taken to improve organisational problem situations, possibly through the introduction of information technologies.

The progress of the 20 to 30 years of research to date, leading to the fundamental understandings outlined above, has been documented and reflected upon in several monographs. The methodology has become less structured and broader as it has developed (Checkland, 1999). The key monographs include:

- **System thinking, systems practice (STSP)** (Checkland, 1981), which describes the early experience of trying to apply system engineering to the problems of management and reports the origin of "system thinking" as an alternative to the reductionism of natural science. It recognises the need for applied system thinking and documents SSM as a seven-stage process of inquiry (see Figure 2).

- **Systems: Concepts, methodologies and applications (SCMA)** (Wilson, 1984) describes a control engineer's view of the experience of the Lancaster research. SCMA represents SSM in terms of an engineering form of logic, presenting a systems engineering approach with the addition of human activity system modelling.

- **Soft system methodology in action (SSMA)** (Checkland & Scholes, 1990) moves beyond the seven-stage model of the methodology and sees SSM as a sense-making approach. It also introduces the "Analysis One, Two, and Three" approaches to understanding an organisation's problem solving, social, and political systems.

- **Information, systems and information systems (ISIS)** (Checkland & Holwell, 1998) relates experiences based on the mature use of SSM to a fundamental reconceptualisation of the field of IS/IT.

Over the years, a number of detailed representations of the broad process of SSM have emerged. The seven-stage model, discussed below, is the most often quoted representation and provides the basis for the studies presented herein.

SSM was originally presented, in STSP, as a sequence of stages with iteration back to previous stages. This seven-stage model is illustrated in Figure 2.

In the seven-stage model of SSM (Figure 2):

- Stages 1 and 2 involve entering the problem situation, finding out about it, and expressing its nature. It does not draw on preconceived problem descriptions but looks at the whole organisational situation with an open mind. **Stage 1** involves finding out who is involved in the organisational problem situation, their perceptions of the situation, their concerns, existing processes, structures, and so on. Then, in **Stage 2**, the problem situation is expressed, often as a set of rich pictures. Rich pictures are a diagrammatic presentation of the organisation and the problem situation. Any appropriate icons, maps, schematic drawings, logos, and the like may be used to describe the situation.

Figure 2. The seven stage model of SSM (As presented by Checkland, 1981)

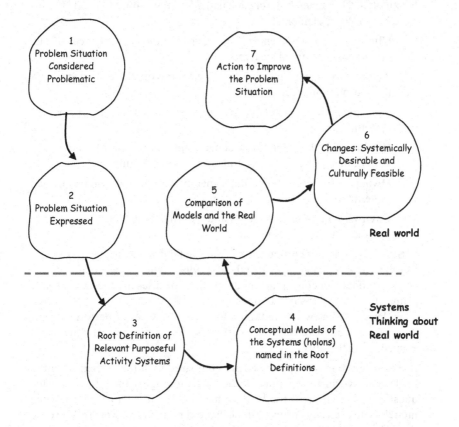

- In **Stage 3**, relevant systems that, if modelled, might provide insight into the problem situation are named. Each named system is expressed as "a system to do xxx." These named systems can be of two broad types:
  - Primary task systems—which are systems that it would be widely agreed represent the transformation of primary concern to those with an interest in the problem situation, for example, for a furniture manufacturer, it would be "a system to make furniture"; and
  - Issue-based systems—which are systems that might provide insights into a particular concern, for example, if the makers of furniture were concerned that there was a lack of trust between them and their timber suppliers, it could "a system to build trust."

For each named system, a concise statement, called a root definition, is formulated. This statement, for each named system, should include the so-called CATWOE elements:

○ **C**lients—those who benefit from, or suffer the consequences of, the outputs of the named system;

○ **A**ctors—those who are involved in carrying out the named system's transformation process;

○ **T**ransformation—the conversion of inputs to outputs for the named system;

○ **W**orldview—the often unstated assumptions relevant to the named system that make the above transformation meaningful;

○ **O**wner—the person with the capacity to close down the named system; and

○ **E**nvironment—the constraints and external influences upon the operation of the named system.

- In **Stage 4**, models are produced for each root definition using approaches described extensively by Checkland (1999). These are called human activity models (or conceptual models). The activities in a model are based primarily on the verbs in the root definition. SSM practitioners also often consider the "5Es" when thinking about the measures of performance of the system they have modelled: efficacy; efficiency; effectiveness; elegance, and ethicality.

- In **Stage 5**, the models produced are compared with the current situation in the real world to structure further questioning of the situation. This questioning often takes the form of asking, about each activity in each model: Is this activity currently done in the perceived real world? Who does this? How is this done? How would we assess if this activity is well done? What actions might we take, relevant to this activity, to improve the situation, possibly involving the application of information technology?

- In **Stage 6**, changes that could improve the situation are identified. The changes must be desirable in principle and feasible to implement given the people involved, the power structures in place, and so on.

- In **Stage 7**, the identified changes are assessed and a set of actions are recommended and taken to improve the problem situation. These changes, once actioned, alter the problem situation, and so, in principle, a new cycle of SSM can begin, with the intention of generating new insights and changes. In this sense, the cycle of learning and improving that is embodied in SSM is never-ending.

The directional arrows that link the seven stages in Figure 2 show the logical structure of the collection of actions, which make up the overall process. Those directional arrows do not necessarily represent the sequence in which the activities are to be executed. The process of analysis may start with any activity, progress in any direction, and use significant iteration at any stage (Checkland, 1981).

It should be recognised that those stages shown "above the line" in Figure 2 employ the language of the real world, and it is expected that broad participation of stakeholders will be encouraged during the execution of all those stages (Stages 1, 2, 5, 6, and 7). The stages "below the line" (Stages 3 and 4) will involve the application of systems thinking principles and will most probably be facilitated and largely carried out by an experienced SSM practitioner.

To illustrate the potential of SSM to support discussions in an SCM workshop environment, an example of the application of SSM to an SCM scenario is presented in the Appendix. This SSM application to a simplified scenario (provided to the authors by the SCM practitioners at the site studied in the research reported herein) was the focus of the practitioner feedback reported in the *Results and Discussion* section of this chapter.

Previous Studies of the Application of SSM to Facilitate SCM Workshops

Very little work has been reported to date on the integration of SCM and SSM. Rigby, Day, Forrester, and Burnett (2000) have highlighted that a gap exists in the literature surrounding the theoretical attention given to interfirm agility. They identify that a difficulty exists in understanding the softer influential elements. Elements such as power, trust, dependency, and certain other human-related factors are not able to be adequately accounted for in analysis. Although it would appear as if soft systems methodology might be able to alleviate many of these concerns by dealing with the softer issues, it is argued by Rigby et al. that "even approaches such as 'soft systems' methodologies cannot capture the essential nature of these relationships and human factors sufficiently to account for 'maverick' episodes" (p. 184). However, detailed studies applying SSM to test this assertion do not appear to have been reported.

On the other hand, the study reported by Smith et al. (2002), which involved the supplementing of established SCM quick response (QR) workshops with a selection of SSM tools and techniques in order to investigate the appropriateness of SSM for identifying social, political, and cultural factors in an SCM context, has been promising. In that study, SCM practitioners were exposed to the possible inclusion of SSM techniques into an SCM QR workshop process model established by Perry and Sohal (2000). In summary, the study of Smith et al. (2002) highlighted the potential of SSM in a workshop setting, with three central themes emerging:

- The SSM techniques allowed the participants to achieve a greater sense of understanding in regard to the supply chain management processes. This was due largely to the fact that the visual nature of rich pictures allowed the participants to see the particular processes involved in the supply chain.

- The utilisation of CATWOE analysis, highlighting the elements of customers, actors, transformation process, ownership, worldview, and environment, allowed for the development of root definitions. Once established, these root definitions were developed into mission statements that reflected each participant's situation and allowed for reanalysis of the cooperative role of the supply chain.

- The value of examining the supply chain from a top-down perspective, through the use of conceptual modelling, was seen to produce a positive effect in the participants' reactions. Instead of each participant developing his or her own activity model, reflecting individual perceptions of the current status of events, an approach undertaken from the top-level allowed for *fresh views* to form, thus broadening perceptions.

One final element of the literature that should be briefly reported is the SCOR approach. This becomes particularly relevant, as will become apparent in the *Results and Discussion* section of this chapter, because the organisation that is the particular focus of the work reported currently follows an approach to reasoning about supply chain problems based on SCOR (Supply-Chain Council, 2005). SCOR is growing in coverage and has earned recognition with near-global coverage, as it aims to describe all of the activities involved in the satisfaction of customer demand. The model contains five basic management processes (plan, source, make, deliver, and return) with various segments that can be applied to describe both simple and complex supply chains. A schematic representation of the SCOR model is presented in Figure 3.

SCOR is a business-process reference model that links process elements, metrics, best practices, and the features associated with the execution of a supply chain. Areas that the model does not span include sales and marketing, research and technology development, product development, and some elements of post-delivery customer support, but acknowledgement is made of those areas. Mention is made that the model has been adjusted in the past and will continue to be so, based on council requirements. SCOR does possess its own set of metrics organised in a hierarchical manner. The metrics are assigned as primary, high-level measures that cross the five business processes, before being

Figure 3. SCOR: Five major management processes (Reported by Supply-Chain Council, 2005)

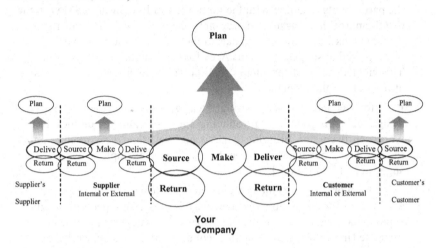

decomposed as diagnostic measures. These level-one metrics (reliability, responsiveness, flexibility, cost, and assets) are linked to what SCOR refers to as *performance attributes*. The performance attributes permit a supply chain to be analysed and evaluated against other supply chains with competing strategies (Supply-Chain Council, 2005).

Research Approach

In order to collect relevant, informed insights into the potential of SSM to facilitate improved strategic decision making in an SCM workshop environment, a short timeframe action-research approach, introducing a selection of SSM techniques to SCM practitioners in a workshop environment, has been applied.

A selection of SSM techniques has been introduced to a workshop of experienced SCM practitioners in two steps:

•   An initial workshop was held with members of the participating firm (Company X) in order to develop an understanding of the current supply chain methods employed by that firm and to inform the participants' initial thinking on the extent to which SSM tools and techniques might facilitate the conduct of a planned second workshop. SSM techniques were presented to the workshop, essentially as outlined earlier in this chapter. Opportunities for applying each of the SSM techniques were discussed with the participants, together with the possibility of integrating SSM with the SCOR approach that is used at present by Company X to facilitate its SCM decision making. In the second part of the first workshop, the participants were invited to suggest a "Focus Area for Consideration in Workshop 2." This yielded the SCM "problem situation" scenario that has been presented at the start of the Appendix.

Prior to a second workshop, thought was given by the researchers to the design of a program for introducing the tools and techniques into a workshop discussion, bringing to the second workshop the worked example (as per the Appendix) built on the fictitious example that had been suggested at Workshop 1.

• A second workshop was then conducted with the participants, introducing a number of SSM techniques as a means of examining aspects of the given supply chain situation that the participants had suggested they would be interested in exploring. During the second part of the second workshop, the participants engaged in what was essentially a focus group to explore their post-workshop reactions to the SSM approach and techniques. It is noteworthy that in this second workshop the participants were, figuratively speaking, wearing two hats, as their opinions on the use of the SSM approach and techniques were obtained from the perspective of both a consultant holding an SCM workshop and the clients participating in a workshop.

Both workshops were audio recorded, and transcriptions of both sessions were subjected to content analysis (Neuman, 2003), clustered around the participants' expectations of the relevance of the various SSM stages and techniques as introduced in Workshop 1, and their subsequent reactions to the second workshop that applied these techniques to the SCM scenario that they had suggested.

Results and Discussion

The Workshop Participants

The organization selected to participate in these studies (Company X) is an international supplier of SCM support services. As such, it was deemed ideal as a site to seek reactions to the possible use of SSM in a SCM context. Company X has established sections within its structure to deal with specific areas including the provision of:

- support, education, and assistance for its clients;
- help to larger businesses to gain the necessary accreditation to issue bar codes; and, most relevant to this study
- assistance with the identification and implementation of both e-commerce and SC management solutions; and
- consultancy services in the dynamic fields of e-commerce and SCM.

The participants for the research study were selected with the help of the General Manager of eTechnology Development at Company X, and were all current employees of Company X, with the exception of one who was a contracted consultant working with the company at the time. Their titles indicate the broad scope of their responsibilities, and include: General Manager eTechnology Development (GM); Knowledge Center Project Manager (KCPM); Industry Services Manager (ISM); Business Analyst (BA); eTechnology Development and Services Manager (DSM); and eTechnology Development and Standards Coordinator (DSC). It should be noted that most of the quotations below come from the KCPM, largely because, as the workshop developed, he summarized the discussion of the group at regular intervals. The abbreviations above are used in the following to identify the sources of particular quotations.

Workshop 1: Initial Reactions to the Possible Use of SSM to Facilitate SCM Strategic Decision-Making

When gathering responses concerning each participant's immediate reactions to the techniques offered by SSM, it became apparent that there were a number of overlaps of SSM with existing methods. SCOR, for example, was described by the KCPM as being "a process model and it looks at processes right across the supply chain at various levels of detail." It was stated by the KCPM, who has deep knowledge of SCOR, that he saw a number of areas of overlap. The KCPM was able make a comparison between the two and identified that "in terms of the five attributes the SCOR model pursues, they don't correspond directly to the five E's, although the efficacy and the efficiency overlap with one or two of the attributes." The KCPM was able to further identify that, based on what he had seen, some of the elements are processes, some are relationships, and some are transactions. "It's a combination of all of these." The DSC was able to draw a comparison with the unified modelling language (UML) but noted that SSM would be used as a higher level strategic approach.

The inherent difficulty in conveying the attributes of SSM in a short workshop scenario would not be fully realised until the participants had a further chance to see the application during the second workshop. When running through the material describing SSM alone and within an SCM context, it became obvious from the participants' comments that the second workshop would be essential in order to allow the participants to see a practical application of the tools and concepts. Some important insights were obtained, however, as to the participants' initial reactions towards where they thought limitations may exist. Specifically, the "rich picture" provoked much conversation as to its applicability in a high-level strategic sense. When discussing initial perceptions, the ISM observed:

Whilst I really like the pretty pictures, the people that we deal with are often in the mindset that it's too creative. My view again is similar to GM that I don't know enough about it... but they could be immediately alienated by what they see, the sort of superficial-type pictures.

The KCPM summarised this discussion by stating, "Where it would fall down is, I think, as the others have mentioned, some people would immediately balk at the cartoon-style pictures." The DSM agreed but was able to look further and suggested that:

I agree that you certainly wouldn't take it to the CEO of Company Y, and get him to start sketching drawings. But I think the small companies... We have very different levels of membership, so I think for some companies that model might work, where they are very simple people. Maybe they've been doing business the same way for years, and want to change and understand, so simple things like this might be of use.

Overall, it was suggested that smaller companies might see some benefit in the utilisation of the rich picture, although the costs of carrying out such workshops may present a limitation. The KCPM suggested:

We have small-type companies and time is one of their drivers, or the lack of it. We are talking about knowledge centers, and talking about bringing them to the Knowledge Center. Are we going to get a three-person band to devote essentially a six-hour program over whatever timeframe, perhaps an hour every time? That's a lot of money to them in the end.

Despite the participants' apprehensive initial opinion of the rich picture technique a number of extremely positive reactions were subsequently recorded on SSM's application in an SCM context. The most prominent of these was that of SSM's mapping of relationships. The KCPM in particular, as an expert on SCOR and quantitative analysis, declared:

The bit that is new and that doesn't overlap with what I have done previously, whether in the SCOR model, or in quantitative analysis of organisational modelling (analytical consulting). The bit that doesn't overlap is the relationship side of it. To be able to map out what the relationships are in an organisation's system and to systematically approach those relationships in terms of their importance, their impact, their 5 E's. To be able to map that out is a very good technique, and that is something that I haven't seen anywhere else.

This identification of a potentially innovative attribute of SSM within an SCM context prompted a discussion of exactly where the participants believed its application might truly lie. The GM was apprehensive and guarded at first when revealing that "my difficulty was to see its application in the general market place. I'm not too sure whether it's applicable to a consultant. I suppose it is, and the difficulty in actually executing it, that's my initial reaction." Later, the KCPM was able to elaborate further on its application in an optimistic sense:

I think you could relabel it CRM and get one of the big software companies to look at it. You'd make a million. Importantly SSM looks at the relationships between the various parties in the organisation, whether it's multiple organisations in the system, or a system within an organization.

The other participants began to open up and view the model as a possible complementary tool to their adopted SCOR approach. The KCPM was able to capture this as a highly analytical perception, as follows:

We could do some kind of cross-mapping there, but how I position the two is that where the SCOR model looks at processes, and it does that fairly rigorously, in a structured way, SSM would sit above that in a more strategic organisational design kind of environmental application.

The final concluding statement made by the GM, after taking into account all of the valuable contributions made, provided a neat summary of the initial perception of SSM's role within an SCM context:

Yes in those applications, where I think it, the window of opportunity, is for those organisations that are not too small, to have no time available for the technique. But on the other hand, not too big, that their system is beyond the capabilities of a bit of butcher's paper. So there is going to be a middle zone, where it is going to work better, both culturally and for complexity reasons. So you stay in that middle zone and you emphasise the strengths that come out of the relationships as the primary outcome of the methodology and don't play, or don't emphasise the process mapping, or the quantitative analysis, which are well covered by other techniques.

Workshop 2: Reactions to the Worked SSM Example

Between the first and second workshops, the researchers developed a sample of SSM in action in an SCM context to share with the participants and to provoke useful discussion, based upon a scenario provided by the workshop participants. That scenario and the fragments of an SSM study based upon it, as put forward for consideration in the second workshop, are presented in the Appendix.

The Rich Picture

The participants were first shown the rich picture (see the Appendix, Figure A1). The notion of drawing the picture together as a group was well received, as it was stated by participants that it would enable the client's conflicts to be identified, as well as showing "how they interact with each other." It was acknowledged that brainstorming was a necessary starting point and the benefits that the rich picture provided were in the structuring of that brainstorming into something more pictorial, something to which the clients can relate. The participants were accustomed to seeing bullet points of ideas, but the dot points and rectangle shapes are replaced in the rich picture by pictures. As the BA put it: ". . .with this one, the picture is growing and you can actually see the relationships, which actually shortens the time-span of decision making." This discussion of the ability of SSM to emphasis the relationships between all of the stakeholders created much enthusiasm. By highlighting the relationships, by drawing more transactional connections and not concentrating on whether the picture actually looks good or not, helpful insights can be obtained.

When introduced to the rich picture in Workshop 1 (refer to the previous section), the participants had felt that the rudimentary drawings in rich pictures would be of little relevance to CEOs or people of high organizational standing. The supportive attitudes that emerged in Workshop 2 were explained by the KCPM:

I think the significant difference between the sample drawing from last time and this time is the proportion of words versus pictures has changed dramatically. The sample here is 60% words and 40% pictures, whereas the last one was 70% pictures and 30% words. I think that this is a significant difference, which for someone who is used to dealing with words and PowerPoint slides, this is far more accessible than the one where it has all pictures.

The participants concluded that if you are a "picture person" the icons may make immediate sense, but you must accommodate those that rely more on words. The principal conclusions drawn were that getting the clients involved in the construction process and highlighting the relationships were the key strengths of the rich picture. As the KCPM summarised:

People do respond well to visual contact especially when we are talking about relationships. Its hard to understand relationships when you read a piece of paper text but if we can draw a picture of a relationship, especially a multi-party relationship like any supply chain is by definition, people are going to respond much faster and with much better insight to a visual representation.

Relevant Systems

By comparison to other SSM techniques that were seen as similar to notations the participants had used previously, the idea of naming relevant systems was an area that required substantial clarification. The named primary task model that was presented (see the Appendix, Stage 3) was described by the KCPM as being a "potentially double-edged sword, as invariably the problem presented to you as an analyst is a system of degree issue and so the question of scope is never in the client's mind." On further discussion, it was decided that it is essential that this issue of "what is the scope" that we are dealing with in a given situation must be prominent in the analyst's mind. For SSM analysts, the scope is usually established implicitly in the defining of the system. The workshop participants felt, however, that there was value in including with any named primary-task system, an explicit statement of the scope of the supply chain operations that it was within the brief of the supply chain managers to consider. "So the wrap up of that is while the primary task statement itself is very useful, it needs to have a related scope statement that establishes the boundary up front and steers the direction." The KCPM went further to conclude that:

The scope has to be done first, leading to the primary task that will have two levels of detail. Then, we do the CATWOE analysis, which effectively sets the components of the system in place, and only then do we drill down the next level of detail where we should talk about SWOT and other analysis.

Root Definition

The CATWOE analysis (Appendix, Stage 3) was received very well by the participants as a substantial and useful way to portray the situation at hand.

... I like the structure of that. I think it's got a much broader base than most methods I've seen, and therefore has the potential to pick up on the soft issues that are usually left out by most other methods. (KCPM)

In discussion of the root definition, however, it was agreed that placing the CATWOE in a paragraph format (see Appendix, Stage 3) was of no particular use. As the KCPM remarked, "the root definition, in my honest opinion, I can't make any sense out of that sentence. I find trying to convert all of that into one sentence doesn't work." Instead, the discussion turned to the removal of the root definition and the inclusion of a statement addressing the overall goals and objectives of the system that would appear at the very beginning of the process. As the KCPM put it:

What were the rules of engagement in the first place for us as consultants to be called in? My experience with different types of consulting projects is that if it is not very clear at the start then not only is the primary task and the scope likely to be skewed; all the work that follows might end up being completely wasted if we are not hitting the right target.

The way that SSM attempts to deal with this is to consider problem situations as opposed to problem statements, so there can not be a danger of locking yourself into a particular statement of the problem early on. For SSM analysts, the goals would emerge later as a result of the learning process mediated by these problem situations. This was accepted by the participants, although it was still firmly decided that:

We need an initial statement of what is the goal, not to lock in but to give a starting point... That's where you then get the problem situation as a collective of the initial stated goal and the real goal to solve the underlying root cause. (KCPM)

Human Activity System (Conceptual) Model

On presentation of the primary task human activity system (conceptual) model (Appendix, Figure A2), it became apparent that it overlapped on many fronts with the SCOR process model, and it was suggested by the KCPM "that in SC terms the process model of all process models was the SCOR model." The SCOR model defines all of the SC activities, with the exception of areas such as recruiting the workforce and the influence on taste and the management of business processes outside of the model. The SCOR model in substantial detail covers everything else inside of the boundary of the activity model that had been developed. As the KCPM stated: "I would actually use the SCOR model to cover 80% of that and then add the other bits." The participants suggested that the SCOR model could be used to cover all of the overlaps, and the activity systems model would be used on the periphery of it, concentrating on the outside issues of marketing, workforce creation, and coordination. Alternatively, it was presented that the same approach and layout used for the activity systems model could remain, with the words in the ellipses 4-11 (refer to Appendix, Figure A2) substituted with the SCOR terminology.

The KCPM was able to express a summary of the overlaps of the SCOR model with the human activity systems model:

There are some fuzzy overlaps with activity 3 and with 12,13 and 14. SCOR doesn't cover marketing so activity 2 is out of bounds while 4 is Plan in the SCOR model directly. 5 is a combination of the supplier's delivery function and the sourcing activity of the business, whilst 6 is the Source and 8 is part of Enable. 7 is not inside the SCOR model but they are currently working on its inclusion as a product designing process. 10 is deliver and 11 is arguably part of the delivery process.

A correlation, therefore, appears between most of the middle section of the developed activity model and SCOR, and potentially on the outer edges. It is the soft edges where there are, for example, decision makers or outside influences on the human activity systems, which SCOR does not model. At those places, the activity model construct of SSM would allow for the identification and labeling of processes, and might be of value in an SCM context.

Analysis/Comparison

Upon discussion of the tabular format of the analysis/comparison (refer Appendix, Figure A3), the participants agreed that it is good to have a structured approach and to systematically work through each of the process elements from the human activity systems model. The part that caused some confusion according to the KCPM was the distinction between the current and possible status. "Where I guess I'm struggling a bit is there doesn't seem to be a distinction between the 'as is' and the 'to be'." Some discussion of how this might be handled by SSM took place, although the participants still considered this a gray area, as the difference between the two may include or may not necessarily include all of the last two columns of the table—possible responses (activities and technologies). The KCPM summarised his impression of the activity analysis, bringing into play the 5 E's:

I'd like to see in this table the five E's which in turn trigger the performance measurement approach. I think the five E's are roughly equivalent to the five performance attributes of the SCOR model and in the SCOR model they are actually introduced right back at the high-level version of the process model.

The Interface between SSM and SCOR

An important theme emerging from the two workshops, and the subject of particular discussion towards the end of the second workshop, was the notion of interfacing SSM with workshop discussions that employed SCOR as a reference.

In summary, the participants in the present study were enthusiastic and displayed genuine interest in both of the workshops conducted. In particular, the KCPM contributed significantly to discussion about the linking of SSM with SCOR and was able to summarise the possible integration of SSM and SCOR at the end of Workshop 1, as follows:

How I position the two is that where the SCOR model looks at processes, and it does that fairly rigorously, in a structured way, SSM would sit above that in a more strategic organisational design kind of environmental application. And for those organisations that are taking seriously these issues, it would be a useful front-end before they embark on process mapping, which in turn comes before they embark on system upgrades and specifications. So, put in the right context, it works best as a precursor to the various other process and technology-orientated tools.

During the second workshop, the participants' views on SSM developed as they had been able to see its practical application to the scenario provided. The following is a summary of the main results that have been reported above, drawn particularly from Workshop 2, related to the way the two methods (SCOR-based and SSM) might be used together. This draws, in particular, upon a body of very useful reflection that took place with the participants near the end of the second workshop.

As a result of the workshop discussions, it emerged that the first step might be the formation of an initial statement of objectives. This statement would establish the rules of engagement of the project and would provide an initial motivation to commence analysis. This would not be a "locked-in" final statement, as later on in the process it would be revisited and potentially revised.

The next step would be the identification of a primary task statement that should capture the key issue of "what system we are looking at." This could come out of a rich picture that could include a heavy use of words to aid in client understanding. The words can then be transformed into cartoon-style pictures, and, as the client's understanding is enhanced, the pictures may be replaced by icons. This is a stage that can be "initiated with flexibility," as the interchange of words, pictures, and icons could be shaped according to client comprehension. The primary task statement may be a short sentence at the highest level, but accompanied by a supporting statement with a few bullet points that "unpack into a second-level tier of detail."

Along with the two-tier definition of the task, we also need a scope or boundary statement to establish clearly "what is in and what is out." This step needs to be clearly spelled out and appear right at the beginning of the activity analysis, as it will have an impact on all of the process design that follows.

The modelling process then begins by undertaking the CATWOE analysis, which, as the participants noted, has a "broader base" than most methods and picks up on the soft issues that are usually left out by other methods. The CATWOE analysis should be accompanied by a discussion of the five E's. Although the five E's appear normally at the end of the activity analysis, it is necessary to draw attention to them at this earlier stage without allocating specific measures. An understanding should be obtained of the impact of each element of the CATWOE on the 5 E's, as we begin to make the conceptual link between the system as we are defining it and the outcomes measured later on by the 5 E's.

At this point, it is then appropriate to go back and reconfirm the goal or objective established in the initial statement. A complete loop has been completed as we have devised a rich picture, Primary Task Definition, and first-round CATWOE analysis. We have looked at the performance attributes, or the five E's, in a preliminary sense and, thus, completed one loop. It is appropriate then to go back and reconfirm the goal or objective to confirm that a full understanding of the situation is held, before the goals of the project are reinforced.

Having set the stage, the next step would be to construct a process model or human activity system model. The participants regarded the way the SSM method approaches the conversion of relationships into activities or processes in high regard. As discussed, "the SCOR model would be used in place of activities 4-11 as a direct correlation appears for most of the middle section." It is the soft edges where there are, for example, decision makers or outside influences on the human activity systems, which SCOR does not model, where an SSM approach would allow for the identification and labelling of additional processes, and therefore would enhance SCOR. This would then be followed by an activity analysis, which drills down into each activity identified.

In order to ensure that ideas that fall outside of the columns in the SSM comparison stage are not lost, a more rigorous approach should be adopted. This could be to add an extra column, "process reengineering," to SSM's tabular comparison format. Process reengineering has more rigor than SSM's current idea of an activity/technology analysis, but this should be applied on a case-by-case basis.

The last step, which is not written into SSM, is that one might need to bring together all of the elements that have been analysed and synthesised and repackage it. This would form a high-level statement of the reengineered or proposed new system.

Conclusion and Outlook

The major outcomes reported in this chapter might be summarized as follows:

- A motivation for research into techniques that might be applied in workshop processes to facilitate the early decision-making processes in addressing SCM concerns has been provided (see *Introduction* and *Background*);
- An introduction to the SSM approach to such problem-solving has been provided (see *Using SSM to Facilitate SCM Decision-making Work-*

shops), including a worked example using a fictitious SCM scenario provided by a group of experienced SCM practitioners (Appendix). Previous applications of SSM in the SCM context have also been briefly reviewed;

- A workshop-based approach to investigate the reactions of SCM professionals to SSM, and to collect their thoughts on the worked example has been described (see Research Approach); and

- A discussion of the data captured within two workshops has been presented. The subject company and the participants involved have been described. An analysis of the data captured in the workshops has been reported, including tentative conclusions on the integration of SCOR with SSM in an SCM workshop context (see *Results and Discussion*).

This study has offered the opportunity to build the theoretical and practical base of both SCM and SSM and, in turn, to open the path for future research, possibly integrating further SSM techniques into SCM practice in a number of varied settings. The results reported have provided enhanced insight into the potential benefits of SSM within a workshop decision-making environment, and have provided valuable guidance to both practitioners and theoreticians alike.

References

Checkland, P. (1981). *Systems thinking, systems practice.* Chichester, UK: John Wiley & Sons.

Checkland, P. (1999). *Systems thinking, systems practice: Includes a thirty-year retrospective.* Chichester, UK: John Wiley & Sons.

Checkland, P., & Holwell, S. (1998). *Information, systems and information systems: Making sense of the field.* Chichester, UK: John Wiley & Sons.

Checkland, P., & Scholes, J. (1990). *Soft systems methodology in action.* Chichester, UK: John Wiley & Sons.

Elmuti, D. (2002). The perceived impact of supply chain management on organisational effectiveness. *Journal of Supply Chain Management, 38*(3),49-57.

Ferguson, B. R. (2000). Implementing supply chain management. *Production and Inventory Management Journal, 41*(2), 64-67.

Neuman, W. (2003). *Social research methods: Qualitative and quantitative approaches.* Boston: Pearson Education.

O'Connell, J. (1999). Streamlining supply chain management processes. *Document World, 4*(1), 40-42.

Perry, M., & Sohal, A. S. (2000). Quick response practices and technologies in developing supply chains: A case study. *International Journal of Physical Distribution and Logistics Management, 30*(7-8), 627-639.

Rigby, C., Day, M., Forrester, P., & Burnett, J. (2000). Agile supply: Rethinking systems thinking, systems practice. *International Journal of Agile Management Systems, 2*(3), 178-186.

Smith, R., Mackay, D., Altmann, G., & Gencoglu, G. (2002). Using SSM to improve supply chain management effectiveness. In G. Ragsdell, D. West, & J. Wilby (Eds.), *Theory and Practice in the Knowledge Age, Proceedings of the 7th International Conference of the UK Systems Society* (pp. 87-96). New York: Kluwer Academic/Plenum Publishers.

Songkhla, N. A. (1997). A soft system approach in introducing information technology: A case study of an international broadcasting programme in Japan. *Information Technology and People, 10*(4), 275-286.

Supply-Chain Council (2005). *Supply-chain operations reference model, Overview of SCOR Version 7.0*. Pittsburgh, PA.

Wilson, B. (1984). *Systems: Concepts, methodologies and applications*. Chichester, UK: John Wiley & Sons.

Appendix

Sample Application of SSM to an SCM Scenario

In the following, the seven-stage SSM approach is applied to a simplified SCM scenario supplied by the SCM practitioners who participated in the study described in this chapter. Note that, although fictitious, the practitioners felt this example was indicative of the types of issues that can emerge in the early stages of strategic discussions with supply chain representatives.

Stage 1: Problem Situation Considered Problematic

Consider the following fictitious scenario. This information may have been put together by speaking with various stakeholders, reading background documentation, and the like.

A number of furniture manufacturers in South Australia have met informally to discuss their on-going viability and the prospect that they might all profit by cooperating with each other and with participants at other points in the furniture manufacturing and retailing supply chain.

Specifically, there are five manufacturers—two are small, involving fewer that 10 employees each; the other three might be termed medium-level enterprises, each having approximately 20 to 30 staff (both furniture makers and accounting/administrative staff). All these manufacturers are each producing small quantities of standard furniture items to their own characteristic designs, as well as custom-designed items for clients who approach them directly. In particular, they each specialise in the use of Australian timbers. Each furniture manufacturer sells directly to the public at their factory warehouse, and a couple have arrangements to sell through specialist furniture outlets that are local to South Australia.

A number of concerns have arisen. Primarily, they are producing more furniture items than they can sell. The large-scale consumer market is being swamped by cheaper imported furniture. They do not see themselves as competing directly against this cheap furniture, however. The major problem is that they have a marketing presence in South Australia for their more costly, higher quality items, but they have no visibility in the eastern states where the majority of buyers are. Indeed, they believe that the South Australian market is essentially saturated. For some of the manufacturers it has become a matter of find new markets or go under!

To go outside their present marketplace, however, they realise that they need to build a framework of organisational and industry cohesion. They need to link in a more efficient fashion to their timber suppliers, to the transport companies (e.g., historically, they have been using local transport companies, but they need to network to larger freight companies across the eastern half of the country), and to furniture retailers who have a presence in the eastern states. In addition, and underlying all this, there is a need to market themselves and the products they offer more vigorously in the eastern states.

They also recognise that if they are to move forward in a more concerted fashion, they need to carry out their operations in a more controlled fashion, tracking the performance of all aspects of their operations to support planning and tuning of all aspects of the operation of their supply chain.

Figure A1. Rich Picture for the "Furniture Manufacturers' Problem Situation"

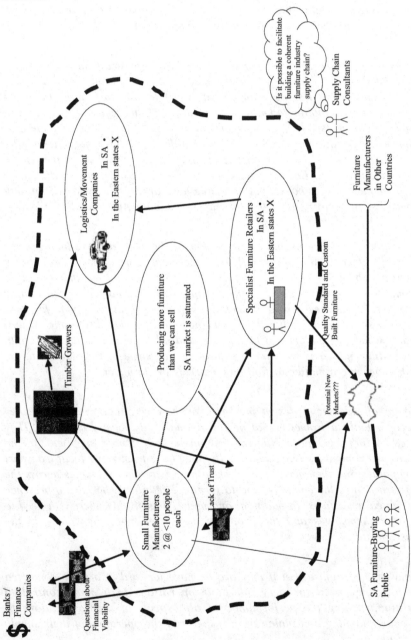

Representatives of each of these five manufacturers have made an appointment with the consultancy team to seek advice and support on how they might, through cooperation across the entire specialist furniture supply chain, build and service markets in the eastern states that will lead to increased profitability for all. To come this far has been a major step, as to date they have been competitors and so have jealously guarded their arrangements with timber suppliers and the designs that make their particular furniture products unique.

Stage 2: Problem Situation Expressed

The analyst, together with stakeholders, might proceed to express the complex situation above as a rich picture, as shown in Figure A1. Note that such rich pictures are most often hand-drawn, as they are intended to open up discussion rather than form substantial study deliverables as might appear in a final report.

Stage 3: Root Definition of Relevant Purposeful Activity Systems

Study of the rich picture might lead the analyst, in discussion with stakeholders, to identify many possible relevant systems that might be modelled. A sample of the relevant systems that might be identified, grouped as primary task and issue-based, include:

Primary Task:
- A system to transform trees into furniture owned by members of the general public
- Others are possible.

Issue-Based:
- A system to market specialized/custom furniture in established areas
- A system to find new marketplaces in new areas
- A system to build trust and cooperation among cooperating partners
- Others are possible.

If the analyst chose to concentrate on the primary task system named above, the following CATWOE elements and root definition might be developed:

CATWOE Analysis—A system to transform trees into furniture owned by members of the general public:

- **(C)lient:** The public that wishes to purchase timber furniture
- **(A)ctor:** Management and employees of all tiers of the timber furniture production and retail supply chain
- **(T)ransformation:** Unharvested Trees → Timber furniture purchased by members of the general public
- **(W)orldview:** Cooperation and coordination of all tiers of the timber furniture production and retail supply chain can be of financial benefit to all participating bodies
- **(O)wner:** The controlling principals of each participating body in the timber furniture production and retail supply chain
- **(E)nvironment:** Skilled workforces at all tiers of the supply chain; and Members of the general public with tastes that can be influenced in timber furniture products and with finite buying power.

Root Definition—*A system to transform trees into furniture owned by members of the general public.* A controlling principals of each participating body in the timber furniture production and retail supply chain owned, management and employees of all tiers of the timber furniture production and retail supply chain operated system to transform unharvested trees into timber furniture purchased by members of the general public, recognising that cooperation and coordination of all tiers of the timber furniture production and retail supply chain can be of financial benefit to all participating bodies. This takes place in an environment of skilled workforces at all tiers of the supply chain, and members of the general public with tastes that can be influenced in timber furniture products and with finite buying power.

Stage 4: Conceptual Models of the Systems (holons) Named in the Root Definitions

Applying the process outlined in the discussion of soft systems methodology in the body of the chapter and discussed by Checkland (1999), to the root definition/ CATWOE above, the analyst might develop a model as shown in Figure A2. (Note: the details of such a model might differ somewhat, depending on the particular ideas that the analyst recognised as worthy of consideration, but one would expect the activities to be broadly as shown.) It is suggested also that there is value in thinking about what might constitute the measures of performance of

Figure A2. Conceptual model of "a system to transform trees into furniture owned by members of the general public"

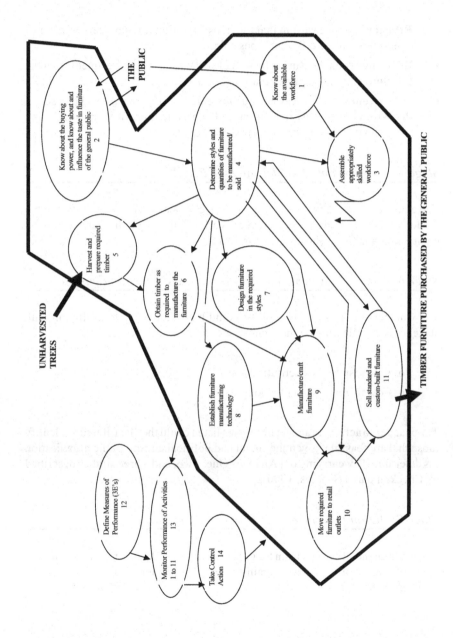

the system defined in the root definition. SSM encourages these measures of performance being expressed as:

- **Efficacy** (i.e., measuring that the transformation takes place): Number of furniture items of different types sold;
- **Efficiency** (i.e., measuring benefit cf cost): Return on investment from the furniture manufacturing operations; and
- **Effectiveness** (i.e., measuring achievement of the purposes expressed in the Worldview): Cost reductions and consequent profit increases arising from enhanced cooperation across the supply chain.

Stage 5: Comparison of Models and the Real World

The analyst and stakeholders could now systematically use the activities in the model to examine the perceived real world. This might be carried out by completing a table as shown in Figure A3.

Stage 6: Changes: Systemically Desirable and Culturally Feasible

The Comparison Table in Figure A3 could be extended, in consultation with stakeholders, reflecting on the comparison, to include the columns:

- Possible responses (Activities); and
- Possible responses (Technology).

The changes to activities and technologies listed could then be filtered to identify those that are feasible, given the social and political culture of the organisation (as determined by carrying out Analysis One, Two, and Three studies described by Checkland and Scholes, 1990).

Stage 7: Action to Improve the Problem Situation

The recommended actions from Stage 6 will then be undertaken. In principle, the cycle of SSM can then begin again to generate further ideas to improve the problem situation.

Figure A3. Sample from possible Comparison Table (only Activities 1 and 2 are shown)

Activity	Currently Done? (Yes/No)	Responsible Party	Present means of assessing performance	Current assessment	Possible responses (Activities)	Possible responses (Technology)
1. Know about the available workforce	Yes—but reactive	Handled separately at each node in the supply chain by managers/HR per-sonnel	Standard HR measures applied at each node on the supply chain	Reactive only—no means of predicting demand and therefore required workforce in advance	Coordinate advance notice of production demand across the supply chain. Introduce processes to monitor and model seasonal demand	EDI supported ordering linking timber mills/movement providers/ furniture manufacturers/ furniture retailers
2. Know about the buying power, and know about and influence the taste in furniture of the general public	Not in place. Some knowledge of taste in furniture vested in individuals, based upon their years of experience. No coordinated marketing	None presently, except sales staff at the factory outlets	Present furniture sales figures	Current performance is poor. SA market appears to be saturated	Establish a joint marketing strategy, funded across all the members of the furniture supply chain	Centralised database of furniture sales figures, supplemented by recent market research

Chapter XI

Integrated E-Enterprise Supply Chain Security Design and Implementation

Stephen C. Shih, Southern Illinois University, USA

Michael Camarata, University of Akron, USA

H. Joseph Wen, Southeast Missouri State University, USA

Abstract

Web technology has enabled many organizations to form an e-enterprise for effective communicating, collaborating, and information sharing. To gain competitive advantages, it is necessary for e-enterprises to integrate the entire lines of business operations and critical business data with external supply chain participants over the Web, which may introduce significant security risks to the organizations' critical assets and infrastructures. This chapter reports a case study of e-service security design and implementation at a leading U.S. company. First, the chapter reviews security concerns and challenges in front-end e-business and back-end supply chain operations. This is followed by the analysis of the company's e-service and its security problems. The case then presents an integrated e-enterprise security methodology to guide the company for meeting its security needs. The results of this case study provides security professionals with practical steps and sustainable solutions for tackling the unique security challenges arising in an open, unbounded e-enterprise supply chain environment.

Introduction

Information technologies (IT) have brought about tremendous changes to the way businesses operate. Many of these changes revolve around and are concerned with the way firms interact with other participants operating as part of their supply chains (Parker & Russell, 2004; Shakir & Viehland, 2005). Competitive pressures are bound to make faster and leaner supply chains a primary goal for manufacturing, distribution, and retail companies. But even as this is occurring, there are further demands to incorporate supply chain agility, adaptation, and alignment all across the system. The potential of using the Internet as a new commercial communication channel has been widely explored. However, a critical assessment of its e-commerce integrated e-enterprise security has just started to receive attention.

Recognizing this vexing security issue, it is obvious that the effective management of e-enterprise security at an organizational level is important (Dess, Rasheed, McLaughlin, & Priem, 1995; Forcht, Saunders, Usry, & Egan, 1997). Nevertheless, due to the wide dispersion of the Internet-based networks, there has been a scarcity of e-enterprise security management guidelines for the e-era organizations. Without proper security management, each type of Internet-based online e-business exchange may raise significant issues and concerns, which threaten the system's fundamental strategic objective of establishing a secure trading environment between the organization and its e-business counterparts (customers, suppliers, and other business partners.

Increased uncertainty and risk threatens to cancel a significant portion of the benefits gained through enhanced supply chain collaboration in the form of increased openness and system-wide information access. Risk increase always carries with it increased costs. Higher risk requires a greater risk premium. Such premium increases are reflected in the total supply chain cost structure as greater value chain costs, which, in turn, lower the realized benefits and added value of systemic transparency.

Over the years, researchers have debated on different perspectives of information security and e-business security (Brunnstein, 1997; Stix, 2005; Yngstrom, 1995). Lichtenstein and Swatman (1997) suggest that the risks must be managed through policies, other management steps, and technical measures. An e-business security policy is the medium by which e-business security requirements for the organization are specified, and the means by which guidance and rules are provided to e-business participants within the business. They further stress that the development of an Internet strategy should direct usage towards the continuous alignment and realignment of business processes with business objectives. Otuteye (2002) stresses the significance of corporate information security management and hypothesizes that effective e-business security decisions have to be part of an overall corporate information security and risk management policy. While most studies in network security to date have emphasized technical solutions, recent literature has been reflecting an emergence of a limited number of studies that incorporate behavioral considerations and technological approaches to security management methods, principles, and models (Guttman & Bagwill, 2003; Lichtenstein & Swatman, 1997; Microsoft Corporation, 2004; Rannenberg, 1994; Tan & Thoen, 2000; U.S. GAO, 1998).

These studies gathered data and learned from "best partnering" experiences and offered "…a process for aligning expectations and determining the level of cooperation that would be most productive…" (Sakaguchi, Nicovich, & Dibrell, 2004, p. 3) to supply chain partners. The data clearly points out that firms wishing to realize performance outcomes that meet expectations must understand their compelling reason(s) for partnering. If parties to any proposed supply chain system partnership understand their unique needs and then share their needs and expectations up front with their partners, levels of anxiety and fear would lessen and a mutuality of interest culture could begin to develop. In a supportive, trusting environment, previously hidden information and actions are brought into the open, driving costs throughout the supply chain lower.

All parties in such a system learn that each participant will be rewarded fairly and equitably in the long run by working within and for a partnership. Such expectations and conclusions are supported by the work of Becker (1960) and Butler (1991, 1995), who found that investments in building social capital build trust and trust provides the foundation for commitment. As the dynamics of the marketplace shift, required changes in the system and incentives for members are adjusted to maintain alignment, equity, and balance. With trust and commitment firmly established, partners can openly signal each other that equity within the system will remain a priority. Equally, suboptimization would be frowned on since it would threaten basic social understanding and commitment and would become an added cost to all players. Thus, agency theory would work to the benefit of the overall performance of the system. Opportunism, once identified, would lead to future system membership exclusion, a very harsh penalty in an increasingly interconnected marketplace.

It is apparent from the direction that current research is moving that behavioral considerations will, of necessity, need to be part of any such system. What is also apparent is that people and their actions are very difficult if not impossible to quantify. Accordingly, relationship and trust building become necessary ingredients to any long-term successful supply chain partnership or alliance. Their part in building a security management framework is aimed more at preventing security breaches internally by building and enhancing intersystem relationships based on trust, commitment, and mutuality of interest.

The remainder of this chapter is organized as follows. An overview of the case company background and the analysis of its security problems are presented next. The following section describes the integrated security solutions that emerged from the analysis phase of the research. The last section briefly concludes this chapter. Issues relating to behavioral based security concerns will be addressed as they become apparent within the context of overall supply chain system analysis and security protocols.

Problem Analysis

HVAC is a leading U.S. company in manufacturing and sales of heating, ventilating, and air conditioning systems and products. Headquartered on the East Coast, the company has over 45,000 employees in 150 countries. With approximate $8.9 billion in annual revenue, the company offers a wide range of choices for air conditioning/heating products and refrigeration units in three major areas: (1) home heating and cooling systems (e.g., air conditioners, heat pumps, furnaces, programmable thermostats, humidifiers, air cleaners, and ventilators), (2) commercial/industrial heating and cooling systems for business office and school buildings, and (3) commercial refrigeration and transport refrigeration systems (i.e., truck/trailer and container refrigeration equipment, and transport air conditioning systems for the bus, rail, and marine industries). With a worldwide network of hundreds of distributors and thousands of dealers who sell, install, and service its products in over 150 countries, the company designs and manufactures its HVAC products in 20 engineering centers and over 100 plants spread across five continents. Within the U.S. and Canada, the company has over 90 service offices, with 12 or so service technicians in each local office. In each office, there are one or more service supervisors and a service administrator.

e-Service Initiatives

In 2001, some of the company's business partners were signing up for the virtual trading marketplace. One of the foremost e-business initiatives of the company has been to deploy the Web-enabled "e-Service" system (Figure 1) for the purpose of enhancing productivity and customer services, specifically for its field service offices in U.S. According to the vice-president of its Global Service Division, "the e-Service has provided a viable mechanism for tracking customers, job sites, equipment, and service contracts." The system also allows office supervisors to effectively assign maintenance tasks to individual technicians and track the progress of those tasks. Furthermore, the system provides supervisors and technicians with the capability of tracking and managing necessary parts, components, and tools on a real-time basis.

The e-Service offers Web-enabled operations and exchanges between the company and its customers, dealers, and components suppliers. It is a worldwide federation of over 600 stores that constitute the world's largest heating, ventilating, air conditioning, and refrigeration supplies organization. These stores make up a true "one-stop online store" for parts and supplies in the industry. Under the centralized management of the company's component replacement center, suppliers, dealers, and customers can access an electronic information catalog of over 100,000 parts.

HVAC has also recognized that wireless connectivity has great potential to revolutionize the industry fundamentally. Recent data show the availability of wireless solutions for mobilizing Web-enabled e-commerce applications. In the company, the growing number of mobile users (mostly field service technicians)

Figure 1. e-Service systems

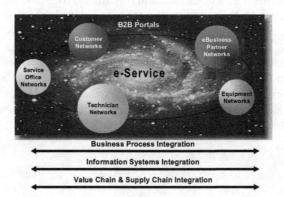

has been triggering wide exploitation of wireless Web. With the marriage of Internet and telecommunications technologies, both the company's employees and business partners are able to access the Web from a greater variety of devices, including both the traditional computer devices and mobile devices like personal digital assistants, mobile cellular telephones, and enhanced pagers. Along the line, a full-scale deployment of mobilized Web-driven applications and services is becoming one of the spotlights in the company. What is missing in its enthusiastic acceptance of the benefits of openness and disclosure is a critical assessment of the potential downside costs in terms of security risk and long-term asset diminishment.

Whipple and Frankel (2000) relate that there is consensus in most industries that as many as 75 % of the participants in alliances felt that the expectations they held going into the alliance were not met. Such outcomes suggest that partici-pants in a supply chain collaboration, which simulates a broad quasi-alliance, should proceed with their eyes wide open. They have access to data and information about potential alliance partners from industry networks and many areas of business that can be used to generate behavioral expectations of both insiders and other parties to the supply chain collaboration. Again, relationship and trustworthiness must be factored in to create a reasoned, balanced approach between granting a new member unbridled openness and access and allowing the member selective sharing adjusted as firm or trusted intermediary experience warrants.

Security Concerns in B2B Supply Chain Interactions

The executive managers of the company have recently recognized the great potential of using the Internet technology as a powerful weapon to increase the company's competitive advantage. Consequently, the company started to pro-vide its business partners with wider access to its critical enterprise information for boosting productivity and operational efficiency and delivering services quickly and satisfactorily—all at the lowest possible cost. As one field service manager puts it:

The caliber to communicate and collaborate with partners, suppliers, customers, and employees anytime and anywhere is now a requirement at the center stage. As a result, deploying the e-Service system is currently the heart of the company's e-business initiatives for effective B2B e-commerce.

Although business-to-business (B2B) commercial medium has been widely explored, a critical assessment of its B2B e-commerce challenges and issues has just started to receive attention. Based on surveys on e-commerce-related security (Cavazos & Morin, 1994; Clarke, 2000; Clarke, 2001; Information Security Magazine, 2000; Rubin & Geer, 1998), the frequency of security attacks, incidents, and breaches is far greater for e-commerce companies. Organizations can not forget that few benefits accrue without some kind of cost, or, to put it more simply, "there is no free lunch." The company of study is not alone in this case. The managers have realized that this new economy of ubiquitous e-commerce may have introduced new risks and challenges to the company. As one information technology (IT) manager noted:

One of the important contributors that resulted in the rise in e-commerce related security incidents has been the "openness" to our business partners. One of our business partners, such as the first-tier suppliers, in the B2B supply chain can have access to the company's highly confidential back-end enterprise resources, like product design and inventory data. As a result, the security challenge is about to migrate from securing of individual network level to protecting the entire virtual network of electronic marketplace.

While implementing and deploying the e-service, various concerns have sur-faced confronting the system's end users, including the field service managers and the company's business partners. Among all the concerns raging about the e-service system, security ranks the highest according to a survey conducted with a sample of the company's service offices in North America. The survey revealed that a majority of the office managers were very concerned about security issues in the developing and deploying e-business environment due to many reported incidents in recent years. In fact, based on the recent incident reports collected in this study, new hostile tactics and more sophisticated means of security threats were reported more frequently than ever before.

Before responding from an "under siege" mentality or in a knee-jerk fashion, firms need to recognize that some degree of their concern can clearly be attributed to fear or lack of trust between alliance partners or to their own level of "trust propensity." Mayer, Davis, and Schoorman, (1995) document this in their model of trust. Three factors are critical in building trust or perceived trustworthiness: (1) ability, (2) benevolence, and (3) integrity. A fourth moder-ating influence is the trustor's propensity to trust (Mayer et al., 1995). Willing-ness to act in the face of perceived risk was shown to shown to be influenced by the presence of trust. Outcomes were, in turn, influenced by relationships that created a willingness to be vulnerable as indicated by risk taking.

A second way of conceiving trust between members of a system is to deconstruct the concept—trust—into three levels: (1) cognitive, (2) affective, and (3) covenantal trust. In this approach, cognitive trust is based on clear evidence of compliance with mutual expectations. It is a quid-pro-quo, tit-for-tat understanding of trust. "A" acts in a way that is acceptable to "B," so "B," based on concrete, observable transactional behavior, trusts "A." Affective trust, however, requires the trusting party, "B," to choose to act favorably towards "A" before "A" actually acts, introducing a willingness on the part of "B" to risk in the face of uncertainty. Often, there may be previous experience with "A" but not within the decision arena facing "B." "B," in the process of choosing to trust "A" in the face of risk, commits to an affective relationship with "A," cementing a deep union between the parties. Assuming "A" acts appropriately and positively toward "B" within the boundaries of the risk taking, the bond is reinforced. Affective commitment is not easily given nor easily broken. In the business setting, the third level of trust, covenantal (intimate) trust, is rare. It sometimes can be seen in the Middle Eastern and Asian concept of "Old Friend."

Recently, the number of business applications and databases being deployed for intranets and extranets in the company's supply chain continues to grow rapidly. However, with the same distributed nature as that of the Internet-based system, an intranet/extranet-driven supply chain network is always a conspicuous target of security attacks. One financial manager related this concern in the following statement:

Doing business through the Web-enabled supply chain network can open the possibilities to some significant security threats. For instance, financial transactions may be interrupted or misdirected by the hackers or crackers. Collaborative supply chain information may introduce the opportunity of revealing sensitive intellectual property to competitors. Logistics information can be illegally used to disrupt normal transportation operations. Attackers can break into an organization's or its partner's supply chain infrastructure and may disrupt or totally paralyze its business operations and functions.

One IT manager further added his comment:

After the 9-11 incident, supply chain security has now involved attacks via global supply chain networks. The company is now forced to reevaluate its security management model, infrastructure, and policies that were already in place and to examine if they should be strengthened or redesigned. The stakes can be extraordinarily high from serious security attacks on the e-

enterprise supply chain network. Accordingly, when our company is reaching out to each other via the Web-based supply chain network, the security should be properly controlled and managed beyond just perimeter protection.

To address these issues, information security analysts and logistics experts have to work together to confront this reality immediately. Eventually, the security measure should cover the entire supply chain of players including manufacturers, suppliers, suppliers, contractors, warehouse providers, and air, sea, and land carriers. A guideline on security recommendations should be available for manufacturers, importers, brokers, air carriers, land carriers, and sea carriers. For manufacturers and importers, these recommendations should cover physical security, access controls, procedural security, personnel security manifest procedures, conveyance security and education and training awareness.

The advent of wireless computing and Internet technologies have significantly changed the way the company's data is stored, accessed, and shared. With the wireless-enabled e-service system, the company is able to implement a more open and distributed information-sharing model for the purpose of leveraging the power of collaboration and network connectivity, as well as enabling closer relations and communications with its customers and partners. Indeed, wireless e-commerce technology is opening up tremendous competitive advantages and exciting opportunities for the company. Unfortunately, this also makes the company far more vulnerable than ever before to security attacks. As one security engineer in the research center commented:

After connecting the company's systems more tightly with those of our business partners via the wireless Web, we are now realizing that the dangers of attacks by intruders become increasingly significant, and the scale of potential damage also rises in magnitude. Mobile workers in particular can be vulnerable, as hackers set off attacks through wireless communications channels against the company's and its business partners' networks.

In other words, the recent proliferation of wireless communications has raised the security stakes further. This phenomenon has made its way firmly into the supply chain applications, such as wireless logistics and warehousing implementations, wireless financial transactions, and sales force automation using mobile devices. Unfortunately, the inherent strengths of wireless access in a supply chain are also the source of its biggest vulnerabilities. This issue was clearly emphasized in a comment made by one IT manager in a discussion session:

Mobility is a clear benefit that wireless communications brings to supply chain communications. However, it can also result in great network exposure and rogue access. Unlike hard-wired systems, unauthorized listeners can easily compromise or tamper data transmitted over wireless media without having to gain physical access to the network infrastructure.

He further remarked on one myth of wireless communications security:

The company has long recognized security as a significant issue in the implementation of B2B e-commerce; nevertheless, for many people, there does not seem to be a related concern with security for wireless communications due to the false perception that wireless technology is inherently safe if the wired infrastructure has been properly safeguarded.

All things considered, this means that the requirements for a complete supply chain security solution must also include the protection of users and resources, whether wired or wireless, as funds are electronically transferred, online trades are made, and sensitive business information is shared between collaborative partners.

Failure to develop a security system that protects users and resources would be catamount to throwing away the potential supply chain gains realized from mutual openness and sharing. Such gains and benefits can be substantial. For example, where openness and sharing is complete, a supplier can maintain supply chain compliance at much lower inventory levels, reducing system costs and increasing system profitability. It has been estimated that as little as a 1% drop in required inventory can translate into millions of dollars in savings in the system. Mutuality of interest creates a sense of belonging that lessens any need for "hidden actions" and lowers the probability for agency theory behaviors to be exercised. The supply chain system belongs to the whole, and like any group that is unified around a super-ordinate goal, it performs both efficiently and effectively.

The Need for an Integrated Security Management and Control Measure

According to the concerns raised by the vast number of managers of the company, security has become an essential part of planning, implementing, and managing the e-service system. Nevertheless, as one executive manager noted, "the security issue that the company faces is very compound and multifaceted."

She explained:

First of all, with wide deployment of distributed client/server and Web-enabled networks, we find it much more difficult and laborious to effectively safeguard our critical networks, applications, and data. Secondly, the need to connect and collaborate with our partners, suppliers, customers, and employees anytime and anywhere has dramatically increased the complexity of managing network and systems security. Thirdly, field service technicians not only work from branch offices, but from the service sites, or from the road. Managing access policies for remote connectivity requires great flexibility to apply proper security policies to different types of connectivity. Finally, security in B2B e-commerce environment involves not only the computer where data start off, but also multiple points throughout various networks through which the data pass.

She further commented, "in the meshes of supply chain networks, a security implementation is only as secure as its weakest link." Because of this truism, security approaches need to recognize that people and their rational and sometimes irrational behavior must be fully considered in the construction of any security management infrastructure. As a result, to take advantage of the benefits from implementing the e-service system, the company needs a secure IT infrastructure that can minimize security risks and further decrease the costs of security management and operations. More than ever, the company needs to leverage state-of-the-art security solutions that will reduce risks while enabling flexibility and adaptability to ensure a proper balance for the corporate security strategy and policy. However, due to no coherent enterprise-wide Web security management method and standard currently existing in the company, the network administrators can only be responsible for various segments of the company's network infrastructure, simply pursuing their own solutions and developing their own autonomous security measures and policies to meet the urgent needs. Addressing this need, an integrated e-enterprise security management methodology is adopted to help the company identify its security exposures and provide the right security tools and controls, especially for a secured e-business environment.

Figure 2. An integrated e-enterprise security methodology

An Integrated e-Enterprise Security Methodology

An e-enterprise security methodology was collaboratively developed by the case study team and several research engineers of the company's research center to address the security needs. The methodology is made up of four major stages: (1) establishment of a baseline model, (2) development of a visual security scenario simulation model and decision-support system, (3) development of security information systems architecture, and (4) demonstration and validation. These major tasks with associated milestones and steps are listed in Figure 2.

The methodology adopted the concept of "survivability" (Lipson & Fisher, 1999) to protect highly distributed enterprise systems and critical organizational assets from being comprised. Survivability is defined as the capability of a system to fulfill its critical mission in a timely manner and in the presence of attacks, failures, or accidents (Mathy, Edwards, & Hutchinson, 2000). Furthermore, the methodology can be considered an "emergent property" (Ellison et al., 1999;

Hinton, 1997) that portrays a notion that an end-to-end security control cannot be achieved at the level of atomic model components, since each component corresponds to a single point of failure for its own survival. In other words, the creation of a reliable security control and management model from atomic components may be less reliable than the composite model. As a result, a holistic approach is embraced to ensure the unification and congruousness of the new security methodology. HVAC accepted the methodology and designed its e-service security accordingly in the following four steps.

Step 1: Security Baseline Establishment

In this initial effort, emphasis is placed on the development of a baseline model to ensure that the identified security concerns and issues are properly addressed. Specifically, this task is composed of three important steps: (1) field research and observations, (2) security requirements definition and baseline development, and (3) emerging security solutions evaluation. Observations and note taking by the field technicians working at the service sites were also made throughout the study. In addition, several interviews were conducted with many office supervisors and service technicians in the Northeastern offices for the purpose of generating an explicit baseline of the intended enterprise-level security model, as well as alternatives to the baseline. The field notes from the observations were used to verify or elaborate on the interview data. Potential obstacles inherent in each alternative were also identified in a brainstorming session. Meanwhile, a development plan was developed for reducing potential risks associated with each alternative. Furthermore, with references to the work of several industry consortia—including the Global Mobile Commerce Forum, the Mobile Wireless Internet Forum, and the WAP (wireless application protocol) Forum—a comprehensive set of wireless security requirements were outlined to address specifically the first findings of the field research report.

As a key milestone, detailed functional requirements for the proposed security model were developed, along with a baseline statement. This document consists of the formulation of essential model functions, assessment of dependencies among various model components, evaluation of alternative solution models, estimation of value, and risk associated with each alternative solution model. As a supplementary effort, part of this task was to evaluate the effectiveness of many real-life security management practices and supply chain security standards in practice. A number of prototype models were developed to perform the benchmarking of these business practices and evaluate the hypotheses.

After a series of discussions, the management team decided that the security solutions for the e-service system should be developed around open industry

Table 1. Partial list of potential security risks and their solutions

Potential security risks	Solutions
Insecure information access	Establish a information access control list (IACI) and encrypt passwords in certain network interfaces
Unauthenticated and unauthorized access	Use multilevel password controls
Multiple-point access controls	Use improved configuration architecture with trusted switches on top of public key infrastructure (PKI)-based authentication

standards and be highly scalable, fully manageable, and extremely resilient. For instance, with regard to WAP security technologies, mobile commerce on WAP-phones should be secured by Java and wireless identity modules (WIM). The WIM will secure Internet transactions by placing encryption and digital signatures to authorize online transactions in the hands of mobile Internet users (field service technicians). With multi-tasking, logical channeling in WIM, mobile users are allowed to pass from one e-service application to another without losing transactions that have already been carried out. In addition, Ericsson's Bluetooth wireless wallet is proposed for development of the payment module for mobile e-commerce. A smart card can be inserted into the wireless wallet, which can then connect to mobile devices through Bluetooth technology. Mobile devices can then communicate via short-range radio frequency rather than cables. Unlike an encryption-enabled browser, the secret keys handling the encryption remain in the user's smart card. Table 1 presents a partial list of suggested security solutions for eliminating a variety of potential security risks.

Step 2: Development of Security Scenario Simulation Models

This task reveals that the exchange of electronic business documents in e-service operations poses a unique set of security challenges, especially on the Internet where parties are often known to each other only through their presence on the network, not in person. To be considered secure, a lab-controlled infrastructure was setup to simulate various scenarios of exchange to address different security concerns. To fully seize the essence of the e-service security model, conducting a series of experimentations is indispensable. This effort is carried out by first formulating pertinent experimental conditions and security incident scenarios under which the security model behavior is simulated. The experimentations helped HVAC management figure out the ways to enhance the model with desirable performances and characteristics.

Two primary Web interactions are simulated in this study: person-to-system (P2S) and system-to-system (S2S). Each e-business transactions can take place in the context of a bilateral (private) or multilateral exchange. In multilateral exchange, the company's customers and suppliers can process online transactions through either private corporation e-business channels or via semiprivate, Web-enabled exchanges. The study shows that each type of exchange may raise different issues threatening the objective of establishing a secure trading environment between the company and its e-business counterparts (customers, suppliers, and dealers). Figure 3 shows the P2S and S2S Web interactions that include the following flow of communications and exchanges.

- **Service Work Order (SWO):** A P2S interaction, including (1) wireless reception of SWO details on mobile device from e-service database, and (2) wireless transmission of work order status.
- **Customer Service Form (CSF):** An S2S interaction, consisting of such tasks as (1) electronic completion of CSF, (2) electronic customer sign-off

Figure 3. Wireless e-service operations

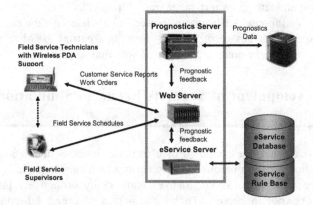

of work done, (3) wireless transmission of completed CSF to e-service database, and (4) storage of CSF information in database.

- **Diagnostics and Prognostics (D&P):** S2S interactions from D&P server to add tasks to existing planned work, as well as interactions from D&P server for raising pure diagnostics and prognostics work orders and pulling in existing schedule jobs.

- **Part ordering transactions between technicians and suppliers/dealers:** P2S and S2S interactions.

- **Communications between service centers and equipment:** S2S interactions.

It is vital to safeguard each point where security can potentially be breached. Identifying the points of vulnerability is one of the keys to securing the company's network infrastructure and critical enterprise resources in an open and distributed computing environment. In order to isolate different points of vulnerability,

Figure 4. e-service operations and security scenario analysis

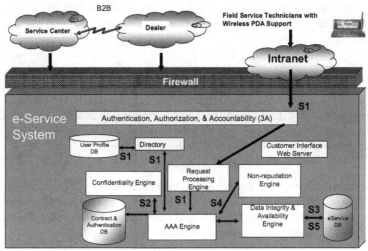

S1 - Authentication, authorization, and accountability
S2 - Confidentiality and privacy
S3 - Data integrity
S4 - Non-repudiation
S5 - Availability

it is essential to analyze the data traveling through the entire e-service networks. There are two basic setups of data flow analysis that ought to be conducted. The first setup is to analyze the data stored on a local computer, the operating system of which is the primary provider of the necessary security services for the protection task. Analyzing data traveling across communication points is the second key scenario to perform for points of vulnerability assessment. Data traveling between network locations should to be secured in a different manner, which mostly entails encrypting the data. Basically, this data traveling the network is in one of two forms: data in the form of network packets coming into a system, or data exiting the system. Protecting data coming into the e-service system involves safeguarding both the data itself and the system against threats posed by the data once it has entered the system. Major protection tasks in this case encompass a system check to ensure that the data comes from an authorized source and that it can execute only authorized tasks. Protecting data departing the system deals with ensuring that it arrives at its destination in exactly the same format in which it was sent. The session and data type, as well as data content, must be undecipherable by a third party to preserve confidentiality.

To better understand the behaviors of each identified security threat, five key security scenario simulation sessions were conducted. They are illustrated in Figure 4. For each simulation session, rules can be configured according to predefined security policies to execute any number of automated actions when a certain simulated security scenario is activated. Meanwhile, multiple responses can be configured for each scenario, ranging from generating notifications delivered via e-mail, pager, or other mobile devices, to setting off automated corrective actions. The five key security scenario simulation sessions are briefly discussed next.

Scenario 1: Authentication, Authorization, and Accountability

Authentication – Testing the entity that the company is dealing with is either the entity it claims to be or an impostor trying to engage in fraudulent activity via authentication of the parties involved in the transaction.

- **Simulation process:** Verifying that users are who they claim to be when logging onto a system. Generally, the use of user names and passwords accomplishes this. More sophisticated verification would involve the use of smart cards and retina scanning.

- **Solutions:** Using a digital certificate issued and verified by a Certificate Authority as part of a public key infrastructure to perform authentication on the Internet. Enhanced authentication services include: on-site verification

Table 2. Comparison of authentication solutions

Proposed Solution	Security Purpose	Implications/concerns	Implementation
smartcards	User identification verification	The trouble and expense of retrofitting the existing corporate infrastructure with smartcard readers	To equip wireless phones and other handheld devices with a slot for a smartcard
the use of proxy servers	Eliminating the Gap in WAP		To eliminate the WAP gap via a client-side WAP proxy server that communicates authentication and authorization details to the wireless network server

and hardware-based authentication. In addition, for means of verifying one's identity, smartcards are proposed for holding digital certificates and private keys. One reason a company might be reluctant to embrace the technology is the trouble and expense of retrofitting the existing corporate infrastructure with smartcard readers. A comparison of authentication solutions in terms of implications and implementation is shown in Table 2.

Authorization – The process of authentication does not grant the user access rights to resources—this is achieved through the authorization process.

- **Simulation process:** Logically, authentication precedes authorization (they may often seem to be combined). The process of allowing only authorized users access to sensitive information. An authorization process uses the appropriate security authority to determine whether a user should have access to resources.

- **Solutions:** Using a digital certificate issued and verified by a Certificate Authority as part of a public key infrastructure is considered likely to become the standard way to perform authentication on the Internet.

Accountability – Ensuring the enforcement of accountability by applying relevant security policy agreements among different systems users via simulation of how the users should be accountable and what proper actions to take.

- **Simulation process:** Authentication, authorization, and accounting (AAA) construct a framework for intelligently controlling access to the enterprise resources, enforcing security management policies, auditing usage, and providing the information necessary to bill for services. These combined processes are considered important for effective network management and security.

- **Solutions:** AAA services are often provided by a dedicated AAA server. A current standard by which network access servers interface with the AAA server is the remote authentication dial-in user service (RADIUS).

Scenario 2: Confidentiality and Privacy

Confidentiality and privacy – Testing and ensuring that confidentiality is protected in communications and that sensitive information remains known only to the parties involved in the transaction.

- **Simulation Process:** To test the causes of confidentiality compromise and poor security measures (e.g., allowing anonymous access to sensitive information or information leaked by personnel). Other simulation scenarios on possible attacks on confidentiality include data aggregation, social engineering, inadvertent disclosure, convert channels, and interception of information.

- **Solutions:** Cryptographic algorithms.

Scenario 3: Data Integrity

Data integrity – Prevention of erroneous modification of information.

- **Simulation process:** This process involves a bidirectional simulation to verify that transactions sent or received in an e-commerce exchange remain exactly as intended, without modification by either fraud or network error. A number of tests are conducted on various attacks of data integrity, including authentication attacks, content-based attacks, protocol attacks, abuse of privilege, exploration of backdoors, and session hijacking. This simulation reveals that authorized users are probably the biggest cause of errors and omissions and alteration of data. Another finding discloses that storing incorrect data within the system can be as bad as losing data.

- **Solutions:** Digital signature.

Scenario 4: Non-Repudiation

Non-repudiation – Ensuring the recipient of an electronic communication that the sender actually sent the information and that it has not been forged.

- **Simulation process:** This process is to simulate the creation of the same level of binding commitment with an electronic communication as with a signed contract, invoice, or other physical document.

- **Solutions:** (1) digital signatures, in conjunction with the digital certificate of the sender, for providing the highest level of assurance regarding the identity of the sender of the document and providing a high degree of certainty that the message was not altered in transit; (2) digital signatures and certificates of the server (to be used in the response messages or notifications sent back to the sender for providing proof that the response is definitely coming from the server); and (3) an event log (stored on the application server) allowing the user or system administrator to track the activity regarding a particular message.

Scenario 5: Availability

Availability – Preventing unauthorized withholding of information or resources.

- **Simulation process:** A series of tests were conducted on simulating the attacks on availability via denial-of-service (DoS), interference, jamming, audit suppression, etc. In addition, the simulation helps ensure that particular system resources, from the level of the individual database that contains data, to the entire network, are fully available to authorized users, but unavailable to anyone else.

Step 3: Development of Security Information System Architecture

Using the simulation results from Step 2, specific information system architectural capabilities were identified for the e-service system to sustain a high-performance, end-to-end security solution to the rigorous requirements in the previous five simulated areas. A conceptual diagram of e-service information system architecture is depicted in Figure 5.

Figure 5. e-Service information system architecture

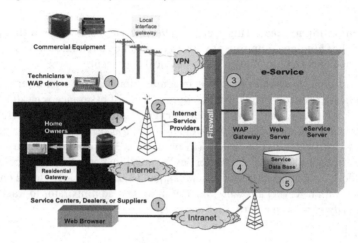

To enable the company to analyze security needs, it is crucial to first assess the entire network architecture as a whole and then separate the architectural structure into separate security entities in physical and conceptual forms. Security exposure can then be identified and, in turn, specific security measure can be performed for each security entity.

Five distinct security entities are identified in the e-service network with regard to possible points of vulnerability: (1) the front-end systems, (2) wireless network, (3) Web-access server, (4) wireless application protocol (WAP) gateway, and (5) back-office systems. These five areas of vulnerability and associated security management strategies constitute the baseline requirement of this case study. Table 3 lists several essential Web security capabilities documented in the baseline report for securing the Web e-service operations in these five areas.

Step 4: Demonstration and Validation

A validation process was performed to test the existing security designs and new ones. Empiricist and rationalist approaches (Law & Kelton, 1991) were adopted to achieve this goal. While an empiricist's approach was used for model-validity checking on the existing designs, a rationalist's approach was employed for the new design components. With the empiricist's approach, the performance results generated by the security management scenario simulations were then compared with historical security incident data in the real-life environment. Hypothesis tests were used to determine if the differences between the various performance results were statistically significant. For the new security designs, since historical security data was unattainable, these designs were closely examined and their assumptions were properly updated and justified.

Conclusion

Complexity is inherent in most real-world problems, including the case study presented in this chapter. The complexity of supply chain management is aggravated by the immense interwoven relationships among vast number of system entities in the inter-enterprise environment. Modeling such a super-complex security system in a supply chain involves mapping out all the potential security risks, threats, uncertainty, and attack scenarios in the simulation models. The integrated security management methodology discussed in this case study provides a viable foundation for building a secure and manageable computing environment. Furthermore, implementing the security management methodology has served to help the security specialists zero in on different critical security management jobs in a sequential but interrelated and logical manner. In turn, in-depth understanding of the potential environmental risks can be properly acquired. The methodology can further help security managers to perform a proactive analysis of the consequences of security breaches in relation to risks. Incorporating security measures into all aspects of the e-enterprise network, a set of meticulously planned security management strategies can then be developed based on the analysis.

As a powerful mechanism, the security management methodology presented in this case study can be adopted by a wide range of business practitioners—from security administrators, network designers, supply chain managers, to e-business managers—who are required to understand, manage, and evaluate security solutions in a complex supply chain environment. Nevertheless, the aim of the methodology is not to provide a recipe book with predetermined steps on security management practices for all possible scenarios. Practically, it renders a unified, structured framework that helps e-enterprise managers develop an actual security plan and solutions. It can also be used to review the current security standards, practices, and configurations in response to special security requirements and long-term e-enterprise needs. Ultimately, it will lead to sound and feasible solutions to the intractable security problems and, in turn, help the organization achieve its security objectives and meet stringent security requirements in a super-complex supply chain environment.

Besides the technical aspect of the security management in a supply chain discussed in this chapter, an equally important organizational issue—trust among business partners—should be dealt with in the future research agenda in order to ensure a truly secure and safer Internet-driven supply chain environment. As outlined in the text, the supply chain system covers a continuum of trust relationships, each having a differing degree of commitment to the overall goals of the system. Because of the variability across the network, both behavioral and technological approaches need to be considered if an overall e-enterprise security system is to be built to effectively prevent system abuse and protect all participants, individually and collectively. The behavioral steps necessary to lessen much of the internal abuse has been discussed previously in this chapter. Taking a balanced, more graduated, approach to openness, building trust and commitment based relationships to lessen or eliminate opportunism, and continually realigning incentives across the supply chain will create lasting win-win situations that turn the goals of the system into super-ordinate goals for all involved. And when each participant realizes it is in his or her best interest to put the system first, risk from internal security breaches will significantly decrease. The remaining possibilities for internal abuse and the external risks of abuse can best be addressed through technology.

To fully utilize the advantages of the open and ubiquitous technology of the Internet, trust enables extensive cooperative and collaborative endeavors among various players in the global supply chain. Trust is a key to positive interpersonal and interorganizational relationships in various supply chain management settings. Furthermore, trust becomes even more central and critical to sustain everlasting business relationships, especially when a great deal of sensitive and/or proprietary business data are required to be shared among business partners over an Internet-based supply chain network. As a result, one of the future research efforts is to focus on conceptualization of business trust model, which should be cross-organizational in nature. Research work in other disciplines (e.g., social science and organizational behavior) on trust will be studied and compared. Ultimately, the development of a trust-driven security management methodology is perceived as one vital future research activity for achieving a truly *trusted and trusting* supply chain environment.

References

Becker, H. S., (1960). Notes on the concept of commitment. *American Journal of Sociology*, 66, 32-40.

Brunnstein, K. (1997, May 14-16). Towards a holistic view of enterprise information and communication technologies: Adapting to a changing paradigm. In L. Yngström & J. Carlsen (Eds.): *Information Security in Research and Business—Proceedings of the 13th International Conference on Information Security (SEC '97)*, Copenhagen, Denmark. London: Chapman & Hall.

Butler, J. K. Jr. (1991). Toward understanding and measuring conditions of trust: Evolution of the conditions of trust inventory. *Journal of Management*, 17, 643-663.

Butler, J. K. Jr. (1995). Behavior, trust, and goal achievement in a win-win negotiating role play. *Group and Organizational Management*, 20(4), 486-501.

Cavazos, E. A., & Morin, G. (1994). *Cyberspace and the law: Your rights and duties in the online world*. Cambridge, MA: MIT Press.

Clarke, R. (2000). *Electronic commerce definitions*. Retrieved April 28, 2006, from http://www.anu.edu.au/people/Roger.Clarke/EC/ECDefns.html

Clarke, R. (2001). *Introduction to information security*. Retrieved April 28, 2006, from http://www.anu.edu.au/people/Roger.Clarke/EC/IntroSecy.html

Dess, G., Rasheed, A., McLaughlin, K., & Priem, R. (1995). The new corporate architecture. *Academy of Management Executive*, 9(3), 7-20.

Ellison, R. J., Fisher, R. C., Linger, H. F., Lispon, H. F., Longstaff, T. A., & Mead, N. R. (1999, May 10-14). Survivable systems: An emerging discipline. In *Proceedings of the 11th Canadian Information Technology Security Symposium* (CITSS, pp. 138-143), Ottawa, Ontario. Communications Security Establishment, Government of Canada.

Forcht, K., Saunders, T., Usry, M. L., & Egan, K. (1997). Control of the Internet. *Information Management & Computer Security*, 5(1), 23-28.

Guttman, B., & Bagwill, R. (2003). Internet security policy: A technical guide. *NIST Special Publication 800-XXX*. Retrieved April 28, 2006, from http://csrc.nist.gov/isptg/html/

Hinton, H. M. (1997, September 23-26). Under-specification, composition and emergent properties. In *Proceedings of the 1997 New Security Paradigms Workshop* (pp. 21-23). Langdale, Cumbria UK. ACM Press.

Information Security Magazine. (2000). *2000 industry survey—Security focused* (pp. 40-68).

Law, A.,& Kelton, W. (1991). *Simulation modeling and analysis* (2nd ed.). New York: McGraw-Hill.

Lichtenstein, S., & Swatman, P. (1997). Issues in e-business security management and policy. In *Proceedings of the 1st Australian Information Security Management Workshop* (pp. 237-242). Geelong, Victoria.

Lipson, H. F., & Fisher, D. A. (1999). Survivability—A new technical and business perspective on security. In *Proceedings of the 1999 New Security Paradigms Workshop*, Ontario, Canada (pp. 198-204). ACM Press.

Mathy, L., Edwards, C., & Hutchison, D. (2000, July-August). The Internet: A global telecommunications solution? *IEEE Network Magazine*, 46-52.

Mayer, R. C., Davis, J. H., & Schoorman, F. D. (1995). An integrative model of organizational trust. *Academy of Management Review*, *20*(3), 709-734.

Microsoft Corporation (2004). *Security management for ASPs*. Microsoft enterprise services white paper. Retrieved April 28, 2006, from http://www.microsoft.com/technet/security/default.mspx

Otuteye, E. (2002). *Framework for e-business information security management*. Retrieved Apirl 28, 2006, from http://ebusinessroundtable.ca/documents/Framework_for_e-business_security.pdf

Parker, D. W., & Russell, K. A. (2004). Outsourcing and inter/intra supply chain dynamics: Strategic management issues. *Journal of Supply Chain Management*, *40*(4), 56-69.

Rannenberg, K. (1994, August 12-17). Recent development in information technology security evaluation—The need for evaluation criteria for multilateral security. In *Proceedings of Security and Control of Information Technology in Society*, IFIP Transactions (pp. 43-48). St. Petersburg, Russia.

Rubin, A. D., & Geer, D. E. Jr. (1998). A survey of Web security. *Computer*, *31*(9), 34-41.

Sakaguchi, T., Nicovich, S. G., & Dibrell, C. C. (2004). Empirical evaluation of an integrated supply chain model for small and medium sized firms. *Information Resources Management Journal*, *17*(3), 1-20.

Shakir, M., & Viehland, D. (2005). The selection of the IT platform: Enterprise system implementation in the NZ Health Board. *Journal of Cases on Information Technology*, *7*(1), 22-34.

Stix, G. (2005, January). Best-kept secrets: Quantum cryptography has marched from theory to laboratory to real products. *Scientific American*, 79-83.

Tan, Y., & Thoen, W. (2000). A logical model of trust in electronic commerce. *EM—Electronic Markets, 10*(4), 32-38.

U.S. GAO (1998). *Information security management: Learning from leading organizations.* Retrieved April 28, 2006, from http://www.gao.gov/special.pubs/ai9868.pdf

Whipple, J. M., & Frankel, R. (2000). Strategic alliance success factors. *Journal of Supply Chain Management, 36*(3), 21-29.

Yngstrom, L. (1995). A holistic approach to IT security. In J. H. P. Eloff & H.S. Von Solms (Eds.), Information security—The next decade. In *Proceedings of the IFIP TC11 11ᵗʰ International Conference on Information Security (IFIP/Sec '95)* (pp. 37-43). London: Chapman and Hall.

Section IV:

Performance Control
and Risk Issues

Chapter XII

Monitoring Supply Chain Flows through Improved Performance Measurement of Extended Processes

Marco Busi, SINTEF Industrial Management,
Norwegian University of Science and Technology, Norway
and University of Strathclyde, UK

Abstract

Increasing strategic importance of logistics-related processes demands a higher integration of performance management and supply chain management. Despite the increasing focus on supply chain management and business collaboration, studies in the area of performance management still narrowly look at the single enterprise and its "within-enterprise" processes. Most of these existing studies are losing relevance in today's industrial dynamics, where business models, such as that of the supply chain, are merely the tip of an emerging trend in new organization alliances, boundary redefinition, and market structures. This chapter goes beyond existing work to develop a better understanding of the issue of performance management from a supply chain management perspective. The goal is to demonstrate how today's manufacturing systems and processes could be measured *and* managed *in the context of the extended business of which they are part—back through the supplier chain and forward into the distribution and customer chain. The chapter's intended major outcomes for its readers are: a clearer understanding of the concept of supply chain management through performance, and a process for designing a supply chain performance measurement system. Additional information emerges throughout the chapter.*

Introduction

Nowadays, market and production globalization and the network- and knowledge-based economy are triggering continuous changes in the way companies are organized and the way they do business. After four decades of focusing on optimization of internal operations, companies have realized that they have to invest in integrating their internal operations with those of their suppliers and customers. In manufacturing, logistics accounts for an ever-increasing percentage of the final product cost, ranging from 6% to 15% of the total turnover. Managers have finally realized that improving logistics and supply chain management (SCM) performance represents an important leverage of competitiveness.

Both management and research emphasis today have, hence, shifted on to:

- Managing flows of information, goods, and knowledge within the supply chain;
- Managing extended processes within and beyond the single company's four walls[1];
- Managing performance from a supply chain perspective;
- Creating and managing multidisciplinary teams;
- Deploying integrated information and communication technologies (ICT) across organizations; and
- Creating and sharing knowledge.

Goal of the Chapter

The goal of this chapter is to clarify what the previously mentioned change in focus means in practice, in terms of the processes, methodologies, and tools needed to support it. It particularly focuses on the process of measuring performance and the methodologies and tools to use the output of this process, namely, the performance levels, to manage supply chains. It highlights how, in the area of business performance measurement, a holistic approach to managing performance from a supply chain perspective is still missing. Hence, this chapter more specifically aims to fill the existing gaps concerning the dynamics, mechanisms, and infrastructure needed for integrated SCM through performance.

To improve understanding of how performance should be measured and managed from a supply chain perspective, this chapter answers two important questions:

- What should be measured?
- How shall it be measured?

The decision of what to measure or how to interpret the performance measures is neither an easy nor a straightforward task. Lack of understanding of which are the key success factors or what is the best measure to adopt would most probably lead to wrong decisions being made. While much has been documented concerning guidelines and rules for the choosing performance measures, there is no recognised methodology in place that allows an organisation to select performance measures in a step-wise, logical fashion. The diverging and often contradictory needs of firms in different business environments are not amenable to the creation of a performance measurement selection tool. Performance measurement selection guidelines are also complicated by the fact that the most relevant measures for a company to adopt change over time.

Structure

This chapter starts with a thorough interdisciplinary study of SCM through performance. Existing knowledge is studied, gathered from relevant disciplines, such as business collaboration, operations management, business performance management, information and communication management, knowledge management, and organizational behaviour. The study highlights the impact of increasing ICT-supported business collaboration on operations and process design and on team and knowledge management; in particular, it looks at the processes of measuring and managing performance. "As-is" and "To-be" situations are defined, highlighting the gaps and the respective future research needs. Throughout the chapter, using the findings from the interdisciplinary study and from observations carried out at a Norwegian manufacturer[2] as a basis, a new concept of SCM through performance measurement is discussed. The three topic issues that define the concept are: the link between supply chain strategy and performance indicators; the use of ICT to gather, analyse, and share performance data; and the indicators' characteristics. The chapter presents the concept discussing these three issues. It continues using the guidelines defined in the first part to present a process for the design of a supply chain performance measurement system.

Contribution

This chapter discusses how performance management can, when supported by existing ICT, translate supply chain strategies into both supply chain- and single-enterprise achievable objectives ("top-down") developing a set of relevant performance indicators, and how important is translating single-enterprise operational performance into valuable inputs to supply chain strategy redefinition ("bottom-up").

The contribution of this chapter is twofold: from one side, presenting a state-of-the-art review of the area of performance management in supply chains, it contributes to academia, clearly indicating gaps and hence needs for future research; from the other side, it contributes to practice by presenting ideas that were developed and tested in an industrial setting by a Norwegian wheel suspensions manufacturer. It could be useful for student and practitioners alike, proposing a supply chain performance measurement system model and delivering a set of management guidelines for managing performance effectively in a supply chain context.

Supply Chain Performance
Management Dictionary

Both in business collaboration and business performance management literature there is a lack of standard understanding of some of the terms used. Neely, Mills, Gregory, and Platts (1995) argue that performance measurement is a topic often discussed but rarely defined. Winston (1999) too complains of a lack of consistency of terms used in performance measurement literature, suggesting that authors often slip from a discussion about performance *measurement* to drawing conclusions about the use of performance *indicators*, and vice versa. Therefore, this paragraph aims to establish a vocabulary common to the author and the reader, of the terms used hereafter:

A *supply chain* can be defined as a network of organizations involved through upstream and downstream linkages in the different processes and activities that produce value in form of products and services in the hands of the ultimate customer (Christopher, 1998). More simply, supply chains are sets of interdependent firms that have agreed to contribute their expertise towards the completion and supply of a common end-product, be that goods or services, and the related information (Jagdev & Thoben, 2001; Simatupang & Sridharan, 2002).

Performance may include *inputs* (e.g., resource costs), *outputs* (e.g., products and services provided to the customer), *intermediate outcomes* (e.g., customer satisfaction and the results of new actions taken within the firm), *end outcomes* (e.g., changes in product volumes or product quality to the customer), and *net impacts* (e.g., the difference a new action—product / process actions, for example—has made). It may also include *unintended outcomes*[3] (e.g., additional costs incurred by the firm in response to process changes) (adapted from Wholey, 1996).

Performance measurement is the systematic assignment of numbers to entities (Zairi, 1994). It is the process of quantifying the efficiency and effectiveness of action (Neely et al., 1995). Measuring performance means evaluating how well organizations are managed and the value they deliver for customers and other stakeholders (Moullin, 2002).

A *performance metric* is a number or value that has been directly measured (e.g., the number of failures per day).

A *performance measure or performance indicator* is a numerical value that shows how well each objective is being met. It is a metric used to quantify the efficiency and/or effectiveness of an action (Neely et al., 1995). That is, performance measures or indicators are measurable characteristics of products, services, processes, and operations that an organization uses to track performance (Bititci, Carrie, & McDevitt, 1997). They represent the "vital signs" of an organization and quantify how well a process or the outputs of a process achieve a specified goal (Hronec, 1993).

A *key performance indicator (KPI)* is the actual measure used to quantitatively assess performance in a limited number of areas in which results, if satisfactory, will ensure successful competitive performance (see also Sinclair & Zairi, 1995). The value of a performance indicator can relate to data collected or calculated from any process or activity, whereas the value of a KPI relates to data collected from a process or activity that is particularly *relevant*. Relevancy is here intended as the ability to show how "good" is that process or activity in relation to the performance objective under study (see also Ahmad & Dhafr, 2002). Performance indicators and KPIs are descriptive; that is, they are derived from the measurement of the performance metric (e.g., percentage of rejects) (Lupton & Dooley, 2003).

A *performance measurement system (PMS)* is a set of metrics used to quantify both the efficiency and effectiveness of actions (Neely et al., 1995); it is a tool for balancing multiple measures across multiple levels (Hronec, 1993).

Performance management is the systematic use of performance measurement information to effect positive change in organizational culture, systems and processes, by helping to set agreed-upon performance goals, allocating and prioritising resources, informing managers to either confirm or change current policy or program directions to meet those goals, and sharing results of performance in pursuing those goals (Amaratunga & Baldry, 2002).

A *performance management framework* provides guidelines on how to measure and manage performance. It assists in the process of performance measurement system building by clarifying performance measurement boundaries and specifying performance measurement dimensions or views, and may also provide initial intuitions into relationships among the performance measurement dimensions. They should not be treated as performance measurement systems, but, nonetheless, form a good starting point for system building as part of theory development (adapted from Rouse & Putterill, 2003).

A *target* is the predetermined desired level of performance against each measure (Sinclair & Zairi, 1995).

Effectiveness refers to the extent to which customer requirements are met (Neely et al., 1995). Effectiveness is comparative; the performance results produced are compared with expected (or actual) results to see how the action is progressing.

Efficiency is a measure of how economically the firm's resources are utilised when providing a given level of customer satisfaction (Neely et al., 1995).

Efficiency examines how the inputs to a process were transformed into outputs and examines the ratios of performance between the inputs and outputs.

Strategy maps enable an organisation to describe and illustrate its strategic goals, initiatives, targets, performance measures, and the cause-and-effect relationships among all the pieces of its strategy (Franco & Bourne, 2003; Kaplan & Norton, 2000).

A last remark concerns the terms *competitive priority, performance objective*, and *performance dimension*. Different authors give slightly different meanings to these terms. This is quite understandable as the borderline between them is blurred. In this chapter, they will be used interchangeably to refer to what Hayes and Wheelwright (1979) refer to as "dominant competitive modes" and "key management tasks." That is, a competitive priority is that performance dimension that, in a particular moment in time and in a particular market and business context, becomes exceptionally more important than others for the survival of a company, and which, therefore, should become the priority of this company's strategy and operations design and control. They represent the dimensions of manufacturing strategy or the content of manufacturing strategy (Fine & Hax, 1985).

Performance Management and its Support to Support Supply Chain Management: A Literature Review

Supply Chain Partners Integration

Due to market and production globalization, technological progress, and ever-more demanding customers, today's marketplace is more fiercely competitive than ever before (Fawcett &Magnan, 2002; Patterson, Grimm, & Thomas, 2003). As a consequence, over the past decade, companies have been forced to continuously restructure themselves (Bititci, Martinez, Albores, & Parung, 2004; Browne & Zhang, 1999; Fawcett & Magnan, 2002; Jagdev & Thoben, 2001; Lee, Cheung, Lau, & Choy, 2003; Lee & Whang, 2001) into more integrated supply chains (Burgess, Gules, & Tekin, 1997), aiming to boost as a whole all those resources and competencies needed to satisfy the end customer (Fawcett & Magnan, 2002). Supply chains, as strategic alliances and partnership, are somewhat in the middle between market and hierarchy,[4] capturing the advantages of both markets and hierarchies, while avoiding the risks of each.

Supply chain integration and partners coordination are today on the forefront of the continuous improvement agenda of several companies. However, empirical data still indicates that these concepts are proving difficult to implement in practice (Sabath & Fontanella, 2002). Considering the very low number of companies having reached a satisfactory stage of integration (Fawcett & Magnan, 2002), and the very high percentage of such initiatives that fail (Wognum & Faber, 2002), supply chain partners integration and coordination are actually still far from being achieved (Holmberg, 2000).

The reason is that new concepts, tools, and techniques—not yet in place—are required to support managers in:

- Managing extended processes within and beyond the single company's boundaries;
- Managing performance from a supply chain perspective;
- Creating and managing cross organisational multidisciplinary teams;
- Deploying integrated ICT across organizations; and
- Creating and sharing knowledge.

Supply Chain Management

Traditional operations management methods, practices, and technologies focus on integration of production activities within one factory. The common belief is that optimizing local performance will eventually lead to overall supply chain performance optimization. On the contrary, a single-firm management style is more likely to obstruct partners' integration (Holmberg, 2000), consequently hindering overall performance optimization. The right approach suggests that optimization of overall supply chain performance will in fact lead to local optimization as well. Innovation of organizational processes and management culture, hence, become a major business challenge critical for success.

In this context, SCM, originally introduced by consultants in the early 1980s, is gaining a lot of attention (Christopher, 1992; Lambert & Cooper, 2000) as the right way to expand the scope of the organisation (Patterson et al., 2003) beyond the enterprise level to include inter-organisational relationships. SCM is responsible for controlling the flows of materials, information, and finances as they move in a process from supplier to manufacturer to wholesaler to retailer to consumer. It emphasises the integration of key business processes from end user through to original suppliers, offering the opportunity for business partners to capture the synergy of intracompany and intercompany integration and management.

The growing acknowledgment that SCM makes firms more responsive to customer demand and, therefore, more profitable is leading managers to make large investments to improve supply chain operations. The driving force of effective SCM is collaboration among all participants in the supply chain, whatever their size, function, or relative position.

Information and Communication Technology

Contributing to partners' integration—and hence supporting SCM—is information technology and, in particular, the Internet. While the most visible manifestation of the Internet has been in the emergence of electronic commerce as a new retail channel, it is likely that the Internet will have an even more profound impact on business-to-business interaction. Information and communication technology nowadays plays a central role in several aspects of SCM becoming a critical organization design issue (Konsynski, 1993). ICT is in fact vital in SCM areas and processes such as: design of business models and operations; definition of business strategy and partners' relationships; design of performance measurement techniques; integration of information, processes, and organizations; planning synchronisation; and workflow coordination (Bowersox & Daugherty, 1995; Patterson et al., 2003).

Figure 1. Evolution of performance measurement and measures

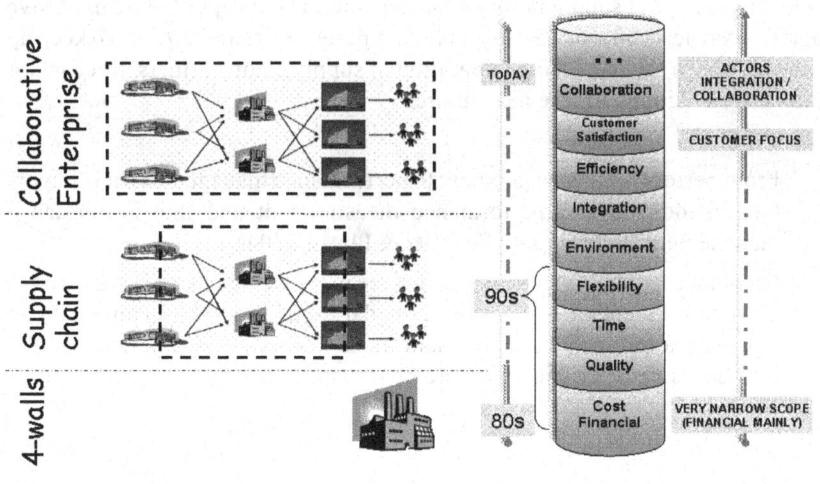

Performance Measurement and Management

Today's performance measurement theories and tools have their roots in Japanese quality management philosophies of the 1940s and 1950s. Ever since then, the history of performance measurement has faced changes in both the focus and use of measures (Figure 1).

The 1980s represent a milestone in the development of today's performance measurement discipline. While up until then, good performance was synonymous with good financial results, during that decade, the increasing dissatisfaction with the financial approach to performance monitoring had fuelled a whole new interest in the area of performance measurement (Dixon, Nanni, & Vollmann, 1990; Eccles, 1991; Ghalayini, Noble, & Crowe, 1997; Goldratt & Cox, 1986; Hayes & Abernathy, 1980; Johnson & Kaplan, 1987; Kaplan & Norton, 1992; Keegan, Eiler, & Jones, 1989; Neely et al., 1995; Thorpe, 2004; Yeniyurt, 2003). Performance measurement eventually stopped being only a part of wider management philosophies and started to gain an identity on its own as "the process of quantifying the efficiency and effectiveness of past actions though acquisition, collation, sorting, analysis, interpretation, and dissemination of appropriate data" (Neely, 1998).

Lately, scientists and practitioners alike are once again questioning the relevance of the measurement principles, measures, and measurement systems developed so far, and their applicability in today's businesses. Even after the performance revolution during the 1980s, the focus of performance measurement has remained on process operations within the organizational boundaries of a firm. Network performance monitoring is still limited to procurement, quality of inbound goods, and suppliers' performance, but the concept of more extensive supply chain performance has not yet fully emerged (Hronec, 1993). To keep up with the pace of the increasing integration of supply chain partners, three major shifts are envisioned for the near future:

- From performance measurement to performance management: it is important to look beyond performance measurement and into performance management (Otley, 1999; Schmitz & Platts, 2004)
- From local to supply chain performance measurement: internal processes are being extended beyond the boundaries of individual companies to encompass the whole supply chain. It is, hence, necessary to widen the limited scope of existing measurement system.

- From lagging to leading performance management: management focus is on the present and the future. Proactive management means foreseeing problems before they occur. To do so, measures are needed in addition to the traditional backward-looking ones that are able to give a real-time picture of ongoing events.

From Performance Measurement to Performance Management

Performance measurement in business serves the purposes of monitoring performance, identifying the areas that need attention, enhancing motivation, improving communications, and strengthening accountability (Waggoner, Neely, & Kennerly, 1999). However, if measures are not used or are used in the wrong way, performance measurement fails to deliver any of the promised benefits. Organizations have started to realize that, in order to reap the benefits of performance measurement, they have to make use of their measures, that is, they have to manage through measures (Amaratunga & Baldry, 2002).

Performance measurement, consequently, becomes merely the practical and technical exercise within the much wider performance management process, whereas performance management is defined by Amaratunga and Baldy (2002) as:

the use of performance measurement information to effect positive change in organizational culture, systems and processes, by helping to set agreed-upon performance goals, allocating and prioritising resources, informing managers to either confirm or change current policy or programme directions to meet those goals, and sharing results of performance in pursuing those goals.

It follows that managing performance involves a cycle of clarifying business goals and then agreeing on individual objectives and standards of performance (Macaulay & Cook, 1994).

From Local to Supply Chain Performance Measurement

Organizations are still unable—or unwilling—to measure and manage performance from a network perspective, failing to understand that:

when limiting their focus to a single organization and neglecting to consider local measurement activities as part of a greater whole, they miss an opportunity to capitalize on how the measurement system could contribute to improving (the business network's) performance by taking waste out of the (business network), not just moving it somewhere else. (Holmberg, 2000)

Therefore, new processes, strategies, measures, and methods to measure and manage performance are needed that would support supply chain managers in monitoring the performance of extended processes and operations within seamless supply chains. Nowadays, it is impossible to ignore those aspects of the organization that extend beyond the traditional or legal boundaries of organizations (Konsynski, 1993).

Monitoring performance in an integrated supply chain context means monitoring both local performance and global network performance (Caplice & Sheffi, 1995). Companies have to enable all chain partners to have access to and share performance information to quickly identify bottlenecks and "weak links" in the network and act in accordance to improve the overall performance (Holmberg, 2000; Ireland & Bruce, 2000; Lummus & Vokurka, 2000; Stank, Dougherty, & Autry, 1999). In other words, companies should be able to realize not only how they are performing as part of their network, but also how changes in each node performance can affect their very performance—and vice versa. To do so, a number of indicators should be defined and maintained that are relevant to the local nodes to understand their contribution to the whole supply chain. These indicators should then feed decision makers who set strategy and targets at the supply chain level.

Difficulties in defining an appropriate balanced set of measures for collaborative performance management have been related to the complexity of overlapping supply chains, trust over information sharing (Lambert & Pholen, 2001) and the unit of analysis (single organizations or many, one product line or many, etc.) (Beamon 1999; Rafele, 2004)

From Lagging to Leading Performance Management

New approaches to performance management are focusing on the use of timely and relevant information made accessible by available technology to increase the ability of decision makers to rely on real-time performance levels (Ghalayini et al., 1997). Traditional PMSs have historically focused on appraising poor performance and identifying improvement areas. In the new business environment, measures must be designed based on continuous input from strategy and must be kept updated based on constant feedback from operations.

A set of new words and phrases is being used such as "proactive" and "passive" performance management, "feedback" and "feedforward" control, and "leading" and "lagging" measures, which reflects this shifting focus. Feedforward control involves the development and deployment of plans and objectives based on leading measures of real-time performance, while feedback control involves the measurement of performance against those objectives through historical lagging measures. Proactive performance management, built upon both feedforward and feedback control, is based on the premise that a balanced set of leading and lagging performance measures should anticipate and not only correct bad performance.

To optimize supply chain performance, partners must be able to access accurate and timely information from all over the network. Selected leading measures, such as aggregate demand and tracking data, showing how products move through each distribution channel (Lee &Whang, 2001), enabling decisions makers to be proactive. This means taking "improvement actions" before "corrective actions" are even needed, thanks to a better understanding of what is going on or what is about to happen (Holmberg, 2000; Schmitz & Platts, 2004).

Conclusions from the Literature Study

Despite the vast amount of literature on performance measurement frameworks and systems, most of the work is concerned with performance measurement within one organization (Schmitz & Platts, 2004). There has been far too little focus on going beyond this previous work to develop a universal framework for designing PMS spanning whole supply chains and using these to support SCM. There is the need to design "a dynamic process for managing strategy and performance [...] which continuously monitors [the supply chain] internal and external operational environment [...] and triggers actions that may change: the direction of the business, the way a business unit competes in its market or the priorities of an operate or support process" (Bititci et al., 2003, Yeniyurt, S. 2003).

Measurement systems should be design to make use of a balanced set of performance measures: (a) that monitor both external relations and the efficiency of internal and extended processes (Euske, Lebas, & McNair, 1993; Kald & Nilsson, 2000); and (b) that will support proactive management based on both feedback and feedforward operations control.

Figure 2. Single node manufacturing business process model

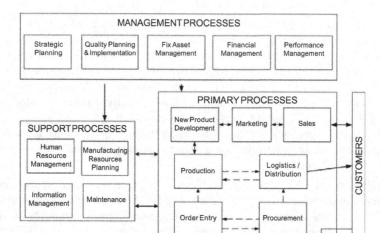

Measuring and Managing
Supply Chain Performance

What Shall Be Measured?

Enterprise processes can be divided into business and secondary processes (Andersen & Fagerhaug, 2002), with logistics being a business process. Or they could be categorized into primary, support, and management processes (Hronec, 1993), with primary processes being directly connected with customers; support processes being those undertaken to support primary ones; and management processes being those that coordinate the interactions between primary and secondary ones. In this latter categorization, logistics would be a primary process.

Based on the work carried out by Hronec (1993) and Andersen and Fagerhaug (2002), the categorization of processes, as shown in Figure 2, is suggested in this chapter. Figure 2 structures and relates relevant manufacturing processes according to the terminology of management, support, and operate processes. The following definitions are provided:

- **Management processes:** these processes concern the management activities undertaken to support the operate processes.

- **Operate processes:** these processes concern the physical material flow within and among the several single nodes in the supply chains.

- **Support processes:** these processes are not directly associated with manufacturing operations, but they indirectly influence the flow of goods and information among and within the single nodes in the supply chain.

Looking beyond the terminology, it is important to realize that logistics is being considered as a core or critical process, regardless of its scope (stand-alone companies vs. supply chain). In manufacturing, logistics account for an ever-increasing percentage of the final product cost, making it an important leverage of competitiveness. SCM, that is, controlling and managing logistics in the network, relies on having visibility of information about stocks, flows, and performance along the supply chain. This information must also be presented in a manner that is easy to assimilate, presents exceptions wherever possible, and most importantly, is based on real-time and accurate data. The key information required tends to break down into three main areas:

1. Performance/efficiency of the internal logistics operation;
2. Stock levels along the chain; and
3. Performance/efficiency of the network logistics operation, namely, SCM.

Figure 3. Levels of analysis of the supply chain

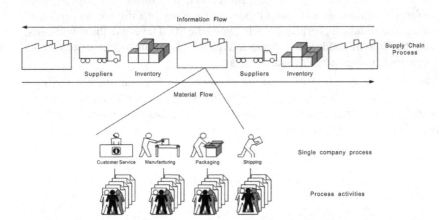

To gather such information, from an actor point of view, operations must be analyzed at the following three levels (Figure 3):

1.   The supply chain process level: process starting with the purchasing of the raw materials from the very first suppliers, to the delivery of the final product to the very last customer.

2.   The single node process level: within the four walls of the company.

3.   The activity level: analysis of the process activities' performance.

Looking at the process model defined earlier in this subsection and the three levels of analysis of the supply chain highlighted in Figure 3, it should be understood that, in the supply chain business model, the management and support processes are extended *vertically*. This means that these processes are carried out at both the single-node and the supply chain level; information related to management and support processes flows from the single-nodes upward to the supply chain level.

Operate processes, on the other hand, are extended *horizontally*. This means that these processes are carried out at each single-node level and extended to the others nodes in the supply chain. In this case, information related to operate processes flows from the very first supplier to the very last customer and vice-versa.

Defining the Scope of Supply Chain Performance Measurement

From the brief discussion in this subsection, it follows that supply chain performance management should monitor the flow of information related to management and support processes between the SCM level and the single units, with the flows of goods and information related to operate processes among the single units being part of the supply chain.

Now that the question of what to measure has been answered, the next subsection will tackle the second important question of supply chain performance management, namely, how is it possible to measure the performance of management, support, and operate processes in a supply chain context?

How Shall It Be Measured?

The Intrinsic Difficulty of Measuring Business Performance

Lord Kelvin (1824-1907) once said: "to know something properly, you must measure it." The problem with Lord Kelvin's statement is that he was a physical scientist, and in physical science, measurement is a much more straightforward procedure. How one measures *something,* in fact, depends on several factors such as: the objective of measurement, the object of measurement, the context conditions, the measuring tool, the personal preferences and bias of the person responsible for carrying out the measurement, and so on.

Major theoretical challenges concern the ownership of the measures being used—different owners have a different perspective on what "good performance" actually is. However, performance needs to be valid and reliable: how can one ensure validity and reliability equally from different perspectives? Different stakeholders play different roles and are consequently interested in different measures. In this view, performance of a supply chain (or a single company) is its relative efficiency and effectiveness towards the stakeholders, based on their subjective view of value (Bredrup, 1995). That is, it is completely relative to the specific interest of the individual stakeholder (Figure 4).

Technical major challenges seem to concern the interoperability of information management system. Human-related challenges are mainly connected both to the need for developing trust prior to sharing performance data among the partners, and to the complexity of the performance measurement process itself. People have to: set the objectives initially; design the system; implement the

Figure 4. The stakeholder model (Adapted from Bredrup, 1995)

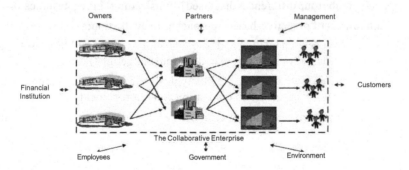

system; bear the responsibility of interpreting the measures obtained; and act on improving the measure (Zairi, 1994). A great deal of subjectivity is involved in each of these activities, and performance measures must be selected to minimize the subjectivity in the measurement result.

Answering the question of how to measure performance in a supply chain context, therefore, means designing the set of performance measure most appropriate to monitor the performance of the business network in relation to its objectives.

Limitation of Traditional Performance Measurement Systems

There has been a considerable amount of criticism concerning the use (and misuse) of PMSs. A number of research scientists have studied existing measures and measurement systems questioning their ability to measures performance of changing processes and organizations (Caplice & Sheffi, 1995; Eccles, 1991; Holmberg, 2000; Kaplan & Norton, 1992). Perrin (1998), although dealing with performance measures and indicators from an evaluation perspective, has pointed out eight inherent flaws and limitations associated with the use of performance indicators that are relevant to all fields of research. These are:

- Varying interpretations of the "same" terms and concepts;
- Goal displacement (i.e., emphasis on "making the numbers" to keep PMS satisfied);
- Use of meaningless and irrelevant measures;
- Cost savings vs. cost shifting (i.e., "performance indicators typically look at individual programs out of context...consequently, 'outcomes' may represent cost shifting rather than true cost savings");
- Critical subgroup differences disguised by misleading aggregate indicators;
- Limitations of objective-based approaches to evaluation;
- Useless for decision making and resource allocation (i.e., PMS is useless, by itself, "for informed decision making and budgeting");
- Less focus on outcome (i.e., "PMS typically leads to less—rather than more—focus on outcome, on innovation and improvement,").
- Table 1 summarizes the major criticisms against traditional measurement systems.

Table 1. Limitations of traditional performance measurement systems

Limitations of traditional PMS
Encourage short-termism
Lack strategic focus and fail to provide data on quality, responsiveness and flexibility
Encourage local optimisation
Do not encourage continuous improvement
Mainly making use of lagging measures (i.e. historical PMS with out-of-date and irrelevant information)
Lack of predictive ability to explain future performance (i.e., lack of leading indicators)
Strategy and measurement are not connected
Inflexible: they have predetermined format
Over-rely on financial aspects
Do not accurately reflect the interest of stakeholders
Missing link between non-financial metrics and financial numbers
Too many isolated and incompatible measures
Lack of appropriate integrated ICT infrastructure
Time consuming (require a large amount of data)
Lack of a structured framework
Inadequate in a supply chain context (be supply chain, virtual enterprise or any other type of enterprise network)
Are not made directly towards the purpose of network performance analysis
Limited in scope (do not provide a complete picture of the network performance)
Report only functional process performance, but not cross-functional, cross-enterprise performance
They do not measure the value create
Traditional metrics do not aggregate from an operational level to a strategic level

Relatively little has been written on the topic of performance measures that extend beyond single businesses. These are considered to be a necessity for future collaboration possibilities, especially to account for integrating activities properly (Lee, 2000). As highlighted in Table 1, traditional PMSs have often been found to be unable to properly assess performance of enterprise networks. Two main explanations are commonly given for this limitation:

1. They do not look at processes as extending beyond the traditional boundaries of a company.

2. They do not use low-level operational measures to redefine high-level enterprise network strategy.

These two points represent the premises for the concept of supply chain performance management as discussed in this chapter, and, in particular, for the supply chain PMS design process that will be discussed later.

Linking Strategy to Performance: The Key to Successful Supply Chain Performance Management

Performance measurement supports SCM, providing useful information at three different levels of analysis and decision making (Figure 5):

1. **Strategic:** long-term decisions regarding supply chain strategic design.

2. **Tactical:** short- to medium-term decisions regarding the definition of the supply chain principles, for example, inventory principles, purchasing principles, production principles, transportation principles, quality polices, and the like.

Figure 5. The three levels of information provided by performance measurement

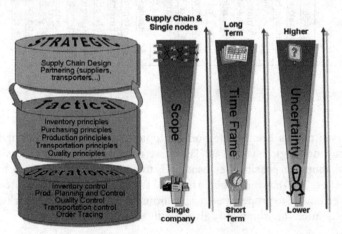

3.   **Operational:** very short- to short-term decisions, such as those involved in operations planning and control, for example, quality control, inventory control, transport quality control, production planning and control, order tracking, and the like.

The final set of selected KPIs that will form the supply chain PMS, therefore, has to be able to translate the strategy defined at higher supply chain level into an operational performance target. Also, the KPIs must be chosen so that they will allow measurement of what is important for the decisions makers to know in order to keep their strategy informed with the actual performance level of the different actors.

Operations in supply chain go from raw material purchase from the n-th tier supplier, to final product delivery to final customer (Child & Faulkner, 1998; Jagdev & Thoben, 2001). Operations must develop capabilities or core competencies that support the supply chain competitive advantages. A strategic planning process can only add value if the dialogue between the centre and the operating units is of high quality (Bungay & Goold, 1991). Effective supply chain strategy planning therefore requires operations to be developed consistently based on: the market, the supply chain mission, core competencies, order winners and order qualifiers, actual performance, and competitors' performance.

The operations strategy is the plan or set of decisions that specifies how operations can provide competitive advantages for a company (Russel & Taylor, 1998). The operations strategy is linked to the supply chain strategy through competitive priorities that enable products to qualify and win orders in the marketplace.

The supply chain strategy formulation must be reviewed periodically, as the customer requirements change over time. Each market/product combination requires operations that enable the product to win orders in the current competitive situation.

Top-Down Approach to Supply Chain Performance Management

According to Kathuria and Partovi (2000), there is a general agreement in the manufacturing strategy literature that the decisions regarding the structure and infrastructure of an organisation should be in line with its competitive priorities (Anderson, Cleveland, & Schroeder, 1989).

Hence, the supply chain strategy definition should be based on an understanding of its competitive priorities. Using techniques likes strategy mapping, the overall

Figure 6. Top-down supply chain performance management

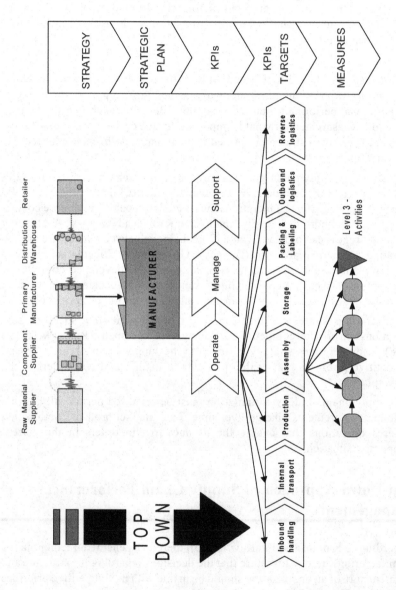

supply chain strategy can be broken down into a more detailed strategic plan, where the strategic objectives are better highlighted. For each of these objectives, a set of KPIs is developed and targets for these indicators are set for the operations.

Such an approach is called "top-down" because it starts from the definition of the supply chain strategy and ends with the definition of the indicators and the indicators targets, namely, the achievable objectives. Figure 6 shows how, from the supply chain strategy, measures for the single activities of the individual

Figure 7. Bottom-up supply chain performance management

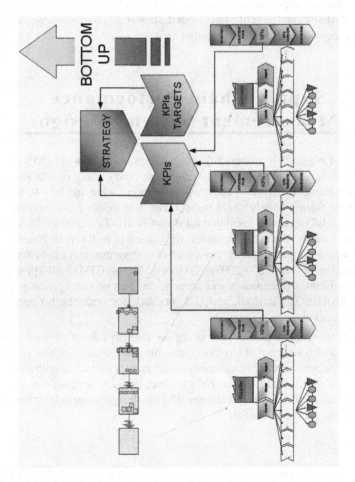

partners (in the simplified example, the manufacturer) are selected and indicators are developed.

Bottom-Up Approach to Supply Chain Performance Management

In the "bottom-up" approach, on the other hand, the starting point for the supply chain strategy definition or adjustment is the lowest level, that is, that of operations and activities. As shown in Figure 7, each actor in the network uses a set of performance indicators and achieves a certain level of performance. Comparing these values with the performance targets set at higher level, the supply chain strategy can be adjusted, for example, using unplanned spare capacity. An additional benefit comes from the possibility for the individual nodes to realign their strategy with the supply chain.

Supply Chain Performance Measurement Systems Design

This section suggests a process to design a supply chain-wide PMS. Such a process was developed based on the interdisciplinary study of literature presented, the answers to the two questions concerning what and how to measure performance from a supply chain perspective, and inputs from industry. It is worth remembering at this point that Raufoss Chassis Technology ASA (RCT) has played a major role in this research. RCT, located in Raufoss, Norway, is a manufacturer acting as a 1st to 2nd tier supplier in the automotive industry. It has a long-term contract ending in 2007 with General Motors (GM) for the production of front and rear aluminium-wheel suspension, part of the Epsilon platform (Vectra, SAAB 93, Vauxhall, and U.S. brands), for both the European and American markets.

RCT first recognized that it was using an inadequate set of performance indicators, which were not of any help in reaching its objective of cost reduction and quality improvement. The company consequently partnered with a research team to develop a state-of-the-art PMS for supply chain performance management. Its contribution to the development of the design process later presented in this chapter has been twofold:

- It has been actively participating in the development of the supply chain performance measurement concept hereby discussed. More specifically, the logistics manager at RCT has given input on the type of indicators it needed, the type of control it wanted to achieve with the new PMS, the type of information it could share and would have expected from its partners, and so on.
- It has served as a "test bed" for the theories and tools being developed.

The remainder of this section first summarizes the key requirements gathered at RCT. It then briefly analyzes the concepts of systems thinking, balanced measurement, and purpose of PMS implementation needed to better understand the design process. Then, it presents the sequence of steps to design a supply chain PMS and the two frameworks devised to select appropriate KPIs.

Input from Industry

When the author begun working with RCT, it was clear that the challenge it set for the future was to develop operations management practices that would eventually cut costs and resource utilization down to 50% of their actual value. The main objective of the research project was to design and develop a template for operations management processes that RCT and its partners could use in the future.

Re-engineering of processes and operations was required to be based on spread utilization of state-of-the-art information management systems integrated along the supply chain. To reach its goals and improvement targets, RCT begun to recognize the need to increase its integration with its value chain partners, based on the supply chain and extended enterprise business models and the lean manufacturing philosophy.

The As-Is situation at RCT concerning performance measurement practices was very close to the general situation described in literature and described earlier, namely:

- Each department (function/processes) operated with lists of several KPIs;
- The KPIs were mainly historical and backward looking and not real-time forward looking; and
- The KPIs were mainly measured internally within the RCT plant in Raufoss.

Table 2. Supply chain PMS—Requirements

Supply Chain PMS: Requirements	
Supply chain PMS should:	
Be balanced	Involve: resource measures, output measures and flexibility measures
Be integrated	Focus on continuous improvement
Be directly related to strategy (Inform and Deploy strategy)	Provide "wholeness"
Target value-adding processes/activities	Primarily use non-financial measures
Include stakeholder contribution	Vary between locations
Change over time as needs (internal & external) change	Spot causes of poor performance
Be inclusive, universal consistent, enable benchmarking	Provide fast feedback to operators and managers
Be simple and easy to use	Be accurate
Provide visual impact	Be relevant
Enable accountability	Involve five perspective: financial, customer, internal processes, and organizational culture and climate
Feature:	
An external monitoring system	
An internal monitoring system	
A review system	
An internal deployment system	

For the future, RCT management required re-engineering of the process of measuring and managing performance, according to the following:

- Reduce the set of KPIs, by identifying some few but highly significant indicators that support controlling the operations throughout the value chain. Change was required from measuring whatever is measurable to measure only what is relevant.

- Select or define a limited number of these KPIs that can give an overall picture of how the company operates within its supply chain (and how the other partners within the same chain operate);

- Expand the view from internal (on RCT own processes) to external (on the process of RCT business network);

- Electronically access performance information in real time.

Comparing and combining the requirements from RCT with the conclusions of the literature review, the following table summarizes the major requirement for a supply chain PMS.

The PMS design process defined later on was defined keeping these requirements in focus at all times.

Supply Chains as Systems

When individual components are combined into a *system*, they show properties that are properties of the whole and not of the constituent components. It follows that, in a supply chain context, PMSs design requires the system-thinking concept to bridge the gaps (both geographical and cultural) between the different nodes in the enterprise network. System thinking advocates the development of

Figure 8. Supply chain performance measurement—Systems concept (Adapted from Homberg, 2000)

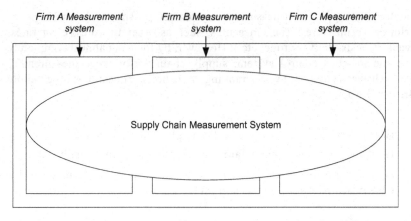

fragmented firm-sized PMS that are ultimately managed at the supply chain level through the coordination of information exchange (Holmberg, 2000). Thus, the supply chain is derived from its fragmented firm-sized PMS, aggregated into a supply chain PMS that has its own individual properties (Holmberg, 2000) (Figure 8).

Balancing the Set of Measures

The system-thinking concept will subsequently be used to "balance" the nodes internal-looking interests and their interests with regard to the external environment.

Kleijnen and Smits (2003) propose the balanced scorecard (Kaplan & Norton, 1992) as a suitable device for supply chain nodes to use, relying upon communication and coordination within the supply chain to overcome the obstacles surrounding the fragmented balanced scorecard developmental process at each node. Brewer and Speh (2000) have further developed the concept of using the balanced scorecard in the supply chain by moving beyond so-called "traditional logistics performance measures" that only measure performance at the interfaces of respective companies in the supply chain. Their work indicates the general use that can be made of the balanced scorecard concept to measure *all* functional areas beyond, but also including, logistics functions. Whereas intraorganisational balanced scorecards maintain a "balance" between financial and nonfinancial performance measures, interorganisational balanced scorecard concepts tend to be "balanced" by the presence of *internal* measures and *external* measures—that is, measures that measure inside the four walls of the company and measures that take into account activities outside the company's walls—that the company's interfaces with its trading partners, and so on (Zimmermann, 2001).

Traditionally, supply chain measurement systems emphasize "traditional logistics performance measures" (i.e., measures, such as order fill rates, error rates, inventory costs, delivery time, etc.). However, by focusing almost completely upon the logistics control system, supply chain performance measurement cannot answer a number of wider-ranging, more holistic questions; for example (Brewer & Speh, 2000):

- How effectively are the firms in the supply chain interacting?
- How does this supply chain fare compared to competing supply chains?
- How flexible is the entire supply chain in responding to requests for customised packages, orders and products?

- To what extent are decisions within the supply chain motivated by power rather than by mutual trust?

Nonetheless, these questions should be tackled in today's increasing integrated supply chains. A renewed approach to supply chain PMSs design should incorporate the structural aspects of traditional PMS and add a number of non-logistic perspectives to its measurement arena (e.g., internal process measures, intangible measures, measures of financial performance, etc.). Traditional measurement systems maintain a more traditional, slightly distant ("at arm's length") relationship with suppliers and customers by requesting data only upon issues of immediate concern from the logistics functions of participating companies. Furthermore, supply chain PMSs may, theoretically, present data from *all* aspects of the participating companies' functions.

As for the more specific matter of selecting KPIs to measure supply chain performance, theories developed in team performance management can be used to approach the supply chain as a team of the company. Doing so, supply chain performance could be measured at three different levels, using extended process measures, collaborating measures, and collaboration management measures.

Purpose of PMS Implementation [5]

A wide range of different possible applications of PMSs and performance data exist. Different applications require different performance data and a different system design. By trying to be everything, there is a risk that the measurement system becomes a less effective compromise between many different considerations. The consequence could be that a PMS must be designed to cover a few core application areas or even that an organization will need more than one system to be able to reap all the benefits. The requirements sets for each application area can possibly be divided into four groups as follows:

- **Simple PMSs** need simple solutions for manual data collection, low data-storage capabilities, require no or very simple calculations, and need not present the user with interactive decision support. Applications covered are typically using KPIs to set and follow strategic direction, using performance data to influence behaviour, assessing supplier performance, evaluating improvement projects, and using performance data for marketing purposes. These can be virtually paper-based, but will most likely appear in the form of simple spreadsheets with manual data input and very little requirements for tailored reports and output.

- **Intermediately advanced PMSs** typically must be able to handle fairly large amounts of data with high accuracy, where the data must be easily available electronically and some integration with others systems can be required, but where there are less needs for calculations, simulations, or interactive decision support. Applications covered are typically developing cost estimates based on past performance, establishing early warning indicators, setting incentives, sharing performance data with customers, and undertaking performance benchmarking. Such systems can rarely be designed using spreadsheets, but must rather be dedicated PMS software or applications that sit on top of ERP, CRM, or other enterprise data systems.

- **Advanced PMSs** must fulfil demands for automatic data capture, secure and flexible data storage and retrieval, broad integration to other systems, support multiple data presentation formats, and allow the users to perform advanced calculations or simulations that offer interactive decision support. Applications covered are typically monitoring overall and enterprise-wide performance, detailed operational planning, production planning based on up-to-date performance data, and determining processes with need for improvement. Such systems are doubtless dedicated PMS software, but might, in some cases, come in the form of advanced modules integrated into an ERP system.

- **Super-advanced and fully-integrated PMSs** must fulfil demands for automatic and geographically distributed data capture, secure and flexible data storage and retrieval from both local as well as central databases, broad integration to other systems, and support multiple data presentation formats. Also, these systems must be able to handle data from several sources and formats and allow the users to perform advanced calculations or simulations that offer interactive decision support. Applications covered are typically monitoring of enterprise networks process and operations, focus on the interfaces between the participating companies, strategy planning at both the overall enterprise network and single-enterprise level, and determining processes or actors with need for improvement. The development of this particular type of system needs to overcome major technological (i.e., integration of systems), and organizational challenges.

There are numerous reports of performance measurement initiatives that fail to deliver their promise of better control and improved performance, both in single-enterprise implementations and certainly in more complex supply chain settings. Carefully studying and understanding the core purpose of the implementation of a PMS should, therefore, be the starting point of any PMS implementation.

The design process includes the following general steps:

1. **Define the PMS application area:** local-nodes have to clearly define the objective of the PMS being implemented.

2. **Process mapping:** local-nodes have to clearly understand the extension (vertical and horizontal) of their business processes to form the supply chain process model. To understand and map processes, a number of tools and techniques do exist, for example, value-stream mapping, cause-and-effect diagrams, relationship mapping, flow charts, and so on. It is usually a good idea to start mapping the processes of the single nodes before moving to the supply chain. This exercise provides an opportunity to look at the interfaces between the internal and external part of one process,

Figure 9. The supply chain wide PMS design process

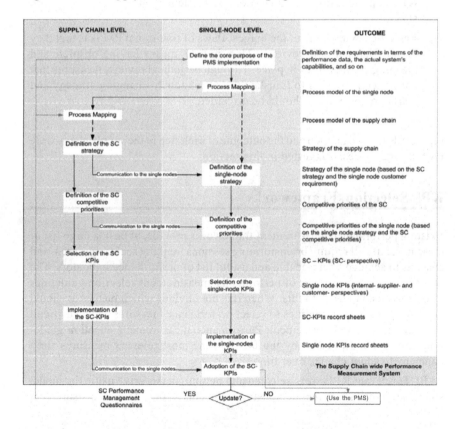

where significant opportunities for supply chain performance improvement usually lay.

3.   **Strategy definition:** it was noted earlier that the decisions regarding the structure and infrastructure of a supply chain should be in line with its strategy. Strategy should be defined at the higher supply chain level and communicated down to the single nodes in the network to allow them to align their local strategies with that of the supply chain.

4.   **Competitive priorities definition:** using techniques like strategy mapping, the overall supply chain strategy is broken down into a more detailed strategic plan where the strategic objectives (or competitive priorities) are better highlighted. Again, the supply chain competitive priorities should be communicated to the single nodes. This allows each node to have a better understanding of the supply chain perspective of its balanced scorecards.

5.   **KPIs selection:** KPIs should be selected using two selection frameworks, as described in the following section.

6.   **KPI implementation:** KPI should be implemented using a KPI record sheet.

7.   **Periodic review:** one of the biggest flaws of traditional PMSs is that they do not plan periodic reviews. This, in turn, means having obsolete and meaningless measures in place. Through periodical review, measures that have become unable to translate the continuously changing strategy and market requirements should be discarded.

Figure 9 displays each step and the outcome of each step in the supply chain-wide PMS design process suggested in this section.

KPI Selection Frameworks

Existing performance measurement frameworks provide, at best, a large list of measures, but still require brainstorming sessions, ranking scales, research, and analysis to achieve a serviceable and useful list of performance indicators. The absence of a formalised set of performance measurement selection guidelines may have much to do with this. When it is not obvious which measures should be adopted, generic guidelines to select performance measures can be difficult to create, never mind implement. Performance measurement selection guidelines are also complicated by the fact that the most relevant measures for a company to adopt change over time.

At RCT, relevant KPIs were selected and put into perspective using the model shown in Figure 10, which demonstrates the cluster of potential measurement

Figure 10. Model used for the selection of the relevant supply chain KPIs

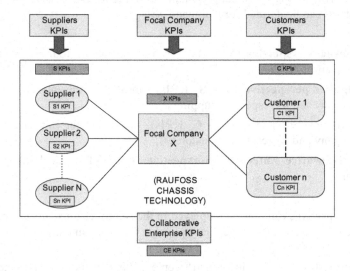

Figure 11. The supply chain balanced scorecard model

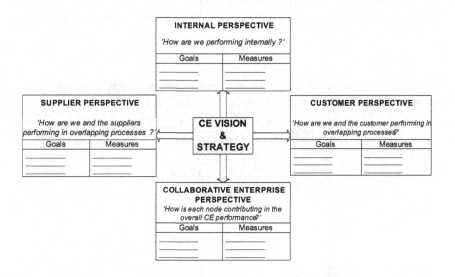

perspectives faced by an individual company (Company X, that is, RCT in the case study) at any tier in the supply chain. From Figure 10, four measurement perspectives can be defined for Company X:

1. **Internal perspective (X KPIs)**—located inside the four walls of the company;
2. **Supplier perspective (S$_1$ - S$_n$ KPIs)**—located at the interface of the company and its respective suppliers;
3. **Customer perspective (C$_1$ - C$_n$ KPIs)**—located at the interface of the company and its respective customers;
4. **Collaborative Enterprise perspective (CE KPIs)**—the holistic system.

These perspectives can now be displayed in the supply chain scorecard model depicted in Figure 11. This model is applicable for each company in the supply chain.

Adapting existing work by Medori and Steeple (2000) with the input from the KPI selection process at RCT, the author suggests using the following two frameworks for KPI selection in the PMS design process:

•   KPI selection at the local node level: concerned with the supplier, internal, and customer perspective of the supply chain balanced scorecard (Figure 10):

Table 3. Forces impacting performance measurement system evolution and change (Adapted from Waggoner et al., 1999)

Force	Examples
Internal influences	Power relationships; Dominant coalition interests; Peer pressure; Search for legitimacy;
External influences	Legislation; Market volatility; Information technology; Nature of work;
Process issues	Manner of implementation; Management of political processes; Innovation saturation; Lack of system design;
Transformational issues	Degree of top-level support; Risk of gain/loss from change; Impact of organisational culture.

○ Stage 1—Define the company's mission and strategy. Important to allow effective translation of the resulting strategy into effective KPIs.

○ Stage 2—Determine the importance of the competitive priorities for each perspective. This must be assessed according to the company's strategy derived in the previous stage. This step is crucial for determining the relevant KPIs.

○ Stage 3—Derive critical success factors and customer requirements from the company's strategy. Using competitive priorities strategy, statements are translated and developed.

○ Stage 4—Select measures. At the end of this stage, a list of KPIs for the internal, supplier, and customer perspective should have been specified under the various competitive priorities.

○ Stage 5—Implementation of KPIs. A performance measure record sheet is produced to standardise the process of actually recording of KPIs used in the company.

○ Stage 6—Periodic review.

- KPI selection at the supply chain level: concerned with the supply chain-perspective in the supply chain balanced scorecard model.

○ Stage 1— Develop the supply chain direction and requirements plan. The supply chain process owners should develop the plan through an examination of the four factors of Waggoner et al. (1999) highlighted in Table 3. Also, the identification of precisely what are the customer's order winners and order qualifiers should be considered. The result of this stage is a document outlining what the plan of the supply chain should be from the final customer's perspective, the internal, supply chain node perspective, and the external environment's perspective.

○ Stage 2—Translate the plan into competitive priorities. This is performed in a fashion similar to Stage 2 of the selection framework for the local-node level.

○ Stage 3—Select measures. At the end of this stage, a list of KPIs for the supply chain perspective is specified under the various macro measures of performance.

○ Stage 4—Implement the supply chain KPIs. This is performed in a fashion similar to Stage 5 of the selection framework for the local-node level.

○ Stage 5—Transmit the developed supply chain KPIs. Having developed the supply chain KPIs that must be used by each node, the supply chain process owners must transmit the KPIs to those parties that require them.

○ Stage 6—Periodic review.

Conclusion

Industries are facing an increasing level of business partner integration. When partners work closely together, processes must be re-engineered. Operations control crosses the traditional company boundaries and extends to the whole network processes. It was highlighted that there is the need to develop new theories and tools to support performance management of integrated supply chain processes. The chapter first analyzed the actual situation concerning SCM, performance measurement and management, and their interrelations. It pinpointed that increasing collaboration and supply chain integration is driving three major shifts in performance measurement practices: from measurement to management, from individual to supply chain measurement, and from feedback to feedforward operations control. The chapter first answered the question: what does supply chain performance management means? Then it answered the two related questions: What shall be measured? and How shall it be measured? Finally a supply chain PMS design process was presented, developed based on the requirements emerging from the previous discussion.

The goal of this chapter was to clarify what measuring and managing performance in a supply chain context mean in practice, in terms of the processes, methodologies, and tools needed to support it. It particularly focused on the process of measuring performance and the methodologies and tools to use to produce the output of this process, namely, the performance levels to manage supply chains.

References

Ahmad, M. M., & Dhafr, N. (2002). Establishing and improving manufacturing performance measures. *Robotics and Computer-Integrated Manufacturing, 18*(3-4), 171-176.

Amaratunga, D., & Baldry, D. (2002). Moving from performance measurement to performance management. *Facilities, 20*(5-6), 217-223.

Andersen, B., & Fagerhaug, T. (2002). *Performance measurement explained: Designing and implementing your state-of-the-art system*. Milwaukee, WI: ASQ Press.

Anderson, J. C., Cleveland, G., & Schroeder, R. G. (1989). Operations strategy: A literature review. *Journal of Operations Management, 8*(2), 133-158.

Beamon, B. M. (1999). Measuring supply chain performance. *International Journal of Operations & Production Management, 19*(3), 275-292.

Bititci, U. S., Carrie, A. S., & McDevitt, L. G. (1997). Integrated performance measurement systems: A development guide. *International Journal of Operations and Production Management, 17*(6), 522-535.

Bititci, U. S., Martinez, V., Albores, P., & Parung, J. (2004). Creating and managing value in collaborative networks. *International Journal of Physical Distribution & Logistics Management, 34*(3-4) 251-268.

Bowersox, D. J., & Daugherty, P. J. (1995). Logistics paradigms: The impact of information technology. *Journal of Business Logistics, 16*(1), 65-80.

Bredrup, H. (1995). *Performance measurement in a changing competitive industrial environment: Breaking the financial paradigm.* Trondheim, Norway: Norwegian Institute of Technology.

Brewer, P., & Speh, T. (2000). Using the balanced scorecard to measure supply chain performance. *Journal of Business Logistics, 21*(1), 75-93.

Browne, J., & Zhang, J. (1999). Extended and virtual enterprises: Similarities and differences. *International Journal of Agile Management Systems, 1*(1), 30-36.

Bungay, S., & Goold, M. (1991). Creating a strategic control system. *Long Range Planning, 24*(3), 32-39.

Burgess, T. F., Gules, H. K., & Tekin, M. (1997). Supply-chain collaboration and success in technology implementation. *Integrated Manufacturing Systems, 8*(5), 323-332.

Busi, M., Alfnes, E., Bolseth, S., & Strandhagen, J. O. (2003, June 16-18). The mobile extended manufacturing enterprise. In G. Spina June et al. (Eds.), *One World? One View of OM? The Challenges of Integrating Research & Practice, Proceedings of the 10th Annual EurOMA Conference,* Cernobbio, Lake Como, Italy (pp. 351-360). Padova: Servizi Grafici Editoriali.

Busi, M., & Strandhagen, J. O. (2004). Monitoring extended enterprise operations using KPIs and a performance dashboard. In *Proceedings of the 2nd World POM Conference on POM,* Cancun, Mexico.

Caplice, C., & Sheffi, Y. (1995). A review and evaluation of logistics performance measurement system. *The International Journal of Logistics Management, 6*(1), 61-74.

Child, J., & Faulkner, D. (1998). *Strategies of co-operation: Managing alliances, networks, and joint ventures.* Oxford, UK: Oxford University Press.

Christopher, M. (1992). *Logistics & supply chain management.* London: Pitsman.

Christopher, M. (1998). *Logistics and supply chain management.* London: Financial Times Prentice Hall.

Dixon, J. R., Nanni, A. J., & Vollmann, T. E. (1990). *The new performance challenge: Measuring operations for world-class competition.* Homewood, IL: Dow Jones-Irwin.

Eccles, R. G. (1991, January-February). The performance measurement manifesto. *Harvard Business Review,* 131-137.

Euske, K. J., Lebas, M. J., & McNair, C. J. (1993, April 28-30). Performance management in an international setting. In *Proceedings of the 16th Annual Congress of the European Accounting Association,* Turku, Finland.

Fawcett, S. E., & Magnan, G. M. (2002). The rhetoric and reality of supply chain integration. *International Journal of Physical Distribution and Logistics Management, 32*(5), 339-361.

Fine, C. H., & Hax, A. C. (1985). Manufacturing strategy: A methodology and an illustration. *Interfaces, 15*(6), 28-46.

Franco, M., & Bourne, M. (2003, June 16-18). Business performance measurement systems: A systematic Review. In G. Spina June et al. (Eds.), *One World? One View of OM? The Challenges of Integrating Research & Practice, Proceedings of the 10th Annual EurOMA Conference,* Cernobbio, Lake Como, Italy (pp. 451-460). Padova: Servizi Grafici Editoriali.

Ghalayini, A. M., Noble, J. S., & Crowe, T. J. (1997). An integrated dynamic performance measurement system for improving manufacturing competitiveness. *International Journal of Production Economics, 48,* 207-225.

Goldratt, E. M., & Cox, J. (1986). *The goal: A process of ongoing improvement.* New York: North River Press.

Hayes, R. H., & Abernathy, W. J. (1980, July-August). Managing our way to economic decline. *Harvard Business Review,* 67-77.

Hayes, R. H., & Wheelwright, S.C. (1979, January-February). Link manufacturing process and product life cycles. *Harvard Business Review,* 133-140.

Holmberg, S. (2000). A system perspective on supply chain measurement. *International Journal of Physical Distribution & Logistics, 30*(10), 847-868.

Hronec, S. M. (1993). *Vital signs: Using quality, time, and performance measurements to chart your company's future.* New York: AMACOM/ American Management Association.

Ireland, R., & Bruce, R. (2000, September-October). CPFR: Only the beginning of collaboration. *Supply Chain Management Review*, 80-88.

Jagdev, H. S., & Thoben, K. D. (2001). Anatomy of enterprise collaborations. *Production Planning & Control*, *12*(5), 437-451.

Johnson, H. T., & Kaplan, R. S. (1987). *Relevance lost: The rise and fall of management accounting*. Boston: Harvard Business School Press.

Kald, M., & Nilsson, F. (2000). Performance measurement at Nordic companies. *European Management Journal*, *18*(1), 113-127.

Kaplan, R. S., & Norton, D. P. (1992, January-February). The balanced scorecard: Measures that drive performance. *Harvard Business Review*.

Kaplan, R. S., & Norton, D. P. (2000, September-October). Having trouble with your strategy? Then map it. *Harvard Business Review*, 167-176.

Kathuria, R., & Partovi, F. Y. (2000). Aligning work force management practices with competitive priorities and process technology: A conceptual examination. *The Journal of High Technology Management Research*, *11*(2), 215-234.

Keegan, D. P., Eiler, R. G., & Jones, C. R. (1989, June). Are your performance measures obsolete? *Management Accounting*, 45-50.

Kleijnen, J., & Smits, M. (2003). Performance metrics in supply chain management. *Journal of the Operational Research Society*, *54*(5), 507-514.

Konsynski, B. R. (1993). Strategic control in the extended enterprise. *IBM Systems Journal*, *32*(1), 111-142.

Lambert, D. M., & Cooper, M. C. (2000). Issues in supply chain management. *Industrial Marketing Management*, *29*(1), 1-19.

Lambert, D. M., & Pholen, T. L. (2001). Supply chain matrix. *International Journal of Logistics Management*, *12*(1), 1-19.

Lee, H. L. (2000, September/October). Creating value through supply chain integration. *Supply Chain Management Review*.

Lee, H. L., & Whang, S. (2001, November). E-business and supply chain integration. *Stanford Global Supply Chain Management Forum*. SGSCMF-W2-2001.

Lee, W. B., Cheung, C. F., Lau, H. C. W., & Choy, K. L. (2003). Development of a Web-based enterprise collaborative platform for networked enterprises. *Business Process Management Journal*, *9*(1), 46-58.

Lummus, R. R., & Vokurka, R. J. (1999). Managing the demand chain through managing the information flow: Capturing 'moments of information.' *Production and Inventory Management Journal*, First Quarter, 16-20.

Lupton, G., & Dooley, L. (2003). Product life cycle performance indicators. In *Proceedings of the 20th International Manufacturers Conference, IMC 20*, Cork, Ireland (pp. 591-597).

Macaulay, S., & Cook, S. (1994). Performance management as the key to customer service, *Industrial and Commercial Training, 26*(11), 3-8.

Medori, D., & Steeple, D. (2000). A framework for auditing and enhancing performance measurement systems. *International Journal of Operations and Production Management, 20*(5), 520-533.

Moullin, M. (2002). *Delivering excellence in health and social care.* Buckingham, UK: Open University Press

Neely, A. D. (1998). *Performance measurement: Why, what and how?* London: Economics Books.

Neely, A. D., Mills, J., Gregory, M., & Platts, K. (1995). Performance measurement system design— A literature review and research agenda. *International Journal of Operations and Production Management, 15*(4), 80-116.

Otley, D. (1999). Performance management: A framework for management control systems research. *Management Accounting Research, 10*(4), 363-382.

Patterson, K. A., Grimm, C. M., & Thomas, M. C. (2003). Adopting new technologies for supply chain management. *Transportation Research Part E, 39*, 95-121.

Perrin, B. (1998). Effective use and misuse of performance measurement. *American Journal of Evaluation, 19*(3), 367-379.

Rafele, C. (2004). Logistic service measurement: A reference framework. *Journal of Manufacturing Technology Management, 15*(3), 280-290.

Rouse, P., & Putterill, M. (2003). An integral framework for performance measurement. *Management Decision, 41*(8), 791-805.

Russell, R., & Taylor III, B. (1998). *Operations management—Focusing on quality and competitiveness.* Upper Saddle River, NJ: Prentice Hall.

Sabath, R., & Fontanella, J. (2002, July-August). The unfulfilled promise of supply chain collaboration, *Supply Chain Management Review*, 24-29.

Schmitz, J., & Platts, K. W. (2004). Supplier logistics performance measurement: Indications from a study in the automotive industry. *International Journal of Production Economics, 89*, 231-243.

Simatupang, T. M., & Sridharan, R. (2002). The collaborative supply chain, *The International Journal of Logistics Management, 13*(1), 15-30.

Sinclair, D., & Zairi, M. (1995). Effective process management through performance measurement, Part III - An integrated model of total quality-based performance measurement. *Business Process Re-Engineering*, *1*(3), 50-65.

Stank, T. P., Dougherty, P. J., & Autry, C. W. (1999). Collaborative planning: Supporting automatic replenishment programs. *Supply Chain Management*, *4*(2), 75-85.

Thorpe, R. (2004). The characteristics of performance management research, implication and challenges. *International Journal of Productivity and Performance Management*, *53*(4), 334-344.

Waggoner, D., Neely. A., & Kennerley, M. (1999). The forces that shape organisational performance measurement systems: An interdisciplinary review. *International Journal of Production Economics*, 60-61, 53-60.

Wholey, J. (1996). Formative and summative evaluation: Related issues in performance measurement. *Evaluation Practice*, *17*(2), 145-149.

Williamson, O. E. (1985). *The economic institutions of capitalism*. New York: The Free Press, Macmillian.

Winston, J. (1999). Performance indicators—Promises unmet: A response to Perrin. *American Journal of Evaluation*, *20*(1), 95-99.

Wognum, P. M., & Faber, E. C. C. (2002). Infrastructures for collaboration in virtual organisations. *International Journal of Networking and Virtual Organizations*, *1*(1).

Yeniyurt, S. (2003). A literature review and integrative performance measurement framework for multinational companies. *Marketing Intelligence & Planning*, *21*(3), 134-142.

Zairi, M. (1994). *Measuring performance for business results*. London: Chapman & Hall.

Zimmermann, K. (2001). Using the balanced scorecard for interorganisational performance management of supply chains—A case study. In S. Seuring & M. Goldbach (Eds), *Cost management in supply chains* (pp. 399-415). Heidelberg: Physica.

Endnotes

[1]   The phrase "a company's four walls" is often used in literature to refer to the physical boundaries of a firm.

2   For the sake of this chapter, it is important to understand that the concepts and methodologies hereby presented and discussed were developed based on observations at Raufoss Chassis Technology ASA, a Norwegian aluminium wheel suspension manufacturer. This chapter will not report these observations in details; for more information please refer to Busi et al. (2003), Busi and Strandhagen (2004).

3   Outcomes can be used to generate measures of effectiveness, while outputs can be used to generate measures of efficiency (Rouse & Putterill, 2003).

4   According to Williamsons (1985), business relationships can be classified as a spectrum of alternatives between market and hierarchy.

5   This section is adapted from the paper entitled "Performance Measurement System Success Depends on Design Alignment with the Core Purpose of Its Implementation" by Henriksen, Andersen, and Busi, available on request to this chapter's author.

Chapter XIII

Supply Chain Risk Management:
A Game Theoretic Analysis

Thorsten Blecker, Hamburg University of Technology, Germany

Wolfgang Kersten, Hamburg University of Technology, Germany

Hagen Späth, Hamburg University of Technology, Germany

Birgit Koeppen, Hamburg University of Technology, Germany

Abstract

This chapter introduces a game-theoretic approach to supply chain risk management. The focus of this study lies on the risk of a single supply chain member defecting from common supply chain agreements, thereby jeopardizing the overall supply chain performance. The chapter goes on to introduce a manual supply chain game, by which dynamic supply chain mechanisms can be simulated and further analyzed using a game-theoretic model. With the help of the game-theoretic model, externalities are identified that negatively impact supply chain efficiency. The conclusion drawn from this chapter is that incentives are necessary to overcome these externalities in order to align supply chain objectives. The authors show that the game-theoretic model, in connection with the supply chain game presented, provides an informative basis for the future development of incentives by which supply chains can be aligned in order to reduce supply chain risks.

Introduction

In recent years, supply chain management (SCM) has experienced considerable attention. Trends, such as lean management, have unleashed outsourcing with the aim of improving corporate efficiency, which, in turn, considerably reduced the vertical range of production. The result is that original equipment manufacturers (OEMs) have outsourced as much as 80% of their value chain. This resulted in an increasing dependency of companies on their suppliers. Intricate supply networks evolved, shifting competition from the single company level to the supply chain level. Thereby, supply chain management became an asset when it comes to guaranteeing efficiency and high service levels (Christopher, 2004).

As a consequence of the interorganizational dependencies, supply chain competition fosters risks. These dependencies and the rising complexity of supply chain networks have increased the importance of supply chain risk management. Although connectivity between the players and transparency across the supply chain are core aspects propagated by SCM in contemporary literature, reality shows that insufficient communication among supply chain participants still prevails. Therefore, interorganizational risks have the potential to become one of the core fields of supply chain risk management (SCRM) research in future.

As supply chain participants are always (potential) competitors, the intensity of collaborative efforts are always a matter of how high single organizations prioritize supply chain alignment. Incentives are a way to overcome the barriers keeping organizations from aligning their objectives. Finding the right incentives for SCRM can turn out to be an extremely hazardous and difficult task for supply chain risk managers. One option is to create mathematical models based on economic settings. However, whether all variables have been considered is only validated the moment the incentive is tested in a realistic setting for a certain period of time. This realistic setting can either be simulated by means of an electronic simulation model, a manual business game, or on a real supply chain. Since it is difficult to analyze the influence of a particular change within a supply chain—particularly due to the vast amount of interactions and the fact that such a change can also negatively influence a chain—the last option can be aborted. The first option does not include the variable that human beings make organizational and interorganizational decisions, which we considered to be central to SCRM. Therefore, we opted for the manual business game. Supply chain risks are evaluated in the so-called supply chain game. The supply chain risks analyzed here are specifically inventory risks, caused by interorganizational drivers. Bringing supply chain networks in connection with strategy and competition addresses a matrix of risk drivers within the locus of this level: horizontal and vertical competition and cooperation. Interorganizational aspects include "co-opetition," a combination of cooperation and competition, as coined by Brandenburger and Nalebuff (1997). This chapter will focus on the vertical organizational and interorganizational risk drivers related to these aspects. To date, SCRM has largely focused on combating the impact of supply chain risks or improving the resilience of supply chains to be able to react to unfavorable changes taking place. Therefore, we can deduct that current SCRM is largely reactive.

Proactive SCRM would require that sources and drivers of supply chain risks are manipulated in a sense that they are, in the best case, avoided, reduced, or at least controlled. Incentives provide the opportunity to do so. However, although incentives have gained wider popularity since the birth of the balanced scorecard (Kaplan & Norton, 1996), they have not yet been implemented as proactive measures in SCRM, and the effects of specific incentives are unclear. In a first step to developing such a proactive incentive framework, it will be shown that the supply chain game enables an ideal test surrounding for testing implications of certain incentives on SCRM. It will be shown that the game correlates to supply chain and market conditions, which justifies it as a reference model. Since natural advantages exist among the supply chain participants, an in-depth analysis can be conducted on their nature. Therefore, a game-theoretic model will be developed based on the findings in the game. The ultimate goal will be to use the model developed in this chapter, which provides the necessary informative basis to deduct incentives to align supply chain objectives.

Background to Supply Chain Risk Management

The effective and efficient management of the supply chain can become a core competency of a company. By definition, SCM is: "the integration of key business processes from end user through original suppliers that provides products, services, and information that add value for customers and other stakeholders" (Stock & Lambert, 2001, p. 54). Simchi-Levi, Kaminsky, and Simchi-Levi (2003) specify the value added as "minimizing system wide costs while satisfying service-level requirements" (p. 2). Poor SCM, therefore, results in the inefficient allocation of resources, which poses a risk, both to the company itself and the entire supply chain. Not only does it pose a threat to the competitive situation of a single enterprise, the entire supply chain is only as strong as its weakest link. It should be comprehensive that in times of decreasing vertical ranges of production, competition no longer is limited to two directly competing enterprises. Competition is increasingly dependent on innovation of suppliers and the effective and efficient management of their processes, as stated above. Therefore, no supply chain would tolerate a weak link over a long period of time, which would pose an unnecessary source of risk to the entire supply chain. We define the term *supply chain risk* as:

an uncertainty or unpredictable event, endogenous or exogenous to the supply chain, affecting one or more of the parties within the supply chain or its business setting, thereby (negatively) influencing the achievement of business objectives.

It is necessary to say that one of the main risk sources is induced by human beings. The importance of risk management arises from the necessity to identify all the potential threats posed to supply chain continuity. It is necessary to translate the basic methodology of risk management into terms of SCM and to develop a framework that addresses the main threats. It is possible to understand that SCRM is the group of activities developed and performed by supply chain managers, encouraged to minimize and, in the best case, to neutralize the effects of these risks. Therefore, SCRM should be seen as an intersection of the risk management theory applied within the framework of SCM.

As stated in the definition above and shown in Figure 1, risks exist that are endogenous and exogenous to the supply chain. Exogenous risks are risks such as geographical, country or national, natural, and market risks. Market risks can be both exogenous and endogenous due to the fact that every supply chain member has an internal and an external customer.

Endogenous risks can be further subdivided into company and relationship risks. As can be deduced from above, risks can be allocated to more than one risk category. As a consequence, the term "risk" as such can have a different meaning depending on the area, company, country, sector, and so on. Supply chain risks can be controlled, avoided, or reduced, which includes sharing and transferring risk. The inventory risk of higher stocks, for example, can be avoided by using modular product design. This this method of complexity management allows storing less product parts, while offering the same number of variants to the customer. Several risks exist that can only be controlled by means of collaborative measures and incentives. Transparency, availability of information, and mutual trust are success factors for the effective anticipation of risks (Blecker, Kersten, Späth, & Bohn, 2005). Christopher (2003) analyzed the

Figure 1. Schematic classification of supply chain risks (Adapted from Pfohl, 2002)

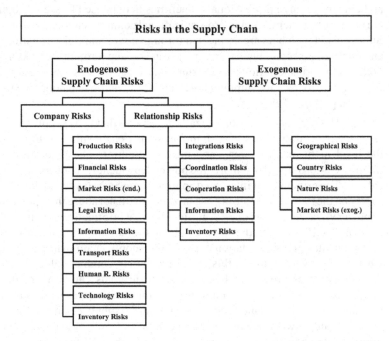

elements influencing risks in supply chains. In his vulnerability report, he identified four different levels at which risk drivers operate in supply chains:

- The first level, the risk drivers related to process and value streams, approaches the supply chain from an idealized integrated end-to-end perspective. From a purely process-based perspective, supply chain risks are principally the financial or commercial risks arising from poor quality, sub-optimal supply chain performance, demand volatility, and shifting marketplace requirements. In reality, supply chains are rarely fixed, discrete, self-propelling, or self-protecting. The adoption of lean and agile practices (particularly JIT delivery) has made them increasingly reliant on the existence of a reliable, secure, and efficient communication, transport, and distribution infrastructure, thereby making supply chains increasingly vulnerable.

- The second level considers assets and infrastructure dependencies. It refers to the implications of loss (temporary or otherwise) of links, nodes, and other essential operating interfaces. To ensure that they continue to operate is likely to fall within the responsibility of logistics, operations, IT, and human resource professionals. Facilities may house IT assets, which are nodes in the internal and interorganizational communications networks. Supply chain members are connected through nodes and links of national and international communications infrastructure and through the links and nodes of the transportation and distribution infrastructures. The links are, for example, roads, rail, shipping lanes, and flight paths, and nodes are rail stations, ports, and airports.

- The third level considers the organizational aspects that view supply chains as interorganizational networks. It moves supply chain vulnerability up to the level of business strategy and microeconomics. The links become trading relationships, particularly the power dependencies between organizations. The principles of integrated approaches to SCM (as set out in Level 1) rely on the premise that strong organizations will not abuse their position of power vis-à-vis weaker ones. Additionally, that information and risk will be shared selflessly for the good of all, within an enduring network of complementary trading relationships. While supply chain managers may work tirelessly to achieve this objective, other commercial interests, competitive pressures, and divergent strategic goals can work against them. Discretionary reconfigurations (e.g., outsourcing), as well as business failures or mergers and acquisitions within the supply chain or industry can all herald network instability at this and lower levels. Where dominant organizations have the power, capabilities, and the will to manage their supply chains in an open and collaborative way, "extended enterprises" will emerge. However, establishing and monitoring close cooperative partnering relationships is resource-intensive. Consequently, large sophisticated customers have reduced the number of direct suppliers, often opting for single sourcing (usually by product line) as the lowest cost way to develop, manage, and monitor their supplier base. The downside of this is that it has given rise to one of the most widely recognized sources of supply chain risk—disruptions caused by the failure of a single source supplier.

- The fourth level considers environmental drivers. Factors for consideration are the political, economic, social, and technological elements of the operating and trading environment, as well as natural phenomenon— geological, meteorological, and pathological. All can affect a supply chain at each of the first three levels of the framework. The sources of risks emanating at this level are likely to be beyond the direct control of supply chain managers, nevertheless the susceptibility of the networks can often be assessed in advance, thus enabling informed decisions to be made regarding the merits of risk avoidance or mitigation strategies. For the further development of this chapter, Level 3, organizational, and

interorganizational networks will be at the centre of the research in the
following sections.

The impacts of supply chain disruptions can be very diverse. The magnitude of
the negative impacts can be very decisive for the way the risks are managed.
Creating an efficient supply chain, therefore, not only concerns cost-reduction
to increase the return on assets (ROA), but also requires sensitive thinking about
shortcomings and sources of risk. Another impact on supply chains resulting out
of supply chain disruption is the loss of clients. It is common to think that the loss
of a client only represents a loss of an order, but this can have bigger
repercussions. It is extremely expensive to win an unhappy client back and, in
addition, the negative publicity can be extremely harmful. Having the product in
the right place, at the right time, at the right quality, and at the right price (4Rs)
represents a core issue in market-oriented supply chain management. It is easier
to win a new client than to recuperate the trust of an existing one. From this point
of view, the effectiveness of the supply chain should avoid this market risk. The
reason why financial risk management is probably the most profound risk
management discipline is that not achieving financial targets set by management
causes the worst outcome of a financial year in respect to a manager's salary
or bonus. Therefore, one of the main objectives in a company is to increase the
shareholder value. It is possible to see that the interaction between the different
participants in the supply chain is a central issue in SCM. However, as shown for
the management of financial risks, managers have the habit of not attending to
a risk or its driver unless an incentive is at hand.

SCRM can only be implemented in a collaborative effort across the entire supply
chain. An example for effects on supply chain performance due to the lack of
coordination, where incentives can counteract inefficiencies, is the bullwhip
effect. Chopra and Meindl (2004) show how the bullwhip effect increases
manufacturing costs, inventory costs, replenishment lead time, transportation
costs, shipping and receiving costs, and decreases the level of product availability
and profitability of the entire supply chain. The barriers to coordination in the
supply chain are among other incentive obstacles. These refer to the incentives
offered to different stages or participants in the supply chain that lead to actions
that increase variability and reduce total supply chain profits. These can be
subdivided into local optimization within functions or stages of a supply chain and
sales force incentives. Local optimization incentives focus only on the local
strategy of a supply chain member, which do not optimize the total supply chain
profits. Improperly structured sales force incentives are significant obstacles to
the coordination in supply chains. In many companies, sales force incentives are
based on the amount sold to the direct customer during an evaluation period. The
manufacturer measures only the quantity he sells to the distributor or retailers
(sell-in), not the quantity sold to the end-consumer (sell-through). An incentive

based on sell-in results in order variability being larger than the customer demand variability. In order to reduce the bullwhip effect and increase profitability, management should consider changing the incentives by aligning them with other supply chain members so that every member works toward maximizing total supply chain profit.

According to Chopra and Meindl (2004), there are three general groups of incentives to align objectives within a supply chain: aligning incentives across functions, pricing for coordination, and changing sales force incentives from sell-in to sell-through. The first involves coordinating the objectives of any function with the firm's overall objective. All facility, transportation, and inventory decisions should be evaluated based on their impact on profitability, not total or local costs. This helps to avoid situations like transportation managers making decisions lowering transportation costs but increasing overall supply chain costs at the same time.

It can be seen that the groups of incentives addressed above can have an impact on supply chain management, since they adhere to basic economic principles. However, most of them have not yet been implemented in industry, and for those that have been, it is not clear precisely which effects they had. Another aspect is that no incentive framework has yet been developed to counteract specific supply chain risks. In the following sections, models are developed whereby the mechanisms within supply chains can best be analyzed. It is important to stress that only models including all relevant variables can be used to ultimately deduct incentives needed to align objectives across functions and organizations in a supply chain, in order to optimize supply chain efficiency and counteract supply chain risks.

Why Model Supply Chain Risks in Business Games?

The aim of this chapter is, as mentioned, the analysis of the interorganizational sources of supply chain risks. Since a supply chain is a very complex system, the approach of modeling and simulating the object of investigation was chosen for this analysis. By simplifying the considered system, a model offers the possibility of elaborating effects and dependencies, which are foreclosed in the real system by many other factors. For analyzing different risks within a supply chain, it is necessary to be able to separate the several effects from each other for analyzing them one-by-one. Another important aspect for using a model and simulating a system is the chance to test strategies and observe their effects in a much shorter period of time than in reality. Also, risky strategies can be tested without fearing extreme or negative results. This aspect is, of course, decisive for analyzing risk management in a supply chain. No real supply chain would be changed according to a strategy that could be damaging to the supply chain performance.

For the concrete modeling of supply chains, many different approaches with different focuses exist. Since the "human factor" is a main cause for supply chain risks, this work focuses on that aspect. Therefore, an approach must be chosen that allows reproducing this non-deterministic human factor. Most models invented in the recent years are computer-based models (for a review of these models, see Chen [2004]). Since these deterministic programs do not allow reproduction of non-deterministic behavior, they are not suitable for the analysis in this work. That is why the approach of a manual business game was chosen for modeling and simulating supply chain risks. In this model, the non-determinism is realized via the human participants of the business game and their unpredictable decisions. The decisions the players have to make during the game correspond to the fundamental decisions in a company, whereby the realistic behavior of a supply chain can be simulated.

The most famous manual business game on SCM is "The Beer Game" invented by MIT in the 1960s (Sterman, 1992). Since this report wants to focus not only on the dependencies and the business competition between the companies *within* a supply chain, but also *between* two supply chains, a new business game based on The Beer Game idea was developed.

Description of the Model

Compared to the MIT Beer Game, a main innovation was included in the developed business game—in the new game, two supply chains are competing with each other with the same product on the same market. The products that are manufactured by the supply chains are tables. The supply chains purchase from the same source, a "forest," by buying trees. At the end, both deliver to the same market, namely, the end-consumer, by selling complete tables. In between, there are three supply chain stations, which represent companies. These are a saw mill, a carpenter, and a dealer. The three stations of the two supply chains will be referred to as agents in the rest of this chapter, and are represented by one to three players each. The forest and the end-consumer are played by the supervisors of the game. As can be seen in Figure 2, each agent has a supplier upstream in the supply chain and a customer downstream in the supply chain.

This constellation of different companies was chosen because the interorganizational sources of risks are the focus of this work. From the game-theoretic approach, the business game was developed on two different game settings that will be analyzed later in this chapter. As can be seen in Figure 3, these are the "Dealer Game" and the "Internal Game."

The first approach contains the competition of the two supply chains against each other for a maximal share of a fixed end-consumer demand. This game can be simplified by considering only the dealer and the end-consumer as agents. The second game setting analyses games within the supply chain, in which single agents compete in two-player games.

Figure 2. Arrangement of the two supply chains

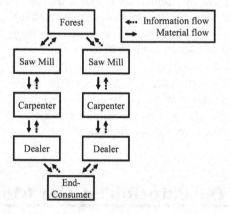

Figure 3. Game theoretic constellations in the supply chain game

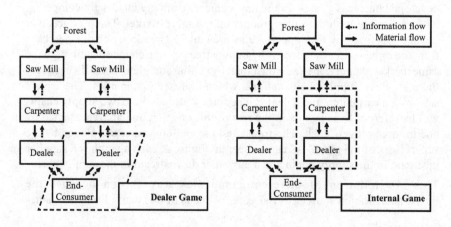

Figure 4. Main parameters of the agents

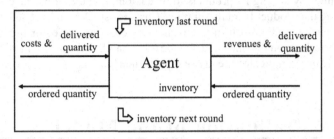

The parameters of the agents, which are relevant for a game-theoretic analysis, are chosen according to the interorganizational focus. In both games, the same inputs and outputs of the agents are identified as significant. These parameters are, as presented in Figure 4, the orders and deliveries, as well as the costs and revenues. Also, the inventory was taken into account, since ineffective stock represents a non-negligible risk of either non-availability of products or high capital lockup.

According to the identified parameters the business game was set on these characteristics as follows:

- The players are only allowed to communicate with each other by sending orders to their supplier and delivering goods to their customer. In each round the agents receive one order and one box with goods and send one of each. In the first ten rounds it takes two rounds until an order or a box reaches its destination. Later it is possible to shorten this time to one round.

- As a core element of the game the agents set a price for their product, that is, one table or the material for one table, respectively. Each agent decides how many products he wants to order from its supplier. Only the forest and the end-consumer have different rules—the price the forest sets for the saw mill is fixed, and the order of the end-consumer depends on an arithmetical function. The function determines the quantity the end-consumer buys from the two dealers in relation to the price the dealers set. Another aspect is included in the function. The end-consumer sets a penalty for the next round, that is, he buys less tables when the dealers are not able to deliver as many tables as the end-consumer ordered. The whole amount of the bought tables is normally fixed, but it is possible to include market growth.

- The intention of each agent is to maximize its profit. The agent gains revenues by selling its products to its customer, subtracting the costs for buying the product from its supplier. Costs for stock also have to be taken into account. The profit of the agent is taken as an indicator for its own performance, on the one hand. On the other hand, the summed profit of the supply chain indicates the group's performance.

Validation of the Model

For validating the model, the development process has to be considered. In the literature, there are two main possible approaches to developing a business model: the deductive logic and the inductive logic (Davis, 2005). Where the inductive model is developed from an empirical analysis of the reality and then generalizing and abstracting the parts of interest, the deductive model is based on a conceptual structure. Basic validated economic functions are combined modularly to generate a new model. In the case of SCRM, a deductive model is advantageous, because this approach allows the analyst to focus on the main points of interest. By designing a model based on validated modules, it is ensured that the model supports these effects and represents them correctly.

For a better assessment of the results, a reference game was developed. In this game, all prices and amounts of ordered and delivered tables are fixed on the starting level. With this construction, it is possible to prove that the rules do not promote or even enforce one result. In the considered case, all agents of both supply chains got the same profit after 30 rounds. So an equal treatment of all agents is ensured. This amount was normalized at 100%.

Since the agents that are closer to the end-consumer have the advantage of noticing changes of the market first, they are expected to profit by minimizing stock. That is why a "handicap" for the downstream agents was implemented by higher stock costs. As a result, when fixing all prices and amounts, the profits from Figure 5 will be reached.

Simulation of the Supply Chain by Business Games

On seven dates, the business game was played with different groups of undergraduate and graduate students under the supervision of the authors. These

Figure 5. Profit of the three agents after thirty rounds (Reference game with handicap)

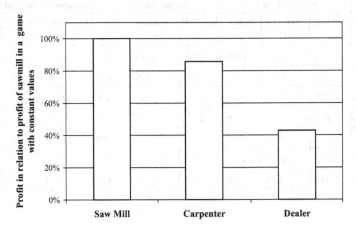

students were not involved in developing the game. In addition, they were not informed about the objectives of this research, and the game was communicated as a teaching instrument so that they should act independently without being influenced.

At each game, 6 to 12 persons took part, and 30 rounds were played. In the first two rounds, all prices and order amounts were fixed, in order to give the players the chance to get into the game. After the fourth round, a market growth was implemented, that is, the amount of tables bought by the end-consumer was increased.

As mentioned, the profits of the agents were used as an indicator for their performance. In Table 1, the result of each supply chain agent after 30 rounds is presented for the seven played games. For each game, the winner and the loser are marked by boldface.

From the results of the games, it is visible that, in most cases (five out of seven), the best and worst results were achieved in the same supply chain. Furthermore, the standard deviations in the right columns show that there are mainly two different cases of supply chain performance. The one is that the agents reach very similar results, that is, the supply chain has a very low standard deviation. This is reached, for example, for Supply Chain 1 in Game 1 or Game 2. In the other case, a high standard deviation occurred, that is, one agent with a very high result benefits from at least one other who achieved a very poor result. This clearly demonstrates two different strategies of working in a supply chain. One

Table 1. Profits of supply chain agents after 30 rounds

	Supply Chain 1			Supply Chain 2			Standard Deviation SC 1	Standard Deviation SC 2
	Saw Mill 1	Carpenter 1	Dealer 1	Saw Mill 2	Carpenter 2	Dealer 2		
Game 1	152%	138%	121%	*199%*	*-29%*	151%	*16%*	120%
Game 2	95%	106%	77%	82%	*54%*	*269%*	*15%*	117%
Game 3	186%	227%	*434%*	*117%*	316%	388%	*133%*	141%
Game 4	*80%*	122%	*261%*	223%	146%	121%	95%	*53%*
Game 5	121%	129%	152%	*32%*	167%	*209%*	*16%*	92%
Game 6	92%	157%	*-19%*	72%	42%	*182%*	89%	*73%*
Game 7	53%	*96%*	*28%*	67%	34%	42%	34%	*17%*

is the cooperative strategy, where all agents try to benefit in equal terms. The other is the non-cooperative strategy, where each agent maximizes its own profit without caring about the others. In this case, higher revenues can be achieved than in the first case, however, normally, only for one agent and mostly for the agent closest to the end-consumer; in five out of seven cases, the dealer won the game. In Figure 6, the average profits for each kind of agent are calculated. It can be seen that the dealers, on average, gained approximately 50% higher profits than the saw mills or the carpenters. It has to be mentioned that this happened although the dealer was handicapped by higher stock costs.

The results of this passage reinforce the intra- and interorganizational risk drivers postulated in the previous section. The fact that the strongest supply chain members reap the highest profits shows that the incentives for local optimization within functions or stages of the supply chain in place are insufficient or not aimed at optimizing the performance of the entire supply chain. The importance of developing the right incentives to encourage the cooperation between the companies is given.

The Game-Theoretic Analysis
of Supply Chain Risks

Analyzed in a game-theoretic context, it is evident that the developed game is a static, multi-period game with time dependence. This is because all players make

Figure 6. Average profits of the three kinds of agents

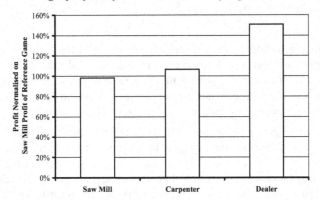

their decisions at the same time, over many periods. Thirty rounds were played in the analyzed games, and some decisions take more than one round to show consequence. Since the game can theoretically go on for more than the 30 rounds played, it is considered to be one with an infinite horizon. The game is subdivided into phases, each consisting of 10 rounds. After each phase, the players can confer about which strategy to use in the next phase. Therefore, we consider the game to be cooperative. The end-consumer demand is set according to a demand function. Therefore, the total demand of tables is fixed, which makes it a zero-sum game.

The aim of this chapter is to find an optimal strategy for the players in this game— a so-called equilibrium—and to compare it to the setting in the played game. Fudenberg and Tirole (1992) summarize: "a Nash equilibrium is a profile of strategies such that each player's strategy is an optimal response to the other buyers' strategies" (p. 11).

The implication of a Nash equilibrium for supply chain risk management (SCRM) is that the configuration of a supply chain is only then optimal to a specific supply chain participant, if it is favorable to all participants. The term "configuration" addresses the organizational and interorganizational constellations and the related risk drivers described in the beginning of this chapter.

The Nash equilibrium is defined by Nash (1950) as:

an n-tuple S_i^* is an equilibrium point if and only if for every i, $\pi_i\left(S_i^*\right) = \max_{all\ r_i}\left[\pi_i\left(S_i^*;r_i\right)\right]$. Thus an equilibrium point is an n-tuple S_i^* such that each player's mixed strategy maximizes his pay-off if the strategies of the *others are held fixed. Thus each player's strategy is optimal against those of the others.* (p. 3)

Subscripts in the definition are: π_i, which are the payoffs of the players i, following mixed strategies r_i. When the term n-tuple is used, we refer to a set of items that are each associated with a mixed strategy. A mixed strategy of a player i, in turn, is a collection of non-negative numbers, which have unit sum and are in one-to-one correspondence with the player's pure strategies.

In the supply chain game, two game settings exist, as shown in Figure 3. In the first, the two supply chains compete against each other, trying to maximize their respective share of the fixed customer demand. This game can be simplified by considering only the dealers as players, that is, an exogenous game constellation. The game shows a two-player game setup, similar to that described by Cachon and Netessine (2004). To simplify the analysis shown in the section "Static, Non-Repetitive Game Analysis," we assume the game to be a unique, single-period game, in which no time-dependency exists. This means that decisions in former games have no influence on decisions in the round analyzed. The aim is to evaluate whether or not a Nash equilibrium for dealer collusions exist. The initial assumption can be relaxed in the section "Exogenous, Infinite-Horizon, Inventory Game Analysis," where time dependency is introduced for a specific infinite-horizon game. Here, the aim will be to analyze which optimality conditions exist for a single dealer in a duopoly described by the supply chain game. The third analysis considers endogenous games, in which single players compete in two-player games. These games are comparable to the inventory-games described by Netessine and Rudi (2003). They will be adjusted to this context in the section "Endogenous, Single Period, Inventory Game Analysis."

Static, Non-Repetitive Game Analysis

In essence, the two-player-game corresponds to the Newsvendor Game that Cachon and Netessine (2004) use as a basis for their analysis. As shown in Figure 7, the game is "symmetric and non-cooperative, which means that the players are indistinguishable, except for their names, and make decisions at the same time" (Morris, 1994, p. 59). The subscripts $i, j \in \{1; 2\}$ are used for the two players or dealers. The price the dealer demands this round is p_i, that of the last round is $\tilde{p}_i$. The pay-offs are π_i.

Every player decides on the price p_i of its product at the beginning of every round. The exogenous demand, symbolized by D_i, is then set according to the demand function of the customer. The price scenario, shown and discussed above, is inextricably intertwined with the following demand function:

Figure 7. Symmetric decision matrix for the dealer game

Dealer 1

		$p_1 < \tilde{p}_2$	$p_1 = \tilde{p}_2$	$p_1 > \tilde{p}_2$
	$p_2 < \tilde{p}_1$	$\pi_1 = \pi_2$	$\pi_1 > \pi_2$	$\pi_1 \gg \pi_2$
Dealer 2	$p_2 = \tilde{p}_1$	$\pi_1 < \pi_2$	$\pi_1 = \pi_2$	$\pi_1 > \pi_2$
	$p_2 > \tilde{p}_1$	$\pi_1 \ll \pi_2$	$\pi_1 < \pi_2$	$\pi_1 = \pi_2$

$$D_i = \frac{\left(\dfrac{p_i + p_j}{2p_i}\right)^3}{\left(\dfrac{p_i + p_j}{2p_i}\right)^3 + \left(\dfrac{p_i + p_j}{2p_j}\right)^3}; \quad i, j \in \{1;2\} \qquad (1)$$

If both players reduce their price, the total monetary market volume shrinks due to the fixed demand in tables within this duopoly, irrespective of the total budget. Conversely, the market grows when both decide to raise their price in equal amounts without changing the demand allocation. Market growth is indicated by the size of the letters in the matrix. The unit costs of the product are c_i and the unit revenues are r_i. The order quantity of the dealer is given by Q_i. In the supply chain game, the products that Dealers 1 and 2 sell are substitutable. As a result, if the demanded price of Dealer 1 is too high, the customer simply buys from Dealer 2.

Each player wants to maximize payoffs by minimizing warehousing costs and maximizing earnings corresponding to demand. Deduced from the general optimization problem, this is a very strong assumption to make. However, relaxing this assumption would change the model to an extent as to make it irrelevant for use on the supply chain game model, where both dealers deliver to the same end-consumer. From the common Newsvendor Game, we arrive at the following optimization problem:

$$\max_{Q_i} \pi_i = \max_{Q_i} E_D[r_i \min(D_i, Q_i) - c_i Q_i] \qquad (2)$$

E_D marks the expected demand. Therefore, the function is a demand maximizing problem in which the variable order quantity Q_i needs to be optimized. In Figure 8, the schematic game setting in the analyzed game is presented.

A strategy in this game is optimal when the best response function in relation to the competitors demand is maximized. The best response function is defined by Cachon and Netessine (2004) as follows: "Given an n-player game, player i's best response (function) to the strategies y_i of the other players is the strategy $y_{i\text{-}}$ that maximizes player i's payoff $\pi_i(y_p, y_{i\text{-}})$" (p. 17). The inventory level is the variable to be optimized by determining the corresponding order quantity Q_i. The ability of a dealer to deliver the exact amount of tables ordered (service reliability) only plays a role in the next games. Therefore, it is assumed here that

Figure 8. Game settings in the single period game

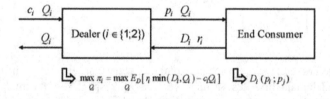

Figure 9. Best response of dealer's price settings in relation to the competitor

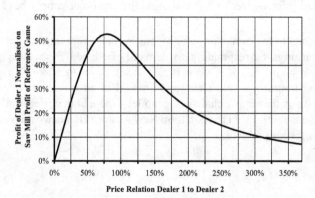

the best response for the dealer is determined by its ability to maximize demand. Since demand is dependent on the price settings in relation to that of the competitor in this duopoly, the optimal price setting of a dealer is where his best response function reaches a local maximum. As Figure 9 shows, the best response for a dealer in this duopolistic game setting would be to choose a price at approximately 78% of the price the competitor chooses.

According to the definitions of Nash (1950) and Fudenberg and Tirole (1992) above, a unique or multiple equilibria exist when the best response functions of the competitors have one or many intersections. Each intersection marks an equilibrium. As can be seen in Figure 10, no equilibrium exists for the duopoly under the assumption above and a single period analysis. Therefore, no ideal price setting can be found for every dealer to maximize his own profit without counteracting the objectives of his competitor.

Collusions might be an alternative arrangement by which every dealer can maximize his profits. In the supply chain game, agents are given the opportunity to agree on a common strategy after every game period, consisting of 10 rounds. Three variations of common strategies were agreed upon in our simulation. The first was that every agent orders the same quantities from its supplier. The second considered fixed prices, so that the supply chain can effectively compete against the other, and the third was free competition among the supply chain members. The quantity agreement was reached only once. However, this strategy failed, as could be expected, because order quantities of the customer result out of the price set by the dealer and, therefore, hardly stay constant. This is a strategy that comes closest to the centralized inventory management model

Figure 10. Best response functions of both dealers

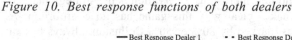
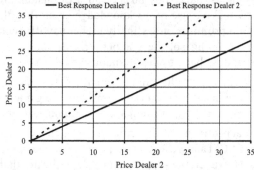

Figure 11. Normalized profits of dealers

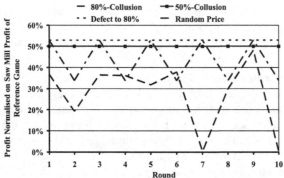

analyzed by Netessine and Rudi (2003). Further analysis of the strategy is abandoned here because it has no significance to the game. The second strategy was more relevant because it showed interesting results. Figure 11 shows the pricing strategy alternatives a dealer has in the supply chain game.

The area under a line represents the accumulated profit of a dealer over 10 rounds. The "Random Price" line shows the realistic pricing equivalent to that made in the supply chain game. As can easily be seen, this strategy amounts to suboptimal revenue developments. It might be added that this is the only of the four strategies that conforms to antitrust regulations. A more optimal outcome to an individual dealer is represented by the case where the two agree to take chances at offering their products at 80% of the other's price. Hence, oscillating revenues result, as the line "80%-Collusion" shows. In the next strategy, both agree to offer their products at the same price, which amounts to a 50% market share for both players. Another interesting observation is the strategy marked "Defect to 80%." This makes clear why this game has no equilibrium. A participant in collusion, as marked by 80% or 50%-Collusion, always has an incentive to defect by making use of his knowledge about the other's pricing strategy, even though it promises only slightly higher payoffs (compare Nash, 1950). However, when doing so, the competitor will soon realize that his competitor defected and go back to the "Random Price" strategy.

Figure 12 shows the realistic results gained from the first simulations with the supply chain game. The data analyzed only considers the games in which the players chose the advanced transportation and communication alternatives.

One would assume that profit and risk sharing among supply chain members, as propagated by modern SCM and SCRM theory, would ultimately increase joined accumulated profits. However, the supply chain game indicates that it is of little

Figure 12. Average agent profits per round

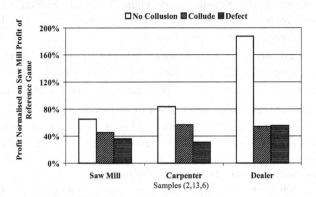

Samples (2,13,6)

advantage to any member. It must be added that the represented amount of simulations is not significant. However, it indicates that free competition is the better option for all agents. One might also add that other reasons for this result might be that important variables of real supply chains, like the importance of innovation out of R&D investments, are missing, and that the games in which supply chains colluded showed less market growth than those with free competition. Future simulations with the supply chain game will have to state whether the first assumptions are correct.

Exogenous, Infinite-Horizon, Inventory Game Analysis

As discussed, the infinite-horizon game is an extension of the single-period game, by introducing time dependency. Netessine, Rudi, and Wang (2004) discuss an inventory-competition model, which is aimed at deducting incentives to backorder. The setup is similar to what we described here, in that they define a duopolistic setup between two suppliers (retailers) competing for orders. However, several assumptions they make are relaxed in this game model. One is that they "assume that the first-choice demand does not depend on any past decisions made by the competing firms" (Netessine et al., 2004, p. 7). In this model, a time dependency is incorporated, which forms a core element in the supply chain games demand allocation. A further deviation marks the exogenous demand function, which is a modification of (1) and which will be discussed later. A restriction to this model is that, implied by the supply chain game, both dealers deliver to only one customer. This does have relevance to real supply chain constellations because there is an abundance of SMEs delivering to only one OEM.

The infinite-horizon model is given by the same subscripts as described in the previous section, "Static, Non-Repetitive Game Analysis." Enhancements to the model above are the periods $t = 1,...,n$ of observation, as indicated in Figure 13. The inventory of a dealer is given by $x_i^t = y_i^{t-1} - d_i^{t-1}$, where $x_i^t \geq 0$. The order quantity of the dealer is symbolized by Q_i^τ, where $\tau = t - (T_T + T_C)$ marks the time delay of deliveries. The time lag in the time dependency is therefore created by transport time, which is given by $T_T \in \{1;2\}$ (rounds) and communication time by $T_C \in \{1;2\}$ (rounds). An assumption for this game-theoretic model, predetermined by the supply chain game, is that the dealer of Supply Chain 1 always orders an order quantity Q_i^τ from the carpenter of Supply Chain 1, who, in turn, buys from the saw mill of Supply Chain 1. In addition, we assume that the supplier (carpenter) always delivers the exact quantity ordered. Inventory replenishment is hence described by $y_i^t = x_i^t + Q_i^\tau$. Constraints to the subscripts are $Q_i^\tau \geq 0$ and $y_i^t \geq x_i^t$. Price per period in the infinite-horizon model is denoted by $p_i^t \geq 0$.

Since this model reduces the customer base of the dealers to one, the exogenous demand $D_i^t(p_i^t; p_j^t)$ denotes the total demand of the customer from both dealers as described by (1). Exogenous demand adheres to the constraint: $D_i^t \geq 0$. Total exogenous demand is fixed at $D^t \in \{20;28\}$, which marks demand before and after "market growth" in round 4. Hence, total exogenous demand is given by $D^t = \overline{D}_i^t + \overline{D}_j^t$. In an infinite-horizon game, whether a dealer ran out of stock in the previous round also matters. This is why a penalty for non-delivery, given by ∂_i^t, is incorporated by $\overline{D}_i^t = \partial_i^t D_i^t$. The penalty has the following characteristics:

$$\partial_i^t(y_i^{t-1}; \overline{D}_i^{t-1}) = \frac{\min\left(y_i^{t-1}; \overline{D}_i^{t-1}\right)}{\overline{D}_i^{t-1}}, \text{where } 0 \leq \partial_i^t \leq 1.$$ The optimization condition aims

Figure 13. Infinite horizon game constellation

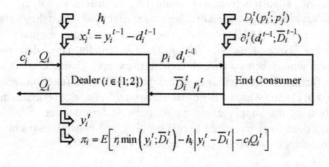

at minimizing negative stock deviation or understocking. The inventory balance equation is: $x_i^{t+1} = \left| y_i^t - \overline{D}_i^t \right|$. A profit maximizing dealer tries to turn over his total inventory once per round, whereby the delivery quantities would equal the inventory levels. When a dealer decides on his inventory level y_i^t for the period, his single-period expected net profit under the lost sale assumption is in correspondence with (2), given by:

$$\pi_i^t = E\left[r_i^t \min\left(y_i^t; \overline{D}_i^t \right) - h_i \left| y_i^t - \overline{D}_i^t \right| - c_i^t Q_i^t \right]; \quad i \in \{1;2\}; \forall t = 1,...,n \qquad (3)$$

Thereby, it becomes a profit-maximizing problem, in which stock deviation from demand needs to be minimized. Corresponding to the last section, "Static, Non-Repetitive Game Analysis," cost and revenue parameters of the dealer are the unit costs c_i^t unit revenues r_i^t and unit inventory holding costs h_i. In analogy to Netessine et al. (2004), the total profit of the dealer over infinite periods, starting with initial inventories $x^1 \equiv (x_1^1; x_2^1)$ as is the case in the supply chain game, amounts to:

$$
\begin{aligned}
\pi_i(y_i^t > \overline{D}_i^t) &= E\sum_{t=1}^{\infty}\left[r_i^t \min\left(y_i^t; \overline{D}_i^t \right) - h_i \left| y_i^t - \overline{D}_i^t \right| - c_i^t Q_i^t \right] \\
&= E\sum_{t=1}^{\infty}\left[r_i^t \min\left(y_i^t; \overline{D}_i^t \right) - h_i \left| y_i^t - \overline{D}_i^t \right| - c_i^t y_i^t + c_i^t x_i^t \right] \\
&= E\left\{ \sum_{t=2}^{\infty}\left[r_i^t \min\left(y_i^t; \overline{D}_i^t \right) - h_i \left| y_i^t - \overline{D}_i^t \right| - c_i^t y_i^t + c_i^{t-1} \left| y_i^{t-1} - \overline{D}_i^{t-1} \right| \right] \right\} \\
&\quad + E\left\{ r_i^1 \min\left(y_i^1; \overline{D}_i^1 \right) - h_i \left| y_i^1 - \overline{D}_i^1 \right| - c_i^1 \left(y_i^1 - x_i^1 \right) \right\} \\
&= E\left\{ \sum_{t=2}^{\infty}\left[r_i^t \min\left(y_i^t; \overline{D}_i^t \right) - h_i \left| y_i^t - \overline{D}_i^t \right| - c_i^t y_i^t + c_i^{t-1} \left| y_i^{t-1} - \overline{D}_i^{t-1} \right| \right] \right\} \\
&\quad + E\left\{ r_i^1 \min\left(y_i^1; \overline{D}_i^1 \right) - h_i \left| y_i^1 - \overline{D}_i^1 \right| - c_i^1 y_i^1 - c_i^1 x_i^1 \right\} \\
&= c_i^1 x_i^1 + E\sum_{t=1}^{\infty}\left[r_i^t \min\left(y_i^t; \overline{D}_i^t \right) - h_i \left| y_i^t - \overline{D}_i^t \right| - c_i^t y_i^t + c_i^t \left| y_i^t - \overline{D}_i^t \right| \right]
\end{aligned}
\qquad (4)
$$

$i \in \{1;2\}, \forall t = 1,...,n$

To derive this result, $Q_i^t = y_i^t - x_i^t$ and $c_i^t x_i^t = c_i^{t-1} \left| y_i^{t-1} - \overline{D}_i^{t-1} \right|$ for $t \geq 2$ are inserted. Further, we assume that the revenue $r_i^t \min(y_i^t; \overline{D}_i^t)$ for $y_i^t > \overline{D}_i^t$ consists of the sold quantity $\left(r_i^t \cdot \overline{D}_i^t \right)$, from which opportunity costs $\left[r_i^t \cdot \left(y_i^t - \overline{D}_i^t \right) \right]$ are subtracted. Substituting the variable part of the optimization results to:

$$\pi_i(y_i^t > \overline{D}_i^t) = c_i x_i^1 + E \sum_{t=1}^{\infty} G_i^t \left(y_i^t \right), \quad i \in \{1;2\}; \forall\, t = 1,\ldots,n \tag{5}$$

where

$$G_i^t \left(y_i^t \right) = \left(r_i^t - c_i^t \right) \overline{D}_i^t - \left(r_i^t - c_i^t \right) \left(\overline{D}_i^t - y_i^t \right) - \left(h_i + c_i^t \right) \left(y_i^t - \overline{D}_i^t \right)$$
$$i \in \{1;2\}; \forall\, t = 1,\ldots,n \tag{6}$$

Now we introduce the notation $u_i^t = r_i^t - c_i^t$ for understocking costs or lost profit (opportunity costs), and $o_i^t = h_i + c_i^t$ for overstocking costs. The expected single-period net profit is therefore:

$$\pi_i^t(y_i^t > \overline{D}_i^t) = E \left[u_i^t \overline{D}_i^t - u_i^t \left(\overline{D}_i^t - y_i^t \right) - o_i^t \left(y_i^t - \overline{D}_i^t \right) \right]$$
$$i \in \{1;2\}; \forall\, t = 1,\ldots,n \tag{7}$$

To determine the single-period profit-maximizing combination, the first derivative is made. Since demand is a function of the order level, the hidden derivate is given by $\overline{D}_i'^t = \dfrac{\partial \overline{D}_i^t}{\partial y_i^t}$. It is assumed that the demand distribution $\overline{D}_i'^t$ can be approximated by a non-linear function with inventory-level dependency. The single-period derivative is:

$$\frac{\partial \pi_i^t}{\partial y_i^t} = u_i^t \overline{D}_i'^t - \left[u_i^t \left(1 - \overline{D}_i'^t \right) + o_i^t \left(1 - \overline{D}_i'^t \right) \right] Br_i^t(\overline{D}_i^t < y_i^t)$$
$$= u_i^t \overline{D}_i'^t - \left[\left(u_i^t + o_i^t \right) \left(1 - \overline{D}_i'^t \right) \right] Br_i^t(\overline{D}_i^t < y_i^t) \tag{8}$$

$Br_i^t \left(\overline{D_i^t} < y_i^t \right)$ defines the best response of i and thereby the profit-maximizing point

with the hidden variable dependencies of y_i^t. For $\dfrac{\partial \pi_i^t}{\partial y_i^t} = 0$ we get:

$$Br_i^t (\overline{D_i^t} < y_i^t) = C \cdot \frac{u_i^t}{u_i^t + o_i^t}; C = \frac{D_i'^t}{1 - D_i'^t} = const.; \quad i \in \{1;2\}; \forall t = 1, ..., n.$$

(9)

It can be seen that the best response function consists of an endogenous part, consisting of the variables for unit costs c_i^t and unit revenues r_i^t, and an exogenous part consisting of the quotient derivative of the non-linear demand distribution. Lippman and McCardle (1997) have demonstrated in their Newsvendor Game that this Nash equilibrium exists. Netessine and Rudi (2003) show that this is a unique and globally stable equilibrium.

Re-introducing the notation $u_i^t = r_i^t - c_i^t$ for understocking cost or lost profit (opportunity cost), and $o_i^t = h_i + c_i^t$ for overstocking cost gives more insight into the optimality condition:

$$Br_i^t (\overline{D_i^t} < y_i^t) = C \cdot \frac{r_i^t - c_i^t}{r_i^t + h_i}; C = \frac{D_i'^t}{1 - D_i'^t} = const.; \quad i \in \{1;2\}; \forall t = 1, ..., n$$

(10)

Figure 14 schematically shows the path of the optimality condition (10). The profit function in the unique Nash equilibrium of this model shows a hyperbolic path and the unit costs function shows a linear path.

Both variables, unit costs c_i^t and unit revenues r_i^t, span a three-dimensional plain, which results in a shift of the exogenous part of the best-response function. For further interpretation of this global Nash equilibrium, refer to the section, "Outcomes." The exogenous part is not considered in the graph and can only be incorporated once precise approximations can be made. Therefore, the graph only represents an idealized path with linear distribution.

Endogenous, Single-Period, Inventory Game Analysis

The supply chain game constellations analyzed up to now show that the main game variable relevant for the optimization of a player's pay-offs is the inventory

Figure 14. Three-dimensional view of profitability against cost and revenue

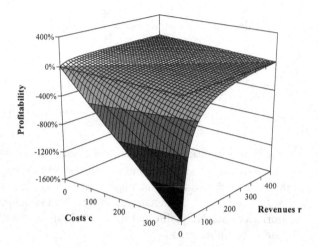

level of an agent *i*. Therefore, this section follows the same approach, analyzing the optimal inventory constellation of an agent *i* within the supply chain. For a model of the interactions within the supply chain as shown in Figure 3, two scenarios are given by Netessine and Rudi (2003). The first is a centralized inventory-management model, where the assumption is made that an overall inventory management is in place. The second is a decentralized-inventory model, in which every agent manages his own inventory. The experience made in the supply chain game shows that it is questionable how high the information connectivity must be to enable a centralized inventory management across the supply chain and to which extent supply chain members are prepared to give these decisions out of hand. The option of centralized inventory management was, therefore, abandoned in this section. The decentralized inventory-management model corresponds to that of Netessine and Rudi (2003). The optimal decision of agent *i* depends on the vector of inventory levels of the other agents in the same supply chain because one agent cannot substitute the product of its supplier against the product of an agent of the other supply chain. Staying with the notation of the analysis above, the inventory level of the agent is given by y_i and that of the other agents by y_i. For simplicity of the model, a single-period model is regarded; therefore, it does not contain time dependency. Demand D_i is then to a great extent influenced by the demand function given by (1). The function determines the demand of the dealer, which, in turn, is biased by the non-delivery penalty. An approximation of the demand distribution in this model D_i is given by a linear demand distribution function of the order quantity of the predecessor, which is a function of the inventory level of agent i. The expected profit of agent i in analogy to (4) is therefore given by:

$$\pi_i(y_i; y_{i-}) = E[u_i D_i - u_i |D_i - y_i| - o_i |y_i - D_i|]$$
$$= E\{u_i D_i - [u_i(y_i - D_i) + o_i(y_i - D_i)]\}; \quad i \in \{1;...;n\}; D_i < y_i$$

$$(11)$$

A game-theoretic situation arises where agent i will employ the best-response strategy $\tilde{y}_i$, which agent i plays to y_{i-} in an competitive environment. The equilibrium condition is therefore given by: $\pi_i(\tilde{y}_i; y_{i-}) = \max_{y_i} \pi_i(y_i; y_{i-})$. The best response will be denoted by $\tilde{y}_i \equiv Br_i(y_{i-})$. Given y_{i-}, it can be verified that π_i is concave in y_i. To obtain the best response, the first derivative of π_i with respect to y_i results in the following expression:

$$\frac{\partial \pi_i}{\partial y_i} = u_i D'_i - [u_i(1 - D'_i) + o_i(1 - D'_i)]Br_i(D_i < y_i)$$
$$= u_i D'_i - [(u_i + o_i)(1 - D'_i)]Br_i(D_i < y_i); \quad i \in \{1;...;n\}$$

$$(12)$$

The best response under the condition that $D'_i = \frac{\partial D'_i}{\partial y_i} = const.$ and $D'_i \geq 0$ is then characterized by the following familiar expression for:

$$Br_i(D_i < y_i) = C \cdot \frac{u_i}{u_i + o_i}; C = \frac{D'_i}{1 - D'_i} = const.; \quad i \in \{1;...;n\}$$

$$(13)$$

Interestingly, the result is the same as it was for the infinite horizon dealer game. This insinuates that the optimality condition of the exogenous game corresponds to that of the endogenous game. For the task of finding globally adequate incentives, this is a very valuable finding.

Outcomes

For the infinite-horizon game model, we have found a unique, globally stable, pure strategy Nash equilibrium, which is characterized by:

$$Br_i^t(\overline{D}_i^t < y_i^t) = C \cdot \frac{u_i^t}{u_i^t + o_i^t}; C = \frac{D_i^{'t}}{1 - D_i^{'t}} = const.; \quad i \in \{1; 2\}; \forall \, t = 1,...,n.$$

(14)

as was the case for the inventory game with:

$$Br_i(D_i < y_i) = C \cdot \frac{u_i}{u_i + o_i}; C = \frac{D_i'}{1 - D_i'} = const.; \quad i \in \{1;...;n\}$$

(15)

As described above, first indications lead us to the assumption that demand for the dealer-game can be approximated by a non-linear function of higher order. Conversely, demand for the internal game can be approximated by a linear function. A comparison of these results shows that the internal best-response function then contains a numeric constant, whereas the dealer game's best response contains the above-named exogenous function of the order greater than zero. Since warehousing and product costs increase to the end of the supply chain, $h_{i\,endo} < h_{i\,exo}$, $c_{i\,endo}^t < c_{i\,exo}^t$ and $r_{i\,endo}^t < r_{i\,exo}^t$. Using the assumption that they differ in equal amounts, we can deduce that:

$$\frac{u_i}{u_i + o_i} \cong \frac{u_i^t}{u_i^t + o_i^t}$$

(16)

If this holds, we can follow from (14) and (15), for a single period that:

$$Br_{exo} = Ext \cdot Br_{endo}$$

(17)

Br_{exo} stands for the best response of the dealer game, and Br_{endo} for that of the inventory game. The term Ext in (17) is the time-dependant, non-linear factor, which characterizes a negative externality to the supply chain. Externalities are effects not directly reflected in the market. In the supply chain, it is the factor causing higher inventory levels upstream in the supply chain, without an equivalent remuneration (Pindyck & Rubinfeld, 1989). In this case, it amounts to the quotient of the endogenous and the exogenous parts of the best-response functions. Since the critical variable in the profit-optimization problem was that of inventory levels, the interpretation of these results shows that $0 < Ext < 1$. This implies that the externality naturally induces higher inventory levels for internal supply chain members in comparison to those members with access to the market. This finding corresponds to the supply chain game, where an extreme profit difference was noted in favor of the downstream supply chain, although the game settings were biased in favor of the upstream supply chain.

As mentioned before, literature in which game theory was applied to supply chain or logistics problems, as shown by Netessine et al. (2004), deducted equilibria for warehousing problems between two agents. Comparing these equilibria for the internal and external case in the researched game, we found that a natural disadvantage exists for upstream supply chain members, which induces a risk for all members. This pinpoints a barrier that in our mind can only be overcome by means of incentives. These need to fulfill two tasks: aligning supply chain objectives, and eliminating the risk that defection is a feasible option for a single supply chain member.

Future Trends

High inventory levels influence the cost reduction capabilities of a supply chain. Inefficient inventory management causes market price increases when over-stocking occurs. On the other hand, understocking causes shipment quantity inaccuracies, a lack of supply availability, and has a negative impact on the volume mix requirements. All are supply risk characteristics as described by Zsidisin (2003) and are directly caused by the bullwhip effect. As we showed in the supply chain game, the bullwhip effect can only be mitigated up to a certain extent when implementing classical supply chain management measures such as improved communication and transportation infrastructure. As long as supply chain members follow different objectives, warehouse management or stocking along the supply chain will be inefficient and ineffective.

Chopra and Meindl (2004) identified three general categories of incentives for SCM by which common supply chain risk management objectives can be coordinated: aligning incentives across functions, pricing for coordination, and changing sales force incentives from sell-in to sell-through. The first involves coordinating the objectives of any function with the firm's overall objective. All facility, transportation, and inventory decisions should be evaluated based on their impact on profitability, not total or local costs. Pricing for coordination shows a model by which the market power of a manufacturer is regarded. If a manufacturer has no market power but large fixed costs associated with each lot, he should use lot-sized quantity discounts to achieve coordination for commodity products. Where the manufacturer has market power, he should introduce price discrimination by using two-part tariffs and volume discounts to help achieve coordination (Besanco, Dranove, Shanley, & Schaefer, 2004). Given demand uncertainty, manufacturers can use buy-back, revenue sharing, and quantity flexibility contracts to spur retailers to provide levels of product availability that maximize supply chain profits. Altering sales force incentives from sell-in to sell-through reduces the incentives for sales persons to push products to the retailer. Linking sales directly to the point-of-sale data can give supply chains a better planning horizon and considerably reduce variation of manufacturer sales compared to end-consumer demand (Blecker et al., 2005). Any such incentive has the potential to further reduce inefficiencies like the bullwhip effect.

As can be seen from our game results, supply chain inefficiencies caused by the bullwhip-effect had a negative impact on supply chains that did not collude. The game showed great standard deviations of revenue for these chains, where the dealers could react fastest to end-consumer demand fluctuations. Thereby, they gained the highest revenues. The game-theoretic models also show that Nash equilibrium exists for the non-cooperative settings. Therefore, the only options supply chain risk managers have to reduce the risk of supply chain members defecting is to impose high penalties on supply chain members who defect, which is not very realistic, or to create incentives, which shift the Nash equilibrium to a more favorable setting.

Conclusion

Competition among single companies is increasingly giving way to competition between supply chains. SCM has, therefore, gained increasing importance in corporate management. However, due to the nature of human interaction, the nonconformity of objectives fosters supply chain risks, which often jeopardize supply chain competitiveness. This stresses the necessity for new SCRM approaches in SCM. Such an approach can be an incentive framework whereby supply chain risk managers can mitigate organizational and interorganizational risk drivers. We have shown in a game, simulating interactions within and among organizations, how supply chain management techniques reach their boundaries when objectives are not aligned. To further analyze and pinpoint the drivers within these interactions, game-theoretic models of sections within and between the supply chains have been generated. These have shown that an external effect exists when comparing the Nash equilibria of the so-called inventory and dealer games. First indications exist that the externality is responsible for the profit gradient along the supply chain. If this is the case, incentives or an incentive framework can be developed to counteract this effect in SCRM.

The analysis of the supply chain game showed that a manual business game can simulate the complex circumstances of supply chains. With this, an excellent testing scenario has been developed on which the incentives could be simulated without unnecessarily risking unfavorable outcomes for entire supply chains or having to wait for a long time before the outcomes can be validated.

Contemporary SCM has paid little attention to the alignment capabilities of incentives. In addition, the risk potential of the nonalignment of supply chains has been neglected. Therefore, effective incentives can enable the alignment of decisions across the entire supply chain, by which the efficiency and service level of the entire supply chain can be maximized while optimizing profitability of all supply chain members. The importance of incentives, therefore, not only becomes an asset to SCM, but, in addition, SCRM gains a new field of research by extending organizational and interorganizational risk drivers by introducing the risk of the defection of single supply chain members when their objectives are not aligned with those of the entire supply chain.

Acknowledgments

We would like to thank Maik Brettschneider and Malte Müller for their tireless support in developing and executing the supply chain business game. In addition, we would like to thank Wendelin Groß for assisting us in the analysis.

References

Besanco, D., Dranove, D., Shanley, M., & Schaefer, S. (2004). *Economics of strategy* (3rd ed.). New York: John Wiley.

Blecker, T., Kersten, W., Späth, H., & Bohn, M. (2005, April 5-6). Finding the optimal postponement approach for demand chain management. In *Proceedings of the 2nd European Forum on Market Driven Supply Chains: From Supply Chains to Demand Chains,* Milan, Italy (EIASM, pp. 1-26).

Brandenburger, A. M., & Nalebuff, B. J., (1997). *Co-opetition: A revolutionary mindset that combines competition and cooperation.* London: HarperCollins Business.

Cachon, G. P., & Netessine, S. (2004). Game theory in supply chain analysis. In D. Simchi-Levi, S. D. Wu, & Z. M. Shen (Eds.), *Handbook of quantitative supply chain analysis: Modeling in the e-business era* (pp. 13-65). Boston: Kluwer.

Chen, Z. L. (2004). Integrated production and distribution operations: Taxonomy, models, and review. In D. Simchi-Levi, S. D. Wu, & Z. M. Shen

(Eds.), *Handbook of quantitative supply chain analysis: Modeling in the e-business era* (pp. 711-745). Boston: Kluwer.

Chopra, S., & Meindl, P. (2004). *Supply chain management: Strategy, planning, and operations, 2nd ed..* Upper Saddle River, NJ: Pearson.

Christopher, M., (2003). *Creating resilient supply chains: A practical guide.* Cranfield, UK: Crown.

Christopher, M., (2004). *Logistics and supply chain management: Strategies for reducing cost and improving service* (6th ed.). London: Prentice Hall

Davis, D. (2005). *Business research for decision making* (6th ed.). Belmont, CA: Thomson.

Fudenberg, D. ,& Tirole, J. (1992). *Game theory.* Cambridge, MA: MIT Press.

Kaplan, R.S., & Norton, D.P. (1996). *The balanced scorecard: Translating strategy into action.* Boston: Harvard Business School Press.

Lippman. S. A., & McCardle, K. F. (1997). The competitive newsboy. *Operations Research, 45,* 54-65.

Morris, P. (1994). *Introduction to game theory.* New York: Springer.

Nash, J. (1950). *Non-cooperative games.* Doctoral dissertation, Princeton University, Princeton, NJ.

Netessine, S., & Rudi, N. (2003). Centralized and competitive inventory models with demand substitution. *Operations Research, 51*(2), 329-335.

Netessine, S., Rudi, N., & Wang, Y. (2004). Inventory *competitions and incentives to backorder.* Retrieved February 10, 2005, from http://www.netessine.com/

Pfohl, H.-C. (2002*). Risiko-und Chancenmanagement in der Supply Chain: Proaktiv—ganzheitlich—nachhaltig.* Berlin: Schmidt.

Pindyck, R. S., & Rubinfeld, L. R. (1989). *Microeconomics* (4th ed.). Upper Saddle River, NJ: Prentice Hall.

Simchi-Levi, D., Kaminsky, P., & Simchi-Levi, E. (2003). *Managing the supply chain: The definitive guide for the business professional.* New York: McGraw-Hill.

Sterman, J. D. (1992, October). Teaching takes off—Flight simulators for management education—"The beer game". *OR/MS Today,* 40-44. Retrieved February 21, 2005, from http://web.mit.edu/jsterman/www/SDG/beergame.html

Stock, J. R., & Lambert, D. M. (2001). *Strategic logistics management.* Boston: McGraw-Hill.

Zsidisin, G. A. (2003). Managerial perceptions of supply risk. *The Journal of Supply Chain Management, 33*(1), 14-25.

Chapter XIV

Smart Integrated eOperations for High-Risk and Technologically Complex Assets:

Operational Networks and Collaborative Partnerships in the Digital Environment

Jayantha P. Liyanage, University of Stavanger, Norway

Mike Herbert, ConocoPhillips, Norway

Jan Harestad, OilCamp AS, Norway

Abstract

As the oil and gas (O&G) production business on the Norwegian Continental Shelf (NCS) stepped into a new development path termed the "3rd efficiency leap" since the year 2003, Smart Integrated eOperations is widely acknowledged as the way forward to deal with this inevitable change. Smart Integrated eOperations appears to be re-engineering the industry *structure. Within the next few years, new policies and practices will establish operational networks and collaborative partnerships between O&G producers and the service-support-supply market through active integration for effective and efficient management of offshore production assets. Adaptation of Smart Integrated eOperations is largely stimulated by rapid development in application technology, large-scale information and communication (ICT) platforms, and the foreseen substantial commercial benefits of well-integrated collaborative industry infrastructure. This is a very novel macro-scale program, and the Norwegian O&G Industry has already launched major initiatives in this regard to realize its fully functional status by the year 2010. The sophisticated information and communication platform called Secure Oil Information Link (SOIL) and Onshore support centres (e.g., ODC and OOC of ConocoPhillips, Norway) represents major icons of this digital era. However, as per the existing circumstances on NCS, this long-range development scenario presents itself with a multitude of challenges, particularly those relating to human and organizational interfaces, which have to be overcome to ensure long-term sustained benefits.*

Introduction and Background

In general, the global business environment today is becoming more and more complex, very dynamic, and highly uncertain. Both short-term and long-term commercial success in this environment call for the adoption of new thinking and innovative solutions to reduce risk and to add value (refer to various insights from Faulkner & Rond, 2001; Hosni & Khalil, 2004; Keen, 1997; Lindgren & Bandhold, 2003; Neef, 2003; Tidd, 2001). In the new era, complexity has defined some unique dimensions for competition, and interconnectivity has already become an imperative (Barabasi, 2003; Lewin, 2001).

North Sea O&G production environment, in particular, has been encountering significant challenges over the last few years particularly from the beginning of year 2000, and subsequently the O&G business activity in Norway is currently undergoing some strategic changes. The major part of the Norwegian O&G production portfolio is gradually approaching the tail-end phase in its production life cycle. An interesting observation is also that many small O&G companies are moving into the Continental shelf with interests on gaining commercial success by improving overall supply levels through development of marginal fields. Major concerns under the existing circumstances mainly relate to cost of ownership and operational efficiency. While technological advancements have been quite catalytic for a range of developments in this respect, the Norwegian O&G

Industry is encountering various other challenges, compelling it to reduce commercial risk and to add more value.

As aforementioned, under the current circumstances, there is an amalgamation of forces that compel a step change within O&G Industry on NCS. Those that are of major impact include:

- Declining oil production and rising operating costs on the Continental Shelf
- Serious focus on volatile oil price and its direct implications on profit performance of offshore production assets
- Subsequent pressure to seek novel ways and means to enhance operational efficiency and reduce cost of operatorship
- Decline in investments and activity level hampering sustained growth on the shelf.

Subsequently, the O&G production scenario on the Norwegian Continental Shelf (NCS) gradually has stepped into its so-called "3rd efficiency leap " since the year 2003. As the Norwegian Oil Industry Association (OLF) points out (OLF, 2003), this "3rd leap" focuses on a new development path to adapt a smarter and a more integrated operational environment within the next few years and towards 2010. Some of the major technical issues of interest, for instance, include:

- Exploiting the advancements in application technologies
- Robust information and communication technology platforms (ICT)
- Adapting novel data management techniques to manage technical and operational data

A unique feature of these developments is that it re-engineers the industry infrastructure that supports the activities in offshore assets. It brings the O&G producers, service contractors, and support & supply organizations closer together, opening up greater opportunities for active cooperation through operational networks and strategic partnerships based on advanced technological capabilities. These developments follow similar trends, for instance, as discussed in Dyre (2000), Spekman (2003), During, Oakey, and Kauser (2004), Tonchia and Tramontano (2004), and the like. On NCS, this new setup led to what is termed Smart Integrated eOperations. Issues related to this new development scenario were also envisioned in the government white paper, "Storting White Paper No. 38 (2003/2004) On Petroleum Activities."

This chapter aims to elaborate on the unique features of *Smart Integrated eOperations*; the nature and scale of integration and collaboration between

O&G producers, service providers, and support & supply organizations; a brief overview of some current settings related to large scale ICT network (*SOIL*); and the successful implementation and use of onshore support centres such as those of ConocoPhillips. Those major support programs with socio-political and macro-industry interests, and major challenges that have to be overcome for realization of full-scale benefits are also being addressed.

The "3rd Efficiency Leap" and the Smart Integrated E-Operating Structure

The "3rd efficiency leap" is characterised by those strategic, tactical, and operational steps that enable a major transition and thus help to realise the long-range development path against the gradual decline scenario of O&G production on NCS (see Figure 1).

The new setting, to a great extent, focuses on:

• Efficient exploitation of marginal (i.e., those with limited reserve prospects) and *mature* (i.e., those with declining production) fields;

• Effective ways and means to manage economical exposure and operating risk for large-scale and small-scale producers;

Figure 1. Reducing commercial risk and enhancing value creation on NCS through 3rd efficiency leap (OLF, 2003)

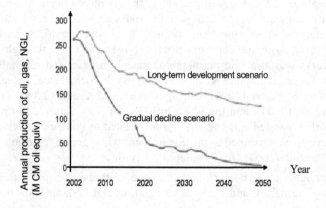

Figure 2. Asset process re-engineering for smart operations through application technology

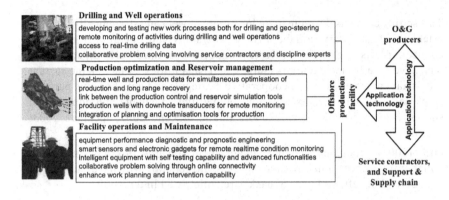

- Strategic use of advanced application technology and joint industry competence to improve offshore activity and productivity; and
- Efficient and effective data management platforms to enhance real-time decision support and work process optimization.

As this writing, major initiatives are underway to refine and re-engineer operational activities across three major asset processes—Drilling and Well Operations, Reservoir Management and Production Optimisation, and Operations and Maintenance. Substantial performance improvements are foreseen through these re-engineering efforts that will subsequently enable online monitoring and real-time collaboration involving major players on the NCS (see Figure 2).

The other supportive processes of this integrated environment encompass mainly license administration and e-commerce (i.e., logistics and procurement). In principle, the long-range development scenario constitutes twofold specific features:

- **Smart integrated setting:** Implies that both offshore assets and onshore support systems (i.e., O&G producers, service contractors, support & supply organizations) are tightly integrated and activities are managed adopting smart tools, techniques, and methods to enhance operational efficiency and cost effectiveness.
- **eOperations:** Provides an indication of the greater reliance on advanced application technology and the digital capability to enhance offshore-

onshore connectivity to ensure that decisions can be made and actions can be implemented in a far more profitable and a safe manner.

This setting compels the industry to look more closely and strategically towards establishing necessary collaborative partnerships and operational networks connecting offshore facilities, O&G producers with third-party organizations who have core competencies, resources, and capabilities. In fact, in the current industrial environment, such cooperative strategies and collaborative partnerships have become cornerstones for competitive advantage and commercial success (see, for instance, Dyer, 2000; Faulkner & Rond, 2001; Spekman, 2003; and the like).

OLF (2003) proclaims that the advancement towards this new integrated collaborative operational setting on NCS, in general, will have substantial commercial benefits. Major paybacks are anticipated in terms of:

- Prolonging commercial lives of offshore production assets;
- Improving recovery and regularity by optimising reservoir, well, and plant performance; and
- Bringing more positive health, safety, and environmental results.

As of this writing, the economical speculations are, in fact, a 10% increment in oil production from the continental shelf and, at the same time, a 30% reduction in overall operating costs.

Towards Operational Networks and Collaborative Partnerships

As aforementioned, Smart Integrated eOperations will redefine and re-engineer the Norwegian O&G Industry structure by establishing tightly integrated online and real-time collaborative partnerships with service contractors, support & supply organizations, and expert services using large-scale ICT platforms, within the next few years. In principle, this looks into systematic integration of core competencies, skills, and resources to build operational capability resorting to an advanced techno-organizational setting. The underlying core interest is in achieving commercial success in the digital era through highly reliable and secure collaborative networks eliminating geographical barriers (see also Hosni & Khalil, 2004; Tonchia & Tramontano, 2004). The new environment on NCS has a major emphasis on creating a synergy among core business sectors and is built upon:

- New forms of interorganizational partnerships and operational cooperation;
- Shared responsibilities and roles, and space for joint competence exploitation;
- Technical integrity, network security, and 24/7 connectivity;
- Rapid access to skills, knowledge, and information; and
- Advanced communication capability to enhance operational intelligence.

To a greater extent, the current activities on NCS are dedicated to acquiring the preliminary digital capability that establishes the secure and reliable network of technical expertise connecting largely dispersed discipline experts and competent organizations for online real-time collaboration. It creates a setting where a formal land-based physical organization is coupled with an active virtual organizational environment (also refer to During, Oakey, & Kauser, 2002; Lipnack & Stamps, 1997; Mankin, Cohen, & Bikson, 1996). Structurally, the new setting on NCS integrates operational and technical data with well-defined strategic sources for knowledge and competencies to retain the technical integrity of offshore assets to reduce underlying commercial risk. Figure 3 illustrates the technical infrastructure of this new setting.

As aforementioned, such an integrated operating environment has sustained benefits at various levels. Those major benefits that it yields in short and long terms, both from a commercial and socio-political standpoint, depend on the following two important issues:

- Level of actual integrity realized and the nature of collaboration agreed upon between active partners; and
- Level of reliability, security, and agility instituted within the collaborative network.

From a pure commercial standpoint, it is important and beneficial insofar as it sets the basis to gradually acquire:

- **Decision optimisation capability through connectivity:** Enabled through joint exploitation of advanced technologies and ICT capabilities for remote monitoring, and real-time operational and technical data sharing.

Figure 3. Operational network and collaborative partnership

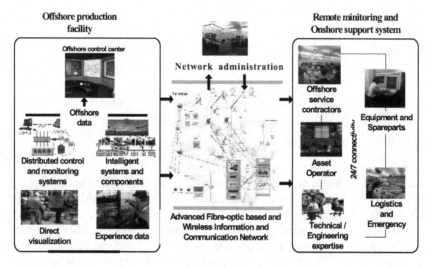

- **Activity optimization capability through integrity:** Enabled through tighter integration of work processes, cooperative decision loops, and effective and efficient division of work between offshore assets and onshore support system.

Decision and activity optimization capability, within the new network and partnership-based environment, is largely strengthened by the application technology. A clear progression is seen today in the technology implementation and exploitation strategies across the industry. Partner industries, particularly those related to electronic and communication technologies in general, have a major role in this digital environment to establish a stable and a reliable technical infrastructure to support decisions and work processes. As of this writing, major technological advancements are visible in the use of, for instance:

- Fiberoptic-based ICT net and wireless communication capability;
- Real-time visualization, 3D visualization, and simulation tools;
- Smart sensors, intelligent transducers, and equipment with advanced functionalities;
- Online diagnostic and prognostic engineering capability;

Figure 4. Core elements for network-based collaborative operational environment

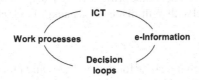

- Process automation and real-time data acquisition techniques; and
- Online video monitoring and conferencing facilities.

While such application technology provides the technical infrastructure to create the operational network, the form of collaboration and level of partnership mainly depend on the extent to which such a technical infrastructure is actively utilized for three purposes (Figure 4):

- Electronic information sharing;
- Decentralization of decision loops; and
- Work process re-engineering.

Producers on the NCS, service providers, and the support & supply organizations have felt the pulse of this change. They have already begun to look more seriously into interorganizational interface development with competence profiling and mapping to create a mutually beneficial work setting that is compatible with the technical demands and organizational needs. The joint effort by various business sectors has already helped towards:

- Challenging conventional organizational barriers between onshore integrated operational centres located at different premises. This is to allow joint monitoring of activities from different locations yet coordinated at the premises of the licensee. The major implication as of this writing is on decision optimisation, where personnel from expert competence sources are more actively involved. At the core of this lies revision of interorganizational partnerships for more coordinated use of dispersed industry's competence
- Integrated use of advanced engineering products, robust information and communication tools and techniques, and data management, and interpretation tools. This introduces new work distribution patterns between

offshore assets and onshore support systems with a great potential to reduce offshore headcount. It creates a more knowledge-based environment and redefines competence profile with subsequent demands for highly educated personnel with multidisciplined backgrounds capable of performing multiple tasks.

The trend and subsequent demands for new policies and practices seem to have direct implications across various corners ranging from coordinated competence management, smart products, to data management and interpretational services. The progression is more towards re-engineering the conventional practice to make it more technology based, information dependent, and knowledge driven, traits acknowledged as the way forward to enhance efficiency and effectiveness of offshore production activity (see also Dyer, 2000; Spekman, 2003; Tonchia & Tramontano, 2004).

In its full operational status, Smart Integrated eOperations will pull together a set of core characteristics within operational, organizational, technological, and human aspects. The resulting operating environment is subsequently expected to be a major enabler for:

- More active collaboration between mutually dependent disciplines (e.g., between health & safety, engineering modifications, budgeting, etc.), and also between partner companies (e.g., major producers, service contractors, and support & supply chain) in an integrated environment.

- Use of more advanced information and communication technology, particularly to bring together discipline experts, producers, and service markets into a more effectively interfaced corporative platform increasing the 24/7 connectivity regardless of the geographical location.

- Use of processes, techniques, and products to effectively and smartly integrate voluminous technical and operational data, experience data, and tacit knowledge into one common operational setting. Real-time access to data (e.g., using such advance tools as 3D visualization, VisiWear, etc.), and a broad spectrum of expertise in tightly integrated networks is expected to facilitate faster and better operational decision making and work-process optimization.

- New formulae for division of work between offshore and onshore organizations, introducing a new work setting that introduces a new culture of responsibility sharing between offshore and onshore organizations, and between major players. It subsequently demands re-engineering of traditional human-technology-organizational interfaces, at both the macro and micro scale.

Figure 5. Major premises for active functionality within the new collaborative network

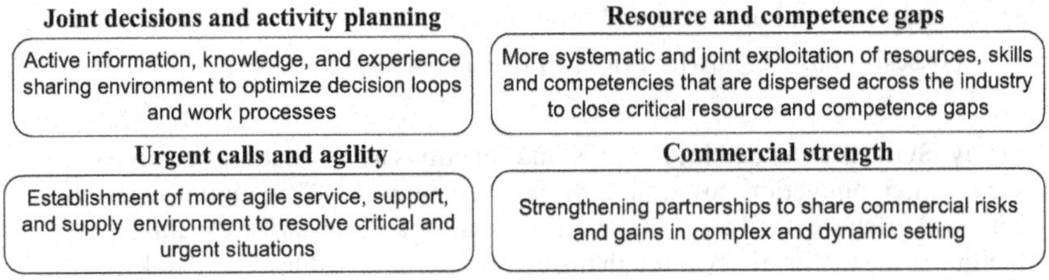

Joint decisions and activity planning	Resource and competence gaps
Active information, knowledge, and experience sharing environment to optimize decision loops and work processes	More systematic and joint exploitation of resources, skills and competencies that are dispersed across the industry to close critical resource and competence gaps

Urgent calls and agility	Commercial strength
Establishment of more agile service, support, and supply environment to resolve critical and urgent situations	Strengthening partnerships to share commercial risks and gains in complex and dynamic setting

- Considerable changes to conventional organizations in order to establish multidisciplinary virtual teams and organizations that consist of skilled and competent personnel from structurally distinctive yet strategically compatible organizations.

Figure 5 illustrates the major premises where such an integrated and a collaborative environment sustain to actively function.

Large-scale fiberoptic-based ICT network termed *"SOIL"* and "Onshore online support centres" remain the major enablers of rapid development today. Such Onshore online support centres have begun to appear both at the premises of major producers (ConocoPhillips, BP, Norsk Hydro, Statoil) and service-support-supply organizations (e.g., BakerHughes INTEQ, OilCamp, RC-DEI, and the like) that allow 24/7 online real-time connectivity with the offshore control rooms, offshore equipment, and activities. Such centers represent principal nodes in the complex digital network.

Secure Oil Information Link (Soil): The "ICT" Nerve

The network-based and collaborative environment requires a highly robust ICT infrastructure to support the core tasks and activities (see reflections from Clarke, Coakes, Hunter, & Wenn, 2003; Gunasekeran, Khalil, & Rahman, 2003; Tonchia & Tramontano, 2004). Secure Oil Information Link (SOIL) introduced in 1998 to the NCS, is the result of the current industry demand to acquire necessary digital capability through a large-scale network and centralized information system. Such a system needs to be:

- highly reliable (stable and dependable);
- secure (control of access and routing); and
- possess a large bandwidth (high-traffic capacity).

Today, SOIL is extended into the UK and functions as a collaboration arena, a secure interconnection point, and an industry network. This digital network between offshore facilities, major producers, and third-party organizations facilitates the connectivity through the use of fiberoptic cables, radio links, and satellite communications (Figure 6). For enhanced services, SOIL provides several shared applications including, for instance, RigCamp and SOIL Directory.

- **RigCamp:** This is a combined network and an application solution based on the Norwegian RigNet Standard that was agreed upon by a group of O&G producers in 1996 to standardize and deliver more efficient IT solutions on offshore rigs in the North Sea. As of this writing, it is a centrally managed data, voice, video, and communication service for the O&G Industry. This enables drilling contractors, O&G producers, and service & supply companies to operate on one common and secure IP network. The solution delivers voice, fax, video, and data over the IP-protocol.
- **SOIL directory:** This is a read-access to a complete directory service with information on member companies and employees. This further allows

Figure 6. Information and communication capability through SOIL

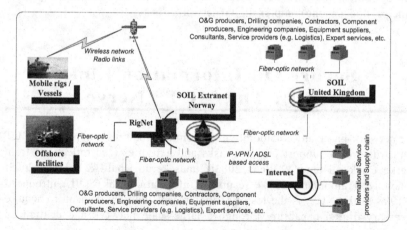

a centralized synchronization service that can synchronize a company's internal directories with that of the SOIL directory, for instance, to enable faster access to personnel to call for specific competencies, services, or expertise under specific circumstances. Directory personnel information is also utilized for secure access to SOIL services from the Internet.

A unique feature of SOIL application today is that it has moved the information sharing and communication capabilities from formal "One-to-One" or "Many-to-Many" project-based setting to a "One-to-Many" collaborative setting.

- **One-to-One or Many-to-Many:** This describes the conventional setting where major O&G producers provide limited access to handle complex technical data only for those contractual business partners on the basis of project-specific applications and/or complex databases.
- **One-to-Many:** This setting, on the other hand, is based on the provision of value-adding collaboration services on top of the established network infrastructure and allows consolidation of the traditional complex network infrastructure into one single hub, building 24/7 online and real-time information-sharing and communication capabilities between O&G producers and their business partners. This is one of the most important application setting for onshore-based remote integrated operations or simply "e-fields."

To enhance the interorganizational connectivity for a fully integrated smart operating environment, SOIL provides some key application services that include:

- **SOIL meeting:** A service enabling virtual meetings between member companies. The users can share applications, a common chat-channel, a common whiteboard, and file-transfer functions. The participants need to use a teleconferencing system during the virtual meeting for better voice quality. SOIL meeting also facilitates cross-company IP-based video services for conferencing in integrated operations.
- **LicenseWeb-based access:** Gives the user a secure login to the LicenseWeb application from the Internet, using a strong authentication provided by Managed User Directory (MUD) of OilCamp.
- **E2E monitoring:** A Web-based application that automatically monitors real-time network performance between operations on offshore rigs and onshore operation centers, providing a live control panel and trend reports.

This supplies the users with vital real-time network status information during remote operations.

- **Proex:** A Web-based solution to structure, define, execute, and follow up on tasks and activities in projects and/or work processes. Such projects can, for instance, involve various partners from different geographical locations, taking up specific roles and responsibilities in the project.

As of this writing, SOIL-based applications are largely used across the Norwegian O&G Industry by major O&G producers, engineering companies, contractors, drilling companies, component producers, equipment suppliers, consultancy services, logistic service providers, and expert services. The membership status has grown from a total of 20 in 1998 to approximately 160 by the end of 2004 just before the extension of SOIL to the UK sector. SOIL has opened up substantial opportunities to build necessary digital information and communication capabilities across the onshore and offshore environment in North Sea.

The O&G Industry, by far, has begun to rely more and more on integrated ICT solutions. Subsequently, the digital capability it requires, demand for more innovative solutions that enable faster decisions and quicker actions. For instance, such smart solutions as VisiWear provide wireless video communication solutions through a simple man-wearable, intrinsically safe conferencing system. It comes in handy and gradually appears to become integrated components of advanced ICT solutions that the industry is willing adapt to manage offshore facilities in the current highly challenging environment. Notably, it also opens up opportunities for manning offshore facilities with relatively fewer cross-trained people who are connected 24/7 with onshore specialist support groups. This has very positive economical and safety implications given the capital-intensive and high-risk nature of offshore activities.

Onshore Support Centers of Conocophillips Norway: An Icon of Success

ConocoPhillips Norway (COPNO) is the third-largest energy company in Norway, with seven production licenses and interests in 25 non-operated licenses. A major share of COPNO's O&G activities are concentrated on the fields in the Ekofisk area that is located in the southern part of the North Sea, some 280 kilometers southwest of Stavanger. The first discovery of O&G at Ekofisk in 1969 converted Norway into one of the world's major petroleum producers. Enormous values and invaluable experience were gained in this area of the North Sea. Ekofisk is still one of Norway's biggest oil-producing fields, and COPNO has drawn major plans to retain it on stream for few more decades. The Ekofisk field has been in production since 1971, and today there are 29 platforms, with 18 of them are currently in operation. The Norwegian Directorate for Cultural Heritage has declared the first Ekofisk platforms as a cultural monument.

COPNO has been working on major plans to enhance the recovery and to optimize production from the Ekofisk area more strategically, particularly exploiting advances in application technology. For instance, the wellhead platform 2/7D Embla is remote operated from the Eldfisk Complex. In 1996, the originally manned production platforms 2/4A and 2/4B were converted for unmanned use and remote operation from the platform 2/4K. These initiatives that brought some early signs of a major transition also brought many positive outcomes, particularly within production, facility maintenance, and operating costs. For instance, in Ekofisk A area, the reduction in cost by 2001 amounted to approximately NOK 47 million in comparison to figures in 1995. However, these technological applications did not introduce notable and significant changes to the operational organization in the Ekofisk Area.

Since 1998, COPNO has been stepping forward and making necessary commitments to make some significant changes to the operating mode in Ekofisk area. It has been gradually building the necessary ICT infrastructure with smart application technology to build remote monitoring capabilities at its premises in Stavanger. Consequently, in early 2003, the Onshore Drilling Center (ODC) came into operation after a dedicated project that spread across a period of seven months, with a total project cost of approximately USD 5.5 million. The ODC is mainly dedicated to drilling activities and well operations in Greater Ekofisk asset, and after a mere 23 months of continuous operations, it has become an icon of success in the exploitation of technology, decision and work process optimization, and multi-disciplinary interorganizational collaboration. Figure 7 is a diagrammatic illustration of the physical layout of a generic onshore support center.

The ODC at COPNO, for instance, is divided into three functional areas, namely:

- **Operational room:** Where online monitoring of offshore activities is enabled. This is equipped with tabletop workstations and back-projected large visual display units (VDUs). Remote work is carried out in this room, and down-hole tools, severs, PCs are all operated remotely.

- **Collaboration room:** Where online communication between offshore facility and onshore support system takes place. This is equipped with

Figure 7. Onshore support center (An illustrative example)

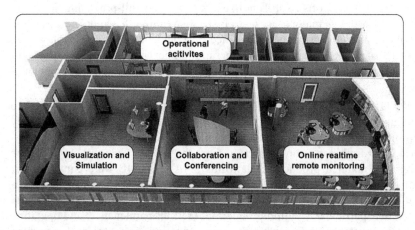

video-conferencing facilities, CCTV, and other advanced technological capabilities (e.g.,VisiWear, Smart boards) for joint decision-making.

- **Visualization room:** Where complex data from reservoir and production/injection wells are processed to enhance visualization. This is equipped with advanced technology to produce 3D images and to run simulations.

The technological capabilities built into ODC, together with the access via the ICT infrastructure enabled by SOIL, has resulted in the establishment of a form of virtual support organization for offshore activities in Ekofisk through a network of collaborative partnership. The current setting has paved the way to establish a 24/7 online real-time connectivity between:

- Offshore and onshore organization of COPNO;
- Different technical disciplines (e.g., data engineers, operation geologists, drilling engineers, reservoir engineers, safety risk analysts, etc.);
- ODC and service providers for Ekofisk (e.g., BakerHughes INTEQ, Halliburton, etc.);
- ODC and ConocoPhillips global (with further expansions to the existing corporate network to receive expert support, for instance, from Aberdeen, UK, Houston, Texas, or Alaska, USA, on an as-needed basis); and
- ODC and other competence centers, both national and international (with further expansions and technical mergers between dispersed application-service providers and network operators).

Figure 8. Digital capabilities for collaboration through partnerships and networks. The setup at ConocoPhillips today for Smart Integrated eOperations through ODC and OOC.

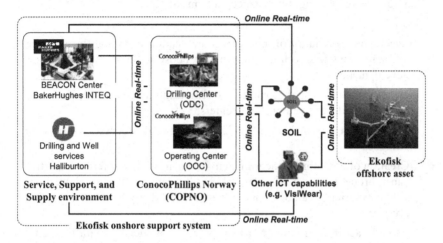

The technical and organizational infrastructure that contributes to further enhance 24/7 connectivity with core-competent third-party sources is still subject to gradual and systematic expansion.

COPNO has taken further initiatives to establish another shore-based support center termed the Onshore Operating Center (OOC) to further enhance collaboration within the Ekofisk operational network. This involves tactical and operational integration of critical support disciplines such as Planning & Scheduling, Logistics, Production optimization, and Operations & Maintenance.

Figure 8 illustrates the current operational configuration that integrates Ekofisk asset and collaborative onshore support system.

The new setting has brought a major change to the operating environment of COPNO. After a very successful effort, the ODC has been in successful operation for a period of over two years. It has brought significant advantages in various technical, organizational, and operational terms. The payback of initial engineering and implementation cost, in pure financial terms, was realized in just seven months. Major savings of up to USD 22 million were reported within the first two years of operations, where a substantial portion relates to improved decision making and resource management. Tangible benefits include reduction in man-days up to 2473, and a subsequent reduction in onshore-offshore transportation logistics of up to 302 helicopter seats.

Obviously, not all the benefits of active integration related to operations of high-risk and capital-intensive assets can financially be justified, particularly those critical, intangible ones. COPNO has achieved other major benefits of the collaborative work setting, for instance, in terms of:

- Successful exploitation of cutting-edge application technology to introduce a change that has resulted in a major boost for a stream of further developments;
- Development of digital capability for remote monitoring and operation of offshore facilities from onshore centers;
- Enhanced decision making and optimization of work processes with proven success;
- Creation of a continuous learning environment where different expertise can be brought to a common platform for joint data analysis and simulation, where experience can be transferred more effectively to solve on-the-job problems;
- Directly addressing current critical problems associated with the aging workforce and the subsequent impact on the tacit and explicit knowledge that gradually leaves the company;
- More flexible use of the best of competence inclusive of those that remain elsewhere within the organization and those that remain external to the organization;
- Substantial reduction in occupational health and safety-related risk with the transfer of personnel from offshore to onshore based monitoring and support environment; and
- Much stronger partnerships that have long-term commercial benefits.

Certainly, the new network-based and collaborative operating environment has already proven its ability to deliver commercial success. The new thinking and practice has brought great potential for expansions on a substantial scale that can lead to a completely different technological setting and operating mode. The ongoing developments, at some stage, will be directly coupled with major technological achievements, for instance, related to down-hole separation, geo-steering, reservoir stimulation, and the like.

Major Programs Under Professional Support Pillars

Given the direct implications of new plans and current activities at the socio-political level, some support initiatives have also been commenced by major state and public institutions. For instance, the actions taken by Norwegian Petroleum Directorate (NPD)/Norwegian Safety Authority (Ptil) and Norwegian Oil Industry Association (OLF) represent serious underlying interests, primarily at the political and macro-industry levels to ensure the achievement of targeted benefits through a smooth transition process. This mainly has a historical standpoint particularly relating to commercial risks (see, for instance, Duffey & Saull, 2003; Perrow, 1999; Wong, 2002).

E-Operations Forum at the Norwegian Petroleum Directorate (NPD)

The introduction of eOperations on the Norwegian shelf represents an important step towards major achievements from the viewpoints of resource exploitation and prudent resource management capability. NPD's primary interest, simply put, is on the new formulae that the new developments introduce to enhance recovery efficiency in the most attractive manner from economical, safety, and environmental perspectives, bridging conventional gaps within the industry.

The government has a major interest in the ongoing developments owing to the long-term implications of the new development scenario. It implies that there are continuing efforts from authorities to actively be involved and to play a strong and supporting role. The government and the authorities seem to have understood that the success in the digital era from high-risk offshore activities calls for an effectively integrated industrial infrastructure that enhances the corporation among various core business sectors. This has major implications on the more strategic use of advanced technological capabilities and bridging the existing gaps among the fairly diversified industry competence. The effective supportive structure needs to be established in such a way that it enables better regulation of the integrated infrastructure through a productive synergy.

Thus, as the authoritative body, NPD has made early arrangements to initiate active collaboration within the O&G Industry to promote more effective and efficient use of eOperations on NCS. This helps target significant results based on meaningful integration and active collaboration among the core business sectors within the industry, breaking the conventional barriers that may pose a real threat due to nonstandard, ill-defined, and inconsistent practices. The NPD, thus, has taken an important initiative establishing a Forum for eOperations ("eDrift Forum"), where licensees, service contractors, support & supply companies, R&D institutions, IT companies, and authorities meet to share information, knowledge, and experience on this subject matter. The aim is to actively look for comprehensive solutions, rather than those that are highly customized with a sole reference to specific internal customs. It also is to ensure that the underlying interests of the Norwegian state are satisfied, yielding the best of benefits through a productive synergy between major players in core business sectors.

Programs and Activities by Norwegian Oil Industry Association (OLF)

The OLF has undertaken the task of addressing some of the important areas, seeking to navigate the new development path through a practice with assured consistency for common standards across the industry. Within the thematic interests of OLF, it has defined some major technical disciplines that provide the necessary basis for a collaborative and a supportive infrastructure. These include:

- Data integration;
- Digital infrastructure;
- ICT security;
- Information quality;
- Knowledge-based industry; and
- Integrated work processes.

OLF has formed a steering group to support the ongoing activities and programs with representatives from core business sectors to work on a 5-10 year road map. This has greater emphasis on creating an industry infrastructure that is cooperative and effective in the best possible way to enhance resource exploitation on NCS, while meeting statutory and regulatory demands. To a greater extent, the task of the steering group relates to the quality of digital services in the new setting that positively contribute to:

- Quality assurance of robust solutions for effective management of real-time data from subsea and top-side facilities, and activities to provide rapid solutions;

- Third-party access to the digital infrastructure on NCS for the development of systems and routines for information safety, particularly on systems where authoritative demands exist, because of the impact on the society;

- Development of a common data-integration platform for various production phases, discipline areas, and organizations, based on international standards and Web technology;

- Development of multidisciplinary digital services on the basis of data integration of various disciplines and active use of multidisciplinary knowledge and competencies; and

- Establishment of an effective dialogue with all interested parties in industry, R&D institutes, and authorities to enhance communication to clarify industrial standpoints in relation to major challenges and critical issues.

To realize the principal expectations, promoting industry-wide cooperation for programs and activities, disciplinary experts are actively involved from O&G producers, service providers, and support & supply organizations. OLF, in particular, has a major role in the establishment of the most productive collaborative environment and professional network bridging the traditional gaps between major players and various sectors across the Norwegian O&G Industry.

Future Development

In general, the entire industry remains optimistic about the future and the positive impact of recent initiatives. With reference to the nature of the ongoing re-engineering process, it appears that the full-scale transition will occur through three successive phases:

- **Integration across core disciplines:** This phase largely focuses on the establishment of onshore support centres, formal division of work and personnel between offshore-onshore organization, competence mapping, and compilation across integrated disciplines that allow greater space for in-sourcing core expertise and competencies from service, and support & supply markets. This is more localized mini-scale integration within the producers' premises, creating a collaborative environment across major disciplines for joint decisions and activity planning.

- **Integration across assets and business sectors:** Here the focus will be on production asset-based integration. The emphasis will mainly be on the establishment of collaborative environment bringing service-support-supply markets closer to the producers' operational environment. Digital ICT capabilities will be used more actively to bridge the dispersed onshore control centres located at the premises of service-support-supply organizations with that of the producers. This has direct implications on the client-service-support-supply interface management. This is more localized micro-scale integration within the industry infrastructure, bringing different business sectors closer together by creating collaborative networks and B2B partnerships.

- **Integration across portfolios and global operational regions:** At the third phase, integration will take place across all the production assets in the portfolios of major producers and across their global operational regions. This enhances the global connectivity through more active use of wireless ICT networks. This is more global macro-scale integration, where critical political and authoritative issues will have to be addressed.

In fact, the level of success that such a systematic and incremental development path can yield will also be defined by the underlying efforts that are required to cross some major hurdles (see discussions, for instance, in Glico & Mohr man, 1990). While development of technology and its successful implementation are challenges themselves, a major requirement is also to resolve those critical issues at the very micro-organizational level that induce major resistance as change impediments. A great proportion of such critical issues remain within human and organizational aspects. Some of those challenges, in general, include:

- Trade union matters related to, for instance, employment conditions, compensations, and so on;
- Division of work between onshore-offshore and implications of headcount reduction;
- Formal offshore work schedules and work handovers;
- Organizational concerns about significant changes in offshore-onshore "customs" and its direct implications on operational risk;
- Organizational infrastructure to support change and change absorption capacity of humans; and
- Security and the reliability of the common ICT infrastructure.

Furthermore, with the forthcoming expansion of activities to a global scale, the path to establish the best practice and thus to achieve commercial excellence has to overcome some critical issues at the macro-organizational level that particularly relate to building strategic interfaces and networking with fairly diversified industry infrastructures in other strategic regions. This includes, for instance:

- Client-service provider strategy and organizational interface;
- Technical interface for extended onshore-based communication network;
- Data filtering logic, data security, and interorganizational trust;
- Political divisions and differences in authoritative regimes;
- Risk- and gain-sharing frameworks and liabilities;
- Performance assessment frameworks and performance incentives;
- Technical standards and consistency in technical language; and
- Rate and scale of change versus change absorption capability.

In general, the industry appears to have already understood that the success in the new setting is defined by a partnership-based network and the level of collaboration. It has already started to break down the conventional barriers between major O&G producers and the service-support-supply organizations. This implies that the industry structure is gradually moving from a demand-supply-based contractual relationship to a more risk- taking and gain-sharing B2B collaborative partnerships (Figure 9).

The new setting will also have notable impact on the compensation format (Figure 10). The formal contractual relationship that agrees on the lowest cost or flat market rate will greatly be challenged to adapt a share-winning policy. Such a policy will be based on a scenario where compensations will be agreed upon based on the extent of risk undertaken and the level of performance enhancements.

Figure 9. From contract-based relationships to B2B collaborative partnerships

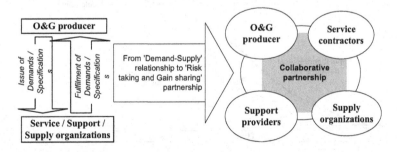

While the most productive interface between O&G producers and the service/support/supply market needs to be carefully addressed and redefined, the industry-push and the technological-pull will continue to directly influence rapid development seeking immediate commercial benefits without too much of risk exposure for all parties involved.

A critical general concern—both at socio-political and industrial levels—is that ill-defined interfaces and increasing complexities of systems and data solutions can lead to unforeseen consequences, greater vulnerability, and greater risk. This pays considerable attention to the important human, organizational, and

Figure 10. From market-based compensation to share-winning policy

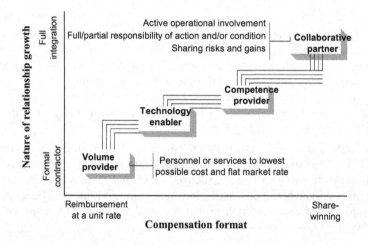

Figure 11. Synchronizing the dispersed development trend

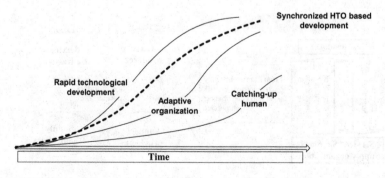

technical aspects. The experience today is that the rate of growth of technological applications is relatively far ahead of the rate of absorption of change and change adaptation by the formal organizational environment and the personnel (Figure 11). It implies that the current development trends along technological, human, and organizational aspects are largely dispersed and the pace of development takes place at different rates and scales. With the growth of realization that this setting will actively contribute to chaos and complexities exposing the stakeholders to greater risks, a major portion of the industry has begun to look more seriously at a more synchronized development path that establishes a harmonized setting across critical human, organizational, and technological aspects.

Even though this has a greater tendency to slightly prolong the integration efforts, the argument is that such a systematic move will have substantial long-term payback rather than a rapid solution that would eventually induce a stream of unforeseen events requiring "ad-hoc solutions" or "quick fixes" that will be too costly to bear (see examples from Chapanis, 1996; Dekker, 2002; Mill, 1992; Noes & Bransby, 2001; Perrow, 1999; Wong, 2002). It implies that there is a growing necessity for more cautious review of the current pace of the development, underlying demands, and a more sensible framework to resolve those strategic, tactical, and operational issues before advancing into a rapid development path. They can remain in the shadow; yet can induce major barriers to active collaboration (for further information, see Liyanage, 2004a, 2004b, 2004c, 2005a, 2005b).

Conclusion

Since 2003, the Norwegian O&G Industry has stepped into a long-term development path termed the "3rd efficiency leap" as the solution to dealing with the gradual decline of O&G activities and production on NCS. This has introduced what is termed Smart Integrated eOperations that greatly emphasize the more active exploitation of application technologies, new data- and knowledge-management techniques, and re-engineering of the industry infrastructure to actively integrating O&G producers with the service-support-supply market during the next few years towards 2010. The principal focus is to enhance cost effectiveness and operational efficiency of offshore O&G production activities for sustained major commercial benefits, capitalizing on smart tools, techniques, methods, and applications to establish a fully integrated environment. The large-scale ICT network called SOIL and onshore remote monitoring centers (e.g. ODC and OOC of ConocoPhillips) represent the major icons of the rapid-change process that currently is in place on NCS. SOIL provides the necessary ICT infrastructure for one-to-many connections and E2E monitoring capability, while onshore control centers represent major nodes of an active network for 24/7 online real-time connectivity. The new setting has already started to introduce major changes within decision loops and work processes, actively involving service contractors, support & supply organizations. Current developments on NCS and underlying long-range plans are typical examples as to how digital capabilities can smartly be exploited to manage high risk and complex production assets to establish operational networks and collaborative partnerships between owners of such assets and service-support-supply organizations in a challenging environment for sustained commercial benefit.

References

Barabasi, A. (2003). *Linked: How everything is connected to everything else and what it means for business, science, and everyday life.* New York: Plume Books.

Becker, J., Kugeler, M., & Rosemann, M. (Eds.). (2003). *Process management: A guide for the design of business process.* New York: Springer.

Chapanis, A. (1996). *Human factors in systems engineering.* New York: John Wiley & Sons.

Clarke, S., Coakes, E., Hunter, G., & Wenn, A. (Eds.) (2003). *Socio-technical and human cognition elements of information systems.* Hershey, PA: Information Science Publishing.

Dekker, S. (2002). *The field guide to human error investigations.* Aldershot, UK: Ashgate Publishing.

Duffey, R. B., & Saull, J. W. (2003). *Know the risk—Learning from errors and accidents: Safety and risk in today's technology.* Burlington, VT: Butterworth Heinemann.

During, W., Oakey, R., & Kauser, S. (Eds.). (2002). *New technology-based firms in the new millennium: Volume III.* New York: Elsevier.

Dyer, J. H. (2000). *Collaborative advantage: Winning through extended enterprise supplier networks.* Oxford, UK: Oxford University Press.

Faulkner, D., & Rond, M. (Eds.). (2001). *Cooperative strategy: Economic, business, and organizational issues.* Oxford, UK: Oxford University Press.

Glinow, M. A., & Mohrman, S. A. (1990). *Managing complexity in high technology organizations.* Oxford University Press.

Gunasekaran, A., Khalil, O., & Rahman, S. (Eds.) (2003). *Knowledge and information technology management: Human and social perspectives.* Hershey, PA: Idea Group Publishing.

Hosni Y. A., & Khalil, T. M. (Eds.) (2004). *Management of technology—Internet economy: Opportunities and challenges for developed and developing regions of the world.* New York: Elsevier.

Keen, P. G. (1997). *The process design: Creating value where it counts.* Cambridge, MA: Harvard Business School Press.

Lewin, R. (2001). *Complexity: Life at the edge of chaos.* Phoenix Mass Market Paperback.

Lindgren, M., & Bandhold, H. (2003). *Scenario planning: The link between future and strategy.* Hampshire, UK: Palgrave Macmillan.

Lipnack, J., & Stamps, J. (1997). *Virtual teams: Reaching across space, time, and organizations with technology.* New York: John Wiley & Sons.

Liyanage, J. P. (2004a). Quality of operations and maintenance performance in sustainable production environments. In *Proceedings of the 5th International Conference on Quality, Reliability, Maintenance (QRM-2004),* University of Oxford, England, (pp 175-178).

Liyanage, J. P. (2004b). Digital future of operations and maintenance in Norwegian oil and gas production environment: Issues, challenges and opportunities. In *Proceedings of the 17th International Congress on Condition Monitoring and Diagnostic Engineering Management (COMADEM-2004),* University of Cambridge, UK (pp 476-486).

Liyanage, J. P. (2004c). Smart integrated OMS: The 3rd leap to manage the integrity of high-risk, capital-intensive, and technologically complex offshore assets on NCS. In *Proceedings of the 4th Asia Pacific Conference on Systems Integrity and Maintenance,* New Delhi, India (pp. 409-414).

Liyanage, J. P. (2005a, August). *Managing integrity of offshore assets through digital capability: Reducing risk and adding value through integrated eOMS in North Sea.* Paper accepted to the 4th International Conference on Quality & Reliability (ICQR-2005), Beijing China.

Liyanage, J. P. (2005b, August). *Reducing risk and adding value through Smart Integrated Assets: Managing complex industrial assets in complex environments.* Paper accepted to the 18th International Congress on Condition Monitoring and Diagnostic Engineering Management (COMADEM-2005), University of Cranfield, UK.

Mankin, D., Cohen, S. G., & Bikson, T. (1996). *Teams and technology: Fulfilling the promise of the new organization.* Cambridge, MA: Harvard Business School Press.

Mill, R. C. (1992). *Human factors in process operations.* Rugby, UK: Institution of Chemical Engineers.

Neef, D. (2003). *Managing corporate reputation and risk: A strategic approach using knowledge management.* New York: Elsevier.

Noyes, J., & Bransby, M. (Eds.) (2001). *People in control: Human factors in control room design.* London: Institution of Electrical Engineers.

OLF (Oljeindustriens landsforening / Norwegian Oil Industry Association). (2003). eDrift for norsk sokkel: det tredje effektiviseringsspranget / eOperations in the Norwegian continental shelf: The third efficiency leap, (in Norwegian).

Perrow, C. (1999). *Normal accidents: Living with high-risk technologies.* Princeton, NJ: Princeton University Press.

Spekman, R. (2003). *Extended enterprise: Creating competitive advantage through collaborative supply chain.* Upper Saddle River, NJ: Prentice Hall.

Tidd, J. (Ed.). (2001). *From knowledge management to strategic competence: Measuring technological, market and organizational innovation.* London, UK: Imperial College Press.

Tonchia, S., & Tramontano, A. (2004). *Process management for the extended enterprise: Organizational and ICT networks.* New York: Springer.

Wong, W. (2002). *How did that happen: Engineering safety and reliability.* London: Professional Engineering Publishing.

About the Authors

William Y. C. Wang (BS, MBA, PhD) is a program director/lecturer in the division of information technology, engineering, and the environment at the University of South Australia. He is also a certified assistant professor by the Taiwanese Ministry of Education. With the experiences of being a telecom and computer engineer, he has been supervising research groups in Australia and Taiwan in the field of B2B integration, interfirm dynamics, and information strategy. He also is a consultant on industrial projects for BRP, global logistics management, and SCM. Focusing on the interaction and business network boundaries, he has done research in the fields of information systems analysis, B2B e-commerce, and supply chain management and configuration for large firms and SMEs. His papers have appeared in the *Journal of Electronic Commerce Research*, *Supply Chain Management*, and the *International Journal of Production Planning and Control*. He has authored chapters in *Electronic Commerce in Small- to Medium-Sized Enterprises: Frameworks, Issues and Implications*, and in proceedings of international conferences.

Michael S. H. Heng is a professor of information systems at Universitas 21 Global, Singapore, and a visiting professor at Fudan University, University of South Australia and the National University of Singapore. His current research interests include globalisation, IS strategy, e-business, IS development, and open source software. He is an associate editor of the *Journal of Electronic Commerce Research*, and a co-chair of the Program Committee of the Pacific Asia Conference on Information Systems 2003. His work has appeared in publications such as *Information and Organization, Information Systems Journal, Journal of Strategic Information Systems, Journal of Electronic Commerce Research, Supply Chain Management,* and *Asia-Pacific Journal of Management Sciences.*

Patrick Y. K. Chau is a professor of information systems at The University of Hong Kong. He received his PhD in business administration from the Richard Ivey School of Business at the University of Western Ontario, Canada. His research interests include IS/IT adoption and implementation, decision support systems, and information presentation and model visualization. He has published papers in journals such as the *MIS Quarterly, Communications of the ACM, Journal of Management Information Systems,* and the *Journal of Organizational Computing and Electronic Commerce.*

* * * *

Graeme Altmann (BCom, MSc, CPA, MACS) is a senior lecturer in the School of Information Systems, Faculty of Business and Law at Deakin University, Australia. For the past decade, he has worked with participants in the Deakin Master of Business Administration program, introducing them to information systems management practices and principles. Graeme works as an IT consultant and is an active researcher in the field of IS. He has recently published and presented papers on IS strategic planning, systems thinking, software quality management, supply chain management and IT entrepreneurship at conferences in Australia and overseas.

Thorsten Blecker is a professor at the Hamburg University of Technology (TUHH), Department of Business Logistics and General Management. He holds a master's degree in business administration and a PhD from the University of Duisburg, Germany. He finished his habilitation thesis in September 2004 at the University of Klagenfurt, Austria. Dr. Blecker is guest-editor of a special issue of *IEEE Transactions on Engineering Management,* and co-editor and author of several books. His main research interests include: business logistics and supply chain management, production/operations management, industrial information systems, Internet-based production systems, mass customization manufacturing systems, strategic management, and virtual organizations.

Marco Busi (MSc, PhD) is the manager of the Centre for Business Process Outsourcing (Glasgow and Invergordon, Scotland), where he is responsible for the development and delivery of research specific to the outsourcing industry and technology and knowledge transfer programs to support industrial performance improvement. He holds a master's degree in industrial management from the Engineering University of Brescia (Italy), and a PhD on collaborative performance management from the Norwegian University of Science and Technology, Trondheim (Norway). He was previously a researcher at SINTEF Technology Management, the largest independent research organization in Scandinavia, where he has been actively involved in Norwegian and European research projects and in contract research for local industry. He was responsible for the work concerning performance management of SCM processes.

Michael Camarata is a visiting professor in the Department of Management at the University of Akron, Ohio. He holds a PhD from Virginia Commonwealth University. Dr. Camarata has published in such academic refereed journals as the *Journal of Business Research* and the *Journal of Business Communication*. He has over twenty years of NGO and public sector senior management experience as a change agent and turn-a-round specialist in organizational and human systems. He is a partner in the management consulting firm of Beckett and Associates. His research interests and areas of proficiency are human systems analysis and change, human network integration, and business policy and strategic management.

Yu Ni Ham (BIS, Hons) is a PhD candidate in the Department of Information Systems at University of Melbourne, Australia. Her main research areas are electronic business, supply chain management, and interorganizational collaboration. Her current research employs qualitative methods to understand how supply chain organizations build relationships and interact in the process of adopting complex interorganizational supply chain management (IOSCM) innovations. She explores why adoption of complex IOSCM innovations has been slow and problematic, and how continual changes in industry and interorganizational environments affect diffusion of IOSCM innovations. She has presented her research at seminars and international conferences in both Australia and Singapore.

Jan Harestad, Chief Executive Officer of OilCamp AS, received a Master of Science in electrical engineering from the Norwegian Technical University (NTNU), Trondheim. He started his career as a research engineer at SINTEF Research Institute, Trondheim, Norway. Afterwards, he held managerial positions related to operations and maintenance in hydroelectric power production companies. He has served as a manager of industrial research at Rogaland Research Institute (RF), Stavanger. He also worked as director of product development at Laerdal Medical in Stavanger, Norway and was later appointed resident of Laerdal California Inc., Long Beach, CA. Moving into the software industry, he took over the position of managing director of the software company Unique AS, Sandnes, Norway. He continued his career as director of technology at ADB Systems AS before joining OilCamp. Both at ADB Systems and OilCamp, Mr. Harestad engaged in using advanced ICT technologies for smart maintenance and remote/integrated operations of remote technical installations such as power plants and offshore oil & gas installations.

Mike Herbert is currently working as the Onshore Drilling Centre advisor for ConocoPhillips, Norway. His main responsibilities include the planning and implementation of the Onshore Drilling Centre (ODC) concept and other remote operation processes. He is also acting as an advisor for the Onshore Operations Centre, which recently has been implemented. He is also working with the company as an advisor on global initiatives relating to remote operations and support. Mr. Herbert has recently been working with the OLF (Norwegian Oil Industry Association) representing ConocoPhillips and led an Oil & Gas Industry work group looking at future developments in integrated operations and e-field on the Norwegian Continental Shelf. He is also a lead party in the OG21 initiative on future oil and gas strategies for Norway. In 1995, he started as a directional drilling coordinator at Sperry Sun, and in 1997, stared to work with remote operations. In 2000, he joined Phillips Petroleum Company Norway as a senior specialist drilling engineer, where he focused on directional drilling, measurement while drilling (MWD), survey management, and real-time operations. Mr. Herbert holds a degree in oceanography and maritime science.

Gert Jan Hofstede is an associate professor in information systems at Wageningen University, Social Science Group, and a regular guest lecturer at the London School of Economics and ETH Zürich. He holds an MSc in biology and a doctorate in production planning, and teaches database design. Hofstede started to use his father Geert's work on national cultures in the mid-nineties to create simulation games, and has since become a well-known speaker and author on cross-cultural communication. He is first author of *Exploring Culture*, a book with practical exercises on cross-cultural communication, and co-author of *Cultures and Organizations (2nd ed.)*. Over the last few years, he has worked on transparency in chains and networks, approaching this topic from a perspective that integrates various theoretical perspectives.

Beverley G. Hope teaches and researches in the School of Information Management, Victoria University of Wellington. She holds a Bachelor of Science and MBA from the University of Kansas and a PhD from the University of Hawaii at Manoa. Her research focuses on quality, particularly in online or multi-channel environments including extranet quality, Web site quality, customer relationship management, performance measurement, and the role of IT in service provision. Other research she has done has examined knowledge management and information systems education and research training. She reviews for and has published in several international conferences and journals.

H. Y. Sonya Hsu is a PhD student majoring in management information systems, at Southern Illinois University, Carbondale (USA). Her primary research interests include knowledge management, supply chain management, telecommunication management, and mobile Internet. She has been published in the *Annual Review of Communication from the International Engineering Consortium* and the *Encyclopedia of Knowledge Management*. She has also made numerous presentations at national and international conferences.

Robert B. Johnston (BSc, Hons.; Dip Ed, MSc, PhD) is an associate professor in the Department of Information Systems at the University of Melbourne, Australia. His main research areas are electronic commerce, supply chain management, and the theoretical foundations of information systems. He currently teaches electronic commerce and research methods. He has over 90 refereed publications, many in leading international journals including *Management Science*, the *European Journal of Information Systems*, the *International Journal of Electronic Commerce*, the *Journal of Strategic Information Systems*, and *Supply Chain Management*. Prior to becoming an academic, he spent 13 years as a consulting analyst/project manager, designing and implementing about 25 large computer systems in a number of leading Australian manufacturing companies.

Wolfgang Kersten is president of the Hamburg School of Logistics and head of the Department of Business Logistics and General Management at the Hamburg University of Technology (TUHH). He graduated in industrial engineering, followed by a doctoral degree at the University of Passau. After several years at DaimlerChrysler in Sindelfingen, he became a senior researcher at the Department of Logistics, Technical University, Munich. His numerous publications focus on variety and complexity management, supply chain management, collaborative engineering, and development management. His main research interests include: logistics and supply chain management, variety and complexity management, and management methods.

Birgit Koeppen is a doctoral candidate and research associate at the Department of Business Logistics and General Management at Hamburg University of Technology (TUHH). She graduated as electrical engineer from the Hamburg

University of Technology. She has participated in several industrial and research projects, covering areas of process management, supply chain management, and business games. Her main research interests are variety and complexity management.

Angela Lin is a lecturer in information systems at the University of Sheffield, UK. Her current teaching and research interests include information systems management; computer supported cooperative work, and e-business, technology, and work.

Jayantha P. Liyanage is an associate professor of asset operations, maintenance technology, and asset management at the University of Stavanger (UiS), Norway. He is also the center leader and a project advisor at the Center for Maintenance and Asset Management (SDV), and a member of the R&D group of the Center for Risk Management and Public Safety (SEROS), UiS. He earned a BSc in production engineering (first class honors), an MSc in human factors (with distinction), and a PhD in offshore engineering (asset operations and maintenance). His PhD thesis addressed operations and maintenance performance in oil and gas production assets. Dr. Liyanage is actively involved in joint industry projects, both at advisory and managerial capacities, and also currently serves as the principal and external advisor on a number of PhD projects. He has published more than 50 publications in various international journals and conferences over the last few years. For his performance, he has received a number of prestigious awards including the University of Peradeniya Award for the Best Performance in Engineering (1995), the Colombo Dockyard Award for the Best Performance in Production Engineering (1995), The Overall Best in Masters (1999), the Lyse Energy Research Award for Excellent Research and Academic Contributions (2001), the Society of Petroleum Engineers Best PhD Award (2003), and the Emerald Literati Club Award for Excellence (2004). He serves as an editorial reviewer and a member of international editorial boards of a number of international journals, and is actively involved in national and international conferences as a program committee member and program chair.

David Mackay (BAgEc, Hons.; MEc, GradDipComp, PhD, MACS, PCP) is an associate professor in the School of Information Systems, Faculty of Business and Law at Deakin University, Australia. In 1995, he completed doctoral studies on the impact of electronic commerce on organizations in the Australian automotive industry. He has undertaken consultancies for both government and private corporations on many aspects relating to the use and expected impact of a range of communication and information technologies, particular relating to how electronic commerce technologies impact organizations.

Lucas Merlo (BCom, Hons.) recently completed research into the application of soft systems methodology in supply chain management during his studies at Deakin University. Merlo has been working in IT support with Rip Curl, an international surfing-products company located in Torquay, Australia.

David Patterson is a business adviser at Business Link South Yorkshire, a UK government-backed organization responsible for improving the competitive performance of SMEs. He specializes in working with ICT developers, e-learning businesses, and computer video games developers. Patterson has been a guest speaker on a number of occasions to give lectures on supply chain management to MSc information systems and MSc information management students in the University of Sheffield, UK.

Asghar Sabbaghi, Associate Dean and Professor of Decision Sciences, has taught for many years at Indiana University South Bend, School of Business and Economics, in the areas of MIS, decision sciences, and production/operations management. His research is in the areas of MIS, supply chain management, decision support systems, economics of information, scarce resource planning, and economics of water resource management. He has reviewed MIS and operation management textbooks and manuscripts for several journals including *MIS Quarterly;* served as editorial Board/Reviewer for *Journal of Economics and Finance, Journal of Microcomputer System Management, and Journal of Information Systems Education;* and served as a paper referee for professional organizations in decision sciences and MIS areas.

Andreas Schroeder is an associate lecturer and PhD scholarship candidate in the School of Information Management, Victoria University of Wellington. He holds a graduate diploma of commerce and BCA (Hons.) from Victoria University of Wellington. In his doctoral research, he examines the governance processes and structures supporting organizational knowledge management initiatives, the impact of leadership, stakeholder involvement, and staff consultation. In addition, he has a strong research interest in the use of ICT in rural communities and its impact on traditional businesses.

Stephen C. Shih is an assistant professor of the School of Information Systems and Applied Technologies at Southern Illinois University, Carbondale, USA. He holds a PhD from The Pennsylvania State University, USA. He has published numerous articles in academic referred journals, as well as national and international conference proceedings. In addition to his established record in academia, he has over six years of industry experience with United Technologies

Research Center, Lucent Technologies/Bell Labs, and SHARP Electronics Co. in leading several supply chain management, knowledge management, and e-business research projects. His research interests and areas of proficiency are supply chain management, knowledge management, lean manufacturing, intelligent information systems design, and e-business security.

Ross Smith (BSc, Hons.; PhD; GDip, CompStud; MACM; MIEEECS; MACS; MISSS; MUKSysSoc) is an associate professor in the School of Information Systems, Deakin University, Australia. Since completing his doctoral studies in computational physics in 1977, he has been a faculty member at the Australian National University, Swinburne University of Technology, and, since 1999, at Deakin University. He has taught widely across the curriculum in areas such as systems analysis and design, software engineering, systems implementation, and software project management. Ross has researched and published widely in systems methodologies, supply chain management, and requirements engineering.

Hagen Späth is a doctoral candidate and research associate at the Department of Business Logistics and General Management at the Hamburg University of Technology. He holds a degree in industrial engineering and general management from the Hamburg University of Technology, the University of Hamburg, and the Hamburg University of Applied Sciences. He has participated in several industrial and research projects, covering areas of supply chain management, logistics and business games. His main research interests are logistics and supply chain management, especially supply chain risk management.

Christine Storer has been a lecturer in agribusiness marketing at Muresk Institute, Curtin University of Technology since 1991. Previously, she worked internationally as an information system analyst and chartered accountant. Her research interests include: information communication systems and management; interorganization, chain and network research; on-farm quality assurance adoption; traceability systems; use of price risk management tools; farmer participation in grower groups; consumer and buyer behavior and attitudes and, more generally, food and fibre marketing, small business, and market analysis. Her research has been published in the *Journal of Chain and Network Science, Journal of Supply Chain Management,* and the *Australasian Agribusiness Review.*

Jeffrey C. F. Tai was a senior industry analyst in the Market Intelligence Center of the Institute for Information Industry, Taiwan (ROC). He received his MS degree in business administration from the National Central University. His research interests include issues in supply chain management, organization theory, and transaction cost economics. His research has appeared in *Information & Management, International Journal of Information Management, Journal of Information Management*, and others.

Ganesh Vaidyanathan, Assistant Professor at Indiana University South Bend, School of Business and Economics, has conducted research in the areas of e-commerce, SCM, project management, knowledge management, innovation, and IT value. He has authored over 20 publications in journals, including *Communications of the ACM*. He has held executive positions at eReliable Commerce, Honeywell, General Dynamics, Lockheed Martin, and Click Commerce. He launched products that include security, payment processing, procurement, logistics, ERP, SCM, and data warehousing. He has consulted with Fortune 100 companies, including United Airlines, Mitsubishi, Motorola, and Honeywell, in technology, business and process reengineering. Dr. Vaidyanathan holds a PhD from Tulane University and an MBA from the University of Chicago.

Eric T. G. Wang is a professor in the Department of Information Management at National Central University, Taiwan (ROC). He received his PhD in business administration, specializing in computer & information systems, from the William E. Simon School of Business Administration, University of Rochester. His research interests include electronic commerce, outsourcing, organizational economics, and the impact of information technology. His research has appeared (and is due to appear) in *Information Systems Research, Management Science, Information Systems Journal, Information & Management, Decision Support Systems, European Journal of Operational Research, Omega*, and others.

Kai Wang was a senior industry analyst and research manager at the e-Business Research Group of the Market Information Center, Institute for Information Industry, Taiwan (ROC). He is responsible for research work on electronic commerce, software industry development, open source software, and information security issues. He received his PhD in business administration, specializing in management information systems, from National Central University. His research interests include online marketing, consumer behavior, and organization theory. His research has appeared in academic journals such as *International Journal of Information*.

H. Joseph Wen is chairperson and associate professor of Management Information Systems, Department of Accounting and Management Information Systems, Harrison College of Business, Southeast Missouri State University. He holds a PhD from Virginia Commonwealth University. He has published over 100 papers in academic refereed journals, book chapters, encyclopedias, and national conference proceedings. He has received over six million dollars in research grants from various State and Federal funding sources. His areas of expertise are Internet research, electronic commerce (EC), transportation information systems, and software development. He has also worked as a senior developer and project manager for various software development contracts since 1988.

Index

A

action-research 265
advanced planning system (APS) 145
affiliate firm 8
agency theory 117
agribusiness 46, 107
anecdotal evidence 244
ascension design 33
authentication 302

B

Beer Game 363
behavioral uncertainty 70
BLSY 24
Bluetooth 299
BSE 114
bullwhip effect 166
business game 363
business intelligence (BI) 6
Business Link South Yorkshire (BLSY) 24
business network 107
business process reengineering (BPR) 4
business-to-business (B2B) 107,
    154, 166, 291
Buyer Power (BP) 83, 85

C

case study 31
CATWOE 262
China Credit Information Services 80
co-managed inventory (CMI) 203, 212
collaboration 216
collaborative planning 14, 30, 67, 138,
    173
competitive advantage 227
competitive priority 319
conceptual model 262
ConocoPhillips Norway (COPNO) 400
cooperation 216
coordination 214
cost of ownership 388
cross docking 173
cryptographic algorithm 304

D

D&P 301
deductive logic 366
dependability 87
digital signature 304
discriminant validity 86, 234
DoS 305

426

downstream information flow 48
DSC 267
DSM 267

E

e-business 107
e-commerce 391
e-enterprise security 287
e-procurement 152
efficiency 318
efficient consumer response (ECR)
    173, 192, 199
Efficient Consumer Response Association
    (ECRA) 198
Ekofisk field 401
electronic data interchange (EDI) 65, 106,
    114, 151, 173, 192, 209
electronic procurement 152
embedded ties 112
endogenous risk 358
engineered-to-order (ETO) 5
enterprise resource planning (ERP) 6, 134,
    139, 151, 172
environmental uncertainty (EU) 82
eOperations 391
EUREP-GAP 114
event log 305
exploratory factor analysis (EFA) 84
extranet 174

F

focal company 66
forecasting and replenishment (CPFR) 173
free-riding phenomenon 166, 167

G

General Food Law 109
global SCM 128
global supply chain forum 136
globalization 129
GlobalNetXchange 192
GM (General Motors) 267
gross domestic product (GDP) 24
grounded theory 198

H

Hazard Analysis Critical Control Points
    (HACCP) 114
history transparency 110
human activity model 262
human activity system (conceptual) model
    273
HVAC 289

I

inductive logic 366
information and communication technology
    (ICT) 25, 65, 169, 314, 389
information distortion 75
information flows 46
information system (IS) 111, 166, 193
information, systems and information
    systems (ISIS) 260
information technology (IT) 2, 47, 150,
    287
information transfer 166
informational distortion 74
integrated product development (IPD) 147
intellectual property rights (IPR) 37
interdependence 78
internal consistency 234
International Organization for Standardiza-
    tion 4
Internet 166
interorganisational structure 210
interorganisational information manage-
    ment system 227
interorganisational structure 205
interorganisational supply chain manage-
    ment (IOSCM) 191, 192
intranet 174
inventory turn 200
item reliability 234

J

Java 299
joint or co-managed inventory (JMI) 210
just-in-time (JIT) 30, 74, 129, 192

K

key performance indicator (KPI) 4, 318
KLICT foundation 115
knowledge management 184

L

Lancaster University 256
local area network (LAN) 151

M

Mad Cow disease 114
made-to-order 5, 201
manufacturing flexibility 87
manufacturing goal 83
measurement model 234
Meat Industry Association 54
Metatek 33
metrics 4, 16, 130, 147, 170, 201
multivariate 234

N

Nash equilibrium 369
NC6 85
NC8 85
NC9 85
netchain 105, 108, 113
network 106
network economy 144
network pole 117
network theory 3
networking 29
normative contract (NC) 83
Norwegian Oil Industry Association 389

O

OECD 132
OLF 389
operational efficiency 388
operational procedure 85
operations transparency 110
organisational boundary 193
organization 25
original equipment manufacturers (OEM)
    64, 128, 140

outsourcing 64

P

partial least squares (PLS) 234, 237
performance 317
performance attribute 265
performance dimension 319
performance indicator 317
performance management 318, 323
performance measurement 317
performance metric 317
person-to-system (P2S) 300
point-of-sale (POS) 174
portal 166, 175
product launch flexibility 143
purchasing price 85

Q

quality 87
quantity flexibility (QF) 145
quasi-alliance 291
Quick Response 192

R

radio frequency identification (RFID) 48
Raytheon Six Sigma 130
relationship intimacy 205, 213
requests for quotation (RFQ) 152
resource-based perspective (RBV) 65
resource-based view 65, 73, 181
responsiveness 136
return on asset (ROA) 201, 361
return on investment 170
rich picture 260
risk 26
root definition 262

S

SCM initiator 12, 14
SCM project 10
SCMA 260
ScorWizard 6
security protocols 289
semi-structured interviews 50, 197
site specificity (SSI1) 85

428

small and medium enterprise (SME) 24,
    115, 128, 131
socio-political 393
soft system methodology in action (SSMA)
    260
soft systems methodology (SSM)
    255, 256, 268
SP 87
special interest group (SIG) 30
spillover 166
stakeholder 46, 122
stakeholder theory 3
strategy map 319
strategy transparency 111
structural equation modelling 234
supplier's specific investments (SSI) 82
supply chain (SC) 2, 108, 205, 317
supply chain integration 46
supply chain management (SCM) 2, 24,
    47, 24, 128, 136, 166, 255, 315, 357
supply chain management system (SCMS)
    167, 176
supply chain operations reference (SCOR)
    3, 254
supply chain performanc 142
supply chain portal (SCP) 166, 175
supply chain risk management (SCRM) 356
supply chain security 293, 295
supply opportunity analysis technique
    (SOAT) 128
SWO 300
system dynamics 67, 135
system thinking, systems practice (STSP)
    260
system-to-system (S2S) 300
systemic transparency 287

T

target 318
theory of swift, even flow 78
traceability 46
Traceability and Assurance Group (TAG)
    48
transaction cost 169
transaction cost analysis (TCA) 68
transaction cost economics 117

transaction cost theory (TCT) 65, 73
transparency 109
trust 26

U

unified modelling language (UML) 268
upstream information flow 48

V

value chain 166
value system 166
vendor managed inventory (VMI) 71, 133,
    171, 210
vertical coordination 75
virtual enterprise network (VEN) 24, 31
virtual integration (VI) 78, 82
virtual organization 25
virtual organizational environment 393
virtuality 25
volume flexibility 143
voluntary inter-industry commerce
    standards (VICS) 138, 198

W

whiplash effect 168
wireless application protocol (WAP) 306
wireless identity module (WIM) 299